Exam Prep Guide for the Postal Exams 460 and 473

v3.5

Updated
June 2008
Dr. Carole Letson

Disclaimer:

The publisher is neither affiliated with nor endorsed by the United States Postal Service or any government agency. This book has been designed to assist individuals to better prepare for the Postal Battery Exam (Exams 460 and 473). The publisher does not guarantee a passing score on the exam nor can we control when or where the USPS offers the exam or when jobs will be available in your area. Passing the Postal Battery Exam is required to be placed on the list of qualified candidates for a position.

While the publisher does not directly process a candidate's Postal Battery Exam (Exams 460 and 473) registration and/or exam date, our materials have been designed to assist individuals in their preparation for the exam. In addition, live operators are available to provide further information, facilitate the registration process, and respond to any questions candidates may have.

Please Note: The United States Postal Service offers study materials free of charge at www.usps.com or your local post office. Publication 60-A is a 32 page orientation guide for Exam 473. Publication 60-E is a 32 page orientation guide for Exam 460.

This book is not from the library of the USPS. The publisher of this book is not responsible for any changes that may have been made to the Postal Battery Exam during or after the printing of this book.

USPS is a registered trademark of the United States Post Office.

Published by Endeavor Media Group, LLC.

ISBN-13:   978-0-9818012-0-9
ISBN-19:   0-9818012-0-X

Copyright © 2008 by Endeavor Media Group, LLC.

Contents

<u>Preface</u>

As you read this book, you will see that great opportunities await you once you have passed the Postal Battery Exam. That's where this book comes in to play. Purchasing these study materials is the first step to success. This text is an excellent tool to help you prepare to take Postal Exams 460 and 473.

If you have purchased this book, you most likely meet the basic hiring requirements for the US Postal Service. Briefly stated, these requirements are:

You must be 18 years of age or older, or 16 if you're already a high school graduate.
If you are a male, between 18 years and 26 years of age, you must be registered with the U.S. Selective Service.
You must be a U.S. citizen or a legal resident alien. (Possess a green card)
If you are applying for a job that requires driving, you must have a valid driver's license and a safe driving record.

Note: Specific positions with the USPS may have additional eligibility requirements that will be defined in the job announcement.

If you meet these requirements and are seeking a job as a rural carrier, you must register to take Exam 460. If you are seeking a job as a city carrier, mail processing clerk, mail handler, or sales, service, and distribution associate, you must register to take Exam 473. Regardless of the position you are interested in, register for an exam. Once you are working for the Postal Service, you may be eligible for other positions as they become available. Most likely, you will register for Exam 460 as this is offered with much more frequency than Exam 473. In general, Exam 460 is offered about twice a year in larger municipalities and Exam 473 is offered once every three (3) or four (4) years. Don't worry if an exam isn't offered the first time you try to apply. The publisher offers a unique service where you can sign up for e-mail notification of job openings in your area. This may be part of the package provided by the reseller that you purchased from, for instructions please see the materials provided by your reseller. If not, you can subscribe to this service for a small fee at the publisher's site www.endeavormediallc.com. New jobs are opened on a regular basis, and it can take as long as six months after registering to receive your notification packet.

Although we are not affiliated with the USPS, you can apply to take the appropriate exam by going online to our website (www.endeavormediallc.com). Follow the directions and links to the postal service to look up exam openings in your state.

You will need to study prior to your exam date; a minimum of two weeks of intense study is suggested. It is a good idea to begin studying as soon as you receive these materials; you will only have about two weeks notice before your test date.

If you do not receive at least a 70, or if you would like to try for a higher score, you can re-take the exam after 12 months. Your test scores are valid for two years so apply for any opening of interest.

The higher you score on the exam, the more rapidly you could be called for an interview.

If you should fail the exam (receive a score lower than 70), you may qualify for a refund of a portion of the purchase price of these materials. This is our guarantee to you that we feel our materials will help you succeed in your job search. Refunds are only available to the original purchaser of the material and only valid if processed through an authorized reseller

We thank you for selecting these study materials.

Good Luck!

Introduction

A career with the United States Postal Service can be very rewarding. It offers a good salary, employee benefits, a good working environment and a secure employment future. Purchasing these book shows that you already know what the U.S. Postal Service offers and why it is an appealing career choice. The very features that make a postal career appealing to you also attract hundreds of other applicants. The only way to get the position you want is to take the Postal Battery Exam and earn the highest possible score.

The idea of having to pass an exam to even get an interview may seem overwhelming, but this book can help. By following the advice given and completing all the practice exams included, you'll perform very well on the actual examination and will earn the high scores required to outperform the other candidates on the list of potential employees.

We recommend that you begin preparing for this exam well in advance of the actual exam date. This will give you time to study each chapter in depth and complete all the practice exams. In addition, you'll have time to do more extensive studying in the areas where your practice exams show that you are weak. No matter how much time you have, you should begin preparing immediately. Start at the beginning of this book and work your way through to the end. Give all your time and attention to this task and you will see results.

This manual is divided into three main sections.

- Background information on the United States Postal Service.
- Study Tips and Practice Exams for Exam 460.
- Study Tips and Practice Exams for Exam 473.

Each of these sections is designed to make the best use of your time as you study for your Postal Battery Exam. Once you have completed and scored each of the practice exams included in this manual, you should feel very confident on your assigned exam day. Study hard and good luck!

1

History of the U. S. Postal Service

In the early days of the country, roads were primitive and scarce. In order to move messages from one point to another, messengers needed to use these roadways or make their own. Inns and taverns were used as makeshift post offices. As a result, the mailing process was slow and not very precise. Something needed to be done.

In 1619, Richard Fairbanks was given the opportunity to process mail. Then, in 1691, Andrew Hamilton started the first national postal system.

In 1707, the British government increased postal rates and basically took over the postal system. This angered American colonists and brought about great opposition to the British government. American postal carriers processed and delivered many letters illegally to avoid charging the higher rates. Benjamin Franklin, American statesman and revolutionary leader, and William Hunter, Postmaster of Williamsburg, Virginia, were appointed Joint Postmasters General in 1751. While Franklin successfully changed the reliability of mail delivery, he was not successful at reducing the cost. Benjamin Franklin was removed from his position when British officials felt he was not as loyal to the Crown as they would like.

When the Revolutionary War began, Mr. Franklin was named Postmaster General of the United States. In 1789, under the new United States Constitution, the federal government took on the task of processing mail and appointed Samuel Osgood the first Postmaster General.

The U.S. Postal Service, which was referred to as the "Post Office" in its early years, made many advances in the 1800's and early 1900's. The post office first required the use of postal stamps in 1847. Pony Express, probably the most famous means of mail delivery in the old west, was founded in 1860.

Although often though to be part of the Post Office, the Pony Express was a complex system of horses, riders, and 190 relay stations founded b y American transportation pioneer William H. Russell. The Pony Express began working under contract as a mail route in July 1861. Riders would live at the stations, eating and sleeping on specific schedules so that each would be prepared when a tired rider arrived at the relay station. The fresh rider and his horse would then run their part of the mail route to the next relay station. This process would be repeated over and over. A system of planned rotation was implemented so that both horses and riders were sufficiently rested and fed. Pony Express service was drastically decreased following the development of transcontinental telegraph service. The emerging national system of steam engines and railroads finally made the Pony Express obsolete in October 1861.

Soon, the relay station stables were replaced by a system of train stations across the country. These stations contained their own post offices. Now, mail could be sorted while onboard moving trains. Postal employees delivered the sorted mail from moving trains by throwing the sacks of mail onto the "catching arms" at the correct train station.

The advances in airplane technology and the advent of air travel in the early 20th century made the delivery of mail even faster and more efficient. Mail was first delivered by airplane in 1911. Today, all mail that needs to travel 100 miles or more to reach its destination is delivered by the use of aircraft.

The now familiar ZIP codes were first used in 1963. The introduction of the ZIP (Zoning Improvement Plan), code allowed the Post Office to sort large volumes of mail faster and decrease the delivery time. While the sorting was done by hand at first, it is now largely done by automated machines.

In 1971, the Post Office was given a face lift with a new name — the United States Postal Service. The Postal Service is now an independent agency within the executive branch of the United States government. The Postal Service became self-financing and actually made a profit in 1983. This was due to raising the cost for first-class mail and the hard-work and dedication of the efficient postal worker.

In 1992, the way our mail was delivered was again updated and streamlined. Along with ZIP codes the mailing process now included bar coding systems. In addition, there was a reorganization of regions, divisions and management sectional centers were replaced by area and district offices for customer service and mail processing.

Today, the USPS delivers mail to almost 138 million homes, businesses and post office boxes. In fact, it is the only delivery service that visits every address in the United States. About 1.7 million new addresses are added each year. United States Postal carriers bring more mail to people over a larger geographic area than any other country. In order to do this, the USPS serves about 7 million customers daily at their 38,000 postal retail outlets.

To keep up with the changing times, the USPS offers limited counter services at more than 4400 privately owned contract retail units and provides stamps on the Internet, by mail, by phone, through 32,000 vending machines and 40,000 commercial retail outlets and ATMs. All of this is done with an annual operating revenue of $65.8 billion.

In order to make all of this possible, this business giant employs 750,000 career employees, including 235,985 veterans and 47,937 employees with disabilities. The Postal Service also invested more than $978 million in new or improved buildings and mail processing equipment in 2002. All this, and they still handle more than 200 billion pieces of mail a year, or five pieces per address per day.

Since the United States Postal Service was formed, the United States and its Postal Service have grown and changed together. Today, the Postal Service fuels the nation's economy and delivers hundreds of millions of messages and billions of dollars in financial transactions each day to 8 million businesses and 290 million Americans. The Postal Service is making history also as it helps lead the way in making the federal government more businesslike and responsive to customer needs.

Although knowing the history of the United States Postal Service may not assist you in scoring higher on this exam, we thought this little bit of information should be passed on to you to acknowledge that the United States Post Office has been here for centuries and surely will be here for centuries more.

You have taken a wise step in educating yourself for a job with United States Postal Service. This is not a job like flipping burgers or pumping gas; this is a career that will last a lifetime.

Chapter 1: Job Descriptions

Rural Carrier Associate (RCA)
(Exam 460)

The Rural Carrier Associate position is a part-time relief position designed to fulfill the duties of a full time career Rural Carrier when the regular carrier is not available due to days off, vacation time, illness, etc. Beginning wages for an RCA were $15.22 per hour as of early 2005. The responsibilities of a Rural Carrier are similar to those of a City Carrier as described below, but in a rural environment as well as additional duties such as selling postage stamps to rural patrons.

An RCA will usually work only a few days each week—perhaps some scheduled days and other days on a call-in basis. RCAs must be very flexible and willing to respond affirmatively almost every time they are called in unexpectedly. Excessive refusals may result in termination.

An RCA should have a reliable vehicle. At some Post Offices, RCAs are required to use their own vehicles to deliver mail. If so, RCAs receive reimbursement for use of their personal vehicle.

It is possible for an RCA to work their way into a full-time career Rural Carrier position. Typically, an RCA will work part-time for several years before a full-time position becomes available. It is possible, but rare, to be hired directly into a full-time Rural Carrier position if there are no available RCAs to fill it.

City Carriers
(Exam 473)

The City Carrier is an entry level career position. City carriers deliver and collect mail. They walk and/or drive trucks. Carriers must be outside in all kinds of weather. Almost all carriers have to carry mailbags on their shoulders that can weigh up to 35 pounds. Carriers have to load and unload sacks of mail weighing as much as 70 pounds. City Carrier applicants must have a current valid state driver's license and are required to have a safe driving record. In some offices, City Carriers are required to work weekends.

Sales and Service Clerk
(Exam 473)

Clerks work indoors. Clerks have to handle parcels, bundles, and sacks of mail weighing as much as 70 pounds. They sort mail by ZIP code or by a memorized plan. Some clerks work at public windows doing such jobs as selling stamps and weighing parcels, and are personally responsible for all money and stamps. Clerks may have to be on their feet all day. They also have to stretch, reach, and bend frequently when distributing mail. In some offices, clerks are required to work at night and on weekends.

Mark-Up Clerk, Automated
(Exam 473)

Mark-Up Clerks enter change-of-address data into a computer base, process mail, and perform other clerical functions. Mark-Up Clerks operate a keyboard in order to process changes. Applicants for Mark-Up Clerk must have good data entry skills and are required to pass a typing test. Free typing tests can be found at www.learn2type.com.

Distribution Clerk, Machine
(Exam 473)

Distribution Clerks, Machine (DCM's) operate a letter-sorting machine to distribute letters by a memorized plan or by reading the ZIP code. They enter distribution codes on a special purpose keyboard at a rate of up to 60 per minute. Applicants must be able to operate this machine at an accuracy rate of 98%. They must have the ability to maintain close visual attention for long periods of time. DCMs must also load and/or unload machines. DCMs are usually required to work nights and weekends.

Flat Sorting Machine Operator
(Exam 473)

Flat Sorting Machine Operators operate a machine to distribute large, flat pieces of mail by a memorized plan or by reading the ZIP code. They enter distribution codes on a special purpose keyboard at a rate of up to 45 per minute. Applicants must be able to operate this machine at an accuracy rate of 98%. They must have the ability to maintain close visual attention for long periods of time. Operators must also load and/or unload machines. Flat Sorting Machine Operators are usually required to work at night and on weekends.

Mail Processor

(Exam 473)

Mail Processors prepare incoming and outgoing mail for distribution. They Examine, sort, and route mail by state, type of mail, or other scheme. They are required to stand for long periods of time loading and unloading mail from a variety of automated mail processing equipment. Mail Processors may also be required to adjust and repair this equipment. Their work is performed in large mail processing facilities in an industrial environment. Mail Processors are normally required to work at night and on weekend.

Mail Handler
(Exam 473)

Mail Handlers load, unload, and move bulk mail and sacks. They may have to be on their feet all day in an industrial environment. They also have to repeatedly lift objects that weigh up to 70 pounds. Applicants must be able to demonstrate their ability to lift by passing a test of strength and stamina. In some offices, Mail Handlers are required to work at night and on weekends.

Regardless of the position, once you are hired by the USPS, you are placed on probation for six (6) months. The purpose of a probationary period is to provide a trial period for the employee to learn the job and for the supervisor to observe and evaluate the employee's performance. If an employee does not meet performance standards and expectations during the probationary period, the employee may be returned to a previous class and/or position, if appropriate. Dismissal is a last resort when the employee does not meet standards and expectations during the probationary period and a change in assignment is not a viable alternative due to the employee's lack of status in another class or documented poor work history.

Chapter 2: The Application

We have spent a good bit of time and space describing the Postal Service positions for which you would elect to take either Exam 460 or Exam 473. Now that you know what these positions involve in terms of ability and dedication, we will take some time to discuss how to apply for an exam and also give you a sample Postal Service Employment application. (You will greatly impress the interviewer if you are completely prepared to fill out the application when you arrive.)

Every year, hundreds of thousands of people apply for jobs with the United States Postal Service. Only a small percentage of these are ever hired. You've taken the first step in gaining a competitive edge for yourself by purchasing this book. Now it's time to take the next step to put yourself in front of the pack.

Becoming a Postal Worker

To be eligible for employment with the United States Postal Service, you must meet certain minimum requirements:

- You must be 18 years of age or older, or 16 if you already have a high school diploma or its equivalent.

- If you are a male between 18 years and 26 years of age, you must be registered with the U.S. Selective Service.

- You must be a U.S. citizen or a legal resident alien (possess a green card).

- If you are applying for a job that requires driving, you must have a valid driver's license and a safe driving record.

If you meet all these requirements you may apply to take a Postal Battery exam. More requirements may have been added after the publication of this manual, and some positions may have more specific requirements.

The first step you need to take is to apply for an exam. The easiest way to apply is go to www.endeavormediallc.com and click on the link that says "Apply"; this link will provide step by step instructions on how to apply and then direct you to the USPS website. Once there, follow the directions and links to begin the application process.

Once you have applied for and taken an exam, as part of your interview preparation, you should familiarize yourself with the Postal Service employment application, included on the next four pages of this book. You can download the actual application from www.usps.com.

This application is included for study purposes only and is not to be filled out and turned in to the United States Postal Service.

UNITED STATES POSTAL SERVICE ®

Application for Employment
The US Postal Service is an Equal Opportunity Employer
(Shaded Areas for Postal Service Use Only)

Rated Application			Veteran preference has been verified through proof that the separation was under honorable conditions, and other proof as required. *(See Section D below.)*	Check One:
Rated For	Rating	Date Rcvd.		☐ 10 pts. CPS
		Time Rcvd.	Type of Proof Submitted & Date Issued	☐ 10 pts. CP
				☐ 10 pts. XP
Signature & Date			Verifier's Signature, Title & Date	☐ 5 pts. TP

A. General Information

1. Name *(First, MI, Last)*	2. Social Security No. (SSN)	3. Home Telephone ( )
4. Mailing Address *(No., Street, City, State, ZIP Code)*	5. Date of Birth	6. Work Telephone ( )
	7. Place of Birth *(City & State or City & Country)*	

8. Kind of Job Applied for and Postal Facility Name & Location *(City & State)*	9. Will You Accept: Temporary/Casual (Noncareer) Work? ☐ Yes ☐ No	10. When Will You Be Available?	11. Are You Willing to Travel? *(Complete only if you are applying for an executive or professional position.)* ☐ Yes ☐ No

B. Educational History

1. Name and Location *(City & State)* of Last High School Attended	2. Are You a High School Graduate? Answer "Yes" if you expect to graduate within the next 9 months, or you have an official equivalency certificate of graduation. ☐ Yes - Month & Year: ☐ No - Highest Grade Completed:

3a. Name and Location of College or University *(City, State, and ZIP Code if known. If you expect to graduate within 9 months, give month and year you expect degree.)*	Dates Attended		No. of Credits Completed		Type Degree (BA, etc.)	Year of Degree
	From	To	Semester Hrs.	Quarter Hrs.		

3b. Chief Undergraduate College Subjects	Semester Hrs. Completed	Quarter Hrs. Completed	3c. Chief Graduate College Subjects	Semester Hrs. Completed	Quarter Hrs. Completed

4. Major Field of Study at Highest Level of College Work

5. Other Schools or Training *(For example, trade, vocational, armed forces, or business. Give for each: Name, City, State, and ZIP Code, if known, of school; dates attended; subjects studied; number of classroom hours of instruction per week; certificates; and any other pertinent information.)*

6. Honors, Awards, and Fellowships Received

7. Special Qualifications and Skills *(Licenses; skills with machines, patents or inventions; publications - do not submit copies unless requested; public speaking; memberships in professional or scientific societies; typing or shorthand speed, etc.)*

PS Form **2591**, March 1999 *(Page 1 of 4)*

This application is included for study purposes only and is not to be filled out and turned in to the United States Postal Service.

Name *(First, MI, Last)*	Social Security No.	Date

C. Work History

(Start with your present position and go back for 10 years or to your 16th birthday, whichever is later. You may include volunteer work. Account for periods of unemployment in separate blocks in order. Include military service. Use blank sheets if you need more space. Include your name, SSN, and date on each sheet.)

May the US Postal Service ask your present employer about your character, qualifications, and employment record? A "No" will not affect your consideration for employment opportunities.

☐ Yes ☐ No

1.

Dates of Employment *(Month & Year)* From To **Present**	Grade If Postal, Federal Service or Military	Starting Salary/Earnings $ per
Exact Position Title Average Hours per Week	Number and Kind of Employees Supervised	Present Salary/Earnings $ per
Name of Employer and Complete Mailing Address	Kind of Business *(Manufacturing, etc.)*	Place of Employment *(City & State)*
	Name of Supervisor	Telephone No. *(If known)* ( )

Reason for Wanting to Leave

Description of Duties, Responsibilities, and Accomplishments

2.

Dates of Employment *(Month & Year)* From To	Grade If Postal, Federal Service or Military	Starting Salary/Earnings $ per
Exact Position Title Average Hours per Week	Number and Kind of Employees Supervised	Present Salary/Earnings $ per
Name of Employer and Complete Mailing Address	Kind of Business *(Manufacturing, etc.)*	Place of Employment *(City & State)*
	Name of Supervisor	Telephone No. *(If known)* ( )

Reason for Leaving

Description of Duties, Responsibilities, and Accomplishments

3.

Dates of Employment *(Month & Year)* From To	Grade If Postal, Federal Service or Military	Starting Salary/Earnings $ per
Exact Position Title Average Hours per Week	Number and Kind of Employees Supervised	Present Salary/Earnings $ per
Name of Employer and Complete Mailing Address	Kind of Business *(Manufacturing, etc.)*	Place of Employment *(City & State)*
	Name of Supervisor	Telephone No. *(If known)* ( )

Reason for Leaving

Description of Duties, Responsibilities, and Accomplishments

PS Form **2591**, March 1999 *(Page 2 of 4)*

This application is included for study purposes only and is not to be filled out and turned in to the United States Postal Service.

Name (First, MI, Last)	Social Security No.	Date

4.	Dates of Employment (Month & Year) From To	Grade If Postal, Federal Service or Military	Starting Salary/Earnings $ per
	Exact Position Title Average Hours per Week	Number and Kind of Employees Supervised	Present Salary/Earnings $ per

Name of Employer and Complete Mailing Address	Kind of Business (Manufacturing, etc.)	Place of Employment (City & State)
	Name of Supervisor	Telephone No. (If known) ( )

Reason for Leaving

Description of Duties, Responsibilities, and Accomplishments

D. Veteran Preference *(Answer all parts. If a part does not apply, answer "No".)*

	Yes	No
1. Have you ever served on active duty in the US military service? *(Exclude tours of active duty for training as a reservist or guardsman.)*		
2. Have you ever been discharged from the armed service under other than honorable conditions? You may omit any such discharge changed to honorable by a Discharge Review Board or similar authority. *(If "Yes," give details in Section F.)*		
3. Do you claim 5-point preference based on active duty in the armed forces? *(If "Yes," you will be required to furnish records to support your claim.)*		
4. Do you claim a 10-point preference? If "Yes," check type of preference claimed and attach Standard Form 15, *Claim for 10-Point Veteran Preference*, together with proof called for in that form.		

☐ Compensable Disability *(Less than 30%)*   ☐ Compensable Disability *(30% or more)*   ☐ Non-Compensable Disability *(includes Receipt of the Purple Heart)*   ☐ Wife/Husband

☐ Widow/Widower   ☐ Mother   ☐ Other:

5. List for All Military Service: *(Enter N/A if not applicable)*

Date (From - To)	Serial/Service Number	Branch of Service	Type of Discharge

THE LAW (39 U.S. CODE 1002) PROHIBITS POLITICAL AND CERTAIN OTHER RECOMMENDATIONS FOR APPOINTMENTS, PROMOTIONS, ASSIGNMENTS, TRANSFERS, OR DESIGNATIONS OF PERSONS IN THE POSTAL SERVICE. Statements relating solely to character and residence are permitted, but every other kind of statement or recommendation is prohibited unless it either is requested by the Postal Service and consists solely of an evaluation of the work performance, ability, aptitude, and general qualifications of an individual or is requested by a government representative investigating the individual's loyalty, suitability, and character. Anyone who requests or solicits a prohibited statement or recommendation is subject to disqualification from the Postal Service and anyone in the Postal Service who accepts such a statement may be suspended or removed from office.

Privacy Act Statement: The collection of this information is authorized by 39 USC 401 and 1001. This information will be used to determine your qualifications and suitability for USPS employment. As a routine use, the information may be disclosed to an appropriate government agency, domestic or foreign, for law enforcement purposes; where pertinent, in a legal proceeding to which the USPS is a party or has an interest; to a government agency in order to obtain information relevant to a USPS decision concerning employment, security clearances, contracts, licenses, grants, permits or other benefits; to a government agency upon its request when relevant to its decision concerning employment, security clearances, security or suitability investigations, contracts, licenses, grants or other benefits; to a congressional office at your request; to an expert, consultant, or other person under contract with the USPS to fulfill an agency function; to the Federal Records Center for storage; to the Office of Management and Budget for review of private relief legislation; to an independent certified public accountant during an official audit of USPS finances; to an investigator, administrative judge or complaints examiner appointed by the Equal Employment Opportunity Commission for investigation of a formal EEO complaint under 29 CFR 1613; to the Merit Systems Protection Board or Office of Special Counsel for proceedings or investigations involving personnel practices and other matters within their jurisdiction; and to a labor organization as required by the National Labor Relations Act. Completion of this form is voluntary; however, if this information is not provided, you may not receive full consideration for a position.

COMPUTER MATCHING: Limited information may be disclosed to a federal, state, or local government administering benefits or other programs pursuant to statute for the purpose of conducting computer matching programs under the Act. These programs include, but are not limited to, matches performed to verify an individual's initial or continuing eligibility for, indebtedness to, or compliance with requirements of a benefit program.

PS Form **2591**, March 1999 *(Page 3 of 4)*

This application is included for study purposes only and is not to be filled out and turned in to the United States Postal Service.

Name *(First, MI, Last)*		Social Security No.	Date

E. Other Information

		Yes	No
1.	Are you one of the following: a United States citizen, a permanent resident alien, a citizen of American Samoa or any other territory owing allegiance to the United States?		
2.	RESERVED FOR OFFICIAL USE		
3.	RESERVED FOR OFFICIAL USE		
If you answer "Yes" to question 4 and/or 5, give details in Section F below. Give the name, address (including ZIP Code) of employer, approximate date, and reasons in each case. ▶	4. Have you ever been fired from any job for any reason?		
	5. Have you ever quit a job after being notified that you would be fired?		
6.	Do you receive or have you applied for retirement pay, pension, or other compensation based upon military, postal, or federal civilian service? *(If you answer "Yes," give details in Section F.)*		
7a.	Have you ever been convicted of a crime or are you now under charges for any offense against the Law? You may omit: (1) any charges that were dismissed or resulted in acquittal; (2) any conviction that has been set aside, vacated, annulled, expunged, or sealed; (3) any offense that was finally adjudicated in a juvenile court or juvenile delinquency proceeding; and (4) any charges that resulted only in a conviction of a non-criminal offense. **All felony and misdemeanor convictions and all convictions in state and federal courts are criminal convictions and must be disclosed. Disclosure of such convictions is required even if you did not spend any time in jail and/or were not required to pay a fine.**		
7b.	While in the military service were you ever convicted by special or general court martial?		
	If you answer "Yes" to question 7a and/or 7b, give details in Section F. Show for each offense: (1) Date of conviction; (2) Charge convicted of; (3) Court and location; (4) Action taken. Note: A conviction does not automatically mean that you cannot be appointed. What you were convicted of, and how long ago, are important. Give all of the facts so that a decision can be made.		
8.	Are you a former Postal Service or Federal Employee not now employed by the US Government?		
	If you answer "Yes," give in Section F, name of employing agency(ies), position title(s), and date(s) employed.		
9.	Does the US Postal Service employ any relative of yours by blood or marriage?		
	Postal officials may not appoint any of their relatives or recommend them for appointment in the Postal Service. Any relative who is appointed in violation of this restriction can not be paid. Thus it is necessary to have information about your relatives who are working for the USPS. These include: mother, father, daughter, son, sister, brother, aunt, uncle, first cousin, niece, nephew, wife, husband, mother-in-law, father-in-law, daughter-in-law, son-in-law, sister-in-law, brother-in-law, stepfather, stepmother, stepdaughter, stepson, stepsister, stepbrother, half sister, and half brother.		
	If you answer "Yes" to question 9, give in section F for such relatives:		
	(1) Full name; (2) Present address and ZIP Code; (3) Relationship; (4) Position title; (5) Name and location of postal installation where employed.		
10.	Are you now dependent on or a user of ANY addictive or hallucinogenic drug, including amphetamines, barbiturates, heroin, morphine, cocaine, mescaline, LSD, STP, hashish, marijuana, or methadone, other than for medical treatment under the supervision of a doctor?		

F. Use This Space for Detailed Answers *(Use blank sheets if you need more space. Include your name, SSN, and date on each sheet.)*

G. Certification

Enter number of additional sheets you have attached as part of this application:

I certify that all of the statements made in this application are true, complete, and correct to the best of my knowledge and belief and are in good faith.	Signature of Applicant	Date Signed

Disclosure by you of your Social Security Number (SSN) is mandatory to obtain the services, benefits, or processes that you are seeking. Solicitation of the SSN by the USPS is authorized under provisions of Executive Order 9397, dated November 22, 1943. The information gathered through the use of the number will be used only as necessary in authorized personnel administration processes.

A false or dishonest answer to any question in this application may be grounds for not employing you or for dismissing you after you begin work, and may be punishable by fine or imprisonment. (US Code, Title 18, Sec. 1001). All information you give will be considered in reviewing your application and is subject to investigation.

PS Form **2591**, March 1999 *(Page 4 of 4)*

Working for the Postal Service

As you may suspect, applicants seeking employment with the United States Postal Service will encounter tough competition for each job available. Although the United States Postal Service is an independent agency of the federal government all employees of the Postal Service are federal employees and enjoy the generous benefits offered by the U.S. government.

These benefits include an automatic raise at least once a year, regular cost-of-living adjustments (or COLA's), paid vacations and sick leaves, life insurance, health care benefits and the opportunity to join a credit union.

At the same time, the operations of the Postal Service are professional, businesslike and independent of politics. Even as government administrations change, postal employee positions are generally secure.

An examination is used to determine the best applicants for available positions. This examination system provides opportunities for those who are qualified and motivated to enter the Postal Service and advance from within.

Any individual who is already employed by the Postal Service may request to take an exam. Current Postal Service employees who have taken the exam for a position and meet the qualifications, will be chosen to fill a vacancy ahead of a person whose name is on the regular list.

It is possible to change careers with the Postal Service. A custodian, janitor or maintenance person, for example, might take the clerk/ carrier exam (Exam 473). A stenographer might choose to become a letter sorting machine operator and a mail handler might choose to enter the personnel department. Accordingly, if the position you want is not immediately available to you, you should strongly consider taking another position, if only for the sake of becoming a postal employee. You can work your way to your desired position inside the Postal Service.

One common type of rapid advancement within the Postal Service is from clerk/carrier, which is a grade level 5 position, to a letter sorting machine operator (LSM), which is a grade level 6 position. Anyone who qualifies as a clerk/carrier is automatically offered the opportunity to become an LSM operator. This position may require another type of test. An LSM operator makes a higher salary due to the higher grade level and increased employment opportunities. Increasingly, most of the routine Postal Service operations are being mechanized and automated. Though most people think of the clerk/carrier when they think of the Postal Service, the real growth area is in the field of automation. In the future, there will be far more openings for LSM operators than there will be for clerks or carriers.

As mentioned previously, the United States Postal Service has also broadened its business to the World Wide Web. Customers can now purchase stamps from vending machines, online, and at some ATM's; as these new ventures grow, the need for new employees to maintain the new technology will also grow.

If, when you attempt to apply for a job, you discover that none are available in your area, you should sign up for our Job Notification Service. If you have not already signed up, please do so now by going to the website provided in your instruction package or you can subscribe for the service at www.endeavormediallc.com, a small fee may apply if your reseller does not offer this serivce on your behalf. In the meantime, you can look in your local newspaper or post office for "Temporary/Casual" announcements. If there is a Temporary/Casual position available you are highly encouraged to apply; not only will this give you a paycheck while you wait to take an exam, but you also may find out about an exam opening that has not been advertised to the general public.

Chapter 3: Postal Employee Benefits

Leave information

The following employees are covered by the USPS leave program: full-time career employees, part-time regular career employees, part-time flexible career employees, and to the extent provided in the USPS National Rural Letter Carriers Association (NRLCA) National Agreement, found at www.nrlca.org, temporary employees assigned to rural carrier duties. Please note that transitional employees are not covered by the leave program, but do earn leave as specified in their union's national agreement. The following employees are *not* covered by the leave program: Postmaster relief/leave replacements, non-career officers in charge, and some other temporary employees, casual employees and those individuals who work on a fee or contract basis.

Annual Leave

Annual leave is the leave time which has traditionally been referred to as vacation. The amount of annual leave each employee receives is determined by the total service time the employee has rendered to the federal government. Employees receive credit for any period of service they may have performed with the armed services or for any other federal agency. Previous federal employment is called "creditable service" and is tallied out to compute the actual status of each worker's leave credits.

If you are a new postal employee (less than 3 years' service), you'll be credited with 13 days of annual leave (4 hours per pay period). If you are a full-time employee, the total amount of vacation you would earn for the year is advanced to you in a lump sum credit at the beginning of the year. That way you can take your leave time whenever you wish, provided that you obtain the consent of your supervisor. If you leave the Postal Service for any reason, however, you will be required to pay back any vacation time you used in advance but did not actually accrue. As your tenure with the USPS increases, you earn more annual leave. For 3–15 years of service, you earn 20 days per year (6 hours per pay period); if you remain with the USPS for 15 or more years, you will earn 26 days of annual leave per year (8 hours per pay period). A certain portion of unused annual leave can be rolled-over to the next year.

Sick Leave

Personal illness, pregnancy or any other conditions requiring medical attention can be grounds for taking sick leave. You can also receive sick leave if you need a medical, dental or optical examination or treatment. Postal employees have an excellent sick leave program. Your unused sick leave can be saved from year to year, which is a smart practice; in case you experience a prolonged illness, your take-home pay will not suffer significantly. As a matter of fact, any sick leave time unused over a long period of time becomes more and more valuable because the value of the sick leave becomes worth more as your salary increases. According to Postal Service regulations, the value of sick leave increases along with your salary and can also be credited toward your retirement benefits.

Full-time employees earn 4 hours of sick leave for each full two-week period worked; this is equal to 13 days per year. Part-time employees earn 1 hour for every 20 hours for which they are paid up to 13 days per year.

Health Care Benefits

Postal employees have the opportunity to protect themselves and their families against the increasing costs of health care. Such benefits are extended to all employees, including those who are in accidents or suffer from severe or prolonged illnesses. The Postal Service pays most of the cost of the plans, with employees paying a smaller portion, or co-payment, through payroll deductions from their paychecks. The system is called the "Federal Employees Health Benefits Program." Postal workers and their spouses become eligible for Medicare at the age of 65.

Postal workers are not required to enroll in the health-care plan. New employees are given an enrollment information guide and a plan comparison chart which will explain the health benefits for each plan, with additional information explaining the various costs and benefits. Postal workers who decide to enroll in a health-care plan may enroll during the annual enrollment sessions or "open enrollment windows, " which are generally held from the second Monday in November through the first Friday in December. Postal workers can sign up for either individual or family coverage. The family members who can be enrolled are the worker's legal spouse and their dependents, which may include all unmarried children under the age of 22, legally adopted children, children born out of wedlock, foster children and children who live in the worker's household. Certain unmarried children, regardless of age, may be covered, as are dependents that are disabled and cannot support themselves. United States Postal Service employees generally receive a much better rate on their health insurance premiums, than other federal employees, because the Postal Service's overall investment in the federal health care program is greater than the contributions of other federal agencies. The amount the worker pays for health insurance and other benefits depends on the plan selected. As a rule, plans that provide greater health-care coverage will have higher monthly premiums.

Life Insurance Information

All postal workers receive basic life insurance coverage, unless they specifically state in writing that they do not need it or if they already have sufficient life insurance from other sources. The U.S. Postal Service pays 100% of the cost of this basic life insurance for its employees.

Two types of basic life insurance are provided through the group policy during employment. The first type is life insurance without a medical examination, and the second is accidental death and injury/dismemberment insurance, which will pay double indemnity for any accidental death and pays for any additional loss of eyesight or the loss of any limbs. The total amount for this kind of insurance is a minimum of $10,000 and a maximum of $92,000.

As a federal employee you have the option to buy additional life insurance. This option will be available to you when you are hired and you will be fully responsible for the cost of the additional coverage. You may wonder, "Why purchase life insurance?" Life insurance is protection for your family against financial loss resulting from your death. In exchange for your timely payment of premiums, insurance companies promise to pay your beneficiary a specific amount of money when you die. Life insurance is protection for your dependents. Your dependents can include children, parents, a spouse, or anyone who depends on you for financial support. Why do you need life insurance? Although you may not think about it, your ability to earn income is a significant asset and life insurance helps replace lost income in the event of your premature death. The death benefit may be used to replace income your family would need to maintain their standard of living after your death, pay off a mortgage loan, or other personal and business debts; create a fund for your children's education; pay final expenses, such as funeral costs and taxes; or create an emergency fund as needed for your family's future.

Salaries

Salaries within the USPS are graded. The amount of time you've been employed, promotions you might have received and whether you work full- or part-time all determine your salary. The following tables illustrate salary levels of various positions with the USPS. Depending on the type of position you fill you are assigned a grade (for example, Grade 5, not that each position has different grade levels). To move between steps (such as from Step B to Step C), you must be at the lower step for a specified number of weeks. More details on these step requirements are defined later.

There are several pay scales in the Postal Service. The pay scale for bargaining unit employees (employees who belong to a union) is presented on the following pages. Special pay scales are also used for rural letter carriers. The Postal Service also pays extra compensation, overtime, and night shift rates. A cost-of-living adjustment is added to the base salary of employees at the rate of one cent per hour for each increase of 0.4 in the Consumer Price Index.

CITY CARRIER WAGE SCHEDULE - EFFECTIVE SEPTEMBER 2, 2006						
Step	Waiting Period to next step (in weeks)	Yearly	Hourly	Bi-Weekly	Regular Overtime	Hourly rate Part-Time Flexibles
A	96	$37,995	$18.2668	$1,461.34	$27.40	$19.00
B	96	$41,445	$19.9255	$1,594.04	$29.89	$20.72
C	44	$42,782	$20.5683	$1,645.46	$30.85	$21.39
D	44	$45,344	$21.8000	$1,744.00	$32.70	$22.67
E	44	$45,698	$21.9702	$1,757.62	$32.96	$22.85
F	44	$46,052	$22.1404	$1,771.23	$33.21	$23.03
G	44	$46,400	$22.3077	$1,784.62	$33.46	$23.20
H	44	$46,753	$22.4774	$1,798.19	$33.72	$23.38
I	44	$47,107	$22.6476	$1,811.81	$33.97	$23.55
J	34	$47,455	$22.8149	$1,825.19	$34.22	$23.73
K	34	$47,809	$22.9851	$1,838.81	$34.48	$23.90
L	26	$48,160	$23.1538	$1,852.30	$34.73	$24.08
M	26	$48,514	$23.3240	$1,865.92	$34.99	$24.26
N	24	$48,868	$23.4942	$1,879.54	$35.24	$24.43
O	-	$49,218	$23.6625	$1,893.00	$35.49	$24.61

Median annual earnings of Postal Service mail carriers were $44,350 in May 2006. The middle 50 percent earned between $40,290 and $28400. The lowest 10 percent earned less than $34,810, while the top 10 percent earned more than $50,830. Rural mail carriers are reimbursed for mileage put on their personal vehicles while delivering mail.

MAIL HANDLER LEVEL 4 WAGE SCHEDULE - EFFECTIVE MARCH 18, 2006

Step	Yearly	Hourly	Bi-Weekly	Regular Overtime
A	$30,810	$14.81	$1,185.00	$22.22
B	$36,967	$17.29	$1,383.35	$25.94
C	$38,404	$18.46	$1,477.08	$27.69
D	$41,992	$20.19	$1,615.08	$30.29
E	$42,281	$20.33	$1,626.19	$30.50
F	$42,576	$20.47	$1,637.54	$30.71
G	$42,863	$20.61	$1,648.58	$30.92
H	$43,155	$20.75	$1,659.81	$31.13
I	$43,446	$20.89	$1,671.00	$31.34
J	$43,742	$21.03	$1,682.38	$31.55
K	$44,030	$21.17	$1,693.46	$31.76
L	$44,321	$21.31	$1,704.65	$31.97
M	$44,613	$21.45	$1,715.88	$32.18
N	$44,902	$21.59	$1,727.00	$32.39
O	$45,193	$21.73	$1,738.19	$32.60

MAIL HANDLER LEVEL 5 WAGE SCHEDULE - EFFECTIVE MARCH 18, 2006

Step	Yearly	Hourly	Bi-Weekly	Regular Overtime
A	$32,260	$15.51	$1,240.77	$23.27
B	$37,771	$18.16	$1,452.73	$27.24
C	$40,276	$19.36	$1,549.08	$29.04
D	$42,700	$20.53	$1,642.31	$30.80
E	$43,012	$20.68	$1,654.31	$31.02
F	$43,329	$20.83	$1,666.50	$31.25
G	$43,637	$20.98	$1,678.35	$31.47
H	$43,952	$21.13	$1,690.46	$31.70
I	$44,269	$21.28	$1,702.65	$31.92
J	$44,579	$21.43	$1,714.58	$32.15
K	$44,893	$21.58	$1,726.65	$32.37
L	$45,202	$21.73	$1,738.54	$32.60
M	$45,519	$21.88	$1,750.73	$32.82
N	$45,832	$22.03	$1,762.77	$33.05
O	$46,144	$22.18	$1,774.77	$33.27

Median annual earnings of Postal Service mail sorters, processors, and processing machine operators were $43,900 in 2006. The middle 50 percent earned between $40,350 and $47,440. The lowest 10 percent had earnings of less than $25,770, while the top 10 percent earned more than $49,570.

CLERK LEVEL 5 WAGE SCHEDULE - EFFECTIVE SEPTEMBER 2, 2006

Step	Yearly	Hourly	Bi-Weekly	Regular Overtime
A	$36,054	$17.33	$1,386.70	$26.00
B	$36,907	$17.74	$1,419.50	$26.21
C	$37,760	$18.15	$1,452.30	$27.23
D	$38,613	$18.56	$1,485.11	$27.84
E	$39,466	$18.97	$1,517.92	$28.46
F	$40,319	$19.38	$1,550.73	$29.08
G	$41,172	$19.79	$1,583.54	$29.69
H	$42,025	$20.20	$1,616.34	$30.31
I	$42,878	$20.61	$1,649.15	$30.92
J	$43,731	$21.02	$1,681.96	$31.54
K	$44,584	$21.43	$1,714.77	$32.15
L	$45,437	$21.84	$1,747.58	$32.77
M	$46,290	$22.25	$1,780.38	$33.38
N	$47,143	$22.66	$1,813.19	$34.00
O	$47,996	$23.07	$1,846.00	$34.61

CLERK LEVEL 6 WAGE SCHEDULE - EFFECTIVE SEPTEMBER 2, 2006

Step	Yearly	Hourly	Bi-Weekly	Regular Overtime
A	$37,825	$18.18	$1,454.81	$27.28
B	$38,630	$18.57	$1,485.77	$27.86
C	$39,435	$18.96	$1,516.73	$28.44
D	$40,240	$19.35	$1,547.70	$29.02
E	$41,045	$19.73	$1,578.66	$29.60
F	$41,850	$20.12	$1,609.62	$30.18
G	$42,655	$20.51	$1,640.58	$30.76
H	$43,460	$20.89	$1,671.54	$31.34
I	$44,256	$21.28	$1,702.50	$31.92
J	$45,070	$21.67	$1,733.46	$32.50
K	$45,875	$22.05	$1,764.42	$33.08
L	$46,680	$22.44	$1,795.38	$33.66
M	$47,485	$22.83	$1,826.34	$34.24
N	$48,290	$23.22	$1,857.30	$34.82
O	$49,095	$23.60	$1,888.27	$35.41

Median annual earnings of Postal Service clerks were $44,800 in 2006.   The middle 50 percent earned between $41,720 and $47,890. The lowest 10 percent had earnings of less than $38,980, while the top 10 percent earned more than $49,750.

As you advance in your selected position within the USPS, you will become eligible for pay increases. To be eligible for a pay increase, an employee must meet the following criteria:

- Must have received and currently be serving under a career appointment.
- Must have performed in a satisfactory or outstanding manner during the waiting period.
- Cannot have received an equivalent increase during the waiting period.
- Must have completed the required waiting period (see the following tables).

Step Increase Waiting Periods for Bargaining Unit Positions

(The number under each grade column indicates the number of weeks an employee must remain in that grade.)

Postal Service (PS) Schedule

Steps (From - To)	Grades 1 - 3	Grades 4 - 7	Grades 8 - 10	Steps (From - To)	Grades 1 - 3	Grades 4 - 7	Grades 8 - 10
A - B	96	-	-	H - I	44	44	44
B - C	88	96	-	I - J	44	44	44
C - D	88	44	-	J - K	34	34	34
D - E	44	44	52	K - L	34	34	34
E - F	44	44	44	L - M	26	26	26
F - G	44	44	44	M - N	26	26	26
G - H	44	44	44	N - O	24	24	24

Mail Handlers' (MH) Schedule

Steps (From - To)	Grades 3	Grades 4 - 6	Steps (From $ To)	Grades 3	Grades 4 - 6
A - B	96	-	H - I	44	44
B -C	88	96	I - J	44	44
C - D	88	44	J - K	34	34
D - E	44	44	K - L	34	34
E - F	44	44	L - M	26	26
F -G	44	44	M - N	26	26
G - H	44	44	N – O	24	24

Note: Wage schedule information is adapted from that found at www.postalreporter.com., and may have changed since the publication of this book. Information regarding median wages can be found on the Bureau of Labor Statistics web site at http://www.bls.gov/oco/ocos141.html.

Chapter 4: Study Hints

Nine Tips for Studying More Effectively

On the following pages, we have listed a number of rules for you to follow to increase efficiency of your study time. If you abide by these rules, you will get the most out of this book.

1. **Make sure you understand the meaning of every word you read.** Your ability to understand what you read is the most important skill needed to pass any test. Therefore, starting now, every time you see a word that you don't fully understand, make certain that you write it down and make note of where you saw it. Then, when you have a chance, look up the meaning of the word in the dictionary. When you think you know what the word means, go back to the reading material which contained the word, and make sure that you fully understand the meaning of the word in its context.

Keep a list of all words you don't know, and periodically review them. Also, try to use these words whenever you can in conversation. If you do this faithfully, you will quickly build an extensive vocabulary which will be helpful to you not only when you take the Postal Battery Exam, but for the rest of your life. In addition, the web site www.dictionary.com allows you to sign up for a word-of-the-day by e-mail. This is an excellent tool to increase your vocabulary. Although you may not think that an expanded vocabulary is important in a clerk or carrier position with the USPS, it will be useful should you ever apply for a promotion to a management or clerical position.

2. **Study uninterrupted for at least 30 minutes.** Unless you can study for at least 30 minutes without stopping, you should not bother to study at all. It is essential that you concentrate for extended periods of time. Remember, the actual exam will take about 2 1/2 hours to complete. You must concentrate just as hard in the last hour of the test as you did in the first. Therefore, as the examination approaches, study for more extended periods of time without interruption. When you take the practice exams in Chapters 6 and 8, complete each examination in one sitting, just as you must at the actual examination.

3. **Simulate examination conditions when studying.** Study under the same conditions as those of the examination, as much as possible. Eliminate as many outside disturbances as you can. If you are a smoker, refrain from smoking while studying since you will most likely *not* be allowed to smoke in the room on the day of your examination.

4. **Make sure you understand the answers to every question in this book.** Answers are accompanied by explanations where appropriate. Whenever you chose the wrong answer to a question, be sure that you understand why you missed it so you won't make the same mistake again. It is equally important to make certain that you have answered a question correctly for the right reason. Therefore, study each answer and any explanation provided as carefully as you study the question itself.

5. **Always follow the recommended technique for answering multiple choice questions.** The next section of this chapter recommends invaluable procedures for handling multiple choice questions.

6. **Always time yourself when doing practice questions.** You can easily avoid running out of time on multiple-choice examinations is a tragic error that is easily avoided. Learn, through practice, to spend a reasonable amount of time on one question, then to move to the next question. Therefore, when you are doing practice questions, always time yourself—and always try to stay within the recommended time limits. The correct use of time during the actual examination is an integral part of the techniques that will be explained in Chapters 5 and 7.

7. **Concentrate your study time in the areas of your greatest weaknesses.** The practice exercises provided in this book will give you an indication of the most difficult types of questions for you. Although you should spend most of your time improving yourself in these areas, be sure to

practice all the types of questions.

8. **Exercise regularly and stay in good physical condition.** Students who are in good physical condition have an advantage over those who are not; good physical health improves the mind's ability to function well, especially when taking lengthy examinations.

9. **Establish a schedule for studying, and stick to it.** Do not put off studying to those times when you have nothing else to do. Schedule your study time, and try not to let anything else interfere with that schedule. If you feel yourself weakening, review the earlier chapters and remind yourself why you would like to work for the USPS.

The Postal Battery Exams are multiple choice. Here are some hints on how to attain a higher score on a multiple choice exam.

Rules for Handling Multiple-Choice Questions

1. **Read the directions.** Do not assume that you know what the directions say without reading them. Make sure you read and understand them. Note particularly whether the directions for one section of the examination are different from the rest.

2. **Make sure you have the complete examination.** Check the examination page by page. Since examination booklets have numbered pages, simply make certain that you have all the pages.

3. **Take a close look at the Answer Grid.** Some Answer Grids are numbered vertically and some horizontally. The Answer Grids for the practice exercises and practice examinations are typical of the ones you will see on your exam. However, do not take anything for granted. Review the directions on each Answer Grid carefully, and familiarize yourself with its format.

4. **Be careful when marking your answers.** Be sure to mark your answers exactly in accordance with the directions.

- Unless indicated otherwise mark only one answer for each question
- Do not make any other marks on your Answer Grid
- Completely darken the space for the answer you choose
- Completely erase any answer you wish to change

5. **Make absolutely certain you are marking the answer to the right question.** Many people have failed multiple-choice exams because of carelessness in this area. All it takes is one mistake. If you mark one answer in the wrong row, you could mark several more rows incorrectly before you realize your error. We recommend you use the following procedure when marking your Answer Grid:

- Select your answer, circle that choice in the test booklet, and connect that answer to the number of the question you are working on.

- If you select choice "C" as the answer for question eleven, circle choice "C" in the test booklet, and say to yourself, "C is the answer to question eleven."

- Then find the space on your Answer Grid for question eleven, and again say "C is the answer to question eleven" as you mark the answer.

While this might seem rather elementary and repetitive, after a while it becomes automatic. If used consistently, this technique guarantees that you will not fail the examination because of a careless mistake.

6. **Make certain that you understand what the question is asking.** Read the stem of the question (the part before the choices) very carefully to make certain that you know what the examiner is asking. In fact, it is wise to read it twice.

7. **Always read all of the choices before you select an answer.** Don't fall for the best distracter, or wrong answer, that comes before the correct choice! Read all choices, then choose the best one.

8. **Never make a choice based on frequency of previous answers.** Some students pay attention to the pattern of answers when taking an exam. Always choose the best answer for each question, whatever the answers to the previous questions have been.

9. **Cross out choices you know are wrong.** As you read through the choices, put an "X" through the letter designation of any choice you know is wrong. After reading through all of the choices, you only have to re-read the ones you did not cross out the first time. If you cross out all but one of the choices, the remaining choice should be the answer. Read the answer one more time to satisfy yourself, put a circle around its letter designation (if you still feel that it is the best answer), and mark it on the Answer Grid. (See the procedure given above under Rule 5.) If you cross out all but two choices when you read through the first time, you only have to re-read the two remaining choices, and make a decision.

Often when you read the remaining choices the second time, the answer is clear. If that happens, cross out the wrong choice, circle the correct one, and transpose the answer to the Answer Grid. If more than two choices are still not crossed out, re-read the stem of the question and make certain you understand it. Then go through the choices again.

10. **Don't dwell too long on any one question.** The first time through the examination, be certain not to spend too much time on any one question. If you cannot decide on an answer to a question within a reasonable time, make an educated guess at the answer, but put a circle around the question number in the test booklet.

11. **Return to questions you guessed at after you finish the rest of the examination.** Once you have answered all the questions on the entire examination, check the time remaining. If time permits, the first thing to do is to return to each question, if any, that you guessed at the first time through, and reread the stem and the choices that are not crossed out. It should be easy to find the questions you guessed at because, as per the instructions in Rule 10, you will have circled their numbers in the test booklet. If the answer is now clear to you, mark it on the Answer Grid, making sure to completely erase any answer choice you wish to change (see Rule 5).

12. **Never leave questions unanswered unless the instructions indicate a penalty for wrong answers.**

You can always create your own sample tests for more practice if you find that there are areas in which you are weak, even after completing all the practice exams included in this book. Remember, our customer care team is available to help with any questions or concerns you may have as you study.

Chapter 5: Exam 460 Basics

Exam 460 is the exam given to those who wish to become Rural Carrier Associates, and with promotion, Rural Carriers. The job description for this position is found in Chapter 1.

This exam is offered with the most frequency; some larger localities have exam openings almost continuously. Even if this is not the position you desire, we recommend you register for and take the exam to get your foot in the door. Once you are working for the Postal Service, you will frequently have opportunities to apply for job openings which are only offered internally.

Exam 460 consists of four (4) parts: address checking, memorization of addresses, number series, and following oral instructions. This chapter contains detailed descriptions of these four sections, followed by some sample exam sections, so that you can familiarize yourself with the type of questions asked before you attempt to take the sample exams.

Chapter 6 contains four full-length sample exams. These exams should be taken under conditions which simulate the actual exam conditions as closely as possible. Your exam date notice packet (which you should receive about 2 weeks before the exam) will include directions on what you need to bring with you, and list a few items that are not allowed in the examination room. These include, but may not be limited to the following instructions:

You should bring:

1. The first page of your scheduling packet.
2. A photo ID.
3. Two sharpened **#2** pencils.

The following items are not allowed in the examination room:

1. Food or drink
2. Cell phones

The descriptions and sample questions you can use to practice for Exam 460 begin on the next page. As you are studying and practicing, if you have any questions, please contact the Customer Care Department for the reseller you ordered the book from. This information should have been part of your original packet.

Address Checking

In this part of the exam, you will have to decide whether two addresses are alike or different. If the two addresses are exactly **alike** darken circle A for the answer. If the two addresses are **different** in any way, darken circle D for the answer.

Your score on the address checking part of the actual exam will be based on the number of wrong answers as well as on the number of right answers. This part of the exam is scored right answers minus wrong answers. Random guessing should not help your score, and may actually hurt it. You will be given 6 minutes to answer 95 questions. Try to answer as many as you can (this is where a lot of practice comes in handy). It is to your advantage to work as quickly and accurately as possible. You will not be expected to be able to answer all the questions in the time allowed.

These first 25 sample questions do not need to be timed.

Mark your answers to these sample questions on the Sample Answer Grid on the next page.

Address Checking Practice

1.	2134 S 20th St.	2134 S 20th St.

1. 2134 S 20th St.   2134 S 20th St.
2. 4608 N Warnock St.   4806 N Warnock St.
3. 1202 W Girard Dr.   1202 W Girard Rd.
4. Chappaqua, NY 10514   Chappaqua, NY 10514
5. 2207 Markland Ave.   2207 Markham Ave.
6. Akron, OH   Akrin, OH
7. Saco, ME   Saco, ME
8. Brooklyn, NY   Brooklyn, FL
9. Main Street   Mane Street
10. 1616 Arbor Street   1666 Arbor Street
11. 123 85th Street   123 85th Street
12. Austin, TX   Austin, TX
13. 1947 Desert Lane   1947 Dessert Lane
14. Miami, FL   Miami, FL
15. 19472 River Rd.   19472 River Ave.
16. Tucson, AZ   Tucson, AZ
17. Apt. 126   Apt. A126
18. Boston, MA   Boston, GA
19. 13 Oak Street   13 Oak Street
20. P.O. Box 147398   P.O. Box 147398
21. New York, NY   New York, NY
22. Kansas City, OH   Kansas City, MO
23. P.O. Box 2111   P.O. Box 211
24. 107 Oak Hill Road   17 Oak Hill Road
25. 100 East North Street   100 North East Street

Sample Answer Grid for Address Checking Practice

1. Ⓐ Ⓓ
2. Ⓐ Ⓓ
3. Ⓐ Ⓓ
4. Ⓐ Ⓓ
5. Ⓐ Ⓓ
6. Ⓐ Ⓓ
7. Ⓐ Ⓓ
8. Ⓐ Ⓓ
9. Ⓐ Ⓓ
10. Ⓐ Ⓓ
11. Ⓐ Ⓓ
12. Ⓐ Ⓓ
13. Ⓐ Ⓓ
14. Ⓐ Ⓓ
15. Ⓐ Ⓓ
16. Ⓐ Ⓓ
17. Ⓐ Ⓓ
18. Ⓐ Ⓓ
19. Ⓐ Ⓓ
20. Ⓐ Ⓓ
21. Ⓐ Ⓓ
22. Ⓐ Ⓓ
23. Ⓐ Ⓓ
24. Ⓐ Ⓓ
25. Ⓐ Ⓓ

Correct Answers – Address Checking Practice

1. Alike
2. Different: the street numbers are different
3. Different: One address is a drive and the other is a road.
4. Alike
5. Different: the street names are different (Markland vs. Markham)
6. Different: Akron is spelled with an "O" in the first column and an "I" in the second.
7. Alike
8. Different: One Brooklyn is in New York and the other is in Florida.
9. Different: Main is spelled differently.
10. Different: the street numbers do not match.
11. Alike
12. Alike
13. Different: The street names are not spelled the same.
14. Alike
15. Different: One address is a road and the other is an avenue.
16. Alike
17. Different: The apartment number in the second column includes a letter.
18. Different: One Boston is in Massachusetts and the other is in Georgia.
19. Alike
20. Alike
21. Alike
22. Different: One Kansas City is in Ohio and the other is in Missouri.
23. Different: The box numbers are not the same.
24. Different: The street numbers are not the same.
25. Different: East and North do not fall in the same position in both columns.

As you can see from this short example, even the most subtle differences are important. This is one reason you want to practice as much as possible. On the following pages are two full-length address checking practice exams. As you practice be sure either to time yourself or to have someone time you. You don't want to get into the habit of taking longer in practice than you will be allowed in the exam. Following these practice exams, once again, the answers are explained for you. When you take the complete practice exam, the answer will not be explained, but we recommend you go back over and look at the "different" answers and determine for yourself what the difference is.

As you proceed through this and the following chapters, you will notice that the Answer Grids follow the questions. You should also notice that the Answer Grids are blank on the reverse so that you may remove them to make copies. This way the book will still be understandable without pages of information missing. If you should choose not to remove those pages, we strongly suggest that the blank pages be used to take notes as you proceed through the tests. Along these lines, any white space in the book should be used for taking notes.

Address Checking – Full-Length Practice #1

(You have 6 minutes to complete this section.)

Directions: If the pair of addresses is alike, darken bubble "A". If the pair is different, darken bubble "D".

1.	1216 W. 9th Ave.	1216 S. 9th Ave.
2.	2020 Poplar Dr.	2020 Popular Dr.
3.	9716 West End Terrace	9716 West End Terrace
4.	Allen, TX 75013	Allan, TX 75013
5.	PO Box 9556	PO Box 9566
6.	611 Main St.	616 Main St.
7.	Rutland, VT 08563	Rutland, VA 08563
8.	PO Box 8587	PO Box 8785
9.	Suite 785	Suite 785
10.	4040 Rock Creek Dr.	4040 Rock Creek Cir.
11.	1912 Elm Hill Rd.	1912 Elm Hill Rd.
12.	PO Box 211	PO Box 217
13.	Seattle, WA 98765	Seettle, WA 98765
14.	Loudon, NH 03067	Lowden, NH 03067
15.	Daytona Beach, FL 95463	Daytona Beach, FL 95643
16.	9856 River Rd.	9856 River Rd.
17.	PO Box 375901	PO Box 375901
18.	Zephyrhills, FL 33539	Zepyrhills, FL 33539
19.	Little Bend, CO 54216	Little Ben, CO 54211
20.	1919 Hickory Way	191919 Hickory Way
21.	Knoxsville, TN 36152	Knoxville, TN 36152
22.	8201 Summerset Place	8201 Sumnerset Place
23.	PO Box 1	PO Box 1
24.	Rural Rte. 427	Rural Rte. 4227
25.	9999 River Bend Way	6666 River Bend Way
26.	Veto, CA 99652	Veto, CA 99652
27.	38045 Northeastern Blvd.	38045 Eastern Blvd. N.
28.	Suite CA 4198	Suite C 4198
29.	Tampa, FL 33560	Tampa, FL 33560
30.	Austin, TX 75089	Astro, TX 75089
31.	1717 W. 1st St.	7171 W. 1st St.
32.	Reno, NV 87412	Reno, NE 87412
33.	Hoboken, NJ 44128	Hobroken, NJ 44128
34.	7109 Deed St.	7109 Deed St.
35.	2525 Riverdale Rd.	2552 Riverdale Rd.
36.	Nashua, NH 03060	Nashuah, NH 03060
37.	14 Brickstone St.	14 BrickStone St.
38.	Apt 24C	Apt C24
39.	Omaha, NE 68154	Omaha, NB 68154
40.	202 North West End	202 West North End
41.	555 Sweet lane	555 Sweet Lane
42.	2929 Hammer Rd.	2929 Hammr Rd.
43.	40 C St.	40 See St.
44.	P.O. Box 02134	PO Box 02134
45.	Pebble, VA	Pebble, VA
46.	12 Arrow Lane	120 Arrow Lane
47.	Little Rock, AR	Little Rock, AK
48.	10 Langholm Dr.	10 Langhome Dr.
49.	Suite B484	Sweet B484
50.	2050 Park Ave.	2050 Park Ave.
51.	Lincoln Park Blvd.	Linkin Park Blvd.

52. 1 Ocean Way	1 Ocean Wy
53. 4 Henry Long Lane	4 Henry Long Lane
54. 887 Broomfield St.	888 Broomfield St.
55. Bronx, NY	Bronks, NY
56. 2 Long Island Rd.	2 Long Iland Rd.
57. Philadelphia, PE	Philadelphia, PA
58. 4 Vein Hwy	4 Vane Hwy
59. Holiday, VT	Holiday, VE
60. 60154 Holliwood St.	60154 Hollywood St.
61. 8269 Hollister Rd.	8269 Hollister Rd.
62. 42 Wilkenson Way	42 Wilkinson Way
63. 6464 Springdale Dr.	6464 SpringDale Dr.
64. 33883 Hopping Trail	33883 Hooping Trail
65. 40 Wild Oak St.	40 Wilds Oak St.
66. 99 Smith St.	99 Smith St.
67. 55 Hopscotch Rd.	55 Hopscoch Rd.
68. 6321 Brook Way	6321 Brooke Way
69. 6 Gordon Dr.	6 Gorden Dr.
70. 4836 Capital St.	4836 Capitol St.
71. Boxborough, MA	Boxboro, MA
72. Rapid City, SD	Rapid City, SC
73. Diamond Rock Park	Diamond Rock Pk
74. 200 Central Ave.	200 Central Ave.
75. 9001 Gliding Rd.	9000 Gliding Rd.
76. 78 Glenwood St.	78 Glennwood St.
77. PO Box 554782	PO Box 554782
78. Hollywood, CA	Hollywood, CL
79. PO Box 6606	PO Box 6666
80. Apt a101	Apt A101
81. Clearwater, FL	Clearwater, FL
82. 734 Quarry Rock Rd.	734 Quary Rock Rd.
83. 1939 North West St.	1939 West North St.
84. Rt. 45 Box 54	Rt. 54 Box 45
85. 258 Smith St.	258 Smyth St.
86. 66 Meadow Lane	66 Meedow Lane
87. Detroit, MI	Detroit, ME
88. San Francisco, CA	San Jose, CA
89. Ocean See Way	Ocean Sea Way
90. Second Ave	Secand Ave
91. 32 Charter St.	23 Charter St.
92. 2469 Webster Way	2469 Webstor Way
93. P.O. Box 45678	P.O. Box 45678
94. 55 Creatave Rd.	55 Creative Rd.
95. 6 Gillman St.	6 Gilman St.

1. Ⓐ Ⓓ
2. Ⓐ Ⓓ
3. Ⓐ Ⓓ
4. Ⓐ Ⓓ
5. Ⓐ Ⓓ
6. Ⓐ Ⓓ
7. Ⓐ Ⓓ
8. Ⓐ Ⓓ
9. Ⓐ Ⓓ
10. Ⓐ Ⓓ
11. Ⓐ Ⓓ
12. Ⓐ Ⓓ
13. Ⓐ Ⓓ
14. Ⓐ Ⓓ
15. Ⓐ Ⓓ
16. Ⓐ Ⓓ
17. Ⓐ Ⓓ
18. Ⓐ Ⓓ
19. Ⓐ Ⓓ
20. Ⓐ Ⓓ
21. Ⓐ Ⓓ
22. Ⓐ Ⓓ
23. Ⓐ Ⓓ
24. Ⓐ Ⓓ
25. Ⓐ Ⓓ
26. Ⓐ Ⓓ
27. Ⓐ Ⓓ
28. Ⓐ Ⓓ
29. Ⓐ Ⓓ
30. Ⓐ Ⓓ
31. Ⓐ Ⓓ
32. Ⓐ Ⓓ

33. Ⓐ Ⓓ
34. Ⓐ Ⓓ
35. Ⓐ Ⓓ
36. Ⓐ Ⓓ
37. Ⓐ Ⓓ
38. Ⓐ Ⓓ
39. Ⓐ Ⓓ
40. Ⓐ Ⓓ
41. Ⓐ Ⓓ
42. Ⓐ Ⓓ
43. Ⓐ Ⓓ
44. Ⓐ Ⓓ
45. Ⓐ Ⓓ
46. Ⓐ Ⓓ
47. Ⓐ Ⓓ
48. Ⓐ Ⓓ
49. Ⓐ Ⓓ
50. Ⓐ Ⓓ
51. Ⓐ Ⓓ
52. Ⓐ Ⓓ
53. Ⓐ Ⓓ
54. Ⓐ Ⓓ
55. Ⓐ Ⓓ
56. Ⓐ Ⓓ
57. Ⓐ Ⓓ
58. Ⓐ Ⓓ
59. Ⓐ Ⓓ
60. Ⓐ Ⓓ
61. Ⓐ Ⓓ
62. Ⓐ Ⓓ
63. Ⓐ Ⓓ
64. Ⓐ Ⓓ

65. Ⓐ Ⓓ
66. Ⓐ Ⓓ
67. Ⓐ Ⓓ
68. Ⓐ Ⓓ
69. Ⓐ Ⓓ
70. Ⓐ Ⓓ
71. Ⓐ Ⓓ
72. Ⓐ Ⓓ
73. Ⓐ Ⓓ
74. Ⓐ Ⓓ
75. Ⓐ Ⓓ
76. Ⓐ Ⓓ
77. Ⓐ Ⓓ
78. Ⓐ Ⓓ
79. Ⓐ Ⓓ
80. Ⓐ Ⓓ
81. Ⓐ Ⓓ
82. Ⓐ Ⓓ
83. Ⓐ Ⓓ
84. Ⓐ Ⓓ
85. Ⓐ Ⓓ
86. Ⓐ Ⓓ
87. Ⓐ Ⓓ
88. Ⓐ Ⓓ
89. Ⓐ Ⓓ
90. Ⓐ Ⓓ
91. Ⓐ Ⓓ
92. Ⓐ Ⓓ
93. Ⓐ Ⓓ
94. Ⓐ Ⓓ
95. Ⓐ Ⓓ

Notes:

1. Different: W in the first column is changed to S in the second.
2. Different: Poplar in first column is changed to Popular in the second.
3. Alike
4. Different: Allen is spelled with an "e" in the first column and an "a" in the second.
5. Different: Box numbers are not the same.
6. Different: Street numbers are not the same.
7. Different: One Rutland is in Vermont, the other is in Virginia.
8. Different: Box numbers are not the same.
9. Alike
10. Different: Drive in the first column is changed to Circle in the second.
11. Alike
12. Different: Box numbers are not the same.
13. Different: Seattle is spelled with an "a" in the first column and two "e's" in the second.
14. Different: Lowden is spelled with a "u" in the first column and a "w" in the second.
15. Different: ZIP codes are not the same.
16. Alike
17. Alike
18. Different: Zephyrhills is spelled with a "ph" in the first column and a "p" in the second.
19. Different: Bend in the first column is changed to Ben in the second.
20. Different: Street numbers are not the same.
21. Different: Knoxville is spelled with an "xs" in the first column and an "x" in the second.
22. Different: Street names are not the same.
23. Alike
24. Different: Route numbers are not the same.
25. Different: Street numbers are not the same.
26. Alike
27. Different: Street names are different.
28. Different: Suite designation is not the same.
29. Alike
30. Different: City name is different.
31. Different: Street number is different.
32. Different: One Reno is in Nevada, the other is in Nebraska.
33. Different: Hoboken is spelled with an "r" in the second column.
34. Alike
35. Different: Street numbers are different.
36. Different: Nashua spelled with an "h" at the end in the second column.
37. Different: Brickstone has a capital "S" in the second column.
38. Different: Apartment numbers are not the same.
39. Different: One Omaha is in Nebraska, the other is in New Brunswick.
40. Different: Street names are not the same.
41. Different: Lane is capitalized in the second column.
42. Different: Hammer is missing the "e" in the second column.
43. Different: Street names are different.
44. Different: Periods in P.O. in the first column and not the second.
45. Alike
46. Different: Street numbers are different.
47. Different: One Little Rock is in Arkansas and the other is in Alaska
48. Different: Street numbers are different.
49. Different: Suite is spelled "Sweet" in the second column.
50. Alike
51. Different: Street names are not the same.
52. Different: Way is abbreviated in the second column.
53. Alike.

54. Different: Street numbers are different.
55. Different: City names are different.
56. Different: Island is missing the "s" in the second column.
57. Different: One Philadelphia is on Prince Edward Island, the other is in Pennsylvania.
58. Different: Vein is spelled differently in the second column.
59. Different: States are different; "VE" is not a valid state abbreviation.
60. Different: Hollywood is spelled with an "i" in the first column and a "y" in the second.
61. Alike
62. Different: Wilkinson is spelled with an "e" in the first column and an "i" in the second.
63. Different: Springdale is spelled with a capital "D" in the second column.
64. Different: Street names are different.
65. Different: "Wild" in first column, "Wilds" in the second.
66. Alike
67. Different: Hopscotch is spelled without the "t" in the second column.
68. Different: Brook is spelled with an "e" on the end in the second column.
69. Different: Gordon is spelled with an "o" in the first column and an "e" in the second.
70. Different: Capital is spelled with an "a" in the first column and an "o" in the second.
71. Different: City names are different.
72. Different: One Rapid City is in South Dakota and the other is in South Carolina.
73. Different: Park is abbreviated in the second column.
74. Alike
75. Different: Street numbers are different.
76. Different: Glenwood is spelled with two "n's" in the second column.
77. Alike
78. Different: States are different; CL is not a valid state abbreviation.
79. Different: Box numbers are different.
80. Different: Lower case "a" in first column, upper case "a" in second column.
81. Alike
82. Different: Quarry is missing an "r" in the second column.
83. Different: Street numbers are different.
84. Different: Route and box numbers are swapped in the second column.
85. Different: Smith is spelled with an "i" in the first column and a "y" in the second.
86. Different: Meadow is spelled with two "e's" in the second column.
87. Different: One Detroit is in Michigan, the other is in Maine.
88. Different: City names are different.
89. Different: See is spelled differently in the second column.
90. Different: Second is spelled with an "o" in the first column and an "a" in the second.
91. Different: Street numbers are different.
92. Different: Webster is spelled with an "er" in the first column and an "or" in the second.
93. Alike
94. Different: Creative is spelled with an "a" in the first column and an "i" in the second.
95. Different: Gillman is spelled with two "l's" in the first column and one in the second.

How many did you answer correctly?

90 or more?	**Awesome**
85-89?	**Still good**
84 or less?	**You should practice a bit more**

Address Checking – Full-Length Practice #2

(You have 6 minutes to complete this section)

Directions: If the pair of addresses is alike, darken bubble "A". If the pair is different, darken bubble "D".

1.	156 Coral Lane	156 Coral Lane
2.	219 Hickory Way	291 Hickory Way
3.	Tempe, AZ	Tempe, AZ
4.	Atlanta, GA	Atlantis, GA
5.	Sioux Falls, SD	Sioux Falls, SD
6.	PO Box 5147	PO Box 5147
7.	Campbell, CA 95008	Cambell, CA 95008
8.	30 Massachusetts Ave.	30 Massechusetts Ave.
9.	Lexington, KY 40512	Lexington, KY 40521
10.	756 John Wayne Lane	756 John Lane Way
11.	Orlando, FL	Orleans, MA
12.	4737 Rodeo Dr.	4737 Rodeo Dr.
13.	San Fransisco, CA	San Francesco, CA
14.	590 Hopkington Way	590 Hopkington Way
15.	Key West, FL	Kee West, FL
16.	918 Truvae Lane	918 Truvay Lane
17.	20817 Northeast Blvd.	20871 Northeast Blvd.
18.	Suite 368	Sweet 368
19.	213 Sumner St.	213 Summer St.
20.	Owensville, AL	Owensville, AL
21.	999 Quincy Ave.	999 Quincy St.
22.	Honolulu, HI	Honolulu, HI
23.	Indianapolis, IN	Indianapolis, IN
24.	576 Oak Hill Rd.	576 Oak Hills Rd.
25.	Marlboro, MA	Marboro, MA
26.	Brooklyn, NY	Brooklyn, NY
27.	899 Government Ave	899 Goverment Ave.
28.	1601 Pennsylvania Ave.	1611 Pennsylvania Ave.
29.	PO Box 310711	PO Box 301711
30.	Charlotte, NC	Charlotte, SC
31.	Buffalo, NY	Buffalo, MO
32.	PO Box 2645545	PO Box 2645455
33.	1111 S. Main St.	1117 S. Main St.
34.	7293 Brittany Lane	7923 Brittany Lane
35.	1901 Pacific Avenue	1901 Pacific Blvd.
36.	231 John Hancock Bldg.	231 John Hancock Blvd.
37.	101 Park Place	101 Park Place
38.	7707 Materials Park	7707 Materiols Park
39.	1364 Quarter Rd.	1364 Quartor Rd.
40.	Fillmore, KA	Fillmore, KS
41.	21 Norman Frank Lane	21 Normand Frank Lane
42.	54789 Madison Sq.	54789 Madison Sq.
43.	187 Parker Hill Rd.	187 Paker Hill Rd.
44.	Brentwood, TN 37219	Brentwood, TN 37219
45.	4554 W 42nd St.	4544 W 42nd St.
46.	Portland, OR	Portland, ME
47.	9000 Jiffy Lane	9000 Jiffy lane
48.	8965 Ridge Rd.	8956 Ridge Rd.
49.	Harvard, MA 01495	Harvard, VA 01495
50.	587 Sartelle St.	587 Sartelle St.

51. Building 1A
52. Hanover, RI
53. 1917 Simmons Pl.
54. Shoals, AL
55. PO Box 555499
56. Miami, FL 36512
57. Oakland, CA 95621
58. PO Box 11111
59. 5542 Algonquin Rd.
60. 6 Wonderstrand Way
61. 317 East St.
62. 419 Haskell Dr.
63. Pittsburg, VA 45621
64. 3001 Carver Way
65. Fairlane, OK 45456
66. Worcester, MA 01499
67. Albany, NY
68. 1 Johns Financial Bldg.
69. PO Box 10001
70. Northern Exposure, TX
71. 558 Gilligan Lane
72. Dade City, FL
73. 3487 W. Campbell Way
74. Hicksville, AK
75. Yuppytown, FL
76. Glenview Station, NY 87246
77. 20304 Government Pl.
78. Braxton, IA
79. 69665 Atlantic Ocean Dr.
80. Boca Raton, FL
81. 8731 Norway Ave.
82. Concord, NH
83. PO Box 171717
84. Burlington, MA
85. 19 Main St.
86. 529 Payton Ave.
87. 1014 Herbert Pl.
88. Ludlow, CA 98721
89. 12 Thomas Jefferson Pl.
90. Suite 154788
91. PO Box 457489
92. Myrtle Beach, SC
93. Yonkers, NY 54698
94. 1216 West St.
95. Finally, MI 56489

Building A
Hanover, CT
1917 Simons Pl.
Shoals, AL
PO Box 554599
Miami, TN 36512
Oakland, CA 95621
PO Box 111111
5542 Algonquin Rd.
6 Wonderstrand Way
311 East St.
419 Haskell St.
Pittsburg, PA 45621
3001 Carver Way
Fairlane, OK 45456
Worchester, MA 01499
Albany, NY
1 Johns Financial Blvd.
PO Box 10101
Northern Exposure, AK
558 Gilian Lane
Dade City, AL
3487 E. Campbell Way
Hicksville, MO
Yuppytown, FL
Glenview Station, NY 87246
20304 Government Pl.
Braxton, IA
69665 Atlantic Ocean Pl.
Boca Raton, FL
8732 Norway Ave.
Concorde, NH
PO Box 177171
Burtlington, VT
19 Main St.
529 Payton Ave.
1014 Hebert Pl.
Ludlow, CT 98721
12 Thomas Jefferson Pl.
Suite 154788
PO Box 457498
Myrtle Beach, SC
Yonkers, NY 54689
1216 West End St.
Finally, MI 56489

1.	Ⓐ	Ⓓ	34.	Ⓐ	Ⓓ	67.	Ⓐ	Ⓓ
2.	Ⓐ	Ⓓ	35.	Ⓐ	Ⓓ	68.	Ⓐ	Ⓓ
3.	Ⓐ	Ⓓ	36.	Ⓐ	Ⓓ	69.	Ⓐ	Ⓓ
4.	Ⓐ	Ⓓ	37.	Ⓐ	Ⓓ	70.	Ⓐ	Ⓓ
5.	Ⓐ	Ⓓ	38.	Ⓐ	Ⓓ	71.	Ⓐ	Ⓓ
6.	Ⓐ	Ⓓ	39.	Ⓐ	Ⓓ	72.	Ⓐ	Ⓓ
7.	Ⓐ	Ⓓ	40.	Ⓐ	Ⓓ	73.	Ⓐ	Ⓓ
8.	Ⓐ	Ⓓ	41.	Ⓐ	Ⓓ	74.	Ⓐ	Ⓓ
9.	Ⓐ	Ⓓ	42.	Ⓐ	Ⓓ	75.	Ⓐ	Ⓓ
10.	Ⓐ	Ⓓ	43.	Ⓐ	Ⓓ	76.	Ⓐ	Ⓓ
11.	Ⓐ	Ⓓ	44.	Ⓐ	Ⓓ	77.	Ⓐ	Ⓓ
12.	Ⓐ	Ⓓ	45.	Ⓐ	Ⓓ	78.	Ⓐ	Ⓓ
13.	Ⓐ	Ⓓ	46.	Ⓐ	Ⓓ	79.	Ⓐ	Ⓓ
14.	Ⓐ	Ⓓ	47.	Ⓐ	Ⓓ	80.	Ⓐ	Ⓓ
15.	Ⓐ	Ⓓ	48.	Ⓐ	Ⓓ	81.	Ⓐ	Ⓓ
16.	Ⓐ	Ⓓ	49.	Ⓐ	Ⓓ	82.	Ⓐ	Ⓓ
17.	Ⓐ	Ⓓ	50.	Ⓐ	Ⓓ	83.	Ⓐ	Ⓓ
18.	Ⓐ	Ⓓ	51.	Ⓐ	Ⓓ	84.	Ⓐ	Ⓓ
19.	Ⓐ	Ⓓ	52.	Ⓐ	Ⓓ	85.	Ⓐ	Ⓓ
20.	Ⓐ	Ⓓ	53.	Ⓐ	Ⓓ	86.	Ⓐ	Ⓓ
21.	Ⓐ	Ⓓ	54.	Ⓐ	Ⓓ	87.	Ⓐ	Ⓓ
22.	Ⓐ	Ⓓ	55.	Ⓐ	Ⓓ	88.	Ⓐ	Ⓓ
23.	Ⓐ	Ⓓ	56.	Ⓐ	Ⓓ	89.	Ⓐ	Ⓓ
24.	Ⓐ	Ⓓ	57.	Ⓐ	Ⓓ	90.	Ⓐ	Ⓓ
25.	Ⓐ	Ⓓ	58.	Ⓐ	Ⓓ	91.	Ⓐ	Ⓓ
26.	Ⓐ	Ⓓ	59.	Ⓐ	Ⓓ	92.	Ⓐ	Ⓓ
27.	Ⓐ	Ⓓ	60.	Ⓐ	Ⓓ	93.	Ⓐ	Ⓓ
28.	Ⓐ	Ⓓ	61.	Ⓐ	Ⓓ	94.	Ⓐ	Ⓓ
29.	Ⓐ	Ⓓ	62.	Ⓐ	Ⓓ	95.	Ⓐ	Ⓓ
30.	Ⓐ	Ⓓ	63.	Ⓐ	Ⓓ			
31.	Ⓐ	Ⓓ	64.	Ⓐ	Ⓓ			
32.	Ⓐ	Ⓓ	65.	Ⓐ	Ⓓ			
33.	Ⓐ	Ⓓ	66.	Ⓐ	Ⓓ			

Notes:

34

1. Alike
2. Different: Street numbers are different.
3. Alike
4. Different: City names are different.
5. Alike
6. Alike
7. Different: Campbell is spelled with a "p" in the first column and with no "p" in the second.
8. Different: Massachusetts is spelled with an "a" in the first column and an "e" in the second.
9. Different: ZIP codes are different.
10. Different: Street names are different.
11. Different: City name and state are both different.
12. Alike
13. Different: San Francisco is spelled with an "si" in the first column and an "ce" in the second.
14. Alike
15. Different: Key is spelled "Kee" in the second column.
16. Different: Truvae is spelled with an "e" in the first column and a "y" in the second.
17. Different: Street numbers are different.
18. Different: Suite is spelled "Sweet" in the second column.
19. Different: Street names are different.
20. Alike
21. Different: Ave in the first column, St in the second
22. Alike
23. Alike
24. Different: "Hill" in the first column, "Hills" in the second.
25. Different: City names are different.
26. Alike
27. Different: There isn't a period at end in the second column.
28. Different: Street numbers are different.
29. Different: Box numbers are different.
30. Different: One Charlotte is in North Carolina, the other is in South Carolina.
31. Different: One Buffalo is in New York, the other is in Missouri.
32. Different: Box numbers are different.
33. Different: Street numbers are different.
34. Different: Street numbers are different.
35. Different: Avenue in the first column, Boulevard in the second.
36. Different: Building in the first column, Boulevard in the second.
37. Alike
38. Different: Materials is spelled with an "a" in the first column and an "o" in the second.
39. Different: Quarter is spelled with an "e" in the first column and an "o" in the second
40. Different: "KA" is not a valid state abbreviation.
41. Different: Street names are different.
42. Alike
43. Different: Street names are different.
44. Alike
45. Different: Street numbers are different.
46. Different: One Portland is in Oregon, the other is in Maine.
47. Different: "lane" is not capitalized in the second column.
48. Different: Street numbers are not the same.
49. Different: One Harvard is in Massachusetts, the other is in Virginia.
50. Alike
51. Different: Building numbers are different.
52. Different: One Hanover is in Rhode Island, the other is in Connecticut.
53. Different: Street names are different.
54. Alike

55. Different: Box numbers are different.
56. Different: One Miami is in Florida, the other is in Tennessee.
57. Alike
58. Different: Box numbers are different.
59. Alike
60. Alike
61. Different: Street numbers are different.
62. Different: Drive in the first column, Street in the second.
63. Different: One Pittsburg is in Virginia, the other is in Pennsylvania.
64. Alike
65. Alike
66. Different: Worchester is spelled without the "h" in the first column.
67. Alike
68. Different: Building in the first column, Boulevard in the second.
69. Different: Box numbers are different.
70. Different: One Northern Exposure is in Texas, the other is in Alaska.
71. Different: Street names are different.
72. Different: One Dade City is in Florida, the other is in Vermont.
73. Different: West in the first column, East in the second.
74. Different: One Hicksville is in Alaska, the other is in Missouri
75. Alike
76. Alike
77. Alike
78. Alike
79. Different: Drive in the first column, Place in the second.
80. Alike
81. Different: Street numbers are different
82. Different: Concord is spelled with an "e" in the second column.
83. Different: Box numbers are different.
84. Different: One Burlington is in Massachusetts, the other is in Alabama.
85. Alike
86. Alike
87. Different: Street names are different.
88. Different: One Ludlow is in California, the other is in Connecticut.
89. Alike
90. Alike
91. Different: Box numbers are different.
92. Alike
93. Different: ZIP codes are different
94. Different: Street names are different.
95. Alike

How many did you answer correctly?

90 or more?	**Awesome**
85-89?	**Still good**
84 or less?	**You should practice a bit more**

After these practice exercises, you should feel fairly confident in your ability to detect the differences between two addresses. In the next chapter, you are given four more opportunities to practice. If after completing all six practice exams, you still are not sure of your abilities, have someone build you some more lists; make sure that they include as many subtle differences as possible.

Let's go on to the next section of the test, the memorization portion. This is probably the most difficult portion of the exam, but don't panic! You will be given plenty of practice and tips to help you to score your very best.

Memory for Addresses

In this part of the exam, you will have to memorize the locations (Boxes A, B, C, D, or E) of 25 addresses shown in five boxes, like those below. For example, "Sardis" is in Box C, "6800 – 6999 Table" is in Box B, etc. The addresses on the actual exam will be different.

During the exam, you will be given three practice exercises to help you memorize the location of addresses shown in five boxes. After the practice exercises, the actual test will be given. Part B is cored right answers minus one-fourth of the wrong answers. Random guessing should not help your score. But, if you can eliminate one or more alternatives, it is to your advantage to guess. For the "Memory for Addresses" part of the exam, you will have five minutes to answer as many of the 88 questions as possible. It will be to your advantage to work as quickly and accurately as you can. You will not be expected to be able to answer all the questions in the time allowed. Remember, as stated in the first sentence of this paragraph, you are given three opportunities to practice before you take the scored exam.

Let's look at some sample questions before going any further.

A	B	C	D	E
4700 – 5599 Table	6800 – 6999 Table	5600 – 6499 Table	6500 – 6799 Table	4400 – 4699 Table
Lismore	Kelford	Joel	Tatum	Ruskin
5600 – 6499 West	6500 – 6799 West	6800 – 6999 West	4400 – 4699 West	4700 – 5599 West
Hesper	Musella	Sardis	Porter	Nathan
4400 – 4699 Blake	5600 – 6499 Blake	6500 – 6799 Blake	4700 – 5599 Blake	6800 – 6999 Blake

Study the locations of the addresses for five minutes. As you study, silently repeat the addresses to yourself. Cover the boxes and try to answer the questions below. Mark your answers for each question by darkening the circle on your Answer Grid corresponding to the letter above the address.

1. Musella
2. 4700 – 5599 Blake
3. 4700 – 5599 Table
4. Tatum
5. 4400 – 4699 Blake
6. Hesper
7. Kelford
8. Nathan
9. 6500 – 6799 Blake
10. Joel
11. 4400 – 4699 Blake
12. 6500 – 6799 West
13. Porter
14. 6800 – 6999 Blake

Sample Answer Grid – Memory for Addresses Practice

1. Ⓐ Ⓑ Ⓒ Ⓓ Ⓔ
2. Ⓐ Ⓑ Ⓒ Ⓓ Ⓔ
3. Ⓐ Ⓑ Ⓒ Ⓓ Ⓔ
4. Ⓐ Ⓑ Ⓒ Ⓓ Ⓔ
5. Ⓐ Ⓑ Ⓒ Ⓓ Ⓔ
6. Ⓐ Ⓑ Ⓒ Ⓓ Ⓔ
7. Ⓐ Ⓑ Ⓒ Ⓓ Ⓔ
8. Ⓐ Ⓑ Ⓒ Ⓓ Ⓔ
9. Ⓐ Ⓑ Ⓒ Ⓓ Ⓔ
10. Ⓐ Ⓑ Ⓒ Ⓓ Ⓔ
11. Ⓐ Ⓑ Ⓒ Ⓓ Ⓔ
12. Ⓐ Ⓑ Ⓒ Ⓓ Ⓔ
13. Ⓐ Ⓑ Ⓒ Ⓓ Ⓔ
14. Ⓐ Ⓑ Ⓒ Ⓓ Ⓔ

Correct Answers – Memory for Addresses Practice

1. B
2. D
3. A
4. D
5. A
6. A
7. B
8. E
9. C
10. C
11. A
12. B
13. D
14. E

How did you do? If you didn't do very well, don't be discouraged; few people do well the first time. The next section gives some suggestions on how to improve your memorization skills and then, as with the Address Checking section, you will be given two opportunities to practice. If you did well, congratulations! You will find this section of the exam to be less challenging than most people and you can probably skip this next section.

Tips to Improve Memorization Skills

Following are three strategies that you can be use to master the Memory for Addresses section. These strategies should enable you to greatly reduce the volume of material to be memorized, to more easily memorize the remaining material, and to answer as many of the 88 questions as possible within the five minutes allowed. You will also have the opportunity to determine which strategy or combination of strategies will work the best for you.

Tip Set #1

1. **Memorize the addresses horizontally across the page**, not vertically down the page. Most people find horizontal memorization to be more natural and manageable.

2. **Memorize only the first four boxes** – Boxes A, B, C, and D. Ignore Box E, the fifth box. As you take the test, mark the addresses that you recognize as having come from Boxes A, B, C, and D. By the process of elimination, the addresses you do not recognize must have come from Box E. Using this strategy, you can correctly answer every question dealing with Box E even though you did not intentionally memorize any of those addresses. This one simple common sense strategy alone reduces the material to be memorized by 20%!

3. **Use imagery and/or association** to memorize the word addresses in Boxes A, B, C, and D. Simply put, tie the words together to form an image, mental picture, phrase, or concept to which you can relate and that you can therefore remember more easily. It helps to form an image or association where the words are imagined to interact with each other in some way. The more realistic, lifelike, or graphic your image or association the better you can remember it. You will see different images or associations in the word addresses based upon your individual personality, experiences, likes, dislikes, etc. It may take a little thought, but you should eventually be able to find an image or association in almost any series of words. It becomes easier with practice. A vivid imagination contributes to your effort; however, the words must be tied together and memorized in the same order as they appear from left to right.

Using the five boxes below, let's try out this strategy. The word addresses in these sample boxes, by the way, are addresses used on actual postal exams.

A	B	C	D	E
4700– 5599 Camp Ishee	6800--6999 Camp Hunter	5600--6499 Camp Dearman	6500--6799 Camp Norwalk	4400--4699 Camp Plank
5600--6499 Sarah Kaytham	6500--6799 Sarah Island	6800--6999 Sarah Carlton	4400--4699 Sarah Nultey	4700--5599 Sarah Airline
4400--4699 Lang	5600--6499 Lang	6500--6799 Lang	4700--5599 Lang	6800--6999 Lang

- The first horizontal row of word addresses from Boxes A, B, C, and D reads as follows.

Ishee Hunter Dearman   Norwalk

- Remember, following the second strategy, we are concentrating only on the first four boxes. Ignore Box E.

An outdoor sports enthusiast friend looked at these four boxes and immediately saw the imagery of "I hunt deer now." To visualize this, let's look at the bold portions of the words:

Ishee Hunter Dearman Nowalk

We took a bit of liberty with the word "dear" out of "Dearman" and used it to refer to the animal "deer". We also played with the sequence of the letters in the word "Norwalk" to come up with the word "now. " Being a hunter, my friend can very easily remember this sentence. Let's say he formerly hunted ducks and wanted to try something different -- so…"I hunt deer now. "

How does this association help? If you see any of the words Ishee, Hunter, Dearman, or Norwalk in a question on the exam, silently recite to yourself the memorized association/sentence "I hunt deer now." If the word in the question is Ishee, which relates to "I", the answer is A. Why? Because since you memorized the words in order from left to right the first word in your memorized sentence must have come from the first box -- Box A; therefore the word in the question relates to the first word in your sentence which relates to the first box -- Box A. If the word in the question is Hunter, the answer will be Box B -- second word in our memorized sentence…second box…Box B. If the word in the question is Dearman, the answer is Box C…third word in the memorized sentence…third box…Box C. And of course, the word Norwalk will relate to your fourth word "now," so the answer would be Box D -- the fourth box. In each case, you should silently recite your sentence which immediately tells you the answer by the position of the word in your sentence -- first/A, second/B, third/C, or fourth/D.

Our staff here has suggested some other sentences for these four street names. We hope they help you to see how this strategy should work.

Is hunting deemed noteworthy?
He's Hunter, a dear man from Norwalk.
Is hunting deer okay in Norwalk?

- Now look at the other horizontal row of word addresses from Boxes A, B, C, and D:

Kaytham Island Carlton Nultey

When taking the exam, you should try to see something in the words that relates to you. Let's say you have a friend named Kay who is a real car nut. She always seems to be trading in her current car for a new one, only to do it again just a few months later. Here's what we saw:

"Kay is (a) car nut."

Notice the bold parts of these words:

Kaytham **Is**land **Car**lton **Nult**ey

As in the previous example, we used parts of words and did a little rearranging of the letters in the word "Nultey". In this case, as you silently recite the sentence, sort of mumble and play down the "a" in the sentence to emphasize that it is not a key word. It is only an aid to help the key words that relate to Boxes A, B, C and D make sense. As before, when you see the words Kaytham, Island, Carlton, or Nultey in a question, silently recite your sentence, and the position of the word in the sentence tells you what box the address came from. First word...first box...Box A; second word...second box...Box B; etc.

Once again we asked our staff for some suggestions, they came up with:

Kay is Carlton's nosey assistant.
Kathy is not yet a liar.

- One additional testing situation you must prepare for is similar word address examples appearing on the same exam. The previous two examples were from different exams. But what if they had been on the same exam? The problem is you have two "I" words: "Ishee" in Box A of the first example and "Island" in Box B of the second example. As a matter of fact, they are both "is" words. This may have caused confusion if you used the sentences we developed earlier. If you do discover such duplication, you should change your imagery or association sentence. In this example, you can go back to the first sentence and use the "she" from "Ishee" rather than the "I"; this would result in the sentence "She hunts deer now."

- You may be thinking, "What if I recite the wrong sentence? What if I recite the one that is supposed to go with the other horizontal row of word addresses?" No problem! The word address in the question should prompt you to recite the proper sentence. But even if you recite the wrong one, don't worry. There are only two of them. If the first one doesn't fit, recite the other one -- it probably will fit. What if the word address in the question doesn't fit either of your memorized sentences? That's okay too. Some of them are not supposed to -- the ones from Box E, which you purposely did not memorize. As we remind you below, you will be able to correctly answer all Box E questions by the process of elimination even though you intentionally did not memorize any of the addresses in Box E.

- As you take the test in this manner, you answer the questions with words you don't recognize simply by marking the answer E. This is part of the plan. By the process of elimination, any word you don't recognize necessarily came from Box E. So, you mark all unrecognized word addresses as "E" and get every one of them right without even trying to memorize them!

4. **Use the "Second Digit Strategy" to memorize the number addresses**. Here's how it works:

Look at the top row of number addresses across the sample boxes horizontally from left to right as shown below. You'll see at least 65 characters that you must memorize:

A	B	C	D	E
4700– 5599 Camp	6800--6999 Camp	5600--6499 Camp	6500--6799 Camp	4400--4699 Camp

By ignoring Box E as we previously discussed, we can reduce the number to something over 50, but that's still a lot. What if we could identify a single key character from each box and memorize only that one item? This would cut the material to be memorized by over 90%. With all the repetition from box to box, is there a key non-repeating element in each case on which we can concentrate? Look at the addresses to see if anything does not repeat...

We can rule out the street names--in our sample boxes the street names Camp, Sarah, and Lang accompany the number addresses and repeat horizontally across all five boxes. What about the numbers themselves? Let's look at the top row of numbers from all five boxes:

A	B	C	D	E
4700– 5599	6800--6999	5600--6499	6500--6799	4400--4699

Look at the first digits from each address in order horizontally as presented in bold above. The character in the first digit location of Box A is the number 4, in Box B it is a 6, in Box C it is a 5, in Box D a 6 and in Box E a 4. Notice that 4 and 6 repeat as first digits.

What about the other digits? The third and fourth digits in each box are 0. In the fifth digit location, 6 repeats three times--in Boxes B, C, and D. The number 9 appears in both the seventh and eighth digit locations of all five boxes. As you see, the numbers repeat all across the board. This is true for all the number addresses in all the boxes.

But what about the second digit numbers? We didn't try them. Let's look at our sample and see:

A	B	C	D	E
4700– 5599	6800--6999	5600--6499	6500--6799	4400--4699

The second digits characters in order horizontally, as in bold above are the numbers 7, 8, 6, 5, and 4. *They don't repeat!* Here is our key non-repeating element. So, how do you use it? First remember you only memorize the first four boxes -- A, B, C, and D. Using our Second Digit Strategy, the only elements you will memorize are the second digit numbers from each address followed by the street name, which means all you want to memorize from this sample is "7865 Camp," which sounds and looks like a single address itself. This is something you can remember easily..."7865 Camp. " Close the book for a moment and silently recite it. See, you've already got it memorized! This is much easier than trying to memorize over 65 characters spread across the top row of five boxes.

So, you have memorized "7865 Camp. " What do you do with it? As you take the test, any time you see a question with the street name Camp, look at the number in the second digit location in the question. Look only at the second digit -- ignore all the other numbers. Let's say that the address in the question is "4700--5599 Camp. " Look at the second digit in the question and see that it is the number 7. Now, silently recite what you memorized -- "7865 Camp. " The second digit in the question (the number 7) matches the first number you memorized which relates to the first box -- Box A. If the second digit of the question matched the fourth number in our series, the answer would be D.

Using the Second Digit Strategy on the other horizontal rows of number addresses in our sample boxes, you would memorize "6584 Sarah" and "4657 Lang." When taking the test, if you find a question with the address "6500--6799 Sarah," the answer is automatically "B." The second digit in the question matches the second number in the series we memorized for Sarah, which relates to the second box -- Box B. If the question is "6500 -- 6799 Lang," the answer is automatically C because the second digit in the question matches the second number in the series you memorized for Lang. With practice, this strategy becomes second nature and allows you to phenomenally increase your Address Memory speed and accuracy.

What if the second digit in the answer doesn't match any of the numbers you memorized? Well, then by process of elimination, the answer is E, the box you did not memorize. You intentionally did not memorize ANY addresses in Box E, so you mark the answer E for any address you don't recognize.

The only position we did not consider was the sixth digit location, which, like the second digit, does not repeat. If necessary, you can use this location in the same way, but the second digit is more convenient to work with.

The first four strategies alone have enabled you to transform the Memory for Addresses section into a manageable task. We have reduced the memorization to the brief list below.

7865 Camp
She hunts deer now.
6584 Sarah
Kay is (a) car nut.
4657 Lang

There are two more strategies for memorizing addresses presented here. Before you begin extensive studying, decide on the one which best suits your study habits and test-taking style.

Tip Set #2

As we discussed earlier, imagery and association techniques can be fun to use and your ability to recall can be substantially extended. Following is another suggestion for memorizing street names using imagery and association.

In this strategy, you are once again using an image based on the street name. Look at the list below for some associations we came up with for the street names. Remember, the associations you come up with have to make sense only to you.

Jorgensen Street- jogger
Phillips Avenue- Phillips screwdriver
Tremont- tree
Tricia- tricycle
Edgewater- edge
Bloomington- bloomers

Carry the process one step further and place those keyword derivatives in a bizarre context, story or situation. Using this process, we have developed the following:

A **jogger** ran through the park with a **Phillips screwdriver** he had found stuck in a **tree**. He came across a **tricycle** at the **edge** of the path with a pair of old **bloomers** on the handlebars.

Sounds ridiculous, doesn't it? However, because of its strong images, you'll not easily forget this kind of story. Another advantage of the imagery technique is that you can remember items in their respective order by simply reviewing where they fit in relation to other items in the story.

Look at each list of street names below and develop a story using imagery. There are no right or wrong keyword derivatives. What is important is that you choose images that conjure up a clear picture in your mind and then interlink.

Work on each of these columns separately:

Oak Hill Road	Echo Street	Hollis Place	Rock Creek Drive
Pleasant Street	Main Street	Boston Road	Anthony Boulevard
Park Street	Northeast Blvd.	First Avenue	Jefferson Place
Oliver Circle	West End Terrace	23rd Street	Green Avenue
Hickory Way	LaVerne Street	Elm Street	Birch Lane

Once you have finished this exercise, cover the street names and see if you can remember all 20 items. If your four stories are bizarre enough, you can have this entire list committed to long-term memory in no time.

As we saw earlier, numbers require a different strategy for memorization. For most people, numbers are difficult to memorize because they are intangible. To solve this problem, transpose numbers into letters so that words can easily be formed and associated accordingly. This strategy uses a system similar to the buttons on your telephone. The numbers 2 through 9 have letters corresponding with them. We will use this association with a slight variation. Starting with the number 0, and ending with the number 9, associate the following letters with each number.

0	B & C		5	N & P
1	D & F		6	Q & R
2	G & H		7	S & T
3	J & K		8	V & W
4	L & M		9	X & Y & Z

You can use these number and letter combinations to help you remember numbers, no matter how large. Let's use 4587632 as our example. Try memorizing that number and walk away for 5 minutes. Get a drink, a snack or just go for a walk. Come back and write the number down on a piece of paper without looking at it.

How did you do? If you remembered it, great; this section may not be very difficult for you. If you didn't remember it, don't feel bad; few people can memorize that quickly.

Now let's try a new technique using the association between the numbers and letters. Since this is a long number, maybe we should dissect it into parts. Using the first two numbers, 4 and 5, we can form a word using the letters associated with the 4 (L & M) and the letters associated with the 5 (N & P). Since the vowels are not used, we can use any vowel to help us form a word. The vowels are "fillers." So, using these letters, we can form the word "LiP" from the 4 and the 5. We can group the next three numbers together also. Using the W from 8, the T from 7, and the R from 6, we can form the word "WaTeR." Finally, we have the 3 and the 2. Using the J from the 3 and the G from the 2, we can form the word "JuG." Put them all together and you have "LiPWaTeR JuG." Using the non-vowel letters, you should be able to come up with the number 4587632.

It may sound hard, but if you try a few numbers and familiarize yourself with this method, it becomes quite simple. If you can form one word using all the numbers, you may find it easier to remember.

Tip Set #3

A third way to memorize addresses is to use the Story Method. This strategy uses imagery/association to create a sentence for each individual box, similar to the first technique suggested. However, you will have to memorize five different sentences rather than one. Here is a set of addresses to try:

A	B	C	D	E
1100-1199 Bugle	3300-3799 Bugle	9000-9499 Bugle	5600-5899 Bugle	4100-4499 Bugle
Patriot	Jefferson	Victory	Carson	Meridian
7500-7799 Major	1000-1599 Major	4200-4799 Major	6100-6499 Major	3300-3799 Major
Marcus	Brown	Hickory	Birch	Elm
5200-5599 Oswald	7800-7999 Oswald	2200-2699 Oswald	4600-4899 Oswald	8200-8699 Oswald

Minimizing the information that you were trying to memorize would likely make a world of difference. Rather than trying to remember 1100-1199 Bugle, why not shorten it to 11 Bugle? To take that one step further, you can shorten all of Box A and make a short memorable sentence. Using the Story Method you can make a short sentence out of the information in the box. Since order does not matter, you can move the information within your sentence to make it easier for you to remember.

For example, you can make the sentence: Marcus, the Patriot that had 11 Bugles, was commanded by 75 Majors to perform the 52 Oswald.

Remembering the sentence should be much easier than recalling all the information in Box A. The sentence you create does not need to make sense to anyone but you. It only needs to help you remember the information. Usually, the more outrageous the sentence, the easier it is to remember. The Story Method should assist you in memorizing the necessary information for this part of the exam. The best way to see if it works for you is to try it.

On the next few pages is a practice exam for memorizing addresses. We suggest you try all three memorization techniques above, and pick the technique that best suits your test-taking style. All three techniques will work equally well, but one may simply come more easily to you, or you may even come up with a technique of your own. But please remember, all three of the strategies above have been used by people to score their best on this portion of Exam 460.

One more study suggestion; do not try to study with all three techniques on the same day. This will simply confuse you and possibly make it hard for you to determine which technique works best for you. Please allow yourself at least three days to determine which technique is best for you. Once you have done the same practice test with each technique, choose the technique which allows you to answer the most questions in the five minutes allowed.

The Answer Grids for this section are designed to be photocopied before use, and are blank on the back so that they can be removed without harming the integrity of the book.

Memory for Addresses Practice – Determination of Best Method

Directions: Study the addresses below for 11 minutes, then turn the page and *from memory* match each address to the correct box.

A	B	C	D	E
1100-1199 Bugle Patriot	3300-3799 Bugle Jefferson	9000-9499 Bugle Victory	5600-5899 Bugle Carson	4100-4499 Bugle Meridian
7500-7799 Major Marcus	1000-1599 Major Brown	4200-4799 Major Hickory	6100-6499 Major Birch	3300-3799 Major Elm
5200-5599 Oswald	7800-7999 Oswald	2200-2699 Oswald	4600-4899 Oswald	8200-8699 Oswald

Memory for Addresses Practice – Determination of Best Method

(You have 5 minutes to complete this section.)

1. Meridian
2. 2200-2699 Oswald
3. Marcus
4. 9000-9499 Bugle
5. 3300-3799 Major
6. Patriot
7. 1000-1599 Major
8. 6100-6499 Major
9. Birch
10. 8200-8699 Oswald
11. Elm
12. 1100-1199 Bugle
13. Jefferson
14. 3300-3799 Major
15. Victory
16. 8200-8699 Oswald
17. Hickory
18. 4100-4499 Bugle
19. 7800-7999 Oswald
20. 7500-7799 Major
21. Carson
22. 4200-4799 Major
23. Marcus
24. Meridian
25. 4600-4899 Oswald
26. 5600-5899 Bugle
27. Patriot
28. 9000-9499 Bugle
29. Birch
30. 2200-2699 Oswald

31. Victory
32. 1000-1599 Major
33. 1100-1199 Bugle
34. Brown
35. 1000-1599 Major
36. Birch
37. Hickory
38. 5200-5599 Oswald
39. 5600-5899 Bugle
40. Marcus
41. Victory
42. Patriot
43. 4100-4499 Bugle
44. 8200-8699 Oswald
45. 7500-7799 Major
46. Carson
47. 9000-9499 Bugle
48. 4200-4799 Major
49. Elm
50. Meridian
51. 3300-3799 Bugle
52. 7800-7999 Oswald
53. Jefferson
54. 8200-8699 Oswald
55. 1100-1199 Bugle
56. Birch
57. 5200-5599 Oswald
58. Hickory
59. 4200-4799 Major
60. 1000-1599 Major

61. Victory
62. 4100-4499 Bugle
63. Brown
64. Marcus
65. Patriot
66. Jefferson
67. Elm
68. 7500-7799 Major
69. Victory
70. 8200-8699 Oswald
71. Carson
72. 5200-5599 Oswald
73. 4100-4499 Bugle
74. Meridian
75. Brown
76. 4200-4799 Major
77. 1100-1199 Bugle
78. Hickory
79. 1000-1599 Major
80. 2200-2699 Oswald
81. Birch
82. 7800-7999 Oswald
83. 6100-6499 Major
84. Patriot
85. 9000-9499 Bugle
86. 3300-3799 Bugle
87. 4600-4899 Oswald
88. Elm

Notes:

Answer Grid – Memory for Addresses – Determination of Best Method

You will need to photocopy this page so that you have three Answer Grids (one for each suggested method of memorization) .

1. Ⓐ Ⓑ Ⓒ Ⓓ Ⓔ
2. Ⓐ Ⓑ Ⓒ Ⓓ Ⓔ
3. Ⓐ Ⓑ Ⓒ Ⓓ Ⓔ
4. Ⓐ Ⓑ Ⓒ Ⓓ Ⓔ
5. Ⓐ Ⓑ Ⓒ Ⓓ Ⓔ
6. Ⓐ Ⓑ Ⓒ Ⓓ Ⓔ
7. Ⓐ Ⓑ Ⓒ Ⓓ Ⓔ
8. Ⓐ Ⓑ Ⓒ Ⓓ Ⓔ
9. Ⓐ Ⓑ Ⓒ Ⓓ Ⓔ
10. Ⓐ Ⓑ Ⓒ Ⓓ Ⓔ
11. Ⓐ Ⓑ Ⓒ Ⓓ Ⓔ
12. Ⓐ Ⓑ Ⓒ Ⓓ Ⓔ
13. Ⓐ Ⓑ Ⓒ Ⓓ Ⓔ
14. Ⓐ Ⓑ Ⓒ Ⓓ Ⓔ
15. Ⓐ Ⓑ Ⓒ Ⓓ Ⓔ
16. Ⓐ Ⓑ Ⓒ Ⓓ Ⓔ
17. Ⓐ Ⓑ Ⓒ Ⓓ Ⓔ
18. Ⓐ Ⓑ Ⓒ Ⓓ Ⓔ
19. Ⓐ Ⓑ Ⓒ Ⓓ Ⓔ
20. Ⓐ Ⓑ Ⓒ Ⓓ Ⓔ
21. Ⓐ Ⓑ Ⓒ Ⓓ Ⓔ
22. Ⓐ Ⓑ Ⓒ Ⓓ Ⓔ
23. Ⓐ Ⓑ Ⓒ Ⓓ Ⓔ
24. Ⓐ Ⓑ Ⓒ Ⓓ Ⓔ
25. Ⓐ Ⓑ Ⓒ Ⓓ Ⓔ
26. Ⓐ Ⓑ Ⓒ Ⓓ Ⓔ
27. Ⓐ Ⓑ Ⓒ Ⓓ Ⓔ
28. Ⓐ Ⓑ Ⓒ Ⓓ Ⓔ
29. Ⓐ Ⓑ Ⓒ Ⓓ Ⓔ
30. Ⓐ Ⓑ Ⓒ Ⓓ Ⓔ
31. Ⓐ Ⓑ Ⓒ Ⓓ Ⓔ
32. Ⓐ Ⓑ Ⓒ Ⓓ Ⓔ
33. Ⓐ Ⓑ Ⓒ Ⓓ Ⓔ

34. Ⓐ Ⓑ Ⓒ Ⓓ Ⓔ
35. Ⓐ Ⓑ Ⓒ Ⓓ Ⓔ
36. Ⓐ Ⓑ Ⓒ Ⓓ Ⓔ
37. Ⓐ Ⓑ Ⓒ Ⓓ Ⓔ
38. Ⓐ Ⓑ Ⓒ Ⓓ Ⓔ
39. Ⓐ Ⓑ Ⓒ Ⓓ Ⓔ
40. Ⓐ Ⓑ Ⓒ Ⓓ Ⓔ
41. Ⓐ Ⓑ Ⓒ Ⓓ Ⓔ
42. Ⓐ Ⓑ Ⓒ Ⓓ Ⓔ
43. Ⓐ Ⓑ Ⓒ Ⓓ Ⓔ
44. Ⓐ Ⓑ Ⓒ Ⓓ Ⓔ
45. Ⓐ Ⓑ Ⓒ Ⓓ Ⓔ
46. Ⓐ Ⓑ Ⓒ Ⓓ Ⓔ
47. Ⓐ Ⓑ Ⓒ Ⓓ Ⓔ
48. Ⓐ Ⓑ Ⓒ Ⓓ Ⓔ
49. Ⓐ Ⓑ Ⓒ Ⓓ Ⓔ
50. Ⓐ Ⓑ Ⓒ Ⓓ Ⓔ
51. Ⓐ Ⓑ Ⓒ Ⓓ Ⓔ
52. Ⓐ Ⓑ Ⓒ Ⓓ Ⓔ
53. Ⓐ Ⓑ Ⓒ Ⓓ Ⓔ
54. Ⓐ Ⓑ Ⓒ Ⓓ Ⓔ
55. Ⓐ Ⓑ Ⓒ Ⓓ Ⓔ
56. Ⓐ Ⓑ Ⓒ Ⓓ Ⓔ
57. Ⓐ Ⓑ Ⓒ Ⓓ Ⓔ
58. Ⓐ Ⓑ Ⓒ Ⓓ Ⓔ
59. Ⓐ Ⓑ Ⓒ Ⓓ Ⓔ
60. Ⓐ Ⓑ Ⓒ Ⓓ Ⓔ
61. Ⓐ Ⓑ Ⓒ Ⓓ Ⓔ
62. Ⓐ Ⓑ Ⓒ Ⓓ Ⓔ
63. Ⓐ Ⓑ Ⓒ Ⓓ Ⓔ
64. Ⓐ Ⓑ Ⓒ Ⓓ Ⓔ
65. Ⓐ Ⓑ Ⓒ Ⓓ Ⓔ
66. Ⓐ Ⓑ Ⓒ Ⓓ Ⓔ

67. Ⓐ Ⓑ Ⓒ Ⓓ Ⓔ
68. Ⓐ Ⓑ Ⓒ Ⓓ Ⓔ
69. Ⓐ Ⓑ Ⓒ Ⓓ Ⓔ
70. Ⓐ Ⓑ Ⓒ Ⓓ Ⓔ
71. Ⓐ Ⓑ Ⓒ Ⓓ Ⓔ
72. Ⓐ Ⓑ Ⓒ Ⓓ Ⓔ
73. Ⓐ Ⓑ Ⓒ Ⓓ Ⓔ
74. Ⓐ Ⓑ Ⓒ Ⓓ Ⓔ
75. Ⓐ Ⓑ Ⓒ Ⓓ Ⓔ
76. Ⓐ Ⓑ Ⓒ Ⓓ Ⓔ
77. Ⓐ Ⓑ Ⓒ Ⓓ Ⓔ
78. Ⓐ Ⓑ Ⓒ Ⓓ Ⓔ
79. Ⓐ Ⓑ Ⓒ Ⓓ Ⓔ
80. Ⓐ Ⓑ Ⓒ Ⓓ Ⓔ
81. Ⓐ Ⓑ Ⓒ Ⓓ Ⓔ
82. Ⓐ Ⓑ Ⓒ Ⓓ Ⓔ
83. Ⓐ Ⓑ Ⓒ Ⓓ Ⓔ
84. Ⓐ Ⓑ Ⓒ Ⓓ Ⓔ
85. Ⓐ Ⓑ Ⓒ Ⓓ Ⓔ
86. Ⓐ Ⓑ Ⓒ Ⓓ Ⓔ
87. Ⓐ Ⓑ Ⓒ Ⓓ Ⓔ
88. Ⓐ Ⓑ Ⓒ Ⓓ Ⓔ

Correct Answers – Memory for Addresses – Determination of Best Method

1. E	31. C	61. C
2. C	32. B	62. E
3. A	33. A	63. B
4. C	34. B	64. A
5. E	35. B	65. A
6. A	36. D	66. B
7. B	37. C	67. E
8. D	38. A	68. A
9. D	39. D	69. C
10. E	40. A	70. E
11. E	41. C	71. D
12. A	42. A	72. A
13. B	43. E	73. E
14. E	44. E	74. E
15. C	45. A	75. B
16. E	46. D	76. C
17. C	47. C	77. A
18. E	48. C	78. C
19. B	49. E	79. B
20. A	50. E	80. C
21. D	51. B	81. D
22. C	52. B	82. B
23. A	53. B	83. D
24. E	54. E	84. A
25. D	55. A	85. C
26. D	56. D	86. B
27. A	57. A	87. D
28. C	58. C	88. E
29. D	59. C	
30. C	60. B	

Before you go on to the full-length practice exams, here are some more Memory for Addresses strategies:

- Answer the 88 questions in order. Do not attempt to go through the test twice (answering only the word address questions the first time and the number address questions the second, or vice versa). Some people find one type of question more manageable than the other and are tempted to answer the ones they find easiest first. Their intent the first time through is to capture the points that come more easily to them and then go back through a second time to work on the ones that are harder for them. Unfortunately, you simply do not have enough time to take the test twice, and that is in effect what you would be doing. Answering 88 questions in 5 minutes is challenging enough; going through the test twice, essentially answering 176 questions in five minutes, is absolutely impossible.

- Speed is just as important as memorization. If you memorize all the addresses perfectly but can only answer half the questions in the time allowed, you have gained nothing. As with the address checking section, practice is absolutely essential to develop the skills and the speed required. You cannot practice too much.

- Complete the Address Memory practice work about two days before your scheduled test date. Do not continue doing Address Memory practice exercises all the way up to the night before. If you do, you may confuse the addresses from this book with those on the real exam -- the address from your practice may still be lingering in your mind as you attempt to take the actual exam. Do not let this happen to you.

By now you should have a very good handle on the Memory for Addresses section of Exam 460. You should have determined the best strategy for your learning style and be ready to tackle the two practice exams which follow. Remember, when you take the actual exam you will be given three chances to memorize and practice before you complete the section for which you are actually scored.

Good luck!

<u>Memory for Addresses – Full-Length Practice #1</u>

Directions: Study the addresses below for 11 minutes, then turn the page and *from memory* match each address to the correct box.

A	B	C	D	E
5100 - 5299 Owen	8700-8899 Owen	3300-3499 Owen	5800-5999 Owen	8200-8300 Owen
Adolph	Walda	Odessa	Sonja	Bayou
3300-3499 Grove	8200-8399 Grove	5800-5999 Grove	5100-5299 Grove	8700-8899 Grove
Brodie	Eddy	Halter	Benoit	Trehern
5800-5999 Tuck	3300-3499 Tuck	8200-8399 Tuck	8700-8899 Tuck	5100-5299 Tuck

Memory for Addresses – Full-Length Practice #1

(You have 5 minutes to complete this section.)

1. 8700-8899 Grove
2. Halter
3. Trehern
4. 5100-5299 Grove
5. 5800-5999 Tuck
6. 8200-8399 Tuck
7. 5800-5999 Owen
8. Walda
9. 8700-8899 Grove
10. Odessa
11. 5800-5999 Tuck
12. Adolph
13. Benoit
14. Walda
15. 3300-3499 Tuck
16. Halter
17. 5100-5299 Owen
18. Bayou
19. 5800-5999 Grove
20. 5100-5299 Tuck
21. 8200-8399 Grove
22. 5800-5999 Owen
23. Trehern
24. 5800-5999 Tuck
25. 5100-5299 Owen
26. Brodie
27. Odessa
28. Benoit
29. 8200-8399 Tuck
30. 3300-3499 Grove
31. 3300-3499 Tuck
32. 8700-8899 Tuck
33. 8200-8399 Grove
34. Bayou
35. 8700-8899 Owen
36. Halter
37. 8200-3899 Grove
38. 5100-5299 Tuck
39. Eddy
40. 5100-5299 Grove
41. 3300-3499 Owen
42. Sonja
43. 8200-8399 Owen
44. 8700-8899 Grove
45. 5800-5999 Grove
46. 3300-3499 Owen
47. Eddy
48. Walda
49. 8700-8899 Tuck
50. Adolph
51. 8200-8399 Owen
52. 5800-5999 Tuck
53. 3300-3499 Tuck
54. Brodie
55. 8700-8899 Tuck
56. 8200-8399 Owen
57. 5800-5999 Grove
58. Benoit
59. Odessa
60. 8200-8399 Grove
61. 3300-3499 Grove
62. 5800-5999 Owen
63. 5100-5299 Tuck
64. Halter
65. Bayou
66. 5100-5299 Tuck
67. Walda
68. 8700-8899 Owen
69. Bayou
70. Sonja
71. 8200-8399 Tuck
72. 5100-5299 Grove
73. Eddy
74. 5800-5999 Grove
75. Brodie
76. 8200-8399 Grove
77. Sonja
78. Benoit
79. 3300-3499 Grove
80. Halter
81. 3300-3499 Owen
82. Trehern
83. Brodie
84. 8200-8399 Owen
85. 8700-8899 Owen
86. 8799-8899 Tuck
87. 8200-8399 Tuck
88. Adolph

Answer Grid – Memory for Addresses–Full-Length Practice #1

1. Ⓐ Ⓑ Ⓒ Ⓓ Ⓔ
2. Ⓐ Ⓑ Ⓒ Ⓓ Ⓔ
3. Ⓐ Ⓑ Ⓒ Ⓓ Ⓔ
4. Ⓐ Ⓑ Ⓒ Ⓓ Ⓔ
5. Ⓐ Ⓑ Ⓒ Ⓓ Ⓔ
6. Ⓐ Ⓑ Ⓒ Ⓓ Ⓔ
7. Ⓐ Ⓑ Ⓒ Ⓓ Ⓔ
8. Ⓐ Ⓑ Ⓒ Ⓓ Ⓔ
9. Ⓐ Ⓑ Ⓒ Ⓓ Ⓔ
10. Ⓐ Ⓑ Ⓒ Ⓓ Ⓔ
11. Ⓐ Ⓑ Ⓒ Ⓓ Ⓔ
12. Ⓐ Ⓑ Ⓒ Ⓓ Ⓔ
13. Ⓐ Ⓑ Ⓒ Ⓓ Ⓔ
14. Ⓐ Ⓑ Ⓒ Ⓓ Ⓔ
15. Ⓐ Ⓑ Ⓒ Ⓓ Ⓔ
16. Ⓐ Ⓑ Ⓒ Ⓓ Ⓔ
17. Ⓐ Ⓑ Ⓒ Ⓓ Ⓔ
18. Ⓐ Ⓑ Ⓒ Ⓓ Ⓔ
19. Ⓐ Ⓑ Ⓒ Ⓓ Ⓔ
20. Ⓐ Ⓑ Ⓒ Ⓓ Ⓔ
21. Ⓐ Ⓑ Ⓒ Ⓓ Ⓔ
22. Ⓐ Ⓑ Ⓒ Ⓓ Ⓔ
23. Ⓐ Ⓑ Ⓒ Ⓓ Ⓔ
24. Ⓐ Ⓑ Ⓒ Ⓓ Ⓔ
25. Ⓐ Ⓑ Ⓒ Ⓓ Ⓔ
26. Ⓐ Ⓑ Ⓒ Ⓓ Ⓔ
27. Ⓐ Ⓑ Ⓒ Ⓓ Ⓔ
28. Ⓐ Ⓑ Ⓒ Ⓓ Ⓔ
29. Ⓐ Ⓑ Ⓒ Ⓓ Ⓔ
30. Ⓐ Ⓑ Ⓒ Ⓓ Ⓔ
31. Ⓐ Ⓑ Ⓒ Ⓓ Ⓔ
32. Ⓐ Ⓑ Ⓒ Ⓓ Ⓔ
33. Ⓐ Ⓑ Ⓒ Ⓓ Ⓔ

34. Ⓐ Ⓑ Ⓒ Ⓓ Ⓔ
35. Ⓐ Ⓑ Ⓒ Ⓓ Ⓔ
36. Ⓐ Ⓑ Ⓒ Ⓓ Ⓔ
37. Ⓐ Ⓑ Ⓒ Ⓓ Ⓔ
38. Ⓐ Ⓑ Ⓒ Ⓓ Ⓔ
39. Ⓐ Ⓑ Ⓒ Ⓓ Ⓔ
40. Ⓐ Ⓑ Ⓒ Ⓓ Ⓔ
41. Ⓐ Ⓑ Ⓒ Ⓓ Ⓔ
42. Ⓐ Ⓑ Ⓒ Ⓓ Ⓔ
43. Ⓐ Ⓑ Ⓒ Ⓓ Ⓔ
44. Ⓐ Ⓑ Ⓒ Ⓓ Ⓔ
45. Ⓐ Ⓑ Ⓒ Ⓓ Ⓔ
46. Ⓐ Ⓑ Ⓒ Ⓓ Ⓔ
47. Ⓐ Ⓑ Ⓒ Ⓓ Ⓔ
48. Ⓐ Ⓑ Ⓒ Ⓓ Ⓔ
49. Ⓐ Ⓑ Ⓒ Ⓓ Ⓔ
50. Ⓐ Ⓑ Ⓒ Ⓓ Ⓔ
51. Ⓐ Ⓑ Ⓒ Ⓓ Ⓔ
52. Ⓐ Ⓑ Ⓒ Ⓓ Ⓔ
53. Ⓐ Ⓑ Ⓒ Ⓓ Ⓔ
54. Ⓐ Ⓑ Ⓒ Ⓓ Ⓔ
55. Ⓐ Ⓑ Ⓒ Ⓓ Ⓔ
56. Ⓐ Ⓑ Ⓒ Ⓓ Ⓔ
57. Ⓐ Ⓑ Ⓒ Ⓓ Ⓔ
58. Ⓐ Ⓑ Ⓒ Ⓓ Ⓔ
59. Ⓐ Ⓑ Ⓒ Ⓓ Ⓔ
60. Ⓐ Ⓑ Ⓒ Ⓓ Ⓔ
61. Ⓐ Ⓑ Ⓒ Ⓓ Ⓔ
62. Ⓐ Ⓑ Ⓒ Ⓓ Ⓔ
63. Ⓐ Ⓑ Ⓒ Ⓓ Ⓔ
64. Ⓐ Ⓑ Ⓒ Ⓓ Ⓔ
65. Ⓐ Ⓑ Ⓒ Ⓓ Ⓔ
66. Ⓐ Ⓑ Ⓒ Ⓓ Ⓔ

67. Ⓐ Ⓑ Ⓒ Ⓓ Ⓔ
68. Ⓐ Ⓑ Ⓒ Ⓓ Ⓔ
69. Ⓐ Ⓑ Ⓒ Ⓓ Ⓔ
70. Ⓐ Ⓑ Ⓒ Ⓓ Ⓔ
71. Ⓐ Ⓑ Ⓒ Ⓓ Ⓔ
72. Ⓐ Ⓑ Ⓒ Ⓓ Ⓔ
73. Ⓐ Ⓑ Ⓒ Ⓓ Ⓔ
74. Ⓐ Ⓑ Ⓒ Ⓓ Ⓔ
75. Ⓐ Ⓑ Ⓒ Ⓓ Ⓔ
76. Ⓐ Ⓑ Ⓒ Ⓓ Ⓔ
77. Ⓐ Ⓑ Ⓒ Ⓓ Ⓔ
78. Ⓐ Ⓑ Ⓒ Ⓓ Ⓔ
79. Ⓐ Ⓑ Ⓒ Ⓓ Ⓔ
80. Ⓐ Ⓑ Ⓒ Ⓓ Ⓔ
81. Ⓐ Ⓑ Ⓒ Ⓓ Ⓔ
82. Ⓐ Ⓑ Ⓒ Ⓓ Ⓔ
83. Ⓐ Ⓑ Ⓒ Ⓓ Ⓔ
84. Ⓐ Ⓑ Ⓒ Ⓓ Ⓔ
85. Ⓐ Ⓑ Ⓒ Ⓓ Ⓔ
86. Ⓐ Ⓑ Ⓒ Ⓓ Ⓔ
87. Ⓐ Ⓑ Ⓒ Ⓓ Ⓔ
88. Ⓐ Ⓑ Ⓒ Ⓓ Ⓔ

Notes:

56

<u>Correct Answers – Memory for Addresses – Full-Length Practice #1</u>

1. E	31. B	61. A
2. C	32. D	62. D
3. E	33. B	63. E
4. D	34. E	64. C
5. A	35. B	65. E
6. C	36. C	66. E
7. D	37. B	67. B
8. B	38. E	68. B
9. E	39. B	69. E
10. C	40. D	70. D
11. A	41. C	71. C
12. A	42. D	72. D
13. D	43. E	73. B
14. B	44. E	74. C
15. B	45. C	75. A
16. C	46. C	76. B
17. D	47. B	77. D
18. E	48. B	78. D
19. C	49. D	79. A
20. E	50. A	80. C
21. B	51. E	81. C
22. D	52. A	82. E
23. E	53. B	83. A
24. A	54. A	84. E
25. A	55. D	85. B
26. A	56. E	86. D
27. C	57. C	87. C
28. D	58. D	88. A
29. C	59. C	
30. A	60. B	

58

Memory for Addresses – Full-Length Practice #2

Directions: Study the addresses below for 11 minutes, then turn the page and *from memory* match each address to the correct box.

A	B	C	D	E
9200-9399 Vada	8500-8699 Vada	6700-6899 Vada	9600-9799 Vada	6300-6499 Vada
Bethel	Parker	Olivia	Lamey	Verde
6700-6899 Bell	6300-6499 Bell	9200-9399 Bell	8500-8699 Bell	9600-9799 Bell
Ford	Finley	Scott	Saratoga	Brady
9600-9799 Lark	9200-9399 Lark	6300-6499 Lark	6700-6899 Lark	8500-8699 Lark

(You have 5 minutes to complete this section.)

1. 6700-6899 Lark
2. Bethel
3. Finley
4. Olivia
5. Scott
6. 9200-9399 Bell
7. Verde
8. 9200-9399 Bell
9. 6300-6499 Lark
10. 6300-6499 Vada
11. Ford
12. 6300-6499 Lark
13. 9200-9399 Lark
14. 6300-6499 Vada
15. 9600-9799 Lark
16. Verde
17. Lamey
18. 6700-6899 Bell
19. 9600-9799 Bell
20. 6700-6899 Lark
21. 9200-9399 Vada
22. 6700-6899 Bell
23. Ford
24. Lamey
25. Parker
26. Saratoga
27. 8500-8699 Bell
28. 6300-6499 Lark
29. Scott
30. Ford
31. 8500-8699 Bell
32. 6300-6499 Bell
33. 9200-9399 Vada
34. 6300-6499 Lark
35. Brady
36. Olivia
37. 9600-9799 Vada
38. 6700-6899 Vada
39. 9200-9399 Lark
40. 9200-9399 Vada
41. 6700-6899 Bell
42. 8500-8699 Bell
43. Scott
44. Parker
45. 6300-6499 Bell
46. 9200-9399 Vada
47. Parker
48. Finley
49. 9600-9799 Lark
50. Bethel
51. 8500-8699 Vada
52. Verde
53. 6300-6499 Vada
54. 9600-9799 Bell
55. 6300-6499 Vada
56. 9600-9799 Bell
57. 6700-6899 Vada
58. 8500-8699 Lark
59. Scott
60. Olivia
61. Scott
62. 9200-9399 Bell
63. 6300-6499 Vada
64. Ford
65. 6300-6499 Lark
66. 8500-8699 Bell
67. 6300-6499 Lark
68. Scott
69. 9200-9399 Vada
70. 6700-6899 Bell
71. Ford
72. Bethel
73. 9600-9799 Bell
74. 6700-6899 Lark
75. 6300-6499 Bell
76. 6300-6499 Vada
77. 6300-6499 Bell
78. 6700-6899 Vada
79. 8500-8699 Vada
80. 8500-8699 Lark
81. Parker
82. 9200-9399 Lark
83. 9600-9799 Vada
84. Lamey
85. 9200-9399 Bell
86. Ford
87. Saratoga
88. Brady

1. Ⓐ Ⓑ Ⓒ Ⓓ Ⓔ
2. Ⓐ Ⓑ Ⓒ Ⓓ Ⓔ
3. Ⓐ Ⓑ Ⓒ Ⓓ Ⓔ
4. Ⓐ Ⓑ Ⓒ Ⓓ Ⓔ
5. Ⓐ Ⓑ Ⓒ Ⓓ Ⓔ
6. Ⓐ Ⓑ Ⓒ Ⓓ Ⓔ
7. Ⓐ Ⓑ Ⓒ Ⓓ Ⓔ
8. Ⓐ Ⓑ Ⓒ Ⓓ Ⓔ
9. Ⓐ Ⓑ Ⓒ Ⓓ Ⓔ
10. Ⓐ Ⓑ Ⓒ Ⓓ Ⓔ
11. Ⓐ Ⓑ Ⓒ Ⓓ Ⓔ
12. Ⓐ Ⓑ Ⓒ Ⓓ Ⓔ
13. Ⓐ Ⓑ Ⓒ Ⓓ Ⓔ
14. Ⓐ Ⓑ Ⓒ Ⓓ Ⓔ
15. Ⓐ Ⓑ Ⓒ Ⓓ Ⓔ
16. Ⓐ Ⓑ Ⓒ Ⓓ Ⓔ
17. Ⓐ Ⓑ Ⓒ Ⓓ Ⓔ
18. Ⓐ Ⓑ Ⓒ Ⓓ Ⓔ
19. Ⓐ Ⓑ Ⓒ Ⓓ Ⓔ
20. Ⓐ Ⓑ Ⓒ Ⓓ Ⓔ
21. Ⓐ Ⓑ Ⓒ Ⓓ Ⓔ
22. Ⓐ Ⓑ Ⓒ Ⓓ Ⓔ
23. Ⓐ Ⓑ Ⓒ Ⓓ Ⓔ
24. Ⓐ Ⓑ Ⓒ Ⓓ Ⓔ
25. Ⓐ Ⓑ Ⓒ Ⓓ Ⓔ
26. Ⓐ Ⓑ Ⓒ Ⓓ Ⓔ
27. Ⓐ Ⓑ Ⓒ Ⓓ Ⓔ
28. Ⓐ Ⓑ Ⓒ Ⓓ Ⓔ
29. Ⓐ Ⓑ Ⓒ Ⓓ Ⓔ
30. Ⓐ Ⓑ Ⓒ Ⓓ Ⓔ
31. Ⓐ Ⓑ Ⓒ Ⓓ Ⓔ
32. Ⓐ Ⓑ Ⓒ Ⓓ Ⓔ
33. Ⓐ Ⓑ Ⓒ Ⓓ Ⓔ
34. Ⓐ Ⓑ Ⓒ Ⓓ Ⓔ

35. Ⓐ Ⓑ Ⓒ Ⓓ Ⓔ
36. Ⓐ Ⓑ Ⓒ Ⓓ Ⓔ
37. Ⓐ Ⓑ Ⓒ Ⓓ Ⓔ
38. Ⓐ Ⓑ Ⓒ Ⓓ Ⓔ
39. Ⓐ Ⓑ Ⓒ Ⓓ Ⓔ
40. Ⓐ Ⓑ Ⓒ Ⓓ Ⓔ
41. Ⓐ Ⓑ Ⓒ Ⓓ Ⓔ
42. Ⓐ Ⓑ Ⓒ Ⓓ Ⓔ
43. Ⓐ Ⓑ Ⓒ Ⓓ Ⓔ
44. Ⓐ Ⓑ Ⓒ Ⓓ Ⓔ
45. Ⓐ Ⓑ Ⓒ Ⓓ Ⓔ
46. Ⓐ Ⓑ Ⓒ Ⓓ Ⓔ
47. Ⓐ Ⓑ Ⓒ Ⓓ Ⓔ
48. Ⓐ Ⓑ Ⓒ Ⓓ Ⓔ
49. Ⓐ Ⓑ Ⓒ Ⓓ Ⓔ
50. Ⓐ Ⓑ Ⓒ Ⓓ Ⓔ
51. Ⓐ Ⓑ Ⓒ Ⓓ Ⓔ
52. Ⓐ Ⓑ Ⓒ Ⓓ Ⓔ
53. Ⓐ Ⓑ Ⓒ Ⓓ Ⓔ
54. Ⓐ Ⓑ Ⓒ Ⓓ Ⓔ
55. Ⓐ Ⓑ Ⓒ Ⓓ Ⓔ
56. Ⓐ Ⓑ Ⓒ Ⓓ Ⓔ
57. Ⓐ Ⓑ Ⓒ Ⓓ Ⓔ
58. Ⓐ Ⓑ Ⓒ Ⓓ Ⓔ
59. Ⓐ Ⓑ Ⓒ Ⓓ Ⓔ
60. Ⓐ Ⓑ Ⓒ Ⓓ Ⓔ
61. Ⓐ Ⓑ Ⓒ Ⓓ Ⓔ
62. Ⓐ Ⓑ Ⓒ Ⓓ Ⓔ
63. Ⓐ Ⓑ Ⓒ Ⓓ Ⓔ
64. Ⓐ Ⓑ Ⓒ Ⓓ Ⓔ
65. Ⓐ Ⓑ Ⓒ Ⓓ Ⓔ
66. Ⓐ Ⓑ Ⓒ Ⓓ Ⓔ
67. Ⓐ Ⓑ Ⓒ Ⓓ Ⓔ
68. Ⓐ Ⓑ Ⓒ Ⓓ Ⓔ

69. Ⓐ Ⓑ Ⓒ Ⓓ Ⓔ
70. Ⓐ Ⓑ Ⓒ Ⓓ Ⓔ
71. Ⓐ Ⓑ Ⓒ Ⓓ Ⓔ
72. Ⓐ Ⓑ Ⓒ Ⓓ Ⓔ
73. Ⓐ Ⓑ Ⓒ Ⓓ Ⓔ
74. Ⓐ Ⓑ Ⓒ Ⓓ Ⓔ
75. Ⓐ Ⓑ Ⓒ Ⓓ Ⓔ
76. Ⓐ Ⓑ Ⓒ Ⓓ Ⓔ
77. Ⓐ Ⓑ Ⓒ Ⓓ Ⓔ
78. Ⓐ Ⓑ Ⓒ Ⓓ Ⓔ
79. Ⓐ Ⓑ Ⓒ Ⓓ Ⓔ
80. Ⓐ Ⓑ Ⓒ Ⓓ Ⓔ
81. Ⓐ Ⓑ Ⓒ Ⓓ Ⓔ
82. Ⓐ Ⓑ Ⓒ Ⓓ Ⓔ
83. Ⓐ Ⓑ Ⓒ Ⓓ Ⓔ
84. Ⓐ Ⓑ Ⓒ Ⓓ Ⓔ
85. Ⓐ Ⓑ Ⓒ Ⓓ Ⓔ
86. Ⓐ Ⓑ Ⓒ Ⓓ Ⓔ
87. Ⓐ Ⓑ Ⓒ Ⓓ Ⓔ
88. Ⓐ Ⓑ Ⓒ Ⓓ Ⓔ

1.	D	31.	D	61.	C
2.	A	32.	B	62.	C
3.	B	33.	A	63.	E
4.	C	34.	C	64.	A
5.	C	35.	E	65.	C
6.	C	36.	C	66.	D
7.	E	37.	D	67.	C
8.	C	38.	C	68.	C
9.	C	39.	B	69.	A
10.	E	40.	A	70.	A
11.	A	41.	A	71.	A
12.	C	42.	D	72.	A
13.	B	43.	C	73.	E
14.	E	44.	B	74.	D
15.	A	45.	B	75.	B
16.	E	46.	A	76.	E
17.	D	47.	B	77.	B
18.	A	48.	B	78.	C
19.	E	49.	A	79.	B
20.	D	50.	A	80.	E
21.	A	51.	B	81.	B
22.	A	52.	E	82.	B
23.	A	53.	E	83.	D
24.	D	54.	E	84.	D
25.	B	55.	E	85.	C
26.	D	56.	E	86.	A
27.	D	57.	C	87.	D
28.	C	58.	E	88.	E
29.	C	59.	C		
30.	A	60.	C		

Number Series

The third section of the Exam 460 involves recognition of patterns in a series of numbers.

For each Number Series question, you are given a series of numbers, which follow some definite order, with answers as five sets of two numbers each. Look at the numbers in the series and figure out what pattern they follow. Then decide what the next two numbers in that series would be if the same pattern continues. It will be to your advantage to answer every question in the Number Series of the exam since your score is based on the number of questions that you answer correctly. Answer the questions which are easiest for you first, being very careful not to lose your place on the Answer Grid. For this part of the test you have 20 minutes to answer as many of the 24 questions as you can.

Number Series Practice

1.   1   2   3   4   5   6   7

    A) 1 2   B) 5 6   C) 8 9   D) 4 5   E) 7 8

2.   15   14   13   12   11   10   9

    A) 2 1   B) 17 16   C) 8 9   D) 8 7   E) 9 8

3.   20   20   21   21   22   22   23

    A) 23 23   B) 23 24   C) 19 19   D) 22 23   E) 21 22

4.   17   3   17   4   17   5   17

    A) 6 17   B) 6 7   C) 17 6   D) 5 6   E) 17 7

5.   1   2   4   5   7   8   10

    A) 11 12   B) 12 14   C) 10 13   D) 12 13   E) 11 13

6.   21   21   20   20   19   19   18

    A) 18 18   B) 18 17   C) 17 18   D) 17 17   E) 18 19

7.   1   22   1   23   1   24   1

    A) 26 1   B) 25 26   C) 25 1   D) 1 26   E) 1 25

8.   1   20   3   19   5   18   7

    A) 8 9   B) 8 17   C) 17 10   D) 17 9   E) 9 18

9.   4   7   10   13   16   19   22

    A) 23 26   B) 25 27   C) 25 26   D) 25 28   E) 24 27

10.   30   2   28   4   26   6   24

    A) 23 9   B) 26 8   C) 8 9   D) 26 22   E) 8 22

11.   5   6   20   7   8   19   9

    A) 10 18   B) 18 17   C) 10 17   D) 18 19   E) 10 11

12. **4   6   9   11   14   16   19**

    A) 21 24   B) 22 25   C) 20 22   D) 21 23   E) 22 24

13. **8   8   1   10   10   3   12**

    A) 13 13   B) 12 5   C) 12 4   D) 13 5   E) 4 12

14. **10   12   50   15   17   50   20**

    A) 50 21   B) 21 50   C) 50 22   D) 22 50   E) 22 24

15. **20   21   23   24   27   28   32   33   38   39**

    A) 45 46   B) 45 52   C) 44 45   D) 44 49   E) 40 46

Answer Grid – Number Series Practice

1. Ⓐ Ⓑ Ⓒ Ⓓ Ⓔ
2. Ⓐ Ⓑ Ⓒ Ⓓ Ⓔ
3. Ⓐ Ⓑ Ⓒ Ⓓ Ⓔ
4. Ⓐ Ⓑ Ⓒ Ⓓ Ⓔ
5. Ⓐ Ⓑ Ⓒ Ⓓ Ⓔ
6. Ⓐ Ⓑ Ⓒ Ⓓ Ⓔ
7. Ⓐ Ⓑ Ⓒ Ⓓ Ⓔ
8. Ⓐ Ⓑ Ⓒ Ⓓ Ⓔ
9. Ⓐ Ⓑ Ⓒ Ⓓ Ⓔ
10. Ⓐ Ⓑ Ⓒ Ⓓ Ⓔ
11. Ⓐ Ⓑ Ⓒ Ⓓ Ⓔ
12. Ⓐ Ⓑ Ⓒ Ⓓ Ⓔ
13. Ⓐ Ⓑ Ⓒ Ⓓ Ⓔ
14. Ⓐ Ⓑ Ⓒ Ⓓ Ⓔ
15. Ⓐ Ⓑ Ⓒ Ⓓ Ⓔ

1. **C** The numbers in this series are increasing by one. If the series were continued for two more numbers, it would read: 1 2 3 4 5 6 7 **8 9**. Therefore the correct answer is C, 8 and 9.

2. **D** The numbers in this series are decreasing by one. If the series were continued for two more numbers, it would read: 15 14 13 12 11 10 9 **8 7**. Therefore the correct answer is D, 8 and 7.

3. **B** The numbers in this series are repeated and then increased by one. If the series were continued for two more numbers, it would read: 20 20 21 21 22 22 23 **23 24**. Therefore the correct answer is B, 23 and 24.

4. **A** This series is the number 17 separated by numbers increasing by one, beginning with the number 3. If the series were continued for two more numbers, it would read: 17 3 17 4 17 5 17 **6 17**. Therefore the correct answer is A, 6 and 17.

5. **E** The numbers in this series are increasing first by one and then by two. If the series were continued for two more numbers, it would read: 1 2 4 5 7 8 10 **11 13**. Therefore the correct answer is E, 11 and 13.

6. **B** Each number in the series repeats itself and then decreases by 1. If the series were to continue for two more numbers, it would read: 21 21 20 20 19 19 18 **18 17**. Therefore the correct answer is B, 18 and 17.

7. **C** The number 1 is separated by numbers which begin with 22 and increase by one. If the series were continued for two more numbers, it would read: 1 22 1 23 1 24 1 **25 1**. Therefore the correct answer is C, 25 and 1.

8. **D** This is best explained by two alternating series – one series starts with 1 and increases by 2; the other series starts with 20 and decreases by 1. If the series were continued for two more numbers, it would read: 1 20 3 19 5 18 7 **16 9**. Therefore the correct answer is D, 16 and 9.

9. **D** The numbers in this series increase by 3. If the series were continued for two more numbers, it would read: 4 7 10 13 16 19 22 **25 28**. Therefore the correct answer is D, 25 and 28.

10. **E** This is best explained as two alternating series – one starts with 30 and decreases by 2; the other starts with 2 and increases by 2. If the series were continued by two more numbers, it would read: 30 2 28 4 26 6 24 **8 22**. Therefore the correct answer is E, 8 and 22.

11. **A** This series is once again two alternating series – one series being sets of two numbers increasing by one, the other being a single number beginning with 20 and decreasing by 1. If the series were continued for two more numbers, it would read: 5 6 20 7 8 19 9 **10 18**. Therefore, the correct answer is A, 10 and 18.

12. **A** This series is created by adding 2 to the first number and then 3 to the second. If the series were continued for two more numbers, it would read: 4 6 9 11 14 16 19 **21 24**. Therefore the correct answer is A, 21 and 24.

13. **B** This series is created by repeating the even numbers beginning at 8 with the repeats separated by numbers increasing by 2 beginning with 1. If the series were continued for two more numbers, it would read: 8 8 1 10 10 3 12 **12 5**. Therefore the correct answer is B, 12 and 5.

14. **D** This series is best described as an alternating series. One series is pairs of numbers separated by the number 50. These pairs of numbers are created by adding two to the first number. The first number of the pair is found by adding three to the second

number of the preceding pair. If the series were continued for two more numbers it would read: 10 12 50 15 17 50 20 **22 50**. Therefore the correct answer is D, 22 and 50.

15. **A** This series is best described as an alternating series. The series are created by taking sequential numbers and adding increasing integers beginning with 2 after each pair. If the series were continued for two more numbers it would read: 20 21 23 24 27 28 32 33 38 39 **45 46**. Therefore, the correct answer is A, 45 and 46.

Now that you have had some practice with the number series questions, here are some hints on the types of questions that are asked and tips on how to quickly recognize the patterns presented.

Number series tests are used to determine your skill at discerning number patterns. For clerks, this directly relates to code recognition as information is typed into a special-purpose keyboard to sort either letters or flats.

Number Series tests are not difficult if you can quickly establish the pattern in the numbers listed. For example, with the question below:

2   4   6   8   10   12   14   16   ___   ___

It should be quite obvious in this example that the following two numbers would be 18 and 20. Each number is two higher then the number before it. In other words, to get the next number you must add two to the number you are on. Therefore, 16 plus two equals 18 and 18 plus two equals 20.

The same can be done using subtraction. Look at the example below and see if you can determine what the last two numbers would be:

33   30   27   24   21   18   15   12   ___   ___

If you begin with the first number (33) and compare that to the second number (30), you should see a difference of three. Subtracting three from your second number (30) would give you the third number (27). Following this pattern throughout the example, you would see that each number, from left to right, has three fewer than the number before it. Subtracting three from the last number you have (12) would give you the first number in question, which is nine. Subtracting three from this number (9) will give you the final number you need in this equation (6).

Multiplication series may be a bit more difficult for some. Some of these equations on the exam may need more thought; the numbers get larger and harder to work in your head. Look at the example below:

1   2   4   8   16   32   64   128   ___   ___

Taking the first two numbers, the 1 and the 2, you may not realize that this was a multiplication problem. Then using the second and third numbers, the 2 and the 4, you may still believe this is just an addition equation. But then, when you get to the third and fourth numbers, the 4 and the 8, it should become more obvious that this is a multiplication equation. Each number is multiplied by 2 to produce the following number. So what did you have for the last two numbers? If you had 256 and 512, you were correct.

The last kind of number series that will appear on the exam is an alternating number series. This kind of number sequence is a little more involved and consequently takes extra time to solve. The series alternates addition and subtraction to create a pattern. A pattern may not be immediately evident, but with a little diligence, it should become apparent. Two examples are given below. Try to determine what the last two numbers would be in each sequence.

0	12	10	3	6	8	6	9	___	___
0	16	17	4	18	19	8	20	___	___

If you guessed 12 and 4 for the first line, and 21 and 12 for the second line, you are correct. You can see how these patterns can become more complicated and less obvious.

When a pattern in an alternating number series is not obvious, there is a method you can use to help you find it. The first step involves determining the differences between each successive number in sequence. Take the following example:

8	12	4	9	14	16	20	19	___	___

To make the differences clearer, you might want to rewrite the problem like this:

8 (+4) **12** (-8) **4** (+5) **9** (+5) **14** (+2) **16** (+4) **20** (-1) **19** ___ ___

Note that there are two +4 and two +5 constants. The next step is to check these differences to see if, indeed, some kind of pattern can be established. Let's start with the + 4 constant. The numbers involved are 8, 12, 16, and 20. What should become evident is that this series of four numbers represents an addition number series pattern. Now, look at the remaining numbers: 4, 9, 14, and 19. Do you see a pattern emerge there? If you determined the series is another addition number series with + 5 as a constant, you are correct again.

If there were one more answer blank, the number 24 would be the right answer. However, the addition number series pattern already established does not encompass the two answer blanks. By continuing with the information you already have, you should notice the pattern with the +5's. It begins with two consecutive numbers with five added to them, then skips two, with the third again larger by five. Looking at the +4 information, you can see the pattern is symmetrical or mirrored. Assuming that the +5 is also mirrored, the numbers in question would be 19 + 5 or 24, and then 24 + 5 or 29. If your answer was 24 and 29, then you are correct. This explanation may be about as clear as mud, but we can rewrite this as two separate series.

8 (+4) **12**   (+4)   **16** (+4) **20**

4 (+5) **9** (+5) **14**   (+5)   **19**

Since there are only 20 minutes on the actual exam to complete 24 number series questions, time is essential. If the answer to an alternating number series question is not apparent within 30 seconds, skip the question and go onto the next one. Be sure to make a **light** mark next to the series you have skipped. If there is time remaining after you have completed the questions that you know, return to the questions you skipped and try to solve them. If you still have trouble determining the answer, systematically plug in each of the answers provided and by the process of elimination you might be able to determine the correct answer. This is somewhat time-consuming, but it is better than just guessing. Guessing should always be a last resort.

On the following pages, you will find some practice exercises using number series.
Once again, the Answer Grid is provided immediately after the questions. The Answer Grids for this section are designed to be photocopied before use, and are blank on the back so that they can be removed without harming the integrity of the book.

Number Series – Full-Length Practice #1

(You have 20 minutes to complete this section.)

Directions: Choose the answer that contains the next two numbers in the series. Darken the appropriate bubble on the Answer Grid.

1.   **7   10   13   16   19   22   __ __**

A) 25 28   B) 23 24   C) 23 27   D) 25 26   E) 27 30

2.   **24   30   36   42   48   54   __ __**

A) 56 66   B) 58 64   C) 60 56   D) 58 66   E) 60 66

3.   **18   27   36   45   54   63   __ __**

A) 70 81   B) 98 110   C) 72 81   D) 71 82   E) 72 83

4.   **4   20   36   52   68   84   __ __**

A) 96 114   B) 98 110   C) 100 110   D) 100 116   E) 110 116

5.   **13   15   17   19   21   23   __ __**

A) 24 25   B) 27 28   C) 25 28   D) 25 27   E) 26 28

6.   **1   18   35   52   69   86   __ __**

A) 105 122   B) 103 120   C) 101 119   D) 103 102   E)105 120

7.   **14   12   10   8   6   4   __ __**

A) 2 0   B) 4 2   C) 2 2   D) 0 2   E) 0 0

8.   **174   150   126   102   78   54   __ __**

A) 40 6   B) 30 4   C) 30 6   D) 28 4   E) 28 2

9.   **45   40   35   30   25   20   __ __**

A) 10 5   B) 15 5   C) 10 15   D) 5 10   E) 15 10

10. **81   72   63   54   45   36   __ __**

A) 18 27   B) 28 17   C) 17 28   D) 26 18   E) 27 18

11. **163   149   135   121   107   93   __ __**

A) 65 79   B) 79 65   C) 81 67   D) 79 59   E) 67 81

12. **1205   1088   971   854   737   620   __ __**

A) 386 503   B) 403 386   C) 503 286   D)503 386   E) 500 286

13. **2   4   8   16   32** ___ ___

A) 32 64   B) 64 32   C) 64 128   D) 60 120   E) 60 128

14. **4   20   100   500   2500** ___ ___

A) 5000 12500 B) 12500 62500 C) 62500 12500 D) 18500 25500 E) 12000 **60000**

15. **3   9   27   81   243** ___ ___

A) 729 2187 B) 715 2180 C) 739 2187 D) 715 2387 E) 723 2187

16. **1   7   49   343** ___ ___

A) 2401 16807 B) 2400 16000 C) 2401 16907 D) 2400 16807 E) 4085/17250

17. **6   12   24   48   96** ___ ___

A) 182 184 B) 190 380 C)192 375 D) 195 380 E) 192 384

18. **2   8   32   128   512** ___ ___

A) 2408 8192 B) 2580 8092 C) 2348 8792 D) 2048 8192 E) 2040 8029

19. **12   10   16   17   8   6   18** ___ ___

A) 19 2   B) 4 19   C) 2 20   D) 19 4   E) 20 3

20. **7   11   3   8   13   15   19   18** ___ ___

A) 25 28   B) 23 28   C) 23 24   D) 21 23   E) 22 28

21. **20   3   6   9   17   14   12   15   18** ___ ___

A) 5 8   B) 7 11   C) 11 8   D) 12 8   E) 8 11

22. **30   20   25   28   30   35   26   40** ___ ___

A) 45 24   B) 46 25   C) 47 24   D) 47 25   E) 41 22

23. **18   14   13   16   12   11   14   10** ___ ___

A) 8 10   B) 9 12   C) 10 9   D) 12 9   E) 10 8

24. **36   42   35   28   45   21   14   7** ___ ___

A) 54 0   B) 36 7   C) 43 14   D) 48 0   E) 48 7

Answer Grid – Number Series – Full-Length Practice #1

1. (A) (B) (C) (D) (E)
2. (A) (B) (C) (D) (E)
3. (A) (B) (C) (D) (E)
4. (A) (B) (C) (D) (E)
5. (A) (B) (C) (D) (E)
6. (A) (B) (C) (D) (E)
7. (A) (B) (C) (D) (E)
8. (A) (B) (C) (D) (E)
9. (A) (B) (C) (D) (E)
10. (A) (B) (C) (D) (E)
11. (A) (B) (C) (D) (E)
12. (A) (B) (C) (D) (E)
13. (A) (B) (C) (D) (E)
14. (A) (B) (C) (D) (E)
15. (A) (B) (C) (D) (E)
16. (A) (B) (C) (D) (E)
17. (A) (B) (C) (D) (E)
18. (A) (B) (C) (D) (E)
19. (A) (B) (C) (D) (E)
20. (A) (B) (C) (D) (E)
21. (A) (B) (C) (D) (E)
22. (A) (B) (C) (D) (E)
23. (A) (B) (C) (D) (E)
24. (A) (B) (C) (D) (E)

Correct Answers – Number Series – Full-Length Practice #1

1. A   (7 10 13 16 19 22 **25 28**)
2. E   (24 30 36 42 48 54 **60 66**)
3. C   (18 27 36 45 54 63 **72 81**)
4. D   (4 20 36 52 68 84 **100 116**)
5. D   (13 15 17 19 12 23 **25 27**)
6. B   (1 18 35 52 69 86 **103 120**)
7. A   (14 21 10 8 6 4 **2 0**)
8. C   (174 150 126 102 78 54 **30 6**)
9. E   (45 40 35 30 25 20 **15 10**)
10. E   (81 72 63 54 45 36 **27 18**)
11. B   (163 149 135 121 107 93 **79 65**)
12. D   (1205 1088 971 854 737 620 **503 386**)
13. C   (2 4 6 8 16 32 **64 128**)
14. B   (4 20 100 500 2500 **12500 62500**)
15. A   (3 9 27 81 243 **729 2187**)
16. A   (1 7 49 343 **2401 16807**)
17. E   (6 12 14 48 96 **192 384**)
18. D   (2 8 32 128 512 **2048 8192**)
19. D   (12 10 16 17 8 6 18 **19 4**)
20. B   (7 11 3 8 13 15 19 18 **23 28**)
21. C   (20 3 6 9 17 14 12 15 18 **11 8**)
22. A   (30 20 25 28 30 35 26 40 **45 24**)
23. B   (18 14 13 16 12 11 14 10 **9 12**)
24. A   (36 42 35 28 45 21 14 7 **54 0**)

How many did you answer correctly?

22 or more?   **Awesome**
20-21?   **Still good**
19 or less?   **You should practice a bit more**

Number Series – Full-Length Practice #2

(You have 20 minutes to complete this section.)

Directions: Choose the answer that contains the next two numbers in the series. Darken the appropriate bubble on the Answer Grid.

1.   **14**   **15**   **16**   **17**   **18**   **19**   ___   ___

     A) 20 23   B) 22 23   C) 20 21   D) 19 20   E) 21 22

2.   **5**   **6**   **8**   **11**   **15**   **20**   ___   ___

     A) 25 34   B) 27 35   C) 26 35   D) 25 31   E) 26 33

3.   **20**   **17**   **10**   **10**   **14**   **11**   **10**   **10**   ___   ___

     A) 9 7   B) 6 7   C) 9 4   D) 8 6   E) 8 5

4.   **2**   **4**   **0**   **6**   **8**   **0**   **10**   ___   ___

     A) 0 14   C) 0 10   C) 12 10   D) 12 14   E) 12 0

5.   **26**   **28**   **30**   **32**   **34**   **36**   ___   ___

     A) 36 38   B) 37 38   C) 40 42   D) 38 42   E) 38 40

6.   **47**   **39**   **31**   **23**   ___   ___

     A) 16 7   B) 15 8   C) 15 7   D) 14 7   E) 13 6

7.   **2**   **15**   **28**   **41**   ___   ___

     A) 54 67   B) 55 68   C) 53 66   D) 55 68   E) 62 71

8.   **5**   **5**   **3**   **5**   **5**   **4**   **5**   **5**   ___   ___

     A) 5 6   B) 6 5   C) 5 5   D) 5 4   E) 5 7

9.   **3**   **6**   **13**   **16**   **23**   ___   ___

     A) 26 33   B) 25 32   C) 26 35   D) 27 36   E) 28 37

10.   **8**   **8**   **10**   **8**   **8**   **9**   **8**   ___   ___

     A) 8 7   B) 8 8   C) 8 6   D) 9 8   E) 8 9

11.   **6**   **5**   **8**   **7**   **10**   **9**   **12**   ___   ___

     A) 10 13   B) 12 14   C) 13 14   D) 11 14   E) 11 15

12.   **75**   **10**   **65**   **20**   **55**   **30**   ___   ___

     A) 45 30   B) 45 40   C) 40 45   D) 55 30   E) 35 40

13. **3   4   4   6   5   8   6 ___ ___**

A) 10 9   B) 12 7   C) 10 8   D) 10 7   E) 11 12

14. **8   3   11   8   14   13   17   18 ___ ___**

A) 20 23   B) 20 24   C) 21 23   D) 22 24   E) 24 26

15. **6   7   9   10   12   13   15 ___ ___**

A) 15 17   B) 16 18   C) 17 19   D) 15 16   E) 16 17

16. **90   60   80   70   70   80 ___ ___**

A) 50 90   B) 40 90   C) 70 90   D) 60 90   E) 50 80

17. **29   25   10   12   21   17   14 ___ ___**

A) 15 12   B) 16 13   C) 17 14   D) 18 5   E) 19 20

18. **7   3   6   14   9   12   21   15 ___ ___**

A) 20 27   B) 22 29   C) 18 27   D) 18 28   E) 23 28

19. **9   9   5   9   9   10   9 ___ ___**

A) 9 15   B) 10 15   C) 9 20   D) 9 17   E) 15 9

20. **34   32   34   33   34   34 ___ ___**

A) 33 36   B) 34 34   C) 34 36   D) 35 35   E) 34 35

21. **8   5   7   16   9   11   24 ___ ___**

A) 12 14   B) 11 14   C) 13 15   D) 14 15   E) 12 13

22. **15   40   20   30   25   20 ___ ___**

A) 20 20   B) 20 10   C) 30 20   D) 40 10   E) 30 10

23. **14   19   16   18   18   17   20   16 ___ ___**

A) 20 13   B) 22 15   C) 24 17   D) 22 16   E) 23 15

24. **6   12   35   18   24   25   30 ___ ___**

A) 37 16   B) 35 15   C) 36 15   D) 30 10   E) 34 15

Notes:

76

Answer Grid – Number Series – Full-Length Practice #2

1. Ⓐ Ⓑ Ⓒ Ⓓ Ⓔ
2. Ⓐ Ⓑ Ⓒ Ⓓ Ⓔ
3. Ⓐ Ⓑ Ⓒ Ⓓ Ⓔ
4. Ⓐ Ⓑ Ⓒ Ⓓ Ⓔ
5. Ⓐ Ⓑ Ⓒ Ⓓ Ⓔ
6. Ⓐ Ⓑ Ⓒ Ⓓ Ⓔ
7. Ⓐ Ⓑ Ⓒ Ⓓ Ⓔ
8. Ⓐ Ⓑ Ⓒ Ⓓ Ⓔ
9. Ⓐ Ⓑ Ⓒ Ⓓ Ⓔ
10. Ⓐ Ⓑ Ⓒ Ⓓ Ⓔ
11. Ⓐ Ⓑ Ⓒ Ⓓ Ⓔ
12. Ⓐ Ⓑ Ⓒ Ⓓ Ⓔ
13. Ⓐ Ⓑ Ⓒ Ⓓ Ⓔ
14. Ⓐ Ⓑ Ⓒ Ⓓ Ⓔ
15. Ⓐ Ⓑ Ⓒ Ⓓ Ⓔ
16. Ⓐ Ⓑ Ⓒ Ⓓ Ⓔ
17. Ⓐ Ⓑ Ⓒ Ⓓ Ⓔ
18. Ⓐ Ⓑ Ⓒ Ⓓ Ⓔ
19. Ⓐ Ⓑ Ⓒ Ⓓ Ⓔ
20. Ⓐ Ⓑ Ⓒ Ⓓ Ⓔ
21. Ⓐ Ⓑ Ⓒ Ⓓ Ⓔ
22. Ⓐ Ⓑ Ⓒ Ⓓ Ⓔ
23. Ⓐ Ⓑ Ⓒ Ⓓ Ⓔ
24. Ⓐ Ⓑ Ⓒ Ⓓ Ⓔ

Notes:

78

1. A
2. E
3. E
4. E
5. E
6. C
7. A
8. C
9. A
10. B
11. D
12. B
13. D
14. B
15. B
16. D
17. B
18. D
19. A
20. E
21. C
22. E
23. B
24. C

Following Oral Instructions

The last section of Exam 460 is "Following Oral Instructions." While this may not be the hardest section of the exam, it may be the most confusing. This test measures your ability to follow directions that are spoken to you. In this part of the test you will be directed to write your answer in a test booklet and then mark your answer on an Answer Grid. The test booklet will have lines of material like the following five samples. **To practice this part of the exam, photocopy or tear out the following page and have someone read the directions to you.** When the reader tells you to darken the space on the Sample Answer Grid, use the grid given. Your score on this part of the exam is based on the number of questions that you answer correctly. Therefore, if you are not sure of an answer, it will be to your advantage to guess. This part of the exam takes about 25 minutes.

Sample 1.   5 ____

Sample 2.   1   6   4   3   7

Sample 3.   D   B   A   E   C

Sample 4.   (8___)   (5___)   (2___)   (9___)   (10___)

Sample 5.   (7___)   [6___]   (1___)   [12___]

Sample Answer Grid for Following Oral Instructions

1. Ⓐ Ⓑ Ⓒ Ⓓ Ⓔ
2. Ⓐ Ⓑ Ⓒ Ⓓ Ⓔ
3. Ⓐ Ⓑ Ⓒ Ⓓ Ⓔ
4. Ⓐ Ⓑ Ⓒ Ⓓ Ⓔ
5. Ⓐ Ⓑ Ⓒ Ⓓ Ⓔ
6. Ⓐ Ⓑ Ⓒ Ⓓ Ⓔ

7. Ⓐ Ⓑ Ⓒ Ⓓ Ⓔ
8. Ⓐ Ⓑ Ⓒ Ⓓ Ⓔ
9. Ⓐ Ⓑ Ⓒ Ⓓ Ⓔ
10. Ⓐ Ⓑ Ⓒ Ⓓ Ⓔ
11. Ⓐ Ⓑ Ⓒ Ⓓ Ⓔ
12. Ⓐ Ⓑ Ⓒ Ⓓ Ⓔ

Following Oral Instructions Practice

Instructions to be Read
(The words in parentheses should not be read aloud)

You are to follow the instructions that I read to you. I cannot repeat them.

- **Look at sample 1**. (Pause slightly) Sample 1 has a number and a line beside it. On the line write A as in Ace. (Pause 2 seconds.) Now on the Sample Answer Grid, find number 5 (Pause 2 seconds) and darken the letter you just wrote on the line. (Pause 2 seconds.)

- **Look at sample 2.** (Pause slightly) Draw a line under the third number. (Pause 2 seconds.) Now look on the Sample Answer Grid, find the number under which you just drew a line and darken B as in Boy. (Pause 5 seconds.)

- **Look at the letters in Sample 3.** (Pause slightly) Draw a line under the third letter in the line. (Pause 2 seconds) Now on your Sample Answer Grid, find number 9 (pause 2 seconds) and darken the letter under which you drew a line.

- **Look at the circles in Sample 4.** Each circle has a number and a line in it. Write D as in Dog on the line in the last circle. (Pause 2 seconds.) Now on the Sample Answer Grid, darken the number-letter combination that is in the circle in which you just wrote. (Pause 5 seconds.)

- **Look at Sample 5.** (Pause slightly.) There are two circles and two boxes of different sizes with numbers in them. (Pause slightly.) If 4 is more than 2 and if 5 is less than 3, write A as in Ace in the smaller circle. (Pause slightly.) Otherwise write C as in Car in the larger box. (Pause 2 seconds.) Now on the Sample Answer Grid, darken the number-letter combination in the box or circle in which you just wrote. (Pause 5 seconds.)

Now, look at the Sample Answer Grid. You should have darkened 4B, 5A, 9A, 10D and 12C on the Sample Answer Grid.

On this section of the test, the Exam Administrator will read questions/instructions aloud to the group of test takers. These oral instructions will direct you to write/mark certain items in your test booklet, which in turn will lead you to the correct answers. Finally, you will be verbally instructed to mark the correct answers on your Answer Grid. You must answer based exclusively upon what you hear – there are no questions for you to read.

The following pages of this practice test are samples of the test booklet pages on which you will mark/write as verbally instructed. Mark your answers on the Answer Grid in the Following Oral Instructions section.

To practice realistically, you must have someone read the questions aloud to you. Do not look over the questions before taking the practice tests. Once you have completed the practice tests, you should then review the questions you missed in order to determine what caused you to miss them. This review should enable you to be more successful on similar questions next time.

Once you have finished the Following Oral Instructions Practice Exams, you are ready to go on to the complete practice exams in the following chapter. These complete exams should be taken as if you were actually in the testing room, so be sure to allow enough time to take the exam in one time period.

Good luck!

Following Oral Instructions – Full-Length Practice #1

1.   C D A B E A D E

2.   (___E)   (___D)   (___A)   (___C)   (___B)

3.   [28___]   [26___]   [33___]   [37___]

4.   XYXY   YXXY   XXYY   XXYX   YYXX

5.   30   58   14   28   42   80   24

6.   (63___)   (79___)   (61___)   Babe   Able   Cad

7.   _____E   _____C

8.   (8:50)   (7:15)   (8:05)   (7:00)   (7:35)
       ___   ___   ___   ___   ___

9.   [85_____]   [49_____]

10.   (Gulfport)   (Biloxi)   (Waveland)
        35___   17___   88___

11.   54   73   9   32   18   49

12.   [51___]   [43___]   [18___]   [21___]   [32___]

13.   [___A]   (___E)   [___D]   (___B)

14.   51___   32___   78___   12___   29___

82

15.   A D D I C T E D
                 __ __ __ __

16.   62   64   86   32   16   75   84   81   26

17.   OOXX   XXOO   XOXO   OXOX   XXXX

18.   ┌──────┐ ┌──────┐ ┌──────┐ ┌──────┐
      │ 23___│ │ 82___│ │ 48___│ │ 23___│
      └──────┘ └──────┘ └──────┘ └──────┘

19.   48 ___   39___   52___

Notes:

Following Oral Instructions – Full-Length Practice #1

Look at Sample 1. (Pause slightly.) Draw a line under the fifth letter from the left. (Pause 3 seconds.) On the Answer Grid, find the number 47, and darken the letter you underlined. (Pause 5 seconds.)

Look at Sample 2. (Pause slightly.) There are five circles, each containing a letter with a line beside it. (Pause slightly.) On the line in the last circle, write the smallest of the following numbers: 82, 78, 59, 64, and 69. (Pause 3 seconds.) On the line in the third circle, write the number 21. (Pause 3 seconds.) On the line in the first circle, do nothing. (Pause slightly.) On the line in the second circle, write the largest of the following numbers: 80, 78, 56, 82, and 79. (Pause 3 seconds.) On the Answer Grid, darken the number-letter combinations you have made. (Pause 5 seconds.)

Look at Sample 3. (Pause slightly.) If there are 365 days in the calendar year, and if Ronald Reagan is the current president of the United States, write a D as in Dog on the line in the fourth box. (Pause 3 seconds.) Otherwise, write a C as in cat on the lines in the second and third boxes. (Pause 3 seconds.) On the Answer Grid, darken the number-letter combination or combinations you have made. (Pause 5 seconds.)

Look at the X's and Y's in Sample 4. (Pause slightly.) Count the number of X's and write that number at the end of the line of X's and Y's. (Pause 4 seconds.) Count the number of Y's, and write that number under the number of X's at the end of the line. (Pause 4 seconds.) Then subtract the number of Y's from the number of X's. (Pause 3 seconds.) Find the resulting number on the Answer Grid, and darken the letter D as in Dog. (Pause 5 seconds.)

Look at the numbers in Sample 5. (Pause slightly.) Draw a line under all of the even numbers that are less than 27. (Pause 3 seconds.) On the Answer Grid, find the numbers you underlined, and darken the letter A as in apple for each. (Pause 5 seconds.)

Look at Sample 5 again. (Pause slightly.) Circle the even numbers that are greater than 56. (Pause 3 seconds.) On the Answer Grid, find the numbers you circled, and darken the letter E as in Egg for each. (Pause 5 seconds.)

Look at Sample 6. (Pause slightly.) There are three circles and three words. (Pause slightly.) Write the first letter of the second word in the second circle. (Pause 3 seconds.) Write the last letter of the first word in the last circle. (Pause 3 seconds.) Write the first letter of the third word in the first circle. (Pause 3 seconds.) On the Answer Grid, darken the number-letter combinations you have made. (Pause 5 seconds.)

Look at Sample 7. (Pause slightly.) Write the number 65 by the letter on the right. (Pause 3 seconds.) Now, on the Answer Grid, darken the number-letter combination you have made. (Pause 5 seconds.)

Look at the circles in Sample 8. (Pause slightly.) If 5 is greater than 3 and 13 is less than 15, write the letter E as in Egg in the last circle. (Pause 3 seconds.) If not, write the letter B as in Boy in the third circle. (Pause 3 seconds.) On the same line in the same circle, write the number that would be created from the last two digits of the time in that circle. (Pause 3 seconds.) On your Answer Grid, darken the number-letter combination you have made. (Pause 5 seconds.)

Look at Sample 8 again. (Pause slightly.) Each circle contains a mail collection time. (Pause slightly.) Write the letter B as in Boy on the line in the circle with the earliest collection time. (Pause 3 seconds.) On the line beside the B, write the number that would be created from the first two digits of the time in that circle (Pause 3 seconds.) On the Answer Grid, darken the number-letter combination you have just made. (Pause 5 seconds.)

Look at the two boxes in Sample 9. (Pause slightly.) In the first box is the number of Priority Mail packages en route to the Jacksonville Post Office. (Pause slightly.) In the second box is the number of Priority Mail packages in route to the Boston Post Office. (Pause slightly.) Write the letter D as in Dog in the box that has the number of Priority Mail packages en route to the Jacksonville Post Office. (Pause 3 seconds.) Now, on the Answer Grid, darken the number-letter combination you have made. (Pause 5 seconds.)

Look at Sample 9 again. (Pause slightly.) Write the letter B as in Boy in the box with the smaller number of Priority Mail packages. (Pause 3 seconds.) On the Answer Grid, darken the number-letter combination you have made. (Pause 5 seconds.)

Look at Sample 10. (Pause slightly.) There are three circles, each containing the name of a city. (Pause slightly.) The city of Gulfport has the latest mail delivery time. (Pause slightly.) The city of Waveland has the earliest delivery time. (Pause slightly.) The city of Biloxi has the middle delivery time. (Pause slightly.) Write the letter C as in Cat in the circle with the city that has the earliest delivery time. (Pause 3 seconds.) On your Answer Grid, darken the number-letter combination you have made. (Pause 5 seconds.)

Look at Sample 11. (Pause slightly.) Write the letter E as in Egg above the largest number. (Pause 3 seconds.) Write the letter D as in Dog below the smallest number. (Pause 3 seconds.) On the Answer Grid, darken the number-letter combinations you have made. (Pause 5 seconds.)

Look at Sample 12. (Pause slightly.) Each of the five boxes contains a number of sacks of mail to be delivered. (Pause slightly.) Write the letter A as in Apple in the box with the smallest number of sacks of mail to be delivered. (Pause 3 seconds.) On the Answer Grid, darken the number-letter combination you have made (Pause 5 seconds.)

Look at Sample 13. (Pause slightly.) If 42 is larger than 39 and 12 is less than 10. Write the number 41 in the larger box. (Pause 3 seconds.) If not, write the number 41 in the smaller box. (Pause 3 seconds.) On the Answer Grid, darken the number-letter combination you have made. (Pause 5 seconds.)

Look at Sample 14. (Pause slightly.) If the letter D as in Dog comes before B as in Boy in the alphabet, write the letter C as in Cat on the line after the third number. (Pause 3 seconds.) If not, write the letter A as in Apple on the line after the second number. (Pause 3 seconds.) On the Answer Grid, darken the number-letter combination you have made. (Pause 5 seconds.)

Look at Sample 15. (Pause slightly.) In Sample 15, there is a word with four lines below it. (Pause slightly.) Write the last letter of the word on the first line. (Pause 3 seconds.) Write the first letter of the word on the last line. (Pause 3 seconds.) Write the number 78 on the third line. (Pause 3 seconds.) On the Answer Grid, darken the number-letter combination you have made. (Pause 5 seconds.)

Look at Sample 16. (Pause slightly.) Draw a line under each of the listed numbers that are greater than 62 but less than 83. (Pause 4 seconds.) On the Answer Grid, find the number or numbers you underlined, and darken the letter B as in Boy for each. (Pause 5 seconds.)

Look at Sample 17. (Pause slightly.) Draw a line over each of the X's in the sequence. (Pause 3 seconds.) Count the number of X's, and write that number at the end of the sequence. (Pause 3 seconds.) Now, count the number of O's in the sequence, and add the number of O's to the number of X's. (Pause 3 seconds.) Write the total at the end of the sequence. (Pause 3 seconds.) On the Answer Grid, find that total number, and darken the letter D as in Dog. (Pause 5 seconds.)

Look at Sample 18. (Pause slightly.) There are four boxes, each containing a number of sacks of mail to be delivered. (Pause slightly.) Write the letter E as in Egg in the boxes that have the same number of sacks of mail to be delivered. (Pause 3 seconds.) On the Answer Grid, darken the number-letter combination you have made.

Look at Sample 19. (Pause slightly.) If 8 is greater than 5 and 3 is less than 4, write the letter A as in Apple on the middle line. (Pause 3 seconds.) Otherwise, write the letter D as in Dog on the last line. (Pause 3 seconds.) On the Answer Grid, darken the number-letter combination you have made.

End of Following Oral Instructions Full-length Practice #1

Notes:

88

Answer Grid – Following Oral Instructions – Full-Length Practice #1

1. Ⓐ Ⓑ Ⓒ Ⓓ Ⓔ
2. Ⓐ Ⓑ Ⓒ Ⓓ Ⓔ
3. Ⓐ Ⓑ Ⓒ Ⓓ Ⓔ
4. Ⓐ Ⓑ Ⓒ Ⓓ Ⓔ
5. Ⓐ Ⓑ Ⓒ Ⓓ Ⓔ
6. Ⓐ Ⓑ Ⓒ Ⓓ Ⓔ
7. Ⓐ Ⓑ Ⓒ Ⓓ Ⓔ
8. Ⓐ Ⓑ Ⓒ Ⓓ Ⓔ
9. Ⓐ Ⓑ Ⓒ Ⓓ Ⓔ
10. Ⓐ Ⓑ Ⓒ Ⓓ Ⓔ
11. Ⓐ Ⓑ Ⓒ Ⓓ Ⓔ
12. Ⓐ Ⓑ Ⓒ Ⓓ Ⓔ
13. Ⓐ Ⓑ Ⓒ Ⓓ Ⓔ
14. Ⓐ Ⓑ Ⓒ Ⓓ Ⓔ
15. Ⓐ Ⓑ Ⓒ Ⓓ Ⓔ
16. Ⓐ Ⓑ Ⓒ Ⓓ Ⓔ
17. Ⓐ Ⓑ Ⓒ Ⓓ Ⓔ
18. Ⓐ Ⓑ Ⓒ Ⓓ Ⓔ
19. Ⓐ Ⓑ Ⓒ Ⓓ Ⓔ
20. Ⓐ Ⓑ Ⓒ Ⓓ Ⓔ
21. Ⓐ Ⓑ Ⓒ Ⓓ Ⓔ
22. Ⓐ Ⓑ Ⓒ Ⓓ Ⓔ
23. Ⓐ Ⓑ Ⓒ Ⓓ Ⓔ
24. Ⓐ Ⓑ Ⓒ Ⓓ Ⓔ
25. Ⓐ Ⓑ Ⓒ Ⓓ Ⓔ
26. Ⓐ Ⓑ Ⓒ Ⓓ Ⓔ
27. Ⓐ Ⓑ Ⓒ Ⓓ Ⓔ
28. Ⓐ Ⓑ Ⓒ Ⓓ Ⓔ
29. Ⓐ Ⓑ Ⓒ Ⓓ Ⓔ
30. Ⓐ Ⓑ Ⓒ Ⓓ Ⓔ
31. Ⓐ Ⓑ Ⓒ Ⓓ Ⓔ
32. Ⓐ Ⓑ Ⓒ Ⓓ Ⓔ
33. Ⓐ Ⓑ Ⓒ Ⓓ Ⓔ
34. Ⓐ Ⓑ Ⓒ Ⓓ Ⓔ
35. Ⓐ Ⓑ Ⓒ Ⓓ Ⓔ

36. Ⓐ Ⓑ Ⓒ Ⓓ Ⓔ
37. Ⓐ Ⓑ Ⓒ Ⓓ Ⓔ
38. Ⓐ Ⓑ Ⓒ Ⓓ Ⓔ
39. Ⓐ Ⓑ Ⓒ Ⓓ Ⓔ
40. Ⓐ Ⓑ Ⓒ Ⓓ Ⓔ
41. Ⓐ Ⓑ Ⓒ Ⓓ Ⓔ
42. Ⓐ Ⓑ Ⓒ Ⓓ Ⓔ
43. Ⓐ Ⓑ Ⓒ Ⓓ Ⓔ
44. Ⓐ Ⓑ Ⓒ Ⓓ Ⓔ
45. Ⓐ Ⓑ Ⓒ Ⓓ Ⓔ
46. Ⓐ Ⓑ Ⓒ Ⓓ Ⓔ
47. Ⓐ Ⓑ Ⓒ Ⓓ Ⓔ
48. Ⓐ Ⓑ Ⓒ Ⓓ Ⓔ
49. Ⓐ Ⓑ Ⓒ Ⓓ Ⓔ
50. Ⓐ Ⓑ Ⓒ Ⓓ Ⓔ
51. Ⓐ Ⓑ Ⓒ Ⓓ Ⓔ
52. Ⓐ Ⓑ Ⓒ Ⓓ Ⓔ
53. Ⓐ Ⓑ Ⓒ Ⓓ Ⓔ
54. Ⓐ Ⓑ Ⓒ Ⓓ Ⓔ
55. Ⓐ Ⓑ Ⓒ Ⓓ Ⓔ
56. Ⓐ Ⓑ Ⓒ Ⓓ Ⓔ
57. Ⓐ Ⓑ Ⓒ Ⓓ Ⓔ
58. Ⓐ Ⓑ Ⓒ Ⓓ Ⓔ
59. Ⓐ Ⓑ Ⓒ Ⓓ Ⓔ
60. Ⓐ Ⓑ Ⓒ Ⓓ Ⓔ
61. Ⓐ Ⓑ Ⓒ Ⓓ Ⓔ
62. Ⓐ Ⓑ Ⓒ Ⓓ Ⓔ
63. Ⓐ Ⓑ Ⓒ Ⓓ Ⓔ
64. Ⓐ Ⓑ Ⓒ Ⓓ Ⓔ
65. Ⓐ Ⓑ Ⓒ Ⓓ Ⓔ
66. Ⓐ Ⓑ Ⓒ Ⓓ Ⓔ
67. Ⓐ Ⓑ Ⓒ Ⓓ Ⓔ
68. Ⓐ Ⓑ Ⓒ Ⓓ Ⓔ
69. Ⓐ Ⓑ Ⓒ Ⓓ Ⓔ
70. Ⓐ Ⓑ Ⓒ Ⓓ Ⓔ

71. Ⓐ Ⓑ Ⓒ Ⓓ Ⓔ
72. Ⓐ Ⓑ Ⓒ Ⓓ Ⓔ
73. Ⓐ Ⓑ Ⓒ Ⓓ Ⓔ
74. Ⓐ Ⓑ Ⓒ Ⓓ Ⓔ
75. Ⓐ Ⓑ Ⓒ Ⓓ Ⓔ
76. Ⓐ Ⓑ Ⓒ Ⓓ Ⓔ
77. Ⓐ Ⓑ Ⓒ Ⓓ Ⓔ
78. Ⓐ Ⓑ Ⓒ Ⓓ Ⓔ
79. Ⓐ Ⓑ Ⓒ Ⓓ Ⓔ
80. Ⓐ Ⓑ Ⓒ Ⓓ Ⓔ
81. Ⓐ Ⓑ Ⓒ Ⓓ Ⓔ
82. Ⓐ Ⓑ Ⓒ Ⓓ Ⓔ
83. Ⓐ Ⓑ Ⓒ Ⓓ Ⓔ
84. Ⓐ Ⓑ Ⓒ Ⓓ Ⓔ
85. Ⓐ Ⓑ Ⓒ Ⓓ Ⓔ
86. Ⓐ Ⓑ Ⓒ Ⓓ Ⓔ
87. Ⓐ Ⓑ Ⓒ Ⓓ Ⓔ
88. Ⓐ Ⓑ Ⓒ Ⓓ Ⓔ

Notes:

90

Following Oral Instructions – Full-Length Practice #1
Correctly Filled-in Answer Grid

1. Ⓐ Ⓑ Ⓒ Ⓓ Ⓔ
2. Ⓐ Ⓑ Ⓒ ● Ⓔ
3. Ⓐ Ⓑ Ⓒ Ⓓ Ⓔ
4. Ⓐ Ⓑ Ⓒ Ⓓ Ⓔ
5. Ⓐ Ⓑ Ⓒ Ⓓ Ⓔ
6. Ⓐ Ⓑ Ⓒ Ⓓ Ⓔ
7. Ⓐ Ⓑ Ⓒ Ⓓ Ⓔ
8. Ⓐ Ⓑ Ⓒ Ⓓ Ⓔ
9. Ⓐ Ⓑ Ⓒ ● Ⓔ
10. Ⓐ Ⓑ Ⓒ Ⓓ Ⓔ
11. Ⓐ Ⓑ Ⓒ Ⓓ Ⓔ
12. Ⓐ Ⓑ Ⓒ Ⓓ Ⓔ
13. Ⓐ Ⓑ Ⓒ Ⓓ Ⓔ
14. ● Ⓑ Ⓒ Ⓓ Ⓔ
15. Ⓐ Ⓑ Ⓒ Ⓓ Ⓔ
16. Ⓐ Ⓑ Ⓒ Ⓓ Ⓔ
17. Ⓐ Ⓑ Ⓒ Ⓓ Ⓔ
18. ● Ⓑ Ⓒ Ⓓ Ⓔ
19. Ⓐ Ⓑ Ⓒ Ⓓ Ⓔ
20. Ⓐ Ⓑ Ⓒ ● Ⓔ
21. ● Ⓑ Ⓒ Ⓓ Ⓔ
22. Ⓐ Ⓑ Ⓒ Ⓓ Ⓔ
23. Ⓐ Ⓑ Ⓒ Ⓓ ●
24. ● Ⓑ Ⓒ Ⓓ Ⓔ
25. Ⓐ Ⓑ Ⓒ Ⓓ Ⓔ
26. Ⓐ Ⓑ ● Ⓓ Ⓔ
27. Ⓐ Ⓑ Ⓒ Ⓓ Ⓔ
28. Ⓐ Ⓑ Ⓒ Ⓓ Ⓔ
29. Ⓐ Ⓑ Ⓒ Ⓓ Ⓔ
30. Ⓐ Ⓑ Ⓒ Ⓓ Ⓔ

31. Ⓐ Ⓑ Ⓒ Ⓓ Ⓔ
32. ● Ⓑ Ⓒ Ⓓ Ⓔ
33. Ⓐ Ⓑ ● Ⓓ Ⓔ
34. Ⓐ Ⓑ Ⓒ Ⓓ Ⓔ
35. Ⓐ Ⓑ Ⓒ Ⓓ ●
36. Ⓐ Ⓑ Ⓒ Ⓓ Ⓔ
37. Ⓐ Ⓑ Ⓒ Ⓓ Ⓔ
38. Ⓐ Ⓑ Ⓒ Ⓓ Ⓔ
39. ● Ⓑ Ⓒ Ⓓ Ⓔ
40. Ⓐ Ⓑ Ⓒ Ⓓ Ⓔ
41. ● Ⓑ Ⓒ Ⓓ Ⓔ
42. Ⓐ Ⓑ Ⓒ Ⓓ Ⓔ
43. Ⓐ Ⓑ Ⓒ Ⓓ Ⓔ
44. Ⓐ Ⓑ Ⓒ Ⓓ Ⓔ
45. Ⓐ Ⓑ Ⓒ Ⓓ Ⓔ
46. Ⓐ Ⓑ Ⓒ Ⓓ Ⓔ
47. Ⓐ Ⓑ Ⓒ Ⓓ ●
48. Ⓐ Ⓑ Ⓒ Ⓓ Ⓔ
49. Ⓐ ● Ⓒ Ⓓ Ⓔ
50. Ⓐ Ⓑ Ⓒ Ⓓ Ⓔ
51. Ⓐ Ⓑ Ⓒ Ⓓ Ⓔ
52. Ⓐ Ⓑ Ⓒ Ⓓ Ⓔ
53. Ⓐ Ⓑ Ⓒ Ⓓ Ⓔ
54. Ⓐ Ⓑ Ⓒ Ⓓ Ⓔ
55. Ⓐ Ⓑ Ⓒ Ⓓ Ⓔ
56. Ⓐ Ⓑ Ⓒ Ⓓ Ⓔ
57. Ⓐ Ⓑ Ⓒ Ⓓ Ⓔ
58. Ⓐ Ⓑ Ⓒ Ⓓ ●
59. Ⓐ ● Ⓒ Ⓓ Ⓔ
60. Ⓐ Ⓑ Ⓒ Ⓓ Ⓔ

61. Ⓐ Ⓑ Ⓒ Ⓓ ●
62. Ⓐ Ⓑ Ⓒ Ⓓ Ⓔ
63. Ⓐ Ⓑ ● Ⓓ Ⓔ
64. Ⓐ ● Ⓒ Ⓓ Ⓔ
65. Ⓐ Ⓑ ● Ⓓ Ⓔ
66. Ⓐ Ⓑ Ⓒ Ⓓ Ⓔ
67. Ⓐ Ⓑ Ⓒ Ⓓ Ⓔ
68. Ⓐ Ⓑ Ⓒ Ⓓ Ⓔ
69. Ⓐ Ⓑ Ⓒ Ⓓ Ⓔ
70. Ⓐ ● Ⓒ Ⓓ Ⓔ
71. Ⓐ Ⓑ Ⓒ Ⓓ Ⓔ
72. Ⓐ Ⓑ Ⓒ Ⓓ Ⓔ
73. Ⓐ Ⓑ Ⓒ Ⓓ ●
74. Ⓐ Ⓑ Ⓒ Ⓓ Ⓔ
75. Ⓐ ● Ⓒ Ⓓ Ⓔ
76. Ⓐ Ⓑ Ⓒ Ⓓ Ⓔ
77. Ⓐ Ⓑ Ⓒ Ⓓ Ⓔ
78. ● Ⓑ Ⓒ Ⓓ Ⓔ
79. ● Ⓑ Ⓒ Ⓓ Ⓔ
80. Ⓐ Ⓑ Ⓒ Ⓓ ●
81. Ⓐ ● Ⓒ Ⓓ Ⓔ
82. Ⓐ Ⓑ Ⓒ ● Ⓔ
83. Ⓐ Ⓑ Ⓒ Ⓓ Ⓔ
84. Ⓐ Ⓑ Ⓒ Ⓓ Ⓔ
85. Ⓐ Ⓑ Ⓒ ● Ⓔ
86. Ⓐ Ⓑ Ⓒ Ⓓ Ⓔ
87. Ⓐ Ⓑ Ⓒ Ⓓ Ⓔ
88. Ⓐ Ⓑ ● Ⓓ Ⓔ

Following Oral Instructions – Full-Length Practice #1
Correct Answers by Sample Number

1. 47E
2. 21A, 59B, 82D
3. 26C, 33C
4. 2D
5. 14A, 24A, 58E, 80E
6. 63C, 79A, 61E
7. 65C
8. 35E, 70B
9. 85D, 49B
10. 88C
11. 73E, 9D
12. 18A
13. 41A
14. 32A
15. 78A
16. 64B, 75B, 81B
17. 20D
18. 23E
19. 39A

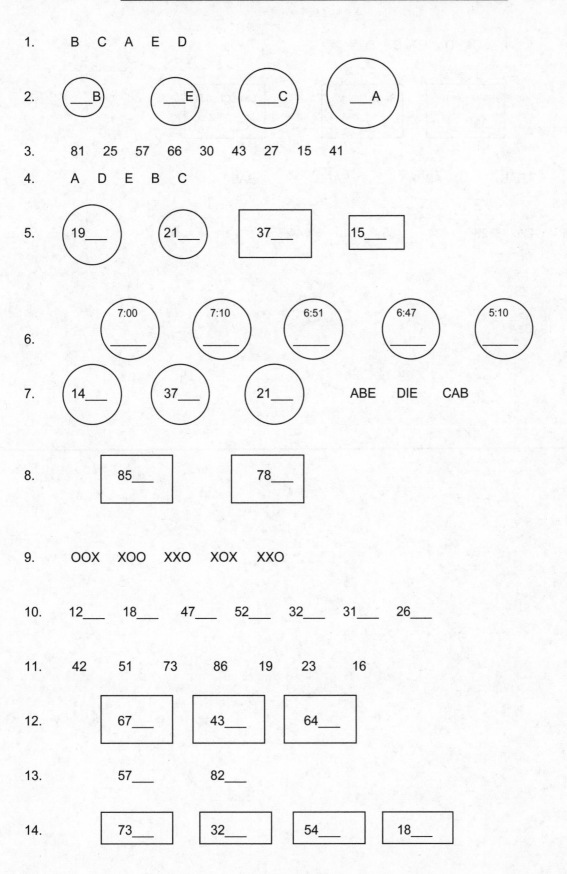

1.   B   C   A   E   D

2.

3.   81   25   57   66   30   43   27   15   41

4.   A   D   E   B   C

5.

6.

7.   ABE   DIE   CAB

8.

9.   OOX   XOO   XXO   XOX   XXO

10.   12___   18___   47___   52___   32___   31___   26___

11.   42   51   73   86   19   23   16

12.

13.   57___   82___

14.

15.   ___B   ___C   ___D   ___E   ___A

16.   A   B   C   D   E   C   D

17. | Monroe | Baton Rouge | Lake Charles |
        | 39___ | 54___ | 58___ |

18.   ABAB   ABBA   BAAB   BABA

19.   22   28   34   35   40   44

Following Oral Instructions – Full-Length Practice #2

(Directions to be Read Aloud)

Look at Sample 1. (Pause slightly.) Underline the fifth letter in the sequence. (Pause 3 seconds.) On the Answer Grid, find the number 44, and darken the letter that you underlined. (Pause 5 seconds.)

Look at Sample 2. (Pause slightly.) There are four circles of different sizes with a letter in each. (Pause slightly.) In the smallest circle, do nothing. (Pause slightly.) In the largest circle, write the number 23. (Pause 3 seconds.) On the Answer Grid, darken the number-letter combination you have made. (Pause 5 seconds.)

Look at the numbers in Sample 3. (Pause slightly.) Draw a line under the numbers which are greater than 27 but less than 43. (Pause 4 seconds.) On the Answer Grid, darken the letter B as in Boy for the numbers you underlined. (Pause 5 seconds.)

Look at Sample 4. (Pause slightly.) If 21 is greater than 27, draw a line under the last letter. (Pause 2 seconds.) Otherwise, draw a line under the third letter. (Pause 2 seconds.) On the Answer Grid, find the number 62, and darken the letter you underlined.

Look at Sample 5. (Pause slightly.) There are two circles and two boxes of different sizes with a number in each. (Pause 2 seconds.) If 6 is greater than 5 and 8 is less than 7, write the letter C as in Cat in the larger box. (Pause 3 seconds.) Otherwise, write the letter A as in Apple in the larger circle. (Pause 3 seconds.) On the Answer Grid, darken the number-letter combination you have made. (Pause 5 seconds.)

Look at the five circles in Sample 6. (Pause slightly.) The circles contain different mail delivery times. (Pause slightly.) Write the letter D as in Dog in the circle that has the latest delivery time. (Pause 3 seconds.) On the Answer Grid, find the number that would be created from the first two numbers of the time in that circle, and darken the letter D as in Dog.

Look at the circles and words in Sample 7. (Pause slightly.) Write the first letter of the last word in the first circle. (Pause 3 seconds.) Write the middle letter of the first word in the second circle. (Pause 3 seconds.) Write the last letter of the second word in the last circle. (Pause 3 seconds.) On the Answer Grid, darken the number-letter combinations you have created. (Pause 5 seconds.)

Look at Sample 8. (Pause slightly.) If March comes before April in the calendar year, write the letter B as in Boy in the first box. (Pause 4 seconds.) Otherwise, write the letter C as in Cat in the second box. (Pause 4 seconds.) Now, on the Answer Grid, darken the number-letter combination you have made. (Pause 5 seconds.)

Look at the X's and O's in Sample 9. (Pause slightly.) Draw a line under each of the X's. (Pause 3 seconds.) Count the number of X's you underlined, and write that number at the end of the series of X's and O's. (Pause 3 seconds.) Now, add 52 to that number. (Pause 3 seconds.) Find the resulting number on the Answer Grid, and darken the letter A as in Apple. (Pause 5 seconds.)

Look at Sample 10. (Pause slightly.) Write the letter D as in Dog next to the numbers that are greater than 12 but less than 32. (Pause 4 seconds.) Now, on the Answer Grid, darken the number-letter combinations you have made. (Pause 5 seconds.)

Look at Sample 11. (Pause slightly.) Draw a line under the sixth number. (Pause 3 seconds.) Draw two lines under the third number. (Pause 3 seconds.) Now, on the Answer Grid, find the number you underlined twice and darken the letter C as in Cat. (Pause 5 seconds.)

Look at Sample 12. (Pause slightly.) There are three boxes with a number in each. (Pause slightly.) The first box has the number of sacks of mail for Portland and Seattle. (Pause slightly.) The second box has the number of sacks of mail for Fargo and Butte. (Pause slightly.) On the line in the third box, write the letter A as in Apple. (Pause 3 seconds.) On the Answer Grid, darken the number-letter combination you have made. (Pause 5 seconds.)

Look at Sample 12 again. (Pause slightly.) Write the letter E as in Egg in the box that has mail for Fargo and Butte. (Pause 3 seconds.) Write the letter B as in Boy in the box that has mail for Portland and Seattle. (Pause 3 seconds.) Now, on the Answer Grid, darken the number-letter combinations you have just made. (Pause 5 seconds.)

Look at Sample 13. (Pause slightly.) Write the letter D as in Dog next to the number on the left side. (Pause 3 seconds.) On the Answer Grid, darken the number-letter combination you have made. (Pause 5 seconds.)

Look at Sample 14. (Pause slightly.) In each box is the number of sacks of mail to be delivered. (Pause slightly.) Write the letter C as in Cat in the box with the second highest number of sacks to be delivered. (Pause 3 seconds.) On the Answer Grid, darken the number-letter combination you have made. (Pause 5 seconds.)

Look at Sample 15. (Pause slightly.) On the fourth line, write the smallest of the following numbers: 31, 12, 15, 27, and 20. (Pause 3 seconds.) Write the number 59 on the first line. (Pause 2 seconds.) Write the largest of the following numbers on the fifth line: 51, 67, 77, 28, and 49. (Pause 3 seconds.) Now, on the Answer Grid, darken the number-letter combinations you have made. (Pause 5 seconds.)

Look at Sample 16. (Pause slightly.) Draw one line under the third letter. (Pause 3 seconds.) Draw two lines under the last letter. (Pause 3 seconds.) On the Answer Grid, find the number 13, and darken the letter under which you drew one line. (Pause 5 seconds.) Then, on the Answer Grid, find the number 52, and darken the letter under which you drew two lines. (Pause 5 seconds.)

Look at Sample 17. (Pause slightly.) Of the cities listed in the three boxes, Baton Rouge has the earliest delivery time. (Pause slightly.) Write the letter A as in Apple on the lines in the other two boxes. (Pause 3 seconds.) On the Answer Grid, darken the number-letter combinations you have made. (Pause 5 seconds.)

Look at Sample 18. (Pause slightly.) Draw a line under each letter B as in Boy that you see in the sequence. (Pause 3 seconds.) Count the number of B's you underlined, and write that number at the end of the sequence. (Pause 3 seconds.) Then, subtract 3 from that number. (Pause 3 seconds.) Now, find the resulting number on the Answer Grid and darken the letter B as in Boy. (Pause 5 seconds.)

Look at Sample 19. (Pause slightly.) Draw a line under the odd number in the sequence. (Pause 3 seconds.) Find that number on the Answer Grid and darken the letter E as in Egg.

End of Following Oral Instructions Practice #2

1. Ⓐ Ⓑ Ⓒ Ⓓ Ⓔ
2. Ⓐ Ⓑ Ⓒ Ⓓ Ⓔ
3. Ⓐ Ⓑ Ⓒ Ⓓ Ⓔ
4. Ⓐ Ⓑ Ⓒ Ⓓ Ⓔ
5. Ⓐ Ⓑ Ⓒ Ⓓ Ⓔ
6. Ⓐ Ⓑ Ⓒ Ⓓ Ⓔ
7. Ⓐ Ⓑ Ⓒ Ⓓ Ⓔ
8. Ⓐ Ⓑ Ⓒ Ⓓ Ⓔ
9. Ⓐ Ⓑ Ⓒ Ⓓ Ⓔ
10. Ⓐ Ⓑ Ⓒ Ⓓ Ⓔ
11. Ⓐ Ⓑ Ⓒ Ⓓ Ⓔ
12. Ⓐ Ⓑ Ⓒ Ⓓ Ⓔ
13. Ⓐ Ⓑ Ⓒ Ⓓ Ⓔ
14. Ⓐ Ⓑ Ⓒ Ⓓ Ⓔ
15. Ⓐ Ⓑ Ⓒ Ⓓ Ⓔ
16. Ⓐ Ⓑ Ⓒ Ⓓ Ⓔ
17. Ⓐ Ⓑ Ⓒ Ⓓ Ⓔ
18. Ⓐ Ⓑ Ⓒ Ⓓ Ⓔ
19. Ⓐ Ⓑ Ⓒ Ⓓ Ⓔ
20. Ⓐ Ⓑ Ⓒ Ⓓ Ⓔ
21. Ⓐ Ⓑ Ⓒ Ⓓ Ⓔ
22. Ⓐ Ⓑ Ⓒ Ⓓ Ⓔ
23. Ⓐ Ⓑ Ⓒ Ⓓ Ⓔ
24. Ⓐ Ⓑ Ⓒ Ⓓ Ⓔ
25. Ⓐ Ⓑ Ⓒ Ⓓ Ⓔ
26. Ⓐ Ⓑ Ⓒ Ⓓ Ⓔ
27. Ⓐ Ⓑ Ⓒ Ⓓ Ⓔ
28. Ⓐ Ⓑ Ⓒ Ⓓ Ⓔ
29. Ⓐ Ⓑ Ⓒ Ⓓ Ⓔ
30. Ⓐ Ⓑ Ⓒ Ⓓ Ⓔ

31. Ⓐ Ⓑ Ⓒ Ⓓ Ⓔ
32. Ⓐ Ⓑ Ⓒ Ⓓ Ⓔ
33. Ⓐ Ⓑ Ⓒ Ⓓ Ⓔ
34. Ⓐ Ⓑ Ⓒ Ⓓ Ⓔ
35. Ⓐ Ⓑ Ⓒ Ⓓ Ⓔ
36. Ⓐ Ⓑ Ⓒ Ⓓ Ⓔ
37. Ⓐ Ⓑ Ⓒ Ⓓ Ⓔ
38. Ⓐ Ⓑ Ⓒ Ⓓ Ⓔ
39. Ⓐ Ⓑ Ⓒ Ⓓ Ⓔ
40. Ⓐ Ⓑ Ⓒ Ⓓ Ⓔ
41. Ⓐ Ⓑ Ⓒ Ⓓ Ⓔ
42. Ⓐ Ⓑ Ⓒ Ⓓ Ⓔ
43. Ⓐ Ⓑ Ⓒ Ⓓ Ⓔ
44. Ⓐ Ⓑ Ⓒ Ⓓ Ⓔ
45. Ⓐ Ⓑ Ⓒ Ⓓ Ⓔ
46. Ⓐ Ⓑ Ⓒ Ⓓ Ⓔ
47. Ⓐ Ⓑ Ⓒ Ⓓ Ⓔ
48. Ⓐ Ⓑ Ⓒ Ⓓ Ⓔ
49. Ⓐ Ⓑ Ⓒ Ⓓ Ⓔ
50. Ⓐ Ⓑ Ⓒ Ⓓ Ⓔ
51. Ⓐ Ⓑ Ⓒ Ⓓ Ⓔ
52. Ⓐ Ⓑ Ⓒ Ⓓ Ⓔ
53. Ⓐ Ⓑ Ⓒ Ⓓ Ⓔ
54. Ⓐ Ⓑ Ⓒ Ⓓ Ⓔ
55. Ⓐ Ⓑ Ⓒ Ⓓ Ⓔ
56. Ⓐ Ⓑ Ⓒ Ⓓ Ⓔ
57. Ⓐ Ⓑ Ⓒ Ⓓ Ⓔ
58. Ⓐ Ⓑ Ⓒ Ⓓ Ⓔ
59. Ⓐ Ⓑ Ⓒ Ⓓ Ⓔ
60. Ⓐ Ⓑ Ⓒ Ⓓ Ⓔ

61. Ⓐ Ⓑ Ⓒ Ⓓ Ⓔ
62. Ⓐ Ⓑ Ⓒ Ⓓ Ⓔ
63. Ⓐ Ⓑ Ⓒ Ⓓ Ⓔ
64. Ⓐ Ⓑ Ⓒ Ⓓ Ⓔ
65. Ⓐ Ⓑ Ⓒ Ⓓ Ⓔ
66. Ⓐ Ⓑ Ⓒ Ⓓ Ⓔ
67. Ⓐ Ⓑ Ⓒ Ⓓ Ⓔ
68. Ⓐ Ⓑ Ⓒ Ⓓ Ⓔ
69. Ⓐ Ⓑ Ⓒ Ⓓ Ⓔ
70. Ⓐ Ⓑ Ⓒ Ⓓ Ⓔ
71. Ⓐ Ⓑ Ⓒ Ⓓ Ⓔ
72. Ⓐ Ⓑ Ⓒ Ⓓ Ⓔ
73. Ⓐ Ⓑ Ⓒ Ⓓ Ⓔ
74. Ⓐ Ⓑ Ⓒ Ⓓ Ⓔ
75. Ⓐ Ⓑ Ⓒ Ⓓ Ⓔ
76. Ⓐ Ⓑ Ⓒ Ⓓ Ⓔ
77. Ⓐ Ⓑ Ⓒ Ⓓ Ⓔ
78. Ⓐ Ⓑ Ⓒ Ⓓ Ⓔ
79. Ⓐ Ⓑ Ⓒ Ⓓ Ⓔ
80. Ⓐ Ⓑ Ⓒ Ⓓ Ⓔ
81. Ⓐ Ⓑ Ⓒ Ⓓ Ⓔ
82. Ⓐ Ⓑ Ⓒ Ⓓ Ⓔ
83. Ⓐ Ⓑ Ⓒ Ⓓ Ⓔ
84. Ⓐ Ⓑ Ⓒ Ⓓ Ⓔ
85. Ⓐ Ⓑ Ⓒ Ⓓ Ⓔ
86. Ⓐ Ⓑ Ⓒ Ⓓ Ⓔ
87. Ⓐ Ⓑ Ⓒ Ⓓ Ⓔ
88. Ⓐ Ⓑ Ⓒ Ⓓ Ⓔ

Notes:

98

#	A	B	C	D	E		#	A	B	C	D	E		#	A	B	C	D	E
1	○	○	○	○	○		31	○	○	○	●	○		61	○	○	○	○	○
2	○	○	○	○	○		32	○	○	○	○	○		62	○	○	○	○	●
3	○	○	○	○	○		33	○	○	○	○	○		63	○	○	○	○	○
4	○	○	○	○	○		34	○	○	○	○	○		64	●	○	○	○	○
5	○	●	○	○	○		35	○	○	○	○	●		65	○	○	○	○	○
6	○	○	○	○	○		36	○	○	○	○	○		66	○	○	○	○	○
7	○	○	○	○	○		37	○	●	○	○	○		67	○	●	○	○	○
8	○	○	○	○	○		38	○	○	○	○	○		68	○	○	○	○	○
9	○	○	○	○	○		39	●	○	○	○	○		69	○	○	○	○	○
10	○	○	○	○	○		40	○	○	○	○	○		70	○	○	○	○	○
11	○	○	○	○	○		41	○	●	○	○	○		71	○	○	○	●	○
12	○	○	○	○	●		42	○	○	○	○	○		72	○	○	○	○	○
13	○	○	●	○	○		43	○	○	○	○	●		73	○	○	●	○	○
14	○	○	●	○	○		44	○	○	○	●	○		74	○	○	○	○	○
15	○	○	○	○	○		45	○	○	○	○	○		75	○	○	○	○	○
16	○	○	○	○	○		46	○	○	○	○	○		76	○	○	○	○	○
17	○	○	○	○	○		47	○	○	○	○	○		77	●	○	○	○	○
18	○	○	○	●	○		48	○	○	○	○	○		78	○	○	○	○	○
19	●	○	○	○	○		49	○	○	○	○	○		79	○	○	○	○	○
20	○	○	○	○	○		50	○	○	○	○	○		80	○	○	○	○	○
21	○	○	○	○	●		51	○	○	○	○	○		81	○	○	○	○	○
22	○	○	○	○	○		52	○	○	○	●	○		82	○	○	○	○	○
23	●	○	○	○	○		53	○	○	○	○	○		83	○	○	○	○	○
24	○	○	○	○	○		54	○	○	●	○	○		84	○	○	○	○	○
25	○	○	○	○	○		55	○	○	○	○	○		85	○	●	○	○	○
26	○	○	○	●	○		56	○	○	○	○	○		86	○	○	○	○	○
27	○	○	○	○	○		57	○	○	○	●	○		87	○	○	○	○	○
28	○	○	○	○	○		58	●	○	○	○	○		88	○	○	○	○	○
29	○	○	○	○	○		59	○	●	○	○	○							
30	○	●	○	○	○		60	●	○	○	○	○							

Following Oral Instructions – Full-Length Practice #2
Correct Answers by Sample Number

1. 44D
2. 23A
3. 30B, 41B
4. 62E
5. 19A
6. 71D
7. 14C, 37B, 21E
8. 85B
9. 60A
10. 18D, 31D, 26D
11. 73C
12. 64A, 43E, 67B
13. 57D
14. 54C
15. 12E, 59B, 77A
16. 13C, 52D
17. 39A, 58A
18. 5B
19. 35E

Chapter 6: Practice 460 Exams

On the following pages you will find four full-length practice exams to help you prepare for Exam 460. The sections of these practice exams are set up in the order they were introduced in the manual and may not reflect the order of the actual exam given.

There are no hints or formulas to use in this section. You will have to rely on what you have learned in Chapter 5 of this manual.

The answers for all sections of each practice exam are located at the end of that exam.

Good Luck!!!!

Notes:

Practice Exam 460 #1

Before beginning, tear out or photocopy the answer grid for each section of the exam.

Address Checking – Practice Exam 460 #1

(You will have 6 minutes to complete this section)

1.	1216 W. 9th Ave.	1216 S. 9th Ave.
2.	2020 Poplar Dr.	2020 Popular Dr.
3.	9716 West End Terrace	9716 West End Terrace
4.	Allen, TX 75013	Allan, TX 75013
5.	PO Box 9556	PO Box 9566
6.	611 Main St.	616 Main St.
7.	Rutland, VT 08563	Rutland, VA 08563
8.	PO Box 8587	PO Box 8785
9.	Suite 785	Suite 785
10.	4040 Rock Creek Dr.	4040 Rock Creek Cir.
11.	1912 Elm Hill Rd.	1912 Elm Hill Rd.
12.	PO Box 211	PO Box 2117
13.	Seattle, WA 98765	Seettle, WA 98765
14.	Louden, NH 03067	Lowden, NH 03067
15.	Daytona Beach, FL 95463	Daytona Beach, FL 95643
16.	9856 River Rd.	9856 River Rd.
17.	PO Box 375901	PO Box 375901
18.	Zephyrhills, FL 33539	Zephyrhills, FL 33539
19.	Little Bend, CO 54216	Little Ben, CO 54211
20.	1919 Hickory Way	191919 Hickory Way
21.	Knoxville, TN 36152	Knoxville, TN 36152
22.	8201 Summerset Place	8201 Sumnerset Place
23.	PO Box 1	PO Box 1
24.	Rural Rte. 427	Rural Rte. 4227
25.	9999 River Bend Way	6666 River Bend Way
26.	Veto, CA 99652	Veto, CA 99652
27.	38045 Northeastern Blvd.	38045 Eastern Blvd. N.
28.	Suite. CA 4198	Suite C 4198
29.	Tampa, FL 33560	Tampa, FL 33560
30.	Austin, TX 75089	Astro, TX 75089
31.	1717 W. 1st St.	17171 W. 1st St.
32.	Reno, NV 87412	Reno, NE 87412
33.	Hoboken, NJ 44128	Hobroken, NJ 44128
34.	7109 Deed St.	7109 Deed St.
35.	2525 Riverdale Rd	2552 Riverdale Rd
36.	Nashua, NH 03060	Nashuah, NH 03060
37.	14 Brockton St.	14 BrickStone St.
38.	Apt 24C	Apt C24
39.	Omaha, NE 68154	Omaha, NB 68154
40.	202 North West End	202 West North End
41.	555 Sweet Lane	555 Sweet Lane
42.	2929 Hammer Rd	2929 Hammr Rd
43.	40 C St	40 See St.
44.	P.O. Box 02134	PO Box 02134
45.	Pebble, VA	Pebble, VA
46.	12 Arrow Lane	120 Arrow Lane
47.	Little Rock, AR	Little Rock, AK

48. 10 Langholm Dr.	10 Langhome Dr.
49. Suite B484	Sweet B484
50. 2050 Park Ave.	2050 Park Ave.
51. Lincoln Park Blvd	Linkin Park Blvd
52. 1 Ocean Way	1 Ocean Wy
53. 4 Henry Long Lane	4 Henry Long Lane
54. 887 Broomfield St	888 Broomfield St
55. Bronx, NY	Bronks, NY
56. 2 Long Island Rd	2 Long Iland Rd
57. Philadelphia, PE	Philadelphia, PA
58. 4 Vein Hwy	4 Vane Hwy
59. Holiday, VT	Holiday, VE
60. 60154 Hollywood St	60154 Hollywood St
61. 8269 Hollister Rd	8269 Hollister Rd
62. 42 Wilkinson Way	42 Wilkinson Way
63. 6464 Springdale Dr.	6464 Springdale Dr.
64. 33883 Hopping Trail	33883 Hoping Trails
65. 40 Wild Oak St.	40 Wilds Oak St.
66. 99 Smith St.	99 Smith St.
67. 55 Hopscotch Rd.	55 Hopscoch Rd.
68. 6321 Brook Way	6321 Brooke Way
69. 6 Gordon Dr.	6 Gorden Dr.
70. 4816 Capital St.	4816 Capitol St.
71. Boxborough, MA	Boxboro, MA
72. Rapid City, SD	Rapid City, SC
73. Diamond Rock Park	Diamond Rock Pike
74. 200 Central Ave	200 Central Ave
75. 9001 Gliding Rd	9000 Gliding Rd
76. 78 Glenwood St.	78 Glennwood St.
77. PO Box 554782	PO Box 554782
78. Hollywood, CA	Hollywood, CL
79. PO Box 6606	PO Box 6666
80. Apt a101	Apt A101
81. Clearwater, FL	Clearwater, FL
82. 734 Quarry Rock Rd	734 Quary Rock Rd
83. 1939 North West St.	1939 West North St.
84. Rt. 45 Box 54	Rt. 54 Box 45
85. 258 Smith St.	258 Smyth St.
86. 66 Meadow Lane	66 Meedow Lane
87. Detroit, MI	Detroit, ME
88. San Francisco, CA	San Jose, CA
89. Ocean See Way	Ocean Sea Way
90. Second Ave	Secand Ave
91. 32 Charter St.	32 Charter St.
92. 2469 Webster Way	2469 Webstor Way
93. P.O. Box 45678	P.O. Box 45678
94. 55 Creatave Rd.	55 Creative Rd.
95. 6 Gellman St.	6 Gilman St.

Answer Grid – Address Checking – Practice Exam 460 #1

1. Ⓐ Ⓓ	33. Ⓐ Ⓓ	65. Ⓐ Ⓓ
2. Ⓐ Ⓓ	34. Ⓐ Ⓓ	66. Ⓐ Ⓓ
3. Ⓐ Ⓓ	35. Ⓐ Ⓓ	67. Ⓐ Ⓓ
4. Ⓐ Ⓓ	36. Ⓐ Ⓓ	68. Ⓐ Ⓓ
5. Ⓐ Ⓓ	37. Ⓐ Ⓓ	69. Ⓐ Ⓓ
6. Ⓐ Ⓓ	38. Ⓐ Ⓓ	70. Ⓐ Ⓓ
7. Ⓐ Ⓓ	39. Ⓐ Ⓓ	71. Ⓐ Ⓓ
8. Ⓐ Ⓓ	40. Ⓐ Ⓓ	72. Ⓐ Ⓓ
9. Ⓐ Ⓓ	41. Ⓐ Ⓓ	73. Ⓐ Ⓓ
10. Ⓐ Ⓓ	42. Ⓐ Ⓓ	74. Ⓐ Ⓓ
11. Ⓐ Ⓓ	43. Ⓐ Ⓓ	75. Ⓐ Ⓓ
12. Ⓐ Ⓓ	44. Ⓐ Ⓓ	76. Ⓐ Ⓓ
13. Ⓐ Ⓓ	45. Ⓐ Ⓓ	77. Ⓐ Ⓓ
14. Ⓐ Ⓓ	46. Ⓐ Ⓓ	78. Ⓐ Ⓓ
15. Ⓐ Ⓓ	47. Ⓐ Ⓓ	79. Ⓐ Ⓓ
16. Ⓐ Ⓓ	48. Ⓐ Ⓓ	80. Ⓐ Ⓓ
17. Ⓐ Ⓓ	49. Ⓐ Ⓓ	81. Ⓐ Ⓓ
18. Ⓐ Ⓓ	50. Ⓐ Ⓓ	82. Ⓐ Ⓓ
19. Ⓐ Ⓓ	51. Ⓐ Ⓓ	83. Ⓐ Ⓓ
20. Ⓐ Ⓓ	52. Ⓐ Ⓓ	84. Ⓐ Ⓓ
21. Ⓐ Ⓓ	53. Ⓐ Ⓓ	85. Ⓐ Ⓓ
22. Ⓐ Ⓓ	54. Ⓐ Ⓓ	86. Ⓐ Ⓓ
23. Ⓐ Ⓓ	55. Ⓐ Ⓓ	87. Ⓐ Ⓓ
24. Ⓐ Ⓓ	56. Ⓐ Ⓓ	88. Ⓐ Ⓓ
25. Ⓐ Ⓓ	57. Ⓐ Ⓓ	89. Ⓐ Ⓓ
26. Ⓐ Ⓓ	58. Ⓐ Ⓓ	90. Ⓐ Ⓓ
27. Ⓐ Ⓓ	59. Ⓐ Ⓓ	91. Ⓐ Ⓓ
28. Ⓐ Ⓓ	60. Ⓐ Ⓓ	92. Ⓐ Ⓓ
29. Ⓐ Ⓓ	61. Ⓐ Ⓓ	93. Ⓐ Ⓓ
30. Ⓐ Ⓓ	62. Ⓐ Ⓓ	94. Ⓐ Ⓓ
31. Ⓐ Ⓓ	63. Ⓐ Ⓓ	95. Ⓐ Ⓓ
32. Ⓐ Ⓓ	64. Ⓐ Ⓓ	

Memory for Addresses – Practice Exam 460 #1

Directions: Study this page for 11 minutes, then turn the page and *from memory*, match each address to the correct box.

A	B	C	D	E
1100-1199 Bugle	3300-3799 Bugle	9000-9499 Bugle	5600-5899 Bugle	4100-4499 Bugle
Patriot	Jefferson	Victory	Carson	Meridian
7500-7799 Major	1000-1599 Major	4200-4799 Major	6100-6499 Major	3300-3799 Major
Marcus	Brown	Hickory	Birch	Elm
5200-5599 Oswald	7800-7999 Oswald	2200-2699 Oswald	4600-4899 Oswald	8200-8699 Oswald

Memory for Addresses – Practice Exam 460 #1

(You will have 5 minutes to complete this section.)

1.	Meridian		45.	7500-7799 Major
2.	2200-2699 Oswald		46.	Carson
3.	Marcus		47.	9000-9499 Bugle
4.	9000-9499 Bugle		48.	4200-4799 Major
5.	3300-3799 Major		49.	Elm
6.	Patriot		50.	Meridian
7.	1000-1599 Major		51.	3300-3799 Bugle
8.	6100-6499 Major		52.	7800-7999 Oswald
9.	Birch		53.	Jefferson
10.	8200-8699 Oswald		54.	8200-8699 Oswald
11.	Elm		55.	1100-1199 Bugle
12.	1100-1199 Bugle		56.	Birch
13.	Jefferson		57.	5200-5599 Oswald
14.	3300-3799 Major		58.	Hickory
15.	Victory		59.	4200-4799 Major
16.	8200-8699 Oswald		60.	1000-1599 Major
17.	Hickory		61.	Victory
18.	4100-4499 Bugle		62.	4100-4499 Bugle
19.	7800-7999 Oswald		63.	Brown
20.	7500-7799 Major		64.	Marcus
21.	Carson		65.	Patriot
22.	4200-4799 Major		66.	Jefferson
23.	Marcus		67.	Elm
24.	Meridian		68.	7500-7799 Major
25.	4600-4899 Oswald		69.	Victory
26.	5600-5899 Bugle		70.	8200-8699 Oswald
27.	Patriot		71.	Carson
28.	9000-9499 Bugle		72.	5200-5599 Oswald
29.	Birch		73.	4100-4499 Bugle
30.	2200-2699 Oswald		74.	Meridian
31.	Victory		75.	Brown
32.	1000-1599 Major		76.	4200-4799 Major
33.	1100-1199 Bugle		77.	1100-1199 Bugle
34.	Brown		78.	Hickory
35.	1000-1599 Major		79.	1000-1599 Major
36.	Birch		80.	2200-2699 Oswald
37.	Hickory		81.	Birch
38.	5200-5599 Oswald		82.	7800-7999 Oswald
39.	5600-5899 Bugle		83.	6100-6499 Major
40.	Marcus		84.	Patriot
41.	Victory		85.	9000-9499 Bugle
42.	Patriot		86.	3300-3799 Bugle
43.	4100-4499 Bugle		87.	4600-4899 Oswald
44.	8200-8699 Oswald		88.	Elm

1. Ⓐ Ⓑ Ⓒ Ⓓ Ⓔ
2. Ⓐ Ⓑ Ⓒ Ⓓ Ⓔ
3. Ⓐ Ⓑ Ⓒ Ⓓ Ⓔ
4. Ⓐ Ⓑ Ⓒ Ⓓ Ⓔ
5. Ⓐ Ⓑ Ⓒ Ⓓ Ⓔ
6. Ⓐ Ⓑ Ⓒ Ⓓ Ⓔ
7. Ⓐ Ⓑ Ⓒ Ⓓ Ⓔ
8. Ⓐ Ⓑ Ⓒ Ⓓ Ⓔ
9. Ⓐ Ⓑ Ⓒ Ⓓ Ⓔ
10. Ⓐ Ⓑ Ⓒ Ⓓ Ⓔ
11. Ⓐ Ⓑ Ⓒ Ⓓ Ⓔ
12. Ⓐ Ⓑ Ⓒ Ⓓ Ⓔ
13. Ⓐ Ⓑ Ⓒ Ⓓ Ⓔ
14. Ⓐ Ⓑ Ⓒ Ⓓ Ⓔ
15. Ⓐ Ⓑ Ⓒ Ⓓ Ⓔ
16. Ⓐ Ⓑ Ⓒ Ⓓ Ⓔ
17. Ⓐ Ⓑ Ⓒ Ⓓ Ⓔ
18. Ⓐ Ⓑ Ⓒ Ⓓ Ⓔ
19. Ⓐ Ⓑ Ⓒ Ⓓ Ⓔ
20. Ⓐ Ⓑ Ⓒ Ⓓ Ⓔ
21. Ⓐ Ⓑ Ⓒ Ⓓ Ⓔ
22. Ⓐ Ⓑ Ⓒ Ⓓ Ⓔ
23. Ⓐ Ⓑ Ⓒ Ⓓ Ⓔ
24. Ⓐ Ⓑ Ⓒ Ⓓ Ⓔ
25. Ⓐ Ⓑ Ⓒ Ⓓ Ⓔ
26. Ⓐ Ⓑ Ⓒ Ⓓ Ⓔ
27. Ⓐ Ⓑ Ⓒ Ⓓ Ⓔ
28. Ⓐ Ⓑ Ⓒ Ⓓ Ⓔ
29. Ⓐ Ⓑ Ⓒ Ⓓ Ⓔ
30. Ⓐ Ⓑ Ⓒ Ⓓ Ⓔ

31. Ⓐ Ⓑ Ⓒ Ⓓ Ⓔ
32. Ⓐ Ⓑ Ⓒ Ⓓ Ⓔ
33. Ⓐ Ⓑ Ⓒ Ⓓ Ⓔ
34. Ⓐ Ⓑ Ⓒ Ⓓ Ⓔ
35. Ⓐ Ⓑ Ⓒ Ⓓ Ⓔ
36. Ⓐ Ⓑ Ⓒ Ⓓ Ⓔ
37. Ⓐ Ⓑ Ⓒ Ⓓ Ⓔ
38. Ⓐ Ⓑ Ⓒ Ⓓ Ⓔ
39. Ⓐ Ⓑ Ⓒ Ⓓ Ⓔ
40. Ⓐ Ⓑ Ⓒ Ⓓ Ⓔ
41. Ⓐ Ⓑ Ⓒ Ⓓ Ⓔ
42. Ⓐ Ⓑ Ⓒ Ⓓ Ⓔ
43. Ⓐ Ⓑ Ⓒ Ⓓ Ⓔ
44. Ⓐ Ⓑ Ⓒ Ⓓ Ⓔ
45. Ⓐ Ⓑ Ⓒ Ⓓ Ⓔ
46. Ⓐ Ⓑ Ⓒ Ⓓ Ⓔ
47. Ⓐ Ⓑ Ⓒ Ⓓ Ⓔ
48. Ⓐ Ⓑ Ⓒ Ⓓ Ⓔ
49. Ⓐ Ⓑ Ⓒ Ⓓ Ⓔ
50. Ⓐ Ⓑ Ⓒ Ⓓ Ⓔ
51. Ⓐ Ⓑ Ⓒ Ⓓ Ⓔ
52. Ⓐ Ⓑ Ⓒ Ⓓ Ⓔ
53. Ⓐ Ⓑ Ⓒ Ⓓ Ⓔ
54. Ⓐ Ⓑ Ⓒ Ⓓ Ⓔ
55. Ⓐ Ⓑ Ⓒ Ⓓ Ⓔ
56. Ⓐ Ⓑ Ⓒ Ⓓ Ⓔ
57. Ⓐ Ⓑ Ⓒ Ⓓ Ⓔ
58. Ⓐ Ⓑ Ⓒ Ⓓ Ⓔ
59. Ⓐ Ⓑ Ⓒ Ⓓ Ⓔ
60. Ⓐ Ⓑ Ⓒ Ⓓ Ⓔ

61. Ⓐ Ⓑ Ⓒ Ⓓ Ⓔ
62. Ⓐ Ⓑ Ⓒ Ⓓ Ⓔ
63. Ⓐ Ⓑ Ⓒ Ⓓ Ⓔ
64. Ⓐ Ⓑ Ⓒ Ⓓ Ⓔ
65. Ⓐ Ⓑ Ⓒ Ⓓ Ⓔ
66. Ⓐ Ⓑ Ⓒ Ⓓ Ⓔ
67. Ⓐ Ⓑ Ⓒ Ⓓ Ⓔ
68. Ⓐ Ⓑ Ⓒ Ⓓ Ⓔ
69. Ⓐ Ⓑ Ⓒ Ⓓ Ⓔ
70. Ⓐ Ⓑ Ⓒ Ⓓ Ⓔ
71. Ⓐ Ⓑ Ⓒ Ⓓ Ⓔ
72. Ⓐ Ⓑ Ⓒ Ⓓ Ⓔ
73. Ⓐ Ⓑ Ⓒ Ⓓ Ⓔ
74. Ⓐ Ⓑ Ⓒ Ⓓ Ⓔ
75. Ⓐ Ⓑ Ⓒ Ⓓ Ⓔ
76. Ⓐ Ⓑ Ⓒ Ⓓ Ⓔ
77. Ⓐ Ⓑ Ⓒ Ⓓ Ⓔ
78. Ⓐ Ⓑ Ⓒ Ⓓ Ⓔ
79. Ⓐ Ⓑ Ⓒ Ⓓ Ⓔ
80. Ⓐ Ⓑ Ⓒ Ⓓ Ⓔ
81. Ⓐ Ⓑ Ⓒ Ⓓ Ⓔ
82. Ⓐ Ⓑ Ⓒ Ⓓ Ⓔ
83. Ⓐ Ⓑ Ⓒ Ⓓ Ⓔ
84. Ⓐ Ⓑ Ⓒ Ⓓ Ⓔ
85. Ⓐ Ⓑ Ⓒ Ⓓ Ⓔ
86. Ⓐ Ⓑ Ⓒ Ⓓ Ⓔ
87. Ⓐ Ⓑ Ⓒ Ⓓ Ⓔ
88. Ⓐ Ⓑ Ⓒ Ⓓ Ⓔ

Notes:

Number Series – Practice Exam 460 #1

(You will have 20 minutes to complete this section.)

1. **7   10   13   16   19   22   ___   ___**
    A. 25 28   B.23 24   C. 23 27   D.25 26   E.27 30

2. **24   30   36   42   48   54   ___   ___**
    A. 56 66   B. 58 64   C. 60 56   D. 58 66   E. 60 66

3. **18   27   36   45   54   63   ___   ___**
    A. 70 81   B. 98 110   C. 72 81   D. 71 82   E. 72 83

4. **4   20   36   52   68   84   ___   ___**
    A. 96 114   B. 98 110   C. 100 110   D. 100 116   E. 110 116

5. **13   15   17   19   21   23   ___   ___**
    A. 24 25   B. 27 28   C. 25 28   D. 25 27   E.26 28

6. **1   18   35   52   69   86   ___   ___**
    A. 105 122   B. 103 120   C. 101 119   D. 103 102   E.105 120

7. **14   12   10   8   6   4   ___   ___**
    A. 2 0   B. 4 2   C. 2 2   D. 0 2   E. 0 0

8. **174   150   126   102   78   54   ___   ___**
    A. 40 6   B. 30 4   C. 30 6   D. 28 4   E. 28 2

9. **45   40   35   30   25   20   ___   ___**
    A. 10 5   B. 15 5   C. 10 15   D. 5 10   E. 15 10

10. **81   72   63   54   45   36   ___   ___**
    A. 18 27   B. 28 17   C. 17 28   D. 26 18   E. 27 18

11. **163   149   135   121   107   93   ___   ___**
    A. 65 79   B. 79 65   C. 81 67   D. 79 59   E. 67 81

12. **1205   1088   971   854   737   620   ___   ___**
    A.386 503   B. 403 386   C. 503 286   D.503 386   E. 500 286

13. **2   4   8   16   32   ___   ___**

   A. 32 64   B. 64 32   C. 64 128   D. 60 120   E. 60 128

14. **4   20   100   500   2500   ___   ___**

   A. 5000 12500 B.12500 62500 C. 62500 12500 D.18500 25500 E. 12000
60000

15. **3   9   27   81   243   ___   ___**

   A. 729 2187   B. 715 2180   C. 739 2187   D. 715 2387   E. 723 2187

16. **1   7   49   343   ___   ___**

   A. 2401 16807   B. 2400 16000   C. 2401 16907   D. 2400 16807   E . 4085 17150

17. **6   12   24   48   96   ___   ___**

   A. 182 384   B. 190 380   C. 192 375   D. 195 380   E. 192 384

18. **2   8   32   128   512   ___   ___**

   A. 2408 8192 B. 2580 8092 C. 2348 8792 D. 2048 8192 E. 2040 8029

19. **12   10   16   17   8   6   18   ___   ___**

   A. 19 2   B. 4 19   C. 2 20   D. 19 4   E. 20 3

20. **7   11   3   8   13   15   19   18   ___   ___**

   A. 25 28   B. 23 28   C.23 24   D. 21 23   E. 22 28

21. **20   3   6   9   17   14   12   5   18   ___   ___**

   A. 5 8   B. 7 11   C. 11 8   D. 12 8   E. 8 11

22. **30   20   25   28   30   35   26   40   ___   ___**

   A. 45 24   B. 46 25   C. 47 24   D. 43 25   E. 41 22

23. **18   14   13   16   12   11   14   10   ___   ___**

   A. 8 10   B. 9 12   C. 10 9   D. 12 9   E. 10 8

24. **36   42   35   28   45   21   14   7   ___   ___**

   A. 54 0   B. 36 7   C. 43 14   D. 48 0   E. 48 7

Answer Grid – Number Series – Practice Exam 460 #1

1. Ⓐ Ⓑ Ⓒ Ⓓ Ⓔ
2. Ⓐ Ⓑ Ⓒ Ⓓ Ⓔ
3. Ⓐ Ⓑ Ⓒ Ⓓ Ⓔ
4. Ⓐ Ⓑ Ⓒ Ⓓ Ⓔ
5. Ⓐ Ⓑ Ⓒ Ⓓ Ⓔ
6. Ⓐ Ⓑ Ⓒ Ⓓ Ⓔ
7. Ⓐ Ⓑ Ⓒ Ⓓ Ⓔ
8. Ⓐ Ⓑ Ⓒ Ⓓ Ⓔ
9. Ⓐ Ⓑ Ⓒ Ⓓ Ⓔ
10. Ⓐ Ⓑ Ⓒ Ⓓ Ⓔ
11. Ⓐ Ⓑ Ⓒ Ⓓ Ⓔ
12. Ⓐ Ⓑ Ⓒ Ⓓ Ⓔ
13. Ⓐ Ⓑ Ⓒ Ⓓ Ⓔ
14. Ⓐ Ⓑ Ⓒ Ⓓ Ⓔ
15. Ⓐ Ⓑ Ⓒ Ⓓ Ⓔ
16. Ⓐ Ⓑ Ⓒ Ⓓ Ⓔ
17. Ⓐ Ⓑ Ⓒ Ⓓ Ⓔ
18. Ⓐ Ⓑ Ⓒ Ⓓ Ⓔ
19. Ⓐ Ⓑ Ⓒ Ⓓ Ⓔ
20. Ⓐ Ⓑ Ⓒ Ⓓ Ⓔ
21. Ⓐ Ⓑ Ⓒ Ⓓ Ⓔ
22. Ⓐ Ⓑ Ⓒ Ⓓ Ⓔ
23. Ⓐ Ⓑ Ⓒ Ⓓ Ⓔ
24. Ⓐ Ⓑ Ⓒ Ⓓ Ⓔ

Notes:

Following Oral Instructions – Practice Exam 460 #1
Samples

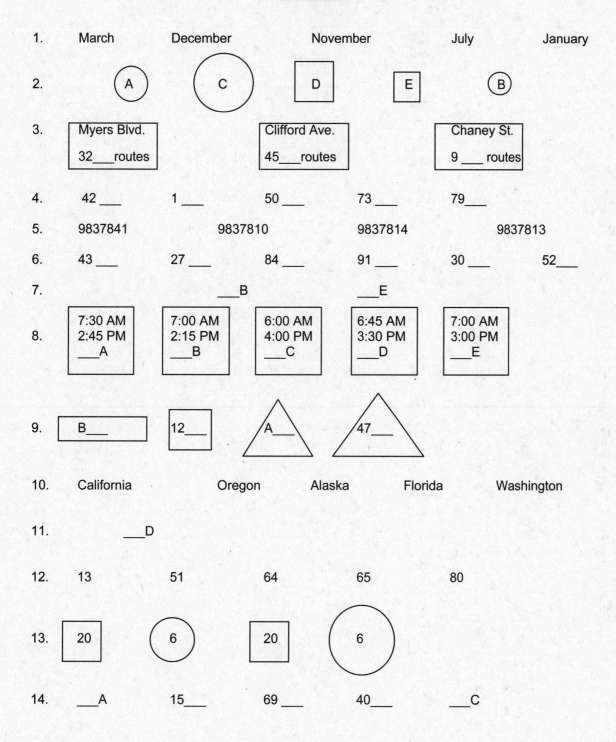

1. March   December   November   July   January

2. (A)   (C)   [D]   [E]   (B)

3. | Myers Blvd. | Clifford Ave. | Chaney St. |
    | 32 ___ routes | 45 ___ routes | 9 ___ routes |

4. 42 ___   1 ___   50 ___   73 ___   79 ___

5. 9837841   9837810   9837814   9837813

6. 43 ___   27 ___   84 ___   91 ___   30 ___   52 ___

7.   ___B   ___E

8. | 7:30 AM 2:45 PM ___A | 7:00 AM 2:15 PM ___B | 6:00 AM 4:00 PM ___C | 6:45 AM 3:30 PM ___D | 7:00 AM 3:00 PM ___E |

9. [B___]   [12___]   A___ (triangle)   47___ (triangle)

10. California   Oregon   Alaska   Florida   Washington

11.   ___D

12. 13   51   64   65   80

13. [20]   (6)   [20]   (6)

14. ___A   15___   69 ___   40___   ___C

115

Following Oral Instructions – Practice Exam 460 #1

(Directions to be Read Aloud)

Examine Sample 1. (Pause slightly.) If any of the months listed in Sample 1 can be categorized as winter months, find number 12 on your Answer Grid and darken the letter E as in Egg. Otherwise, find number 14 on your Answer Grid and darken the letter A as in Apple. (Pause 7 seconds.)

Examine Sample 1 again. (Pause slightly.) If more than two months begin with the letter J as in Jack, go to number 15 on your Answer Grid and darken the letter B as in Boy. Otherwise, darken the letter C as in Cat at number 5 on your Answer Grid. (Pause 7 seconds.)

Examine Sample 2. (Pause slightly.) Write the number 17 in the smallest circle shown. Darken the resulting number-letter combination on your Answer Grid only if there are two larger circles shown in the sample. (Pause 10 seconds.) Otherwise, write the number 16 in square D as in Dog, and darken the number-letter combination on your Answer Grid. (Pause 10 seconds.)

Examine Sample 3. (Pause slightly.) This sample illustrates the respective number of routes originating from each of three postal substations in a metropolitan area. Select the largest substation, designated by the highest number of routes, and write the letter C as in Cat beside it. (Pause 7 seconds.) Darken the resulting number-letter combination you have selected on your Answer Grid. (Pause 7 seconds.)

Examine Sample 3 again. (Pause slightly.) If the Chaney Street station has more routes than the Myers Boulevard station, write the letter B as in Boy beside the Clifford Avenue station. (Pause 5 seconds.) If not, write the letter A as in Apple beside the Myers Boulevard station. (Pause 5 seconds.) Darken the number-letter combination you have selected on your Answer Grid. (Pause 7 seconds.)

Examine Sample 4. (Pause slightly.) If the third number is greater than the second number, but less than the fifth number, write the letter A as in Apple beside the number 42. (Pause 5 seconds.) Otherwise write the letter D as in Dog beside the fourth number. (Pause 5 seconds.) Darken the number-letter combination that you have selected on your Answer Grid (Pause 7 seconds.)

Examine Sample 3 again. (Pause slightly.) Darken the letter D as in Dog at number 9 on the Answer Grid if the Chaney Street substation has the smallest number of routes. (Pause 7 seconds.) Otherwise, go to number 82 on your Answer Grid and darken the letter D as in Dog. (Pause 7 seconds.)

Examine Sample 4 again. (Pause slightly.) If there are any numbers greater than 53, but less than 70, write the letter B as in Boy beside that number and darken the resulting number-letter combination(s) on your Answer Grid. (Pause 7 seconds.) Otherwise, write the letter E as in Egg beside the second number of the sample and darken that number letter combination on your Answer Grid. (Pause 10 seconds.)

Examine Sample 5. (Pause slightly.) This sample shows four numbers, each representing a combined ZIP code and route direct number. The first five digits of each number identify the ZIP code and the last two digits represent intercity route numbers. If all of the ZIP codes in Sample 5 are the same and there is not a route number higher than 50, darken the letter A as in Apple at number 50 on your Answer Grid. (Pause 10 seconds.) Otherwise darken the letter C as in Cat at number 49 on your Answer Grid. (Pause 7 seconds.)

Examine Sample 6. (Pause slightly.) Write the letter A as in Apple beside the lowest number if the first number in the sample is less than the last number in the sample, and if there is a number greater than 91. (Pause 7 seconds.) Otherwise write the letter E as in Egg beside the number 30. (Pause 5 seconds.) Darken the number-letter combination you have selected on your Answer Grid. (Pause 7 seconds.)

Examine Sample 6 again. (Pause slightly.) Write the letter B as in Boy beside the number 84 if the preceding number is less than 84. (Pause 5 seconds.) Otherwise, write the letter C as in Cat beside 84. (Pause 5 seconds.) Darken the number-letter combination you have chosen on your Answer Grid. (Pause 7 seconds.)

Examine Sample 6 one more time. (Pause slightly.) If there is a number that is greater than 43, but less than 53, write the letter D as in Dog beside it. Darken that number-letter combination on your Answer Grid. (Pause 10 seconds.) If not, go to number 14 on your Answer Grid and darken the letter B as in Boy. (Pause 7 seconds.)

Examine Sample 7. (Pause slightly.) If Los Angeles is located in Florida, and Washington, D.C., is in California, write the number 16 on the line beside the letter E as in Egg. (Pause 5 seconds.) If the preceding statement is false, write the number 16 beside the letter E as in Egg anyway, and darken the resulting number-letter combination on your Answer Grid. (Pause 10 seconds.)

Examine Sample 8. (Pause slightly.) These five boxes show the starting and finishing times of five rural routes on a particular day. The time at the top is the rural carriers' starting time and the time listed below shows when they finished for the day. Find the carrier whose route takes the longest time and write the number 10 beside the letter representing that carrier. (Pause 10 seconds.) Darken your Answer Grid with this number-letter combination. (Pause 7 seconds.)

Examine Sample 8 again. (Pause slightly.) If carrier A as in Apple finished for the day before Carrier B as in Boy write the number 2 beside the letter A as in Apple. (Pause 5 seconds.) Otherwise, find which of the carriers had the latest starting time and write the number 7 beside the letter representing that carrier. (Pause 7 seconds.) Darken the number-letter combination you have chosen on your Answer Grid. (Pause 7 seconds.)

Examine Sample 8 one last time. (Pause slightly.) Write the number 11 beside the letter representing the carrier with the second latest finishing time. (Pause 7 seconds.) Darken that number-letter combination on your Answer Grid. (Pause 7 seconds.)

Examine Sample 9. (Pause slightly.) Write the letter E as in Egg beside the number that is in the circle and darken the resulting number-letter combination. (Pause 5 seconds.) If there is no circle in the sample, write the number 47 beside the letter within the rectangle and darken that number-letter combination on your Answer Grid.

Examine Sample 10. (Pause slightly.) If any one of the states shown in the sample is not located in the western part of the United States, go to number 36 on your Answer Grid and darken the letter E as in Egg. (Pause 7 seconds.) Otherwise, go to number 3 on your Answer Grid and darken the letter B as in Boy. (Pause 7 seconds.)

Examine Sample 10 again. (Pause slightly.) If any of the states listed begins with the letter C as in Cat go to number 49 on your Answer Grid and darken the letter C as in Cat. (Pause 7 seconds.)

Examine Sample 11. (Pause slightly.) If 9 is greater than 7 and 20 is less than 21, write the number 60 on the line provided and darken that number-letter combination on your Answer Grid. (Pause 10 seconds.) Otherwise, go to number 23 on your Answer Grid and darken the letter B as in Boy.

Examine Sample 12. (Pause slightly.) Find the number that is greater than 13 and less than 64; go to that number on your Answer Grid and darken the letter E as in Egg. (Pause 7 seconds.)

Examine Sample 13. (Pause slightly.) Choose the number that is shown in identically sized shapes; go to that number on your Answer Grid and darken the letter E as in Egg. (Pause 10 seconds.)

Examine Sample 14. (Pause slightly.) If 40 is less than 69 and greater than 15, go to 40 on your Answer Grid and darken the letter A as in Apple. (Pause 7 seconds.) If not, write the letter C as in Cat beside the number 15 in the sample. (Pause 5 seconds.) Darken that number-letter combination on your Answer Grid. (Pause 7 seconds.)

End of Following Oral Instructions Practice Exam 460 #1

Notes:

1. Ⓐ Ⓑ Ⓒ Ⓓ Ⓔ
2. Ⓐ Ⓑ Ⓒ Ⓓ Ⓔ
3. Ⓐ Ⓑ Ⓒ Ⓓ Ⓔ
4. Ⓐ Ⓑ Ⓒ Ⓓ Ⓔ
5. Ⓐ Ⓑ Ⓒ Ⓓ Ⓔ
6. Ⓐ Ⓑ Ⓒ Ⓓ Ⓔ
7. Ⓐ Ⓑ Ⓒ Ⓓ Ⓔ
8. Ⓐ Ⓑ Ⓒ Ⓓ Ⓔ
9. Ⓐ Ⓑ Ⓒ Ⓓ Ⓔ
10. Ⓐ Ⓑ Ⓒ Ⓓ Ⓔ
11. Ⓐ Ⓑ Ⓒ Ⓓ Ⓔ
12. Ⓐ Ⓑ Ⓒ Ⓓ Ⓔ
13. Ⓐ Ⓑ Ⓒ Ⓓ Ⓔ
14. Ⓐ Ⓑ Ⓒ Ⓓ Ⓔ
15. Ⓐ Ⓑ Ⓒ Ⓓ Ⓔ
16. Ⓐ Ⓑ Ⓒ Ⓓ Ⓔ
17. Ⓐ Ⓑ Ⓒ Ⓓ Ⓔ
18. Ⓐ Ⓑ Ⓒ Ⓓ Ⓔ
19. Ⓐ Ⓑ Ⓒ Ⓓ Ⓔ
20. Ⓐ Ⓑ Ⓒ Ⓓ Ⓔ
21. Ⓐ Ⓑ Ⓒ Ⓓ Ⓔ
22. Ⓐ Ⓑ Ⓒ Ⓓ Ⓔ
23. Ⓐ Ⓑ Ⓒ Ⓓ Ⓔ
24. Ⓐ Ⓑ Ⓒ Ⓓ Ⓔ
25. Ⓐ Ⓑ Ⓒ Ⓓ Ⓔ
26. Ⓐ Ⓑ Ⓒ Ⓓ Ⓔ
27. Ⓐ Ⓑ Ⓒ Ⓓ Ⓔ
28. Ⓐ Ⓑ Ⓒ Ⓓ Ⓔ
29. Ⓐ Ⓑ Ⓒ Ⓓ Ⓔ
30. Ⓐ Ⓑ Ⓒ Ⓓ Ⓔ
31. Ⓐ Ⓑ Ⓒ Ⓓ Ⓔ
32. Ⓐ Ⓑ Ⓒ Ⓓ Ⓔ
33. Ⓐ Ⓑ Ⓒ Ⓓ Ⓔ
34. Ⓐ Ⓑ Ⓒ Ⓓ Ⓔ

35. Ⓐ Ⓑ Ⓒ Ⓓ Ⓔ
36. Ⓐ Ⓑ Ⓒ Ⓓ Ⓔ
37. Ⓐ Ⓑ Ⓒ Ⓓ Ⓔ
38. Ⓐ Ⓑ Ⓒ Ⓓ Ⓔ
39. Ⓐ Ⓑ Ⓒ Ⓓ Ⓔ
40. Ⓐ Ⓑ Ⓒ Ⓓ Ⓔ
41. Ⓐ Ⓑ Ⓒ Ⓓ Ⓔ
42. Ⓐ Ⓑ Ⓒ Ⓓ Ⓔ
43. Ⓐ Ⓑ Ⓒ Ⓓ Ⓔ
44. Ⓐ Ⓑ Ⓒ Ⓓ Ⓔ
45. Ⓐ Ⓑ Ⓒ Ⓓ Ⓔ
46. Ⓐ Ⓑ Ⓒ Ⓓ Ⓔ
47. Ⓐ Ⓑ Ⓒ Ⓓ Ⓔ
48. Ⓐ Ⓑ Ⓒ Ⓓ Ⓔ
49. Ⓐ Ⓑ Ⓒ Ⓓ Ⓔ
50. Ⓐ Ⓑ Ⓒ Ⓓ Ⓔ
51. Ⓐ Ⓑ Ⓒ Ⓓ Ⓔ
52. Ⓐ Ⓑ Ⓒ Ⓓ Ⓔ
53. Ⓐ Ⓑ Ⓒ Ⓓ Ⓔ
54. Ⓐ Ⓑ Ⓒ Ⓓ Ⓔ
55. Ⓐ Ⓑ Ⓒ Ⓓ Ⓔ
56. Ⓐ Ⓑ Ⓒ Ⓓ Ⓔ
57. Ⓐ Ⓑ Ⓒ Ⓓ Ⓔ
58. Ⓐ Ⓑ Ⓒ Ⓓ Ⓔ
59. Ⓐ Ⓑ Ⓒ Ⓓ Ⓔ
60. Ⓐ Ⓑ Ⓒ Ⓓ Ⓔ
61. Ⓐ Ⓑ Ⓒ Ⓓ Ⓔ
62. Ⓐ Ⓑ Ⓒ Ⓓ Ⓔ
63. Ⓐ Ⓑ Ⓒ Ⓓ Ⓔ
64. Ⓐ Ⓑ Ⓒ Ⓓ Ⓔ
65. Ⓐ Ⓑ Ⓒ Ⓓ Ⓔ
66. Ⓐ Ⓑ Ⓒ Ⓓ Ⓔ
67. Ⓐ Ⓑ Ⓒ Ⓓ Ⓔ
68. Ⓐ Ⓑ Ⓒ Ⓓ Ⓔ

69. Ⓐ Ⓑ Ⓒ Ⓓ Ⓔ
70. Ⓐ Ⓑ Ⓒ Ⓓ Ⓔ
71. Ⓐ Ⓑ Ⓒ Ⓓ Ⓔ
72. Ⓐ Ⓑ Ⓒ Ⓓ Ⓔ
73. Ⓐ Ⓑ Ⓒ Ⓓ Ⓔ
74. Ⓐ Ⓑ Ⓒ Ⓓ Ⓔ
75. Ⓐ Ⓑ Ⓒ Ⓓ Ⓔ
76. Ⓐ Ⓑ Ⓒ Ⓓ Ⓔ
77. Ⓐ Ⓑ Ⓒ Ⓓ Ⓔ
78. Ⓐ Ⓑ Ⓒ Ⓓ Ⓔ
79. Ⓐ Ⓑ Ⓒ Ⓓ Ⓔ
80. Ⓐ Ⓑ Ⓒ Ⓓ Ⓔ
81. Ⓐ Ⓑ Ⓒ Ⓓ Ⓔ
82. Ⓐ Ⓑ Ⓒ Ⓓ Ⓔ
83. Ⓐ Ⓑ Ⓒ Ⓓ Ⓔ
84. Ⓐ Ⓑ Ⓒ Ⓓ Ⓔ
85. Ⓐ Ⓑ Ⓒ Ⓓ Ⓔ
86. Ⓐ Ⓑ Ⓒ Ⓓ Ⓔ
87. Ⓐ Ⓑ Ⓒ Ⓓ Ⓔ
88. Ⓐ Ⓑ Ⓒ Ⓓ Ⓔ
89. Ⓐ Ⓑ Ⓒ Ⓓ Ⓔ
90. Ⓐ Ⓑ Ⓒ Ⓓ Ⓔ
91. Ⓐ Ⓑ Ⓒ Ⓓ Ⓔ
92. Ⓐ Ⓑ Ⓒ Ⓓ Ⓔ
93. Ⓐ Ⓑ Ⓒ Ⓓ Ⓔ
94. Ⓐ Ⓑ Ⓒ Ⓓ Ⓔ
95. Ⓐ Ⓑ Ⓒ Ⓓ Ⓔ

You have just completed the first of four practice Exam 460's found in this manual. Before you proceed to the remaining three, we have a few more suggestions.

1. Use the answer keys on the next five pages to score the exam you have just completed. If you do not feel that you can be objective about your answers, have someone else score them.

2. Once you know your score, go back over the study tips for the sections you did not do well on.

3. Take a break. It is not a good idea to try to complete more than one exam on any given day.

<u>Correct Answers – Address Checking – Practice Exam 460 #1</u>

1. D
2. D
3. A
4. D
5. D
6. D
7. D
8. D
9. A
10. D
11. A
12. D
13. D
14. D
15. D
16. A
17. A
18. A
19. D
20. D
21. A
22. D
23. A
24. D
25. D
26. A
27. D
28. D
29. A
30. D
31. D
32. D
33. D
34. A
35. D
36. D
37. D
38. D
39. D
40. D
41. A
42. D
43. D
44. D
45. A
46. D
47. D
48. D
49. D
50. A
51. D
52. D
53. A

54. D
55. D
56. D
57. D
58. D
59. D
60. A
61. A
62. A
63. A
64. D
65. D
66. A
67. D
68. D
69. D
70. D
71. D
72. D
73. D
74. A
75. D
76. D
77. A
78. D
79. D
80. D
81. A
82. D
83. D
84. D
85. D
86. D
87. D
88. D
89. D
90. D
91. A
92. D
93. A
94. D
95. D

Correct Answers – Memory for Addresses – Practice Exam 460 #1

1.	E	56.	D
2.	C	57.	A
3.	A	58.	C
4.	C	59.	C
5.	E	60.	B
6.	A	61.	C
7.	B	62.	E
8.	D	63.	B
9.	D	64.	A
10.	E	65.	A
11.	E	66.	B
12.	A	67.	E
13.	B	68.	A
14.	E	69.	C
15.	C	70.	E
16.	E	71.	D
17.	C	72.	A
18.	E	73.	E
19.	B	74.	E
20.	A	75.	B
21.	D	76.	C
22.	C	77.	A
23.	A	78.	C
24.	E	79.	B
25.	D	80.	C
26.	D	81.	D
27.	A	82.	B
28.	C	83.	D
29.	D	84.	A
30.	C	85.	C
31.	C	86.	B
32.	B	87.	D
33.	A	88.	E
34.	B		
35.	B		
36.	D		
37.	C		
38.	A		
39.	D		
40.	A		
41.	C		
42.	A		
43.	E		
44.	E		
45.	A		
46.	D		
47.	C		
48.	C		
49.	E		
50.	E		
51.	B		
52.	B		
53.	B		
54.	E		
55.	A		

Correct Answers – Number Series – Practice Exam 460 #1

1. A   (7 10 13 16 19 22 **25 28**)
2. E   (24 30 36 42 48 54 **60 66**)
3. C   (18 27 36 45 54 63 **72 81**)
4. D   (4 20 36 52 68 84 **100 116**)
5. D   (13 15 17 19 21 23 **25 27**)
6. B   (1 18 35 52 69 86 **103 120**)
7. A   (14 12 10 8 6 4 **2 0**)
8. C   (174 150 126 102 78 54 **30 6**)
9. E   (45 40 35 30 25 20 **15 10**)
10. E   (81 72 63 54 45 36 **27 18**)
11. B   (163 149 135 121 107 93 **79 65**)
12. D   (1205 1088 971 854 737 620 **503 386**)
13. C   (2 4 6 8 16 32 **64 128**)
14. B   (4 20100 500 2500 **12500 62500**)
15. A   (3 9 27 81243 **729 2187**)
16. A   (1 7 49 343 **2401 16807**)
17. E   (6 12 24 48 96 **192 384**)
18. D   (2 8 32 128 512 **2048 8192**)
19. D   (12 10 16 17 8 6 18 **19 4**)
20. B   (7 11 3 8 13 15 19 18 **23 28**)
21. C   (20 3 6 9 17 14 12 15 18 **11 8**)
22. A   (30 20 25 28 30 35 26 40 **45 24**)
23. B   (18 14 13 16 12 11 14 10 **9 12**)
24. A   (36 42 35 28 45 21 14 7 **54 0**)

Following Oral Instructions – Practice Exam 460 #1
Correctly Filled-in Answer Grid

1. Ⓐ Ⓑ Ⓒ Ⓓ ●
2. Ⓐ Ⓑ Ⓒ Ⓓ Ⓔ
3. Ⓐ Ⓑ Ⓒ Ⓓ Ⓔ
4. Ⓐ Ⓑ Ⓒ Ⓓ Ⓔ
5. Ⓐ Ⓑ Ⓒ Ⓓ Ⓔ
6. Ⓐ Ⓑ Ⓒ Ⓓ Ⓔ
7. ● Ⓑ Ⓒ Ⓓ Ⓔ
8. Ⓐ Ⓑ Ⓒ Ⓓ Ⓔ
9. Ⓐ Ⓑ Ⓒ ● Ⓔ
10. Ⓐ Ⓑ ● Ⓓ Ⓔ
11. Ⓐ Ⓑ Ⓒ ● Ⓔ
12. Ⓐ Ⓑ Ⓒ Ⓓ ●
13. Ⓐ Ⓑ Ⓒ Ⓓ Ⓔ
14. Ⓐ Ⓑ Ⓒ Ⓓ Ⓔ
15. Ⓐ ● Ⓒ Ⓓ Ⓔ
16. Ⓐ Ⓑ Ⓒ Ⓓ ●
17. Ⓐ ● Ⓒ Ⓓ Ⓔ
18. Ⓐ Ⓑ Ⓒ Ⓓ Ⓔ
19. Ⓐ Ⓑ Ⓒ Ⓓ Ⓔ
20. Ⓐ Ⓑ Ⓒ Ⓓ ●
21. Ⓐ Ⓑ Ⓒ Ⓓ Ⓔ
22. Ⓐ Ⓑ Ⓒ Ⓓ Ⓔ
23. Ⓐ Ⓑ Ⓒ Ⓓ Ⓔ
24. Ⓐ Ⓑ Ⓒ Ⓓ Ⓔ
25. Ⓐ Ⓑ Ⓒ Ⓓ Ⓔ
26. Ⓐ Ⓑ Ⓒ Ⓓ Ⓔ
27. Ⓐ Ⓑ Ⓒ Ⓓ Ⓔ
28. Ⓐ Ⓑ Ⓒ Ⓓ Ⓔ
29. Ⓐ Ⓑ Ⓒ Ⓓ Ⓔ
30. Ⓐ Ⓑ Ⓒ Ⓓ ●
31. Ⓐ Ⓑ Ⓒ Ⓓ Ⓔ
32. ● Ⓑ Ⓒ Ⓓ Ⓔ
33. Ⓐ Ⓑ Ⓒ Ⓓ Ⓔ
34. Ⓐ Ⓑ Ⓒ Ⓓ Ⓔ

35. Ⓐ Ⓑ Ⓒ Ⓓ Ⓔ
36. Ⓐ Ⓑ Ⓒ Ⓓ ●
37. Ⓐ Ⓑ Ⓒ Ⓓ Ⓔ
38. Ⓐ Ⓑ Ⓒ Ⓓ Ⓔ
39. Ⓐ Ⓑ Ⓒ Ⓓ Ⓔ
40. ● Ⓑ Ⓒ Ⓓ Ⓔ
41. Ⓐ Ⓑ Ⓒ Ⓓ Ⓔ
42. ● Ⓑ Ⓒ Ⓓ Ⓔ
43. Ⓐ Ⓑ Ⓒ Ⓓ Ⓔ
44. Ⓐ Ⓑ Ⓒ Ⓓ Ⓔ
45. Ⓐ Ⓑ ● Ⓓ Ⓔ
46. Ⓐ Ⓑ Ⓒ Ⓓ Ⓔ
47. Ⓐ ● Ⓒ Ⓓ Ⓔ
48. Ⓐ Ⓑ Ⓒ Ⓓ Ⓔ
49. Ⓐ Ⓑ ● Ⓓ Ⓔ
50. ● Ⓑ Ⓒ Ⓓ Ⓔ
51. Ⓐ Ⓑ Ⓒ Ⓓ ●
52. Ⓐ Ⓑ Ⓒ ● Ⓔ
53. Ⓐ Ⓑ Ⓒ Ⓓ Ⓔ
54. Ⓐ Ⓑ Ⓒ Ⓓ Ⓔ
55. Ⓐ Ⓑ Ⓒ Ⓓ Ⓔ
56. Ⓐ Ⓑ Ⓒ Ⓓ Ⓔ
57. Ⓐ Ⓑ Ⓒ Ⓓ Ⓔ
58. Ⓐ Ⓑ Ⓒ Ⓓ Ⓔ
59. Ⓐ Ⓑ Ⓒ Ⓓ Ⓔ
60. Ⓐ Ⓑ Ⓒ ● Ⓔ
61. Ⓐ Ⓑ Ⓒ Ⓓ Ⓔ
62. Ⓐ Ⓑ Ⓒ Ⓓ Ⓔ
63. Ⓐ Ⓑ Ⓒ Ⓓ Ⓔ
64. Ⓐ Ⓑ Ⓒ Ⓓ Ⓔ
65. Ⓐ Ⓑ Ⓒ Ⓓ Ⓔ
66. Ⓐ Ⓑ Ⓒ Ⓓ Ⓔ
67. Ⓐ Ⓑ Ⓒ Ⓓ Ⓔ
68. Ⓐ Ⓑ Ⓒ Ⓓ Ⓔ

69. Ⓐ Ⓑ Ⓒ Ⓓ Ⓔ
70. Ⓐ Ⓑ Ⓒ Ⓓ Ⓔ
71. Ⓐ Ⓑ Ⓒ Ⓓ Ⓔ
72. Ⓐ Ⓑ Ⓒ Ⓓ Ⓔ
73. Ⓐ Ⓑ Ⓒ Ⓓ Ⓔ
74. Ⓐ Ⓑ Ⓒ Ⓓ Ⓔ
75. Ⓐ Ⓑ Ⓒ Ⓓ Ⓔ
76. Ⓐ Ⓑ Ⓒ Ⓓ Ⓔ
77. Ⓐ Ⓑ Ⓒ Ⓓ Ⓔ
78. Ⓐ Ⓑ Ⓒ Ⓓ Ⓔ
79. Ⓐ Ⓑ Ⓒ Ⓓ Ⓔ
80. Ⓐ Ⓑ Ⓒ Ⓓ Ⓔ
81. Ⓐ Ⓑ Ⓒ Ⓓ Ⓔ
82. Ⓐ Ⓑ Ⓒ Ⓓ Ⓔ
83. Ⓐ Ⓑ Ⓒ Ⓓ Ⓔ
84. Ⓐ ● Ⓒ Ⓓ Ⓔ
85. Ⓐ Ⓑ Ⓒ Ⓓ Ⓔ
86. Ⓐ Ⓑ Ⓒ Ⓓ Ⓔ
87. Ⓐ Ⓑ Ⓒ Ⓓ Ⓔ
88. Ⓐ Ⓑ Ⓒ Ⓓ Ⓔ
89. Ⓐ Ⓑ Ⓒ Ⓓ Ⓔ
90. Ⓐ Ⓑ Ⓒ Ⓓ Ⓔ
91. Ⓐ Ⓑ Ⓒ Ⓓ Ⓔ
92. Ⓐ Ⓑ Ⓒ Ⓓ Ⓔ
93. Ⓐ Ⓑ Ⓒ Ⓓ Ⓔ
94. Ⓐ Ⓑ Ⓒ Ⓓ Ⓔ
95. Ⓐ Ⓑ Ⓒ Ⓓ Ⓔ

Following Oral Instructions – Practice Exam 460 #1
Correct Answers by Sample Number

1. 12E, 15B
2. 17B
3. 45C, 32A, 9D
4. 42A, 1E
5. 50A
6. 30E, 84B, 52D
7. 16E
8. 10C, 7A, 11D
9. 47B
10. 36E, 49C
11. 60D
12. 51E
13. 20E
14. 40A

End of Practice Exam 460 #1

Practice Exam 460 #2

Before beginning, tear out or photocopy the answer grid for each section of the exam.

Address Checking – Practice Exam 460 #2

(You will have 6 minutes to complete this section.)

1. 156 Coral Lane		156 Coral Lane
2. 219 Hickory Way		291 Hickory Way
3. Tempe, AZ		Tempe, AZ
4. Atlanta, GA		Atlantis, GA
5. Sioux Falls, SD		Sioux Falls, SD
6. PO Box 5147		PO Box 5147
7. Campbell, CA 95008		Cambell, CA 95008
8. 30 Massachusetts Ave		30 Massachusetts Ave.
9. Lexington, KY 40512		Lexington, KY 40512
10. 756 John Wayne Lane		756 John Lane Way
11. Orlando, FL		Orleans, MA
12. 4737 Rodeo Dr.		4737 Rodeo Dr.
13. San Francisco, CA		San Francesco, CA
14. 590 Hopkinton Way		590 Hopkinton Way
15. Key West, FL		Kee West, FL
16. 918 Truvae Lane		918 Trove Lane
17. 20817 Northeast Blvd.		20871 Northeast Blvd.
18. Suite 368		Sweet 368
19. 213 Sumner St		213 Summers St.
20. Owensville, AL		Owensville, AL
21. 999 Quincy Ave		999 Quincy St
22. Honalulu, HI		Honalulu, HI
23. Indianapolis, IN		Indianapolis, IN
24. 576 Oak Hill Rd		576 Oak Halls Rd
25. Marlboro, MA		Marboro, MA
26. Brooklyn, NY		Brooklyn, NY
27. 899 Government Ave		899 Goverment Ave.
28. 1601 Pennsylvania Ave.		1611 Pennsylvania Ave.
29. PO Box 310711		PO Box 301711
30. Charlotte, NC		Charlotte, SC
31. Buffalo, NY		Buffalo, MO
32. PO Box 2645545		PO Box 2645455
33. 1111 S. Main St.		1117 S. Main St.
34. 7293 Brittany Lane		7923 Brittany Lane
35. 1901 Pacific Avenue		1901 Pacific Blvd.
36. 231 John Hancock Bldg.		231 John Hancock Blvd.
37. 101 Park Place		101 Park Place
38. 7707 Materials Park		7707 Materiols Park
39. 1364 Quarter Rd.		1364 Quartor Rd.
40. Fillmore, KA		Fillmore, KS
41. 21Norman Frank Lane		21 Normand Frank Lane
42. 54789 Madison Sq.		54789 Madison Sq.
43. 187 Parker Hill Rd.		187 Paker Hill Rd.
44. Brentwood, TN 37219		Brentwood, TN 37219
45. 4554 W 42nd St		4544 W 42nd St
46. Portland, OR		Portland, ME
47. 9000 Jiffy Lane		9000 Jiffy Lane

48. 8965 Ridge Rd.	8956 Ridge Rd.
49. Harvard, MA 01495	Harvard, VA 01495
50. 587 Sartell St.	587 Sartell St.
51. Building 1A	Building A
52. Hanover, RI	Hanover, CT
53. 1917 Simmons Pl.	1917 Simons Pl.
54. Shoals, AL	Shoals, AL
55. PO Box 555499	PO Box 554599
56. Miami, FL 36512	Miami, TN 36512
57. Oakland, CA 95621	Oakland, CA 95621
58. PO Box 11111	PO Box 111111
59. 5542 Algonquin Rd.	5542 Algonquin Rd.
60. 6 Wonderstrand Way	6 Wonderstrand Way
61. 317 East St.	311 East St.
62. 419 Haskell Dr.	419 Haskell St.
63. Pittsburg, VA 45621	Pittsburgh, PA 45621
64. 3001 Carver Way	3001 Carver Way
65 Fairland, OK 45456	Fairland, OK 45456
66. Worcester, MA 01499	Worchester, MA 01499
67. Albany, NY	Albany, NY
68. 1 Johns Financial Bldg.	1 Johns Financial Blvd.
69. PO Box 10001	PO Box 10101
70. Northern Exposure, TX	Northern Exposure, AK
71. 558 Gilligan Lane	558 Gilian Lane
72. Dade City, FL	Dade City, AL
73. 3487 W. Campbell Way	3487 E. Campbell Way
74. Hicksville, AK	Hicksville, MO
75. Yuppytown, FL	Yuppytown, FL
76. Glenview Station, NY 87246	Glenview Station, NY 87246
77. 20304 Government Pl.	20304 Government Pl.
78. Braxton, IA	Braxton, IA
79. 69665 Atlantic Ocean Dr.	69665 Atlantic Ocean Pl.
80. Boca Raton, FL	Boca Raton, FL
81. 8731 Norway Ave.	8732 Norway Ave.
82. Concord, NH	Concorde, NH
83. PO Box 171717	PO Box 177171
84. Burlington, MA	Burtlington, VT
85. 19 Main St.	19 Main St.
86. 529 Payton Ave.	529 Payton Ave.
87. 1014 Herbert Pl.	1014 Hebert Pl.
88. Ludlow, CA 98721	Ludlow, CT 98721
89. 12 Thomas Jefferson Pl.	21 Thomas Jefferson Pl.
90. Suite 154788	Suite 154788
91. PO Box 457489	PO Box 457498
92. Myrtle Beach, SC	Myrtle Beach, SC
93. Yonkers, NY 54698	Yonkers, NY 54689
94. 1216 West St.	1216 West End St.
95 Finally, MI 56489	Finally, MI 56489

1. Ⓐ Ⓓ		36. Ⓐ Ⓓ		71. Ⓐ Ⓓ	
2. Ⓐ Ⓓ		37. Ⓐ Ⓓ		72. Ⓐ Ⓓ	
3. Ⓐ Ⓓ		38. Ⓐ Ⓓ		73. Ⓐ Ⓓ	
4. Ⓐ Ⓓ		39. Ⓐ Ⓓ		74. Ⓐ Ⓓ	
5. Ⓐ Ⓓ		40. Ⓐ Ⓓ		75. Ⓐ Ⓓ	
6. Ⓐ Ⓓ		41. Ⓐ Ⓓ		76. Ⓐ Ⓓ	
7. Ⓐ Ⓓ		42. Ⓐ Ⓓ		77. Ⓐ Ⓓ	
8. Ⓐ Ⓓ		43. Ⓐ Ⓓ		78. Ⓐ Ⓓ	
9. Ⓐ Ⓓ		44. Ⓐ Ⓓ		79. Ⓐ Ⓓ	
10. Ⓐ Ⓓ		45. Ⓐ Ⓓ		80. Ⓐ Ⓓ	
11. Ⓐ Ⓓ		46. Ⓐ Ⓓ		81. Ⓐ Ⓓ	
12. Ⓐ Ⓓ		47. Ⓐ Ⓓ		82. Ⓐ Ⓓ	
13. Ⓐ Ⓓ		48. Ⓐ Ⓓ		83. Ⓐ Ⓓ	
14. Ⓐ Ⓓ		49. Ⓐ Ⓓ		84. Ⓐ Ⓓ	
15. Ⓐ Ⓓ		50. Ⓐ Ⓓ		85. Ⓐ Ⓓ	
16. Ⓐ Ⓓ		51. Ⓐ Ⓓ		86. Ⓐ Ⓓ	
17. Ⓐ Ⓓ		52. Ⓐ Ⓓ		87. Ⓐ Ⓓ	
18. Ⓐ Ⓓ		53. Ⓐ Ⓓ		88. Ⓐ Ⓓ	
19. Ⓐ Ⓓ		54. Ⓐ Ⓓ		89. Ⓐ Ⓓ	
20. Ⓐ Ⓓ		55. Ⓐ Ⓓ		90. Ⓐ Ⓓ	
21. Ⓐ Ⓓ		56. Ⓐ Ⓓ		91. Ⓐ Ⓓ	
22. Ⓐ Ⓓ		57. Ⓐ Ⓓ		92. Ⓐ Ⓓ	
23. Ⓐ Ⓓ		58. Ⓐ Ⓓ		93. Ⓐ Ⓓ	
24. Ⓐ Ⓓ		59. Ⓐ Ⓓ		94. Ⓐ Ⓓ	
25. Ⓐ Ⓓ		60. Ⓐ Ⓓ		95. Ⓐ Ⓓ	
26. Ⓐ Ⓓ		61. Ⓐ Ⓓ			
27. Ⓐ Ⓓ		62. Ⓐ Ⓓ			
28. Ⓐ Ⓓ		63. Ⓐ Ⓓ			
29. Ⓐ Ⓓ		64. Ⓐ Ⓓ			
30. Ⓐ Ⓓ		65. Ⓐ Ⓓ			
31. Ⓐ Ⓓ		66. Ⓐ Ⓓ			
32. Ⓐ Ⓓ		67. Ⓐ Ⓓ			
33. Ⓐ Ⓓ		68. Ⓐ Ⓓ			
34. Ⓐ Ⓓ		69. Ⓐ Ⓓ			
35. Ⓐ Ⓓ		70. Ⓐ Ⓓ			

Memory for Addresses – Practice Exam 460 #2

Directions: Study the addresses below for 11 minutes, then turn the page and *from memory*, match each address to the correct box.

A	B	C	D	E
3700 – 3799 Boston	4300 – 4399 Boston	4000 – 4099 Boston	3500 – 3599 Boston	5100 – 5199 Boston
Eagle Ct.	Michigan Ave.	Alderwood	Falkner Dr.	Stevens Ln.
9000 – 9099 Sievers	9400 – 9499 Sievers	8200-8299 Sievers	8700-8799 Sievers	8000 – 8099 Sievers
Swanson Ave.	Caldwell	Mt. Springs	Apache Jct.	Benchard Dr.
0900 – 0999 St. John	2500 – 2599 St. John	1000 – 1099 St. John	0400-0499 St. John	2200-2299 St. John

Memory for Addresses – Practice Exam 460 #2

(You will have 5 minutes to complete this section.)

1. 8700 – 8799 Sievers
2. 4300 – 4399 Boston
3. 2200 – 2299 St. John
4. Apache Jct.
5. Alderwood
6. Stevens Ln.
7. Swanson Ave.
8. Michigan Ave.
9. 4000 – 4099 Boston
10. 3700 – 3799 Boston
11. 4300 – 4399 Boston
12. 8200 – 8299 Sievers
13. 3500 – 3599 Boston
14. Michigan Ave.
15. 2500 – 2599 St. John
16. 8200 – 8299 Sievers
17. 0400 – 0499 St. John
18. Alderwood
19. Eagle Ct.
20. Benchard Dr.
21. Mt. Springs
22. Michigan Ave.
23. 3700 – 3799 Boston
24. Eagle Ct.
25. Apache Jct.
26. 9000 – 9099 Sievers
27. Benchard Dr.
28. 8000 – 8099 Sievers
29. 2200 – 2299 St. John
30. 9000 – 9099 Sievers
31. 2500 – 2599 St. John
32. 5100 – 5199 Boston
33. 2200 -- 2299 St. John
34. Caldwell
35. Stevens Ln.
36. Falkner Dr.
37. 5100 – 5199 Boston
38. 1000 – 1099 St. John
39. 3500 -- 3599 Boston
40. Apache Jct.
41. Stevens Ln.
42. Benchard Dr.
43. 8000-8099 Sievers
44. Mt. Springs
45. 3700 – 3799 Boston
46. 2500 – 2599 St. John
47. Caldwell
48. Mt. Springs
49. 8000-8099 Sievers
50. 3700-3799 Boston
51. Falkner Dr.
52. 0900 – 0999 St. John
53. 8700-8799 Sievers
54. Eagle Ct.
55. 4000-4099 Boston
56. Michigan Ave.
57. Stevens Ln.
58. 1000-1099 St. John
59. 4000-4099 Boston
60. 8700 – 8799 Sievers
61. Falkner Dr.
62. 3500-3599 Boston
63. 3700-3799 Boston
64. Swanson Ave.
65. Alderwood
66. 9400 – 9499 Sievers
67. Michigan Ave.
68. 0400 – 0499 St. John
69. Alderwood
70. 0900 – 0999 St. John
71. 1000 – 1099 St. John
72. Falkner Dr.
73. Apache Jct.
74. Mt. Springs
75. 9000-9099 Sievers
76. Swanson Ave.
77. 5100 – 5199 Boston
78. 4300 – 4399 Boston
79. Michigan Ave.
80. Eagle Ct.
81. 2500 – 2599 St. John
82. 2200 – 2299 St. John
83. Caldwell
84. 4300 – 4399 Boston
85. 0400 – 0499 St. John
86. 3700 – 3799 Boston
87. Falkner Dr.
88. Swanson Ave.

Answer Grid – Memory for Addresses – Practice Exam 460 #2

1. Ⓐ Ⓑ Ⓒ Ⓓ Ⓔ	35. Ⓐ Ⓑ Ⓒ Ⓓ Ⓔ	69. Ⓐ Ⓑ Ⓒ Ⓓ Ⓔ
2. Ⓐ Ⓑ Ⓒ Ⓓ Ⓔ	36. Ⓐ Ⓑ Ⓒ Ⓓ Ⓔ	70. Ⓐ Ⓑ Ⓒ Ⓓ Ⓔ
3. Ⓐ Ⓑ Ⓒ Ⓓ Ⓔ	37. Ⓐ Ⓑ Ⓒ Ⓓ Ⓔ	71. Ⓐ Ⓑ Ⓒ Ⓓ Ⓔ
4. Ⓐ Ⓑ Ⓒ Ⓓ Ⓔ	38. Ⓐ Ⓑ Ⓒ Ⓓ Ⓔ	72. Ⓐ Ⓑ Ⓒ Ⓓ Ⓔ
5. Ⓐ Ⓑ Ⓒ Ⓓ Ⓔ	39. Ⓐ Ⓑ Ⓒ Ⓓ Ⓔ	73. Ⓐ Ⓑ Ⓒ Ⓓ Ⓔ
6. Ⓐ Ⓑ Ⓒ Ⓓ Ⓔ	40. Ⓐ Ⓑ Ⓒ Ⓓ Ⓔ	74. Ⓐ Ⓑ Ⓒ Ⓓ Ⓔ
7. Ⓐ Ⓑ Ⓒ Ⓓ Ⓔ	41. Ⓐ Ⓑ Ⓒ Ⓓ Ⓔ	75. Ⓐ Ⓑ Ⓒ Ⓓ Ⓔ
8. Ⓐ Ⓑ Ⓒ Ⓓ Ⓔ	42. Ⓐ Ⓑ Ⓒ Ⓓ Ⓔ	76. Ⓐ Ⓑ Ⓒ Ⓓ Ⓔ
9. Ⓐ Ⓑ Ⓒ Ⓓ Ⓔ	43. Ⓐ Ⓑ Ⓒ Ⓓ Ⓔ	77. Ⓐ Ⓑ Ⓒ Ⓓ Ⓔ
10. Ⓐ Ⓑ Ⓒ Ⓓ Ⓔ	44. Ⓐ Ⓑ Ⓒ Ⓓ Ⓔ	78. Ⓐ Ⓑ Ⓒ Ⓓ Ⓔ
11. Ⓐ Ⓑ Ⓒ Ⓓ Ⓔ	45. Ⓐ Ⓑ Ⓒ Ⓓ Ⓔ	79. Ⓐ Ⓑ Ⓒ Ⓓ Ⓔ
12. Ⓐ Ⓑ Ⓒ Ⓓ Ⓔ	46. Ⓐ Ⓑ Ⓒ Ⓓ Ⓔ	80. Ⓐ Ⓑ Ⓒ Ⓓ Ⓔ
13. Ⓐ Ⓑ Ⓒ Ⓓ Ⓔ	47. Ⓐ Ⓑ Ⓒ Ⓓ Ⓔ	81. Ⓐ Ⓑ Ⓒ Ⓓ Ⓔ
14. Ⓐ Ⓑ Ⓒ Ⓓ Ⓔ	48. Ⓐ Ⓑ Ⓒ Ⓓ Ⓔ	82. Ⓐ Ⓑ Ⓒ Ⓓ Ⓔ
15. Ⓐ Ⓑ Ⓒ Ⓓ Ⓔ	49. Ⓐ Ⓑ Ⓒ Ⓓ Ⓔ	83. Ⓐ Ⓑ Ⓒ Ⓓ Ⓔ
16. Ⓐ Ⓑ Ⓒ Ⓓ Ⓔ	50. Ⓐ Ⓑ Ⓒ Ⓓ Ⓔ	84. Ⓐ Ⓑ Ⓒ Ⓓ Ⓔ
17. Ⓐ Ⓑ Ⓒ Ⓓ Ⓔ	51. Ⓐ Ⓑ Ⓒ Ⓓ Ⓔ	85. Ⓐ Ⓑ Ⓒ Ⓓ Ⓔ
18. Ⓐ Ⓑ Ⓒ Ⓓ Ⓔ	52. Ⓐ Ⓑ Ⓒ Ⓓ Ⓔ	86. Ⓐ Ⓑ Ⓒ Ⓓ Ⓔ
19. Ⓐ Ⓑ Ⓒ Ⓓ Ⓔ	53. Ⓐ Ⓑ Ⓒ Ⓓ Ⓔ	87. Ⓐ Ⓑ Ⓒ Ⓓ Ⓔ
20. Ⓐ Ⓑ Ⓒ Ⓓ Ⓔ	54. Ⓐ Ⓑ Ⓒ Ⓓ Ⓔ	88. Ⓐ Ⓑ Ⓒ Ⓓ Ⓔ
21. Ⓐ Ⓑ Ⓒ Ⓓ Ⓔ	55. Ⓐ Ⓑ Ⓒ Ⓓ Ⓔ	
22. Ⓐ Ⓑ Ⓒ Ⓓ Ⓔ	56. Ⓐ Ⓑ Ⓒ Ⓓ Ⓔ	
23. Ⓐ Ⓑ Ⓒ Ⓓ Ⓔ	57. Ⓐ Ⓑ Ⓒ Ⓓ Ⓔ	
24. Ⓐ Ⓑ Ⓒ Ⓓ Ⓔ	58. Ⓐ Ⓑ Ⓒ Ⓓ Ⓔ	
25. Ⓐ Ⓑ Ⓒ Ⓓ Ⓔ	59. Ⓐ Ⓑ Ⓒ Ⓓ Ⓔ	
26. Ⓐ Ⓑ Ⓒ Ⓓ Ⓔ	60. Ⓐ Ⓑ Ⓒ Ⓓ Ⓔ	
27. Ⓐ Ⓑ Ⓒ Ⓓ Ⓔ	61. Ⓐ Ⓑ Ⓒ Ⓓ Ⓔ	
28. Ⓐ Ⓑ Ⓒ Ⓓ Ⓔ	62. Ⓐ Ⓑ Ⓒ Ⓓ Ⓔ	
29. Ⓐ Ⓑ Ⓒ Ⓓ Ⓔ	63. Ⓐ Ⓑ Ⓒ Ⓓ Ⓔ	
30. Ⓐ Ⓑ Ⓒ Ⓓ Ⓔ	64. Ⓐ Ⓑ Ⓒ Ⓓ Ⓔ	
31. Ⓐ Ⓑ Ⓒ Ⓓ Ⓔ	65. Ⓐ Ⓑ Ⓒ Ⓓ Ⓔ	
32. Ⓐ Ⓑ Ⓒ Ⓓ Ⓔ	66. Ⓐ Ⓑ Ⓒ Ⓓ Ⓔ	
33. Ⓐ Ⓑ Ⓒ Ⓓ Ⓔ	67. Ⓐ Ⓑ Ⓒ Ⓓ Ⓔ	
34. Ⓐ Ⓑ Ⓒ Ⓓ Ⓔ	68. Ⓐ Ⓑ Ⓒ Ⓓ Ⓔ	

Notes:

Number Series Practice Exam 460 #2

(You will have 20 minutes to complete this section.)

1. **10   15   20   15   25   30   20   35   __   __**

   A. 40 20   B. 40 25   C. 25 40   D. 40 30   E. 35 40

2. **39   30   32   37   40   42   35   50   __   __**

   A. 33 45   B. 33 52   C. 52 33   D. 45 33   E. 45 45

3. **7   0   1   2   23   7   2   3   __   __**

   A. 7 4   B. 5 7   C. 6 7   D. 4 7   E. 6 6

4. **0   1   172   49   3   __   __**

   A. 4 343   B. 340 9   C. 9 340   D. 349 4   E. 343 4

5. **12   10   11   108   9   86   __   __**

   A. 8 9   B. 6 7   C. 10 11   D. 8 8   E. 7 6

6. **75   63   71   67   67   71   63   __   __**

   A. 75 59   B. 75 63   C. 70 59   D. 70 73   E. 62 59

7. **51   53   57   54   56   60   57   __   __**

   A. 59 63   B. 57 63   C. 59 59   D. 59 62   E. 62 59

8. **8   98   8   98   7   8   98   6   7   8   __   __**

   A. 8 9   B. 9 8   C. 10 8   D. 10 9   E. 10 10

9. **43   47   44   40   44   41   37   41   __   __**

   A. 37 34   B. 38 34   C. 39 33   D. 40 35   E. 38 33

10. **25   30   30   28   22   25   27   21   19   16   __   __**

    A. 23 10   B. 20 8   C. 24 10   D. 23 8   E. 20 20

11. **3   18   6   17   9   15   12   12   __   __**

    A. 8 8   B. 14 7   C. 15 8   D. 14 9   E. 15 10

12. **69   75   3   93   __   __**

    A. 103 115   B. 100 112   C. 103 117   D. 105 119   E. 98 110

13. **70   55   66   51   62   __   __**

    A. 47 58   B. 45 56   C. 45 58   D. 58 47   E. 48 57

14. 52   33   52   38   45   44   45   51   ___   ___

   A. 35 56   B. 59 38   C. 36 58   D. 38 59   E. 59 40

15. 6   1   2   12   4   8   18   16   ___   ___

   A. 30 24   B. 32 20   C. 30 26   D. 34 24   E. 32 24

16. 87   69   75   61   63   53   51   ___   ___

   A. 46 39   B. 47 39   C. 45 39   D. 45 38   E. 44 38

17. 20   23   23   23   25   25   26   27   27   ___   ___

   A. 27 29   B. 29 29   C. 30 30   D.28 28   E. 28 29

18. 77   87   88   88   81   89   88   88   85   91   88   88

___ ___

   A. 89 92   B. 88 89   C. 90 93   D. 90 94   E. 89 93

19. 1   4   3   2   9   4   9   2   3   4   ___   ___

   A. 3 2   B. 1 2   C. 2 3   D. 1 4   E. 1 5

20. 54   38   37   35   45   32   28   23   36   17   10   ___

___

   A. 2 27   B. 10 27   C. 27 3   D. 27 2   E. 4 25

21. 1   5   5   9   9   13   ___   ___

   A. 9 13   B. 13 16   C.13 17   D. 13 18   E. 13 20

22. 8   10   10   12   11   11   16   12   ___   ___

   A.12 18   B.18 12   C. 20 14   D. 12 20   E.14 20

23. 29   34   27   32   25   ___   ___

   A. 30 24   B. 24 17   C. 28 22   D. 30 23   E. 30 20

24. 30   28   32   38   40   42   46   52   60   60   64   68
74   82   ___   ___

   A. 90 90   B. 92 90   C. 90 92   D. 94 86   E. 86 94

1. Ⓐ Ⓑ Ⓒ Ⓓ Ⓔ
2. Ⓐ Ⓑ Ⓒ Ⓓ Ⓔ
3. Ⓐ Ⓑ Ⓒ Ⓓ Ⓔ
4. Ⓐ Ⓑ Ⓒ Ⓓ Ⓔ
5. Ⓐ Ⓑ Ⓒ Ⓓ Ⓔ
6. Ⓐ Ⓑ Ⓒ Ⓓ Ⓔ
7. Ⓐ Ⓑ Ⓒ Ⓓ Ⓔ
8. Ⓐ Ⓑ Ⓒ Ⓓ Ⓔ
9. Ⓐ Ⓑ Ⓒ Ⓓ Ⓔ
10. Ⓐ Ⓑ Ⓒ Ⓓ Ⓔ
11. Ⓐ Ⓑ Ⓒ Ⓓ Ⓔ
12. Ⓐ Ⓑ Ⓒ Ⓓ Ⓔ
13. Ⓐ Ⓑ Ⓒ Ⓓ Ⓔ
14. Ⓐ Ⓑ Ⓒ Ⓓ Ⓔ
15. Ⓐ Ⓑ Ⓒ Ⓓ Ⓔ
16. Ⓐ Ⓑ Ⓒ Ⓓ Ⓔ
17. Ⓐ Ⓑ Ⓒ Ⓓ Ⓔ
18. Ⓐ Ⓑ Ⓒ Ⓓ Ⓔ
19. Ⓐ Ⓑ Ⓒ Ⓓ Ⓔ
20. Ⓐ Ⓑ Ⓒ Ⓓ Ⓔ
21. Ⓐ Ⓑ Ⓒ Ⓓ Ⓔ
22. Ⓐ Ⓑ Ⓒ Ⓓ Ⓔ
23. Ⓐ Ⓑ Ⓒ Ⓓ Ⓔ
24. Ⓐ Ⓑ Ⓒ Ⓓ Ⓔ

Notes:

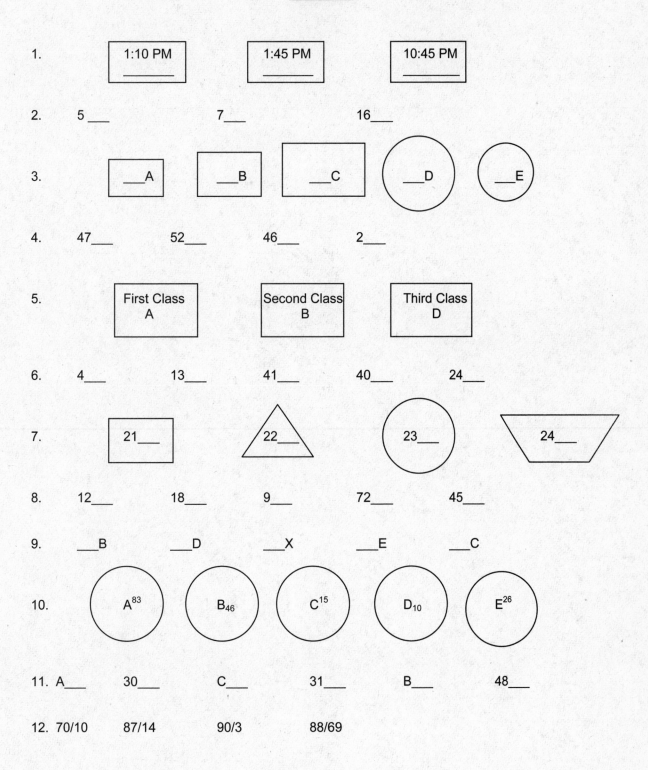

1. [1:10 PM ____]   [1:45 PM ____]   [10:45 PM ____]

2. 5 ___   7___   16___

3. [___A]   [___B]   [___C]   (___D)   (___E)

4. 47___   52___   46___   2___

5. [First Class A]   [Second Class B]   [Third Class D]

6. 4___   13___   41___   40___   24___

7. [21___]   △22___   (23___)   ⬡24___

8. 12___   18___   9___   72___   45___

9. ___B   ___D   ___X   ___E   ___C

10. (A^{83})   (B$_{46}$)   (C^{15})   (D$_{10}$)   (E^{26})

11. A___   30___   C___   31___   B___   48___

12. 70/10   87/14   90/3   88/69

141

Notes:

142

Following Oral Instructions – Practice Exam 460 #2

(Directions to be Read Aloud)

Examine Sample 1. (Pause slightly) The figures shown represent postal drop boxes, each showing respective collection times. Write the letter B as in Boy in the box that has the earliest collection time. (Pause 5 seconds.) Find the number that represents the minutes of the collection time you have selected. Go to that number on your Answer Grid and darken that letter-number combination. (Pause 7 seconds.)

Examine Sample 2. (Pause slightly) Write the letter E as in Egg beside 16 if 16 is greater than 7. (Pause 5 seconds) Otherwise, write an A as in Apple beside number 7. (Pause 5 seconds.) Darken your chosen number-letter combination on the Answer Grid. (Pause 7 seconds.)

Examine Sample 2 again. (Pause slightly.) If 30 is more than 27, and 40 is less than 41, write the letter C as in Cat beside number 5 in the sample. (Pause 5 seconds.) If not, write the letter E as in Egg beside number 16. (Pause 5 seconds.) Darken the selected number-letter combination on your Answer Grid. (Pause 7 seconds.)

Examine Sample 3. (Pause slightly.) There are three squares and two circles of different proportions. In the second-largest square write the number 75. (Pause 7 seconds.) Darken that number-letter combination on your Answer Grid. (Pause 7 seconds.)

Examine Sample 3 again. (Pause slightly.) If 10 divided by 5 equals 3, then write the number 76 in square C as in Cat. (Pause 5 seconds.) If not, write number 81 in the larger circle. (Pause 5 seconds.) Darken the number-letter combination you have created on your Answer Grid.

Examine Sample 4. (Pause slightly.) Write the letter A as in Apple beside the second-largest number and the letter D as in Dog beside the largest number. (Pause 10 seconds.) Of the remaining two numbers, write the letter E as in Egg beside the smaller number of the two. (Pause 5 seconds.) Darken the number-letter combinations you have just created.

Examine Sample 5. (Pause slightly.) The three boxes shown in this sample represent different classes of mail; each is assigned a letter. If Box D as in Dog has a cheaper means of mailing advertisements than Box A as in Apple find number 15 on your Answer Grid and darken the letter D as in Dog. (Pause 7 seconds.) If Box D as in Dog is a more expensive means of mailing advertisements, then find number 3 on your Answer Grid and darken the letter A as in Apple. (Pause 7 seconds.)

Examine Sample 6. (Pause slightly.) This sample shows five numbers, each representing the length of a different mail route in terms of mileage. Write the letter C as in Cat beside the third longest route if it is over 25 miles in length. (Pause 5 seconds.) Otherwise, write the letter A as in Apple beside the smallest route. (Pause 5 seconds.) Darken the number-letter combination you have created on your Answer Grid.

Examine Sample 6 again. (Pause slightly.) Pick out the route that is more than 14 miles long, yet less than 40 miles long. (Pause 5 seconds.) Write the letter A as in Apple beside it. (Pause 5 seconds.) Darken the resulting number-letter combination on your Answer Grid. (Pause 7 seconds.)

Examine Sample 6 one more time. (Pause slightly.) If the longest mail route is exactly 37 miles longer than the shortest route, go to number 3 on your Answer Grid and darken the letter C as in Cat. (Pause 10 seconds.) If it is not exactly 37 miles longer, then find number 8 on your Answer Grid and darken the letter E as in elephant. (Pause 10 seconds.)

Examine Sample 7. (Pause slightly.) Write the letter B as in Boy in the triangle and the letter C as in Cat in the circle. (Pause 10 seconds.) If the trapezoid represented by the number 24 has more sides than a square, darken the number-letter combination on your Answer Grid that lies in the triangle.

(Pause 10 seconds.) Otherwise, darken the number-letter combination that lies in the circle. (Pause 10 seconds.)

Examine Sample 8. (Pause slightly.) This sample shows five different numbers. Each number represents the number of parcels delivered by each of five carriers on a particular day.   Consider 72 the largest number and 9 the smallest number. If the second-largest number is more than 50, write the letter C as in Cat, beside number 12. (Pause 5 seconds.) Darken this number-letter combination on your Answer Grid. (Pause 7 seconds.) If the second-smallest number of parcels is less than 11, write the letter E as in Egg beside the number 45 and darken that number-letter combination on your Answer Grid. (Pause 10 seconds.) If none of the previous statements is true, then write the letter C as in Cat beside the number 9 and darken your Answer Grid accordingly. (Pause 10 seconds.)

Examine Sample 9. (Pause slightly.) Write the number 20 beside letter B as in Boy if Chicago is located in Alaska. (Pause 5 seconds.) If not, write the number 6 beside the letter C as in Cat and darken that number-letter combination on your Answer Grid. (Pause 10 seconds.)

Examine Sample 9 again. (Pause slightly.) If the product of 3 times 3 is greater than the sum of 4 plus 4 then write the number 17 beside the letter E as in Egg. (Pause 7 seconds.) Otherwise, write the number 82 beside the letter E as in Egg. (Pause 5 seconds.) Darken your Answer Grid with the number-letter combination that you have created. (Pause 7 seconds.)

Examine Sample 10.   (Pause slightly.) Sample 10 shows five Mail Volume Index figures. Index numbers shown as superscripts indicate an above-average mail volume. Index numbers shown as subscripts indicate a below-average mail volume. If circles C as in Cat and E as in Egg each illustrate a below-average Index figure, find number 27 on your Answer Grid and darken the letter D as in Dog. (Pause 10 seconds.) However, if circle A as in Apple and C as in Cat show above average figures, find number 14 on your Answer Grid and darken the letter A as in Apple. (Pause 10 seconds)

Examine Sample 10 again. (Pause slightly.) On your Answer Grid darken the number-letter combination of the highest Mail Volume Index figure.

Examine Sample 10 once again. (Pause slightly.) If circle A as in Apple has a higher Index figure than circle D as in Dog find the number 27 on your Answer Grid and darken the letter B as in Boy. (Pause 7 seconds.) If not, find number 10 on your Answer Grid and darken the letter D as in Dog. (Pause 7 seconds.)

Examine Sample 11. (Pause slightly.) If 30 is greater than 31, write the number 30 on the line beside the letter C as in Cat. Darken that number-letter combination on your Answer Grid. (Pause 10 seconds.) If not, then write the number 30 on the line beside the letter B as in Boy, and darken your Answer Grid accordingly. (Pause 10 seconds.)

Examine Sample 9 again. (Pause slightly.) Go to the fourth letter from the right side of the sample and write the number 32 beside it. (Pause 5 seconds.) Darken this number-letter combination on your Answer Grid. (Pause 7 seconds.)

Examine Sample 11 again. (Pause slightly.) Write the letter C as in Cat beside number 30. Darken the number-letter combination on your Answer Grid only if 30 is the largest number in the sample. (Pause 10 seconds.) Otherwise, write the letter A as in Apple beside number 48. Darken your answer on the Answer Grid. (Pause 7 seconds.)

Examine Sample 12. (Pause slightly.) This sample has four pairs of numbers, each measuring the quantity of letters dropped in a test collection box on four consecutive Mondays. The first number in each pair represents the number of out-of-town letters and the second number represents the number of local delivery letters. If there are more out-of-town letters than local letters in each of the pairs, and the testing is conducted on Tuesday, go to number 93 on your Answer Grid and darken the letter A as in Apple. (Pause 7 seconds.) Otherwise, go to number 69 on your Answer Grid and darken the letter B as in Boy. (Pause 7 seconds.)

Examine Sample 12 again. (Pause slightly.) Write the letter C as in Cat beside the second highest out-of-town mail count and darken that number-letter combination on your Answer Grid. (Pause 10 seconds.)

End of Following Oral Instructions – Practice Exam 460 #2

The answer keys for Practice Exam 460 #2 are found on the next five pages.

<u>Correct Answers – Address Checking – Practice Exam 460 #2</u>

1. A
2. D
3. A
4. D
5. A
6. A
7. D
8. D
9. D
10. D
11. D
12. A
13. D
14. A
15. D
16. D
17. D
18. D
19. D
20. A
21. D
22. A
23. A
24. D
25. D
26. A
27. D
28. D
29. D
30. D
31. D
32. D
33. D
34. D
35. D
36. D
37. A
38. D
39. D
40. D
41. D
42. A
43. D
44. A
45. D
46. D
47. A
48. D
49. D
50. A
51. D
52. D
53. D
54. A

55. D
56. D
57. A
58. D
59. A
60. A
61. D
62. D
63. D
64. A
65. A
66. D
67. A
68. D
69. D
70. D
71. D
72. D
73. D
74. D
75. A
76. A
77. A
78. A
79. D
80. A
81. D
82. D
83. D
84. D
85. A
86. A
87. D
88. D
89. A
90. A
91. D
92. A
93. D
94. D
95. A

1.	D	56.	B
2.	B	57.	E
3.	E	58.	C
4.	D	59.	C
5.	C	60.	D
6.	E	61.	D
7.	A	62.	D
8.	B	63.	A
9.	C	64.	A
10.	A	65.	C
11.	B	66.	B
12.	C	67.	B
13.	D	68.	D
14.	B	69.	C
15.	B	70.	A
16.	C	71.	C
17.	D	72.	D
18.	C	73.	D
19.	A	74.	A
20.	E	75.	A
21.	C	76.	A
22.	B	77.	E
23.	A	78.	B
24.	A	79.	B
25.	D	80.	A
26.	A	81.	B
27.	E	82.	E
28.	E	83.	B
29.	E	84.	B
30.	A	85.	D
31.	B	86.	A
32.	E	87.	D
33.	E	88.	A
34.	B		
35.	E		
36.	D		
37.	E		
38.	C		
39.	D		
40.	D		
41.	E		
42.	E		
43.	E		
44.	C		
45.	A		
46.	B		
47.	B		
48.	C		
49.	E		
50.	A		
51.	D		
52.	A		
53.	D		
54.	A		
55.	C		

1. B   (10 15 20 15 25 30 20 35 **40 25**)
2. C   (39 30 32 37 40 42 35 50 **52 33**)
3. D   (7 0 1 2 71 2 3 4 **7**)
4. E   (0 1 1 7 2 49 3 **343 4**)
5. E   (12 10 11 10 8 9 8 6 **7 6**)
6. A   (75 63 71 67 67 71 63 **75 59**)
7. A   (51 53 57 54 56 60 57 **59 63**)
8. B   (8 9 8 8 9 8 7 8 9 8 6 7 8 **9 8**)
9. B   (43 47 44 40 44 47 37 41 **38 34**)
10. C   (25 30 30 28 22 25 27 21 19 16 **24 10**)
11. C   (3 18 6 17 9 15 12 12 **15 8**)
12. D   (69 75 83 93 **105 119**)
13. A   (70 55 66 51 62 **47 58**)
14. D   (52 33 52 38 45 44 45 51 **38 59**)
15. E   (6 1 2 12 4 8 18 16 **32 24**)
16. C   (87 69 75 61 63 53 51 **45 39**)
17. B   (20 23 23 23 25 25 26 27 27 **29 29**)
18. E   (77 87 88 88 87 89 88 88 85 91 88 88 **89 93**)
19. B   (1 4 3 2 9 4 9 2 3 4 **1 2**)
20. A   (54 38 37 35 45 32 28 23 36 17 10 **2 27**)
21. C   (1 5 5 9 9 13 **13 17**)
22. D   (8 10 10 12 11 11 16 12 **12 20**)
23. D   (29 34 27 32 25 **30 23**)
24. B   (30 28 32 38 40 42 46 52 60 60 64 68 74 82 **92 90**)

Following Oral Instructions – Practice Exam 460 #2
Correctly Filled in Answer Grid

1. Ⓐ Ⓑ Ⓒ Ⓓ Ⓔ
2. Ⓐ Ⓑ Ⓒ Ⓓ ●
3. Ⓐ Ⓑ ● Ⓓ Ⓔ
4. ● Ⓑ Ⓒ Ⓓ Ⓔ
5. Ⓐ Ⓑ ● Ⓓ Ⓔ
6. Ⓐ Ⓑ ● Ⓓ Ⓔ
7. Ⓐ Ⓑ Ⓒ Ⓓ Ⓔ
8. Ⓐ Ⓑ Ⓒ Ⓓ Ⓔ
9. Ⓐ Ⓑ ● Ⓓ Ⓔ
10. Ⓐ ● Ⓒ Ⓓ Ⓔ
11. Ⓐ Ⓑ Ⓒ Ⓓ Ⓔ
12. Ⓐ Ⓑ Ⓒ Ⓓ Ⓔ
13. Ⓐ Ⓑ Ⓒ Ⓓ Ⓔ
14. ● Ⓑ Ⓒ Ⓓ Ⓔ
15. Ⓐ Ⓑ Ⓒ ● Ⓔ
16. Ⓐ Ⓑ Ⓒ Ⓓ ●
17. Ⓐ Ⓑ Ⓒ Ⓓ ●
18. Ⓐ Ⓑ Ⓒ Ⓓ Ⓔ
19. Ⓐ Ⓑ Ⓒ Ⓓ Ⓔ
20. Ⓐ Ⓑ Ⓒ Ⓓ Ⓔ
21. Ⓐ Ⓑ Ⓒ Ⓓ Ⓔ
22. Ⓐ Ⓑ Ⓒ Ⓓ Ⓔ
23. Ⓐ Ⓑ ● Ⓓ Ⓔ
24. ● Ⓑ Ⓒ Ⓓ Ⓔ
25. Ⓐ Ⓑ Ⓒ Ⓓ Ⓔ
26. Ⓐ Ⓑ Ⓒ Ⓓ Ⓔ
27. Ⓐ ● Ⓒ Ⓓ Ⓔ
28. Ⓐ Ⓑ Ⓒ Ⓓ Ⓔ
29. Ⓐ Ⓑ Ⓒ Ⓓ Ⓔ
30. Ⓐ ● Ⓒ Ⓓ Ⓔ
31. Ⓐ Ⓑ Ⓒ Ⓓ Ⓔ
32. Ⓐ Ⓑ Ⓒ ● Ⓔ
33. Ⓐ Ⓑ Ⓒ Ⓓ Ⓔ
34. Ⓐ Ⓑ Ⓒ Ⓓ Ⓔ

35. Ⓐ Ⓑ Ⓒ Ⓓ Ⓔ
36. Ⓐ Ⓑ Ⓒ Ⓓ Ⓔ
37. Ⓐ Ⓑ Ⓒ Ⓓ Ⓔ
38. Ⓐ Ⓑ Ⓒ Ⓓ Ⓔ
39. Ⓐ Ⓑ Ⓒ Ⓓ Ⓔ
40. Ⓐ Ⓑ Ⓒ Ⓓ Ⓔ
41. Ⓐ Ⓑ Ⓒ Ⓓ Ⓔ
42. Ⓐ Ⓑ Ⓒ Ⓓ Ⓔ
43. Ⓐ Ⓑ Ⓒ Ⓓ Ⓔ
44. Ⓐ Ⓑ Ⓒ Ⓓ Ⓔ
45. Ⓐ Ⓑ Ⓒ Ⓓ Ⓔ
46. Ⓐ Ⓑ Ⓒ Ⓓ Ⓔ
47. ● Ⓑ Ⓒ Ⓓ Ⓔ
48. ● Ⓑ Ⓒ Ⓓ Ⓔ
49. Ⓐ Ⓑ Ⓒ Ⓓ Ⓔ
50. Ⓐ Ⓑ Ⓒ Ⓓ Ⓔ
51. Ⓐ Ⓑ Ⓒ Ⓓ Ⓔ
52. Ⓐ Ⓑ Ⓒ ● Ⓔ
53. Ⓐ Ⓑ Ⓒ Ⓓ Ⓔ
54. Ⓐ Ⓑ Ⓒ Ⓓ Ⓔ
55. Ⓐ Ⓑ Ⓒ Ⓓ Ⓔ
56. Ⓐ Ⓑ Ⓒ Ⓓ Ⓔ
57. Ⓐ Ⓑ Ⓒ Ⓓ Ⓔ
58. Ⓐ Ⓑ Ⓒ Ⓓ Ⓔ
59. Ⓐ Ⓑ Ⓒ Ⓓ Ⓔ
60. Ⓐ Ⓑ Ⓒ Ⓓ Ⓔ
61. Ⓐ Ⓑ Ⓒ Ⓓ Ⓔ
62. Ⓐ Ⓑ Ⓒ Ⓓ Ⓔ
63. Ⓐ Ⓑ Ⓒ Ⓓ Ⓔ
64. Ⓐ Ⓑ Ⓒ Ⓓ Ⓔ
65. Ⓐ Ⓑ Ⓒ Ⓓ Ⓔ
66. Ⓐ Ⓑ Ⓒ Ⓓ Ⓔ
67. Ⓐ Ⓑ Ⓒ Ⓓ Ⓔ
68. Ⓐ Ⓑ Ⓒ Ⓓ Ⓔ

69. Ⓐ ● Ⓒ Ⓓ Ⓔ
70. Ⓐ Ⓑ Ⓒ Ⓓ Ⓔ
71. Ⓐ Ⓑ Ⓒ Ⓓ Ⓔ
72. Ⓐ Ⓑ Ⓒ Ⓓ Ⓔ
73. Ⓐ Ⓑ Ⓒ Ⓓ Ⓔ
74. Ⓐ Ⓑ Ⓒ Ⓓ Ⓔ
75. Ⓐ ● Ⓒ Ⓓ Ⓔ
76. Ⓐ Ⓑ Ⓒ Ⓓ Ⓔ
77. Ⓐ Ⓑ Ⓒ Ⓓ Ⓔ
78. Ⓐ Ⓑ Ⓒ Ⓓ Ⓔ
79. Ⓐ Ⓑ Ⓒ Ⓓ Ⓔ
80. Ⓐ Ⓑ Ⓒ Ⓓ Ⓔ
81. Ⓐ Ⓑ Ⓒ ● Ⓔ
82. Ⓐ Ⓑ Ⓒ Ⓓ Ⓔ
83. ● Ⓑ Ⓒ Ⓓ Ⓔ
84. Ⓐ Ⓑ Ⓒ Ⓓ Ⓔ
85. Ⓐ Ⓑ Ⓒ Ⓓ Ⓔ
86. Ⓐ Ⓑ Ⓒ Ⓓ Ⓔ
87. Ⓐ Ⓑ Ⓒ Ⓓ Ⓔ
88. ● Ⓑ Ⓒ Ⓓ Ⓔ
89. Ⓐ Ⓑ Ⓒ Ⓓ Ⓔ
90. Ⓐ Ⓑ Ⓒ Ⓓ Ⓔ
91. Ⓐ Ⓑ Ⓒ Ⓓ Ⓔ
92. Ⓐ Ⓑ Ⓒ Ⓓ Ⓔ
93. Ⓐ Ⓑ Ⓒ Ⓓ Ⓔ
94. Ⓐ Ⓑ Ⓒ Ⓓ Ⓔ
95. Ⓐ Ⓑ Ⓒ Ⓓ Ⓔ

1. 10B
2. 16E, 5C
3. 75B, 81D
4. 2E, 52D, 47A
5. 15D
6. 4A, 24A, 3C
7. 23C
8. 9C
9. 6C, 17E, 32D
10. 14A, 27B, 83A
11. 30B, 48A
12. 69B, 88C

End of Practice Exam 460 #2

Practice Exam 460 #3

Before beginning, tear out or photocopy the answer grid for each section of the exam.

Address Checking – Practice Exam 460 #3

(You will have 6 minutes to complete this section.)

1.	8757 Lee Blvd.	8757 Lee Blvd
2.	Roundfield, MA 78645	Roundfield, MA 78654
3.	109 Boggs Circle SW	109 Boggs Circle SW
4.	315 E. Fourth St.	315 E. Fourth St.
5.	Lurch, AZ 22344	Lurch, AZ 23344
6.	555 Van Buren Ave.	55 Van Buren Ave.
7.	2343 Camron Mills	2343 Canron Mills
8.	Rolling Fork, MS 39255	Rolling Fork, MS 23255
9.	Hinds, NH	Hinds, NH
10.	456 Cuevas Dr	546 Cuevas St
11.	Shasta Place #242 W	Shasta Place #424 W
12.	6226 Heibenheim Ct.	6262 Heibenhein Ct.
13.	7445 Highview Dr.	7445 Highview Dr.
14.	Yorkshire N Apt. 66	Yorkshire N Apt. 66
15.	Muskego, OH 35426	Muskego, OH 35246
16.	91 W. Vandenburg Heights #68	W Vandenburg Heights #86
17.	1 E. Rustwood St	1 E. Rustwood St.
18.	7864 Knollwood Dr.	7684 Knollwood Dr.
19.	9572 Waycross Dr.	9572 Waycross Dr.
20.	Vandenburg, VA 67495	Vandenburg, VA 67945
21.	303-D Sweeney Dr.	303-B Sweeney Dr.
22.	1724 Maple Ct.	1742 Maple Ct.
23.	231-B Menarney St.	321-B Menarney St.
24.	6010 Area Blvd.	6001 Area Blvd.
25.	Orange Grove, FL 40097	Orange Grove, FL 40097
26.	909 Sinwell Market St.	909 Sinwell Market St.
27.	4763 Oak Pl. Apt. 6-B	4763 Oak Ct. Apt 6-B
28.	6749 Beach Ct.	6794 Beach Ct.
29.	9834 Wellings NW	9834 Willings NW
30.	982 Brymnawr Ave	982 Brynmawr Ave
31.	Kinston, SC 77896	Kingston, SC 77896
32.	212 Columbia Rd.	212 Columbia Rd.
33.	2000 Sylva Mannor Dr.	2000 Sylva Mannor Dr.
34.	305 Park Row	305 Park Row
35.	1335 Main Road East	1334 Main Road East
36.	999 Jefferson Davis Cir.	999 Jefferson Davis Cir.
37.	Mt. Olive, NS 35074	Mt. Olive, NS 35047
38.	878 St. George Sq.	878 St. George Sq.
39.	215 Beaumont Dr. West	215 Beaumont Dr. East
40.	Summit, WA 94590	Summitt, WA 94590
41.	5064 E. Mission Lane	5064 E. Mission Lane
42.	217 Leigh St. NW	217 Lee St. NW
43.	4004 Oak Place	404 Oak Place
44.	504 Gulf View N	405 Gulf View N
45.	303 Mesa Villa Rd	303 Mesa Vila Rd
46.	1952 Bilmar Dr.	1952 Bilmar Dr.

47. St. Bay Louis, MI 78655	St. Bay Louis, MI 58556
48. 956 Powers Pl.	956 Powers Pl.
49. 209 Jeff Davis SE	209 Jeff Davis SE
50. 102 Trautman Ave.	102 Trautman Dr.
51. 101 Westwood Pl.	1010 Westwood Pl.
52. 905 Coutel Blvd. N	95 Coutel Blvd. North
53. Miller, WV 56655	Miller, WV 55665
54. 3007 Memory Lane	3007 Memory Lane
55. 605 Camp Ave.	605 Camp Ave.
56. 255 Ann St. South	255 Ane St. South
57. Eaton Village, OK	Eaton Village, OK
58. 1001 Mitchell Blvd. NW	1001 Mitchell Blvd. NE
59. 106 Carroll Ave. South	106 Carrol Ave South
60. 104-A N. Island View	104-A N. Island View
61. 1133 Mockingbird Lane	1313 Mockingbird Lane
62. 1221 North Street East	1221 East Street North
63. 905 Morse Code Rd.	590 Morse Code Rd.
64. Portland, OR 95580	Portland, OR 95580
65. 6242 Lynnwood Cir East	6244 Linnwood Cir East
66. 220 West Beach	220 West Beach
67. Great Andes, CA 99033	Great Andes, CA 99033
68. Beach Oaks Apts. NW	Beach Oak Apts. NE
69. 4234 Newton Park	4324 Newton Park
70. 205 B Ranch Road East	205-B Ranch Road East
71. Houston, TX 77055	Houston, TX 77050
72. 489 East Old Pass Rd.	4089 East Old Pass Rd.
73. 515 W. Nicholson Ave.	515 W. Nicholson Ave.
74. 7523 Bienville Dr.	7253 Bienville Dr.
75. Holly Hills, KY 38572	Holly Hills, KY 38572
76. 399 Santa Maria Cr.	339 Santa Maria Cr.
77. 3097 Rodenburg Ave.	3097 Rodenburg Ave.
78. 132 Regency Blvd.	123 Regency Blvd.
79. Merigold, MA 68975	Merrigold, MA 69557
80. 212 South Shore St.	212 South Shore Ct.
81. Kensington, LA 57391	Kensington, LA 57931
82. 696 Camp Wilkes	696 Camp Willie
83. 1658 Cherry Circle	1658 Cheery Circle
84. Sycamore, NY 76983	Sycamore, NY 76983
85. 60 De Mountluzin Ave.	600 De Montluzin Ave.
86. 44-B Daisy Vestry Rd.	44-B Daisy View Rd.
87. 717 Acacia Apt. A	717 Acacia Apt A
88. 397 N. Paradise Pt.	379 N. Paradise Pt.
89. 112 Felicity View W.	122 Felicity View W.
90. 435 Ballentine N.	453 Ballentine W.
91. 17 S. Crawford Ct.	17 S. Crawfish Ct.
92. Lameuse, TX 48275	Lameuse, Texas 48725
93. 47-C Rolling Hills Ave.	47-C Rolling Hills Ave.
94. Everbreeze, SD 29402	Evergreen, SD 29402
95. Rock Chester, NJ 79538	Rock Chester, NM 79538

Answer Grid – Address Checking – Practice Exam 460 #3

1. Ⓐ Ⓓ	35. Ⓐ Ⓓ	69. Ⓐ Ⓓ
2. Ⓐ Ⓓ	36. Ⓐ Ⓓ	70. Ⓐ Ⓓ
3. Ⓐ Ⓓ	37. Ⓐ Ⓓ	71. Ⓐ Ⓓ
4. Ⓐ Ⓓ	38. Ⓐ Ⓓ	72. Ⓐ Ⓓ
5. Ⓐ Ⓓ	39. Ⓐ Ⓓ	73. Ⓐ Ⓓ
6. Ⓐ Ⓓ	40. Ⓐ Ⓓ	74. Ⓐ Ⓓ
7. Ⓐ Ⓓ	41. Ⓐ Ⓓ	75. Ⓐ Ⓓ
8. Ⓐ Ⓓ	42. Ⓐ Ⓓ	76. Ⓐ Ⓓ
9. Ⓐ Ⓓ	43. Ⓐ Ⓓ	77. Ⓐ Ⓓ
10. Ⓐ Ⓓ	44. Ⓐ Ⓓ	78. Ⓐ Ⓓ
11. Ⓐ Ⓓ	45. Ⓐ Ⓓ	79. Ⓐ Ⓓ
12. Ⓐ Ⓓ	46. Ⓐ Ⓓ	80. Ⓐ Ⓓ
13. Ⓐ Ⓓ	47. Ⓐ Ⓓ	81. Ⓐ Ⓓ
14. Ⓐ Ⓓ	48. Ⓐ Ⓓ	82. Ⓐ Ⓓ
15. Ⓐ Ⓓ	49. Ⓐ Ⓓ	83. Ⓐ Ⓓ
16. Ⓐ Ⓓ	50. Ⓐ Ⓓ	84. Ⓐ Ⓓ
17. Ⓐ Ⓓ	51. Ⓐ Ⓓ	85. Ⓐ Ⓓ
18. Ⓐ Ⓓ	52. Ⓐ Ⓓ	86. Ⓐ Ⓓ
19. Ⓐ Ⓓ	53. Ⓐ Ⓓ	87. Ⓐ Ⓓ
20. Ⓐ Ⓓ	54. Ⓐ Ⓓ	88. Ⓐ Ⓓ
21. Ⓐ Ⓓ	55. Ⓐ Ⓓ	89. Ⓐ Ⓓ
22. Ⓐ Ⓓ	56. Ⓐ Ⓓ	90. Ⓐ Ⓓ
23. Ⓐ Ⓓ	57. Ⓐ Ⓓ	91. Ⓐ Ⓓ
24. Ⓐ Ⓓ	58. Ⓐ Ⓓ	92. Ⓐ Ⓓ
25. Ⓐ Ⓓ	59. Ⓐ Ⓓ	93. Ⓐ Ⓓ
26. Ⓐ Ⓓ	60. Ⓐ Ⓓ	94. Ⓐ Ⓓ
27. Ⓐ Ⓓ	61. Ⓐ Ⓓ	95. Ⓐ Ⓓ
28. Ⓐ Ⓓ	62. Ⓐ Ⓓ	
29. Ⓐ Ⓓ	63. Ⓐ Ⓓ	
30. Ⓐ Ⓓ	64. Ⓐ Ⓓ	
31. Ⓐ Ⓓ	65. Ⓐ Ⓓ	
32. Ⓐ Ⓓ	66. Ⓐ Ⓓ	
33. Ⓐ Ⓓ	67. Ⓐ Ⓓ	
34. Ⓐ Ⓓ	68. Ⓐ Ⓓ	

Notes:

Memory for Addresses – Practice Exam 460 #3

Directions: Study the addresses below for 11 minutes, then turn the page and *from memory* match each address to the correct box.

A	B	C	D	E
6800-7599 Beach	8900-8999 Beach	8600-8799 Beach	7700-8499 Beach	6500-6699 Beach
Island View	Galloway	Alexander	Mathison	Clifford
7700-8499 West	8600-8799 West	8900-8999 West	6500-6699 West	6800-7599 West
Carroll	Runnels	Driftwood	Pirate	Lynwood
6500-6699 Samuel	7700-8499 Samuel	8600-8799 Samuel	6800-7599 Samuel	8900-8999 Samuel

Memory for Addresses – Practice Exam 460 #3

(You will have 5 minutes to complete this section.)

1. 8600-8799 West
2. Alexander
3. 6500-6699 West
4. Mathison
5. 6800-7599 Beach
6. 8900–8999 Samuel
7. Carroll
8. 7700-8499 Samuel
9. Lynwood
10. Island View
11. 6500-6699 Samuel
12. 8900-8999 Beach
13. Pirate
14. 7700-8499 West
15. Clifford
16. 6500 – 6699 Beach
17. 8900 – 8999 West
18. 7700 – 8499 Samuel
19. Driftwood
20. 6800 – 7599 Samuel
21. Galloway
22. Mathison
23. 8600 – 8799 Samuel
24. 6800 – 7599 Beach
25. 6500 – 6699 Beach
26. Runnels
27. 7700 – 8499 Samuel
28. 7700 – 8499 West
29. 6800-7599 West
30. Pirate
31. 6500 – 6699 West
32. Lynwood
33. Alexander
34. 8900 – 8999 West
35. 7700 – 8499 Samuel
36. 6500 – 6699 Beach
37. 6500-6699 Samuel
38. 8900 – 8999 Beach
39. 8600 – 8799 West
40. 6800 – 7599 Samuel
41. Island View
42. Carroll
43. 7700 – 8499 West
44. Driftwood
45. Galloway
46. 6800 – 7599 West
47. 8900 – 8999 Samuel
48. Mathison
49. Clifford
50. 6800 – 7599 West
51. 6500 – 6699 Samuel
52. 8600 – 8799 Samuel
53. Island View
54. 7700-8499 Samuel
55. Runnels
56. Lynwood
57. 8600 – 8799 West
58. 6500 – 6699 West
59. Pirate
60. 6500 – 6699 Beach
61. Galloway
62. 8900 – 8999 Beach
63. 7700 – 8499 West
64. Clifford
65. 8600 – 8799 Beach
66. 6800 – 7599 Samuel
67. Alexander
68. Mathison
69. 7700 – 8499 West
70. 6500 – 6699 Samuel
71. 8900 – 8999 West
72. 7700 – 8499 Samuel
73. Driftwood
74. 6500 – 6699 West
75. Carroll
76. Driftwood
77. 6800 – 7599 Beach
78. Island View
79. 8900 – 8999 Samuel
80. 6800 – 7599 West
81. 7700 – 8499 Beach
82. Galloway
83. Clifford
84. 8600 – 8799 Samuel
85. 8900 – 8999 Beach
86. 6800 – 7599 Beach
87. Lynwood
88. 8600 – 8799 West

1. Ⓐ Ⓑ Ⓒ Ⓓ Ⓔ
2. Ⓐ Ⓑ Ⓒ Ⓓ Ⓔ
3. Ⓐ Ⓑ Ⓒ Ⓓ Ⓔ
4. Ⓐ Ⓑ Ⓒ Ⓓ Ⓔ
5. Ⓐ Ⓑ Ⓒ Ⓓ Ⓔ
6. Ⓐ Ⓑ Ⓒ Ⓓ Ⓔ
7. Ⓐ Ⓑ Ⓒ Ⓓ Ⓔ
8. Ⓐ Ⓑ Ⓒ Ⓓ Ⓔ
9. Ⓐ Ⓑ Ⓒ Ⓓ Ⓔ
10. Ⓐ Ⓑ Ⓒ Ⓓ Ⓔ
11. Ⓐ Ⓑ Ⓒ Ⓓ Ⓔ
12. Ⓐ Ⓑ Ⓒ Ⓓ Ⓔ
13. Ⓐ Ⓑ Ⓒ Ⓓ Ⓔ
14. Ⓐ Ⓑ Ⓒ Ⓓ Ⓔ
15. Ⓐ Ⓑ Ⓒ Ⓓ Ⓔ
16. Ⓐ Ⓑ Ⓒ Ⓓ Ⓔ
17. Ⓐ Ⓑ Ⓒ Ⓓ Ⓔ
18. Ⓐ Ⓑ Ⓒ Ⓓ Ⓔ
19. Ⓐ Ⓑ Ⓒ Ⓓ Ⓔ
20. Ⓐ Ⓑ Ⓒ Ⓓ Ⓔ
21. Ⓐ Ⓑ Ⓒ Ⓓ Ⓔ
22. Ⓐ Ⓑ Ⓒ Ⓓ Ⓔ
23. Ⓐ Ⓑ Ⓒ Ⓓ Ⓔ
24. Ⓐ Ⓑ Ⓒ Ⓓ Ⓔ
25. Ⓐ Ⓑ Ⓒ Ⓓ Ⓔ
26. Ⓐ Ⓑ Ⓒ Ⓓ Ⓔ
27. Ⓐ Ⓑ Ⓒ Ⓓ Ⓔ
28. Ⓐ Ⓑ Ⓒ Ⓓ Ⓔ
29. Ⓐ Ⓑ Ⓒ Ⓓ Ⓔ
30. Ⓐ Ⓑ Ⓒ Ⓓ Ⓔ
31. Ⓐ Ⓑ Ⓒ Ⓓ Ⓔ
32. Ⓐ Ⓑ Ⓒ Ⓓ Ⓔ
33. Ⓐ Ⓑ Ⓒ Ⓓ Ⓔ
34. Ⓐ Ⓑ Ⓒ Ⓓ Ⓔ

35. Ⓐ Ⓑ Ⓒ Ⓓ Ⓔ
36. Ⓐ Ⓑ Ⓒ Ⓓ Ⓔ
37. Ⓐ Ⓑ Ⓒ Ⓓ Ⓔ
38. Ⓐ Ⓑ Ⓒ Ⓓ Ⓔ
39. Ⓐ Ⓑ Ⓒ Ⓓ Ⓔ
40. Ⓐ Ⓑ Ⓒ Ⓓ Ⓔ
41. Ⓐ Ⓑ Ⓒ Ⓓ Ⓔ
42. Ⓐ Ⓑ Ⓒ Ⓓ Ⓔ
43. Ⓐ Ⓑ Ⓒ Ⓓ Ⓔ
44. Ⓐ Ⓑ Ⓒ Ⓓ Ⓔ
45. Ⓐ Ⓑ Ⓒ Ⓓ Ⓔ
46. Ⓐ Ⓑ Ⓒ Ⓓ Ⓔ
47. Ⓐ Ⓑ Ⓒ Ⓓ Ⓔ
48. Ⓐ Ⓑ Ⓒ Ⓓ Ⓔ
49. Ⓐ Ⓑ Ⓒ Ⓓ Ⓔ
50. Ⓐ Ⓑ Ⓒ Ⓓ Ⓔ
51. Ⓐ Ⓑ Ⓒ Ⓓ Ⓔ
52. Ⓐ Ⓑ Ⓒ Ⓓ Ⓔ
53. Ⓐ Ⓑ Ⓒ Ⓓ Ⓔ
54. Ⓐ Ⓑ Ⓒ Ⓓ Ⓔ
55. Ⓐ Ⓑ Ⓒ Ⓓ Ⓔ
56. Ⓐ Ⓑ Ⓒ Ⓓ Ⓔ
57. Ⓐ Ⓑ Ⓒ Ⓓ Ⓔ
58. Ⓐ Ⓑ Ⓒ Ⓓ Ⓔ
59. Ⓐ Ⓑ Ⓒ Ⓓ Ⓔ
60. Ⓐ Ⓑ Ⓒ Ⓓ Ⓔ
61. Ⓐ Ⓑ Ⓒ Ⓓ Ⓔ
62. Ⓐ Ⓑ Ⓒ Ⓓ Ⓔ
63. Ⓐ Ⓑ Ⓒ Ⓓ Ⓔ
64. Ⓐ Ⓑ Ⓒ Ⓓ Ⓔ
65. Ⓐ Ⓑ Ⓒ Ⓓ Ⓔ
66. Ⓐ Ⓑ Ⓒ Ⓓ Ⓔ
67. Ⓐ Ⓑ Ⓒ Ⓓ Ⓔ
68. Ⓐ Ⓑ Ⓒ Ⓓ Ⓔ

69. Ⓐ Ⓑ Ⓒ Ⓓ Ⓔ
70. Ⓐ Ⓑ Ⓒ Ⓓ Ⓔ
71. Ⓐ Ⓑ Ⓒ Ⓓ Ⓔ
72. Ⓐ Ⓑ Ⓒ Ⓓ Ⓔ
73. Ⓐ Ⓑ Ⓒ Ⓓ Ⓔ
74. Ⓐ Ⓑ Ⓒ Ⓓ Ⓔ
75. Ⓐ Ⓑ Ⓒ Ⓓ Ⓔ
76. Ⓐ Ⓑ Ⓒ Ⓓ Ⓔ
77. Ⓐ Ⓑ Ⓒ Ⓓ Ⓔ
78. Ⓐ Ⓑ Ⓒ Ⓓ Ⓔ
79. Ⓐ Ⓑ Ⓒ Ⓓ Ⓔ
80. Ⓐ Ⓑ Ⓒ Ⓓ Ⓔ
81. Ⓐ Ⓑ Ⓒ Ⓓ Ⓔ
82. Ⓐ Ⓑ Ⓒ Ⓓ Ⓔ
83. Ⓐ Ⓑ Ⓒ Ⓓ Ⓔ
84. Ⓐ Ⓑ Ⓒ Ⓓ Ⓔ
85. Ⓐ Ⓑ Ⓒ Ⓓ Ⓔ
86. Ⓐ Ⓑ Ⓒ Ⓓ Ⓔ
87. Ⓐ Ⓑ Ⓒ Ⓓ Ⓔ
88. Ⓐ Ⓑ Ⓒ Ⓓ Ⓔ

Notes:

<u>Number Series – Practice Exam 460 #3</u>

(You will have 20 minutes to complete this section.)

1. **12**   **11**   **10**   **9**   **8**   **7**   **6**   ___   ___

   A) 4   5   B) 5   4   C) 2   7   D) 5   5   E) 10   10

2. **14**   **16**   **18**   **20**   **22**   **24**   ___   ___

   A) 26   28   B) 29   30   C) 28   26   D) 26   24   E) 14   16

3. **4**   **9**   **14**   **19**   **24**   ___   ___

   A) 4   9   B) 25   29   C) 29   35   D) 29   34   E) 8   34

4. **2**   **5**   **3**   **11**   **4**   **17**   ___   ___

   A) 7   11   B) 5   23   C) 23   5   D) 5   9   E) 23   25

5. **3**   **8**   **11**   **13**   **19**   **18**   ___   ___

   A) 27   23   B) 23   28   C) 28   41   D) 33   48   E) 48   51

6. **28**   **25**   **10**   **12**   **22**   **19**   **14**   ___   ___

   A) 14   15   B) 12   16   C) 16   16   D) 25   30   E) 33   16

7. **33**   **66**   **44**   **55**   **55**   **44**   ___   ___

   A) 65   32   B) 68   90   C) 66   77   D) 66   33   E) 33   22

8. **21**   **87**   **24**   **85**   **27**   **83**   ___   ___

   A) 30   90   B) 28   40   C) 81   96   D) 30   81   E) 40   40

9. **10**   **30**   **15**   **20**   **35**   **25**   **30**   ___   ___

   A) 40   35   B) 35   20   C) 20   35   D) 40   25   E) 36   15

10. **75**   **8**   **75**   **15**   **75**   **22**   ___   ___

    A) 29   15   B) 75   8   C) 15   22   D) 29   8   E) 75   29

11. **1**   **9**   **8**   **1**   **9**   **8**   ___   ___

    A) 1   9   B) 8   1   C) 9   8   D) 9   9   E) 1   5

12. **13**   **15**   **90**   **35**   **37**   **87**   ___   ___

    A) 57   37   B) 89   59   C) 90   37   D) 57   59   E) 59   90

13. **1**   **2**   **4**   **5**   **7**   **8**   **10**   ___   ___

    A) 13   8   B) 11   4   C) 13   7   D) 11   7   E) 11   13

14. **41**   **36**   **63**   **68**   **31**   **26**   **73**   ___   ___

A) 78 68   B) 78 21   C) 21 41   D) 78 31   E) 21 73

15. **7**   **12**   **37**   **17**   **22**   **40**   **27**   ___   ___

A) 32 43   B) 43 37   C) 22 43   D) 32 17   E) 27 27

16. **14**   **14**   **14**   **26**   **17**   **17**   **17**   **40**   **20**   ___   ___

A) 20 40   B) 17 17   C) 20 20   D) 14 26   E) 20 17

17. **24**   **22**   **21**   **34**   **20**   **19**   **44**   ___   ___

A) 43 42   B) 17 18   C) 18 17   D) 23 43   E) 43 23

18. **1**   **3**   **4**   **7**   **11**   **18**   ___   ___

A) 11 47   B) 18 4   C) 29 47   D) 29 32   E) 7 4

19. **2**   **7**   **12**   **17**   ___   ___

A) 27 27   B) 22 12   C) 20 11   D) 17 7   E) 22 27

20. **13**   **14**   **44**   **42**   **40**   **15**   **16**   **38**   ___   ___

A) 36 34   B) 44 40   C) 34 14   D) 15 36   E) 15 38

21. **9**   **10**   **30**   **28**   **11**   **12**   ___   ___

A) 30 26   B) 26 24   C) 28 12   D) 11 20   E) 24 30

22. **33**   **32**   **31**   **31**   **29**   **30**   **27**   ___   ___

A) 28 26   B) 29 29   C) 29 25   D) 25 23   E) 31 29

23. **10**   **30**   **29**   **28**   **9**   **27**   **26**   **25**   **8**   ___   ___

A) 23 22   B) 25 30   C) 29 24   D) 24 23   E) 32 21

24. **8**   **45**   **40**   **28**   **35**   **30**   **48**   ___   ___

A) 24 19   B) 21 26   C) 32 40   D) 22 34   E) 25 20

1. Ⓐ Ⓑ Ⓒ Ⓓ Ⓔ
2. Ⓐ Ⓑ Ⓒ Ⓓ Ⓔ
3. Ⓐ Ⓑ Ⓒ Ⓓ Ⓔ
4. Ⓐ Ⓑ Ⓒ Ⓓ Ⓔ
5. Ⓐ Ⓑ Ⓒ Ⓓ Ⓔ
6. Ⓐ Ⓑ Ⓒ Ⓓ Ⓔ
7. Ⓐ Ⓑ Ⓒ Ⓓ Ⓔ
8. Ⓐ Ⓑ Ⓒ Ⓓ Ⓔ
9. Ⓐ Ⓑ Ⓒ Ⓓ Ⓔ
10. Ⓐ Ⓑ Ⓒ Ⓓ Ⓔ
11. Ⓐ Ⓑ Ⓒ Ⓓ Ⓔ
12. Ⓐ Ⓑ Ⓒ Ⓓ Ⓔ
13. Ⓐ Ⓑ Ⓒ Ⓓ Ⓔ
14. Ⓐ Ⓑ Ⓒ Ⓓ Ⓔ
15. Ⓐ Ⓑ Ⓒ Ⓓ Ⓔ
16. Ⓐ Ⓑ Ⓒ Ⓓ Ⓔ
17. Ⓐ Ⓑ Ⓒ Ⓓ Ⓔ
18. Ⓐ Ⓑ Ⓒ Ⓓ Ⓔ
19. Ⓐ Ⓑ Ⓒ Ⓓ Ⓔ
20. Ⓐ Ⓑ Ⓒ Ⓓ Ⓔ
21. Ⓐ Ⓑ Ⓒ Ⓓ Ⓔ
22. Ⓐ Ⓑ Ⓒ Ⓓ Ⓔ
23. Ⓐ Ⓑ Ⓒ Ⓓ Ⓔ
24. Ⓐ Ⓑ Ⓒ Ⓓ Ⓔ

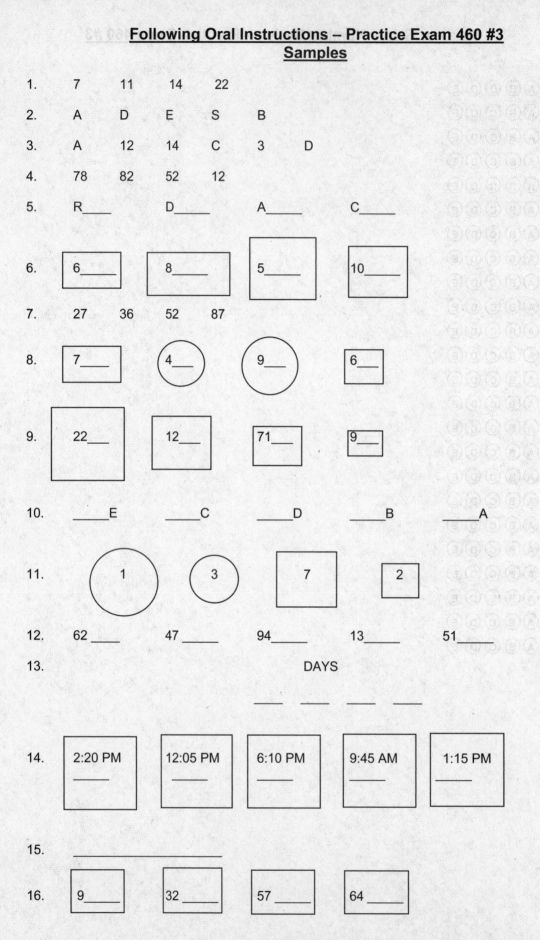

1.   7   11   14   22

2.   A   D   E   S   B

3.   A   12   14   C   3   D

4.   78   82   52   12

5.   R____   D____   A____   C____

6.   6____   8____   5____   10____

7.   27   36   52   87

8.   7___   4___   9___   6___

9.   22___   12___   71___   9___

10.   ____E   ____C   ____D   ____B   ____A

11.   1   3   7   2

12.   62____   47____   94____   13____   51____

13.   DAYS

    ___ ___ ___ ___

14.   2:20 PM   12:05 PM   6:10 PM   9:45 AM   1:15 PM
       ____   ____   ____   ____   ____

15.   _____

16.   9____   32____   57____   64____

162

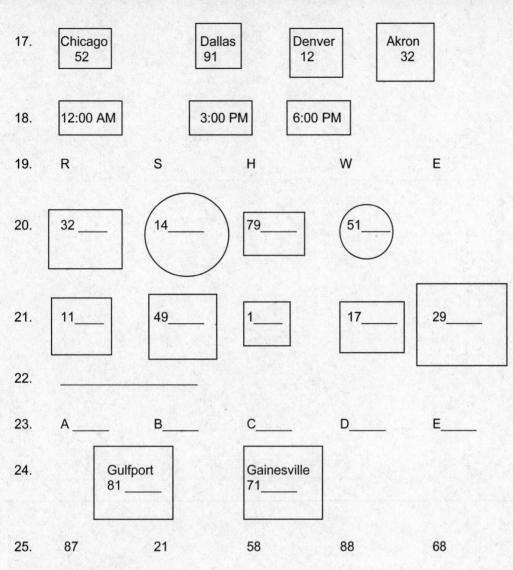

17. | Chicago 52 | | Dallas 91 | | Denver 12 | | Akron 32 |

18. 12:00 AM   3:00 PM   6:00 PM

19. R   S   H   W   E

20. 32 ____   14 ____   79 ____   51 ____

21. 11 ____   49 ____   1 ____   17 ____   29 ____

22. _____

23. A _____   B _____   C _____   D _____   E _____

24. Gulfport 81 _____   Gainesville 71 _____

25. 87   21   58   88   68

26. Math Problem

Notes:

164

Following Oral Instructions – Practice Exam 460 #3

(Directions to be Read Aloud)

1. **Look at Sample 1.** (Pause slightly.) Draw a line under the second number. (Pause 3 seconds.) On the Answer Grid, find that number and darken the letter A, as in Apple. (Pause 5 seconds.)

2. **Look at Sample 2.** (Pause slightly.) Draw a circle around the last letter. (Pause 3 seconds.) On the Answer Grid, find the number 78 and darken the letter you just circled. (Pause 5 seconds.)

3. **Look at Sample 3.** (Pause slightly.) There are three letters and three numbers. (Pause slightly.) Underline the first letter and last number. (Pause 4 seconds.) On the Answer Grid, darken the number-letter combination you just underlined. (Pause 5 seconds.)

4. **Look at Sample 4.** (Pause slightly.) Circle the largest number. (Pause 3 seconds.) Now, on the Answer Grid, find that number and darken the letter B as in Boy. (Pause 5 seconds.)

5. **Look at Sample 5.** (Pause slightly.) Find the letter A as in Apple and write the number 8 beside it. (Pause 3 seconds.) On the Answer Grid, darken the number-letter combination that they make. (Pause 5 seconds.)

6. **Look at Sample 6.** (Pause slightly.) There are four different size boxes, each with a different number in it. (Pause slightly.) In the next to last box, write the letter B as in Boy next to the number. (Pause 3 seconds.) On the Answer Grid, darken the number-letter combination that you have made. (Pause 5 seconds.)

7. **Look at Sample 7.** (Pause slightly.) There are four numbers in sample 7. (Pause slightly.) If 68 is less than 86 and the letter C as in Cat comes before the letter D as in Dog, underline the first number. (Pause 3 seconds.) Otherwise, underline the last number. (Pause 3 seconds.) On the Answer Grid, find the number you underlined and darken the letter A as in Apple. (Pause 5 seconds.)

8. **Look at Sample 8.** (Pause slightly.) There are two squares and two circles. (Pause slightly.) If 5 is greater than 2 and 9 is less than 12, write the letter C as in Cat in the smaller circle. (Pause 3 seconds.) If not, write the letter A as in Apple in the larger square. (Pause 3 seconds.) On the Answer Grid, darken the number-letter combination that you have made. (Pause 5 seconds.)

9. **Look at Sample 9.** (Pause slightly.) Write the letter D as in Dog in the smallest box. (Pause 3 seconds.) On the Answer Grid, darken the number letter combination you have created. (Pause 5 seconds.)

10. **Look at Sample 10.** (Pause slightly.) There are five letters with a line before each. (Pause slightly.) If the second letter in the line comes before the first letter alphabetically, write the number 36 on the line before the first letter. (Pause 4 seconds.) Otherwise, write the number 47 on the last line. (Pause 3 seconds.) On the Answer Grid, darken the number-letter combination you have made. (Pause 5 seconds.)

11. **Look at Sample 11.** (Pause slightly.) There are boxes and circles in this sample. (Pause slightly.) Write the letter B as in Boy in the second box. (Pause 4 seconds.) On the Answer Grid, darken B as in Boy for the number in the box. (Pause 5 seconds.)

12. **Look at Sample 11 again.** (Pause slightly.) Write the letter C as in Cat in the largest box. (Pause 3 seconds.) On the Answer Grid, find the number 33 and darken the letter E as in Egg. (Pause 5 seconds.)

13. **Look at Sample 12.** (Pause slightly.) There are five numbers in Sample 12. (Pause slightly.) If the second number is larger than the last number, write the letter D as in Dog by the last number. (Pause 2 seconds.) Otherwise, write the letter D as in Dog next to the first number. (Pause 4

seconds.) On the Answer Grid, darken the number letter combination you have just made. (Pause 5 seconds.)

14. **Look at Sample 13.** (Pause slightly.) Sample 13 has a word with four lines underneath it. (Pause slightly.) On the first line, write the last letter of the word. (Pause 2 seconds.) On the last line, write the second letter of the word. (Pause 3 seconds.) Write the first letter on the second line, and write the third letter on the third line. (Pause 5 seconds.) Find the number 54 on the Answer Grid and darken the letter you wrote on the last line. (Pause 5 seconds.)

15. **Look at Sample 14.** (Pause slightly.) Listed in the five boxes are postal delivery times. Write the letter A as in Apple in the box containing the latest delivery time. (Pause 3 seconds.) On the Answer Grid, find the number that corresponds to the last two digits in that time. (Pause slightly.) Darken the letter E as in Egg on the Answer Grid. (Pause 5 seconds.)

16. **Look at Sample 15.** (Pause slightly.) In Sample 15 there is a line; if 33 is greater than 22 and 44 is less than 11, write the number 11 on the line. (Pause 4 seconds.) Otherwise, write the number 44 on the line. (Pause 3 seconds.) On the Answer Grid, find the number that you wrote and darken the letter C as in Cat. (Pause 5 seconds.)

17. **Look at Sample 16.** (Pause slightly.) Each box has a number of letters to be postmarked. Find the greatest number of letters to be postmarked. (Pause 3 seconds.) Write the letter B as in Boy in that box. (Pause 2 seconds.) On the Answer Grid, darken the number-letter combination you have just made. (Pause 5 seconds.)

18. **Look at Sample 17.** (Pause slightly.) You will see the names of four cities each with the number of parcels to be delivered to that city. (Pause slightly.) Find the city with the largest number of parcels going to it and circle the first letter in that city's name. (Pause 4 seconds.) On the Answer Grid, find the number 17 and darken the letter you just circled. (Pause 5 seconds.)

19. **Look at Sample 17 again.** (Pause slightly.) If 56 is greater than 23 but less than 95, underline the second letter in the name of the city with the least number of parcels. (Pause 3 seconds.) Then find the number 39 on the Answer Grid and darken the letter you just underlined. (Pause 4 seconds.) Otherwise, darken the letter A on number 39 on the Answer Grid. (Pause 5 seconds.)

20. **Look at Sample 18.** (Pause slightly.) There are three boxes with the time of day in each. (Pause slightly.) Find the box with the latest time in it. (Pause 3 seconds.) On the Answer Grid, find the number that would be created by using the digits before the colon in that time, and darken the letter B as in Boy. (Pause 5 seconds.)

21. **Look at Sample 19.** (Pause slightly.) If the first letter is an R as in Rat, then look at the last letter. (Pause 2 seconds.) If the last letter is a C as in Cat, darken the letter C at number 75 on the Answer Grid. (Pause 4 seconds.) Otherwise, darken the letter A as in Apple at number 75. (Pause 5 seconds.)

22. **Look at Sample 20.** (Pause slightly.) There are two boxes and two circles of different sizes with numbers in each. (Pause slightly.) Find the smallest box and write the letter A as in Apple in that box. (Pause 3 seconds.) Find the smallest circle, and write the letter E as in Egg in that circle. (Pause 3 seconds.) On the Answer Grid, darken the number-letter combinations you have made. (Pause 5 seconds.)

23. **Look at Sample 21.** (Pause slightly.) There are five boxes of different sizes with a number in each. (Pause slightly.) If the largest box contains the largest number, write the letter C as in Cat in that box. (Pause 3 seconds.) Otherwise, write the letter C in the next to largest box. (Pause 3 seconds.) On the Answer Grid, darken the number-letter combination you have made. (Pause 5 seconds.)

24. **Look at Sample 21 again.** (Pause slightly.) In the box with the smallest number, write the letter B as in Boy if the number is greater than 5. (Pause 4 seconds.) Otherwise, write the letter D as in

Dog in that box. (Pause 4 seconds.) Darken the number-letter combination for the box in which you just wrote. (Pause 5 seconds.)

25. **Look at Sample 22.** (Pause slightly.) Write the number 22 on the line if the letter A as in Apple comes before Z as in Zebra in the alphabet. (Pause 4 seconds.) If you wrote the number 22 on the line, find that number on the Answer Grid and darken the letter C as in Cat. (Pause 4 seconds.) If you did not write the number 22 on the line, darken 63 A on the Answer Grid. (Pause 5 seconds.)

26. **Look at Sample 23.** (Pause slightly.) If 12 is greater than 8 and 25 is less than 32, write the number 12 behind the second letter. (Pause 2 seconds.) If not, write the number 15 behind the fourth letter. (Pause 2 seconds.) On the Answer Grid, darken the number-letter combination you have made. (Pause 5 seconds.)

27. **Look at Sample 24.** (Pause slightly.) Each of the two boxes contains the name of a city. (Pause slightly.) Of the two cities, the city of Gulfport has the earliest delivery time. (Pause slightly.) Write an E as in Egg in the box containing the city with the latest delivery time. (Pause 3 seconds.) On the Answer Grid, darken the number-letter combination you have made. (Pause 5 seconds.)

28. **Look at Sample 25.** (Pause slightly.) Write the letter B as in Boy below the largest number. (Pause 3 seconds.) On the Answer Grid, darken the number-letter combination you have made. (Pause 5 seconds.)

29. **Look at Sample 26.** (Pause slightly.) Sodas come 6 cans to a package. (Pause slightly.) How many packages must you buy to have 36 cans of soda? (Pause 3 seconds.) Take this number and add one to it. (Pause 3 seconds.) Find the resulting number on the Answer Grid and darken the letter C as in Cat. (Pause 5 seconds.)

End of Following Oral Instructions Practice Exam 460 #3

End of Practice Exam 460 #3. Use the answer keys on the next five pages to score your work.

Notes:

Answer Grid – Following Oral Instructions – Practice Exam 460 #3

#						#						#					
1.	A	B	C	D	E	36.	A	B	C	D	E	71.	A	B	C	D	E
2.	A	B	C	D	E	37.	A	B	C	D	E	72.	A	B	C	D	E
3.	A	B	C	D	E	38.	A	B	C	D	E	73.	A	B	C	D	E
4.	A	B	C	D	E	39.	A	B	C	D	E	74.	A	B	C	D	E
5.	A	B	C	D	E	40.	A	B	C	D	E	75.	A	B	C	D	E
6.	A	B	C	D	E	41.	A	B	C	D	E	76.	A	B	C	D	E
7.	A	B	C	D	E	42.	A	B	C	D	E	77.	A	B	C	D	E
8.	A	B	C	D	E	43.	A	B	C	D	E	78.	A	B	C	D	E
9.	A	B	C	D	E	44.	A	B	C	D	E	79.	A	B	C	D	E
10.	A	B	C	D	E	45.	A	B	C	D	E	80.	A	B	C	D	E
11.	A	B	C	D	E	46.	A	B	C	D	E	81.	A	B	C	D	E
12.	A	B	C	D	E	47.	A	B	C	D	E	82.	A	B	C	D	E
13.	A	B	C	D	E	48.	A	B	C	D	E	83.	A	B	C	D	E
14.	A	B	C	D	E	49.	A	B	C	D	E	84.	A	B	C	D	E
15.	A	B	C	D	E	50.	A	B	C	D	E	85.	A	B	C	D	E
16.	A	B	C	D	E	51.	A	B	C	D	E	86.	A	B	C	D	E
17.	A	B	C	D	E	52.	A	B	C	D	E	87.	A	B	C	D	E
18.	A	B	C	D	E	53.	A	B	C	D	E	88.	A	B	C	D	E
19.	A	B	C	D	E	54.	A	B	C	D	E						
20.	A	B	C	D	E	55.	A	B	C	D	E						
21.	A	B	C	D	E	56.	A	B	C	D	E						
22.	A	B	C	D	E	57.	A	B	C	D	E						
23.	A	B	C	D	E	58.	A	B	C	D	E						
24.	A	B	C	D	E	59.	A	B	C	D	E						
25.	A	B	C	D	E	60.	A	B	C	D	E						
26.	A	B	C	D	E	61.	A	B	C	D	E						
27.	A	B	C	D	E	62.	A	B	C	D	E						
28.	A	B	C	D	E	63.	A	B	C	D	E						
29.	A	B	C	D	E	64.	A	B	C	D	E						
30.	A	B	C	D	E	65.	A	B	C	D	E						
31.	A	B	C	D	E	66.	A	B	C	D	E						
32.	A	B	C	D	E	67.	A	B	C	D	E						
33.	A	B	C	D	E	68.	A	B	C	D	E						
34.	A	B	C	D	E	69.	A	B	C	D	E						
35.	A	B	C	D	E	70.	A	B	C	D	E						

Notes:

Correct Answers – Address Checking – Practice Exam 460 #3

1.	A	56.	D
2.	D	57.	A
3.	A	58.	D
4.	A	59.	D
5.	D	60.	A
6.	D	61.	D
7.	D	62.	D
8.	D	63.	D
9.	A	64.	A
10.	D	65.	D
11.	D	66.	A
12.	D	67.	A
13.	A	68.	D
14.	A	69.	D
15.	D	70.	D
16.	D	71.	D
17.	D	72.	D
18.	D	73.	A
19.	A	74.	D
20.	D	75.	A
21.	D	76.	D
22.	D	77.	A
23.	D	78.	D
24.	D	79.	D
25.	A	80.	D
26.	A	81.	D
27.	D	82.	D
28.	D	83.	D
29.	D	84.	A
30.	D	85.	D
31.	A	86.	D
32.	D	87.	D
33.	A	88.	D
34.	A	89.	D
35.	D	90.	D
36.	A	91.	D
37.	D	92.	D
38.	A	93.	A
39.	D	94.	D
40.	D	95.	D
41.	A		
42.	D		
43.	D		
44.	D		
45.	D		
46.	A		
47.	D		
48.	A		
49.	A		
50.	D		
51.	D		
52.	D		
53.	D		
54.	A		
55.	A		

1.	B	45.	B
2.	C	46.	E
3.	D	47.	E
4.	D	48.	D
5.	A	49.	E
6.	C	50.	E
7.	D	51.	A
8.	B	52.	C
9.	A	53.	A
10.	E	54.	B
11.	A	55.	B
12.	D	56.	E
13.	E	57.	B
14.	B	58.	D
15.	A	59.	D
16.	C	60.	E
17.	C	61.	B
18.	B	62.	B
19.	C	63.	A
20.	D	64.	E
21.	B	65.	C
22.	D	66.	D
23.	C	67.	C
24.	A	68.	D
25.	E	69.	A
26.	B	70.	A
27.	B	71.	C
28.	A	72.	B
29.	E	73.	C
30.	D	74.	D
31.	D	75.	A
32.	E	76.	C
33.	C	77.	A
34.	C	78.	A
35.	B	79.	E
36.	E	80.	E
37.	A	81.	D
38.	B	82.	B
39.	B	83.	E
40.	D	84.	C
41.	A	85.	B
42.	A	86.	A
43.	A	87.	E
44.	C	88.	B

1. B
2. A
3. D
4. B
5. A
6. C
7. D
8. D
9. A
10. A
11. E
12. D
13. E
14. B
15. A
16. C
17. C
18. C
19. E
20. A
21. B
22. C
23. D
24. E

1. Ⓐ Ⓑ Ⓒ ● Ⓔ
2. Ⓐ ● Ⓒ Ⓓ Ⓔ
3. ● Ⓑ Ⓒ Ⓓ Ⓔ
4. Ⓐ Ⓑ ● Ⓓ Ⓔ
5. Ⓐ ● Ⓒ Ⓓ Ⓔ
6. Ⓐ ● Ⓒ Ⓓ Ⓔ
7. Ⓐ Ⓑ ● Ⓓ Ⓔ
8. ● Ⓑ Ⓒ Ⓓ Ⓔ
9. Ⓐ Ⓑ Ⓒ ● Ⓔ
10. Ⓐ Ⓑ Ⓒ Ⓓ ●
11. ● Ⓑ Ⓒ Ⓓ Ⓔ
12. Ⓐ ● Ⓒ Ⓓ Ⓔ
13. Ⓐ Ⓑ Ⓒ Ⓓ Ⓔ
14. Ⓐ Ⓑ Ⓒ Ⓓ Ⓔ
15. Ⓐ Ⓑ Ⓒ Ⓓ Ⓔ
16. Ⓐ Ⓑ Ⓒ Ⓓ Ⓔ
17. Ⓐ Ⓑ Ⓒ ● Ⓔ
18. Ⓐ Ⓑ Ⓒ Ⓓ Ⓔ
19. Ⓐ Ⓑ Ⓒ Ⓓ Ⓔ
20. Ⓐ Ⓑ Ⓒ Ⓓ Ⓔ
21. Ⓐ Ⓑ Ⓒ Ⓓ Ⓔ
22. Ⓐ Ⓑ ● Ⓓ Ⓔ
23. Ⓐ Ⓑ Ⓒ Ⓓ Ⓔ
24. Ⓐ Ⓑ Ⓒ Ⓓ Ⓔ
25. Ⓐ Ⓑ Ⓒ Ⓓ Ⓔ
26. Ⓐ Ⓑ Ⓒ Ⓓ Ⓔ
27. ● Ⓑ Ⓒ Ⓓ Ⓔ
28. Ⓐ Ⓑ Ⓒ Ⓓ Ⓔ
29. Ⓐ Ⓑ Ⓒ Ⓓ Ⓔ
30. Ⓐ Ⓑ Ⓒ Ⓓ Ⓔ
31. Ⓐ Ⓑ Ⓒ Ⓓ Ⓔ
32. Ⓐ Ⓑ Ⓒ Ⓓ Ⓔ

33. Ⓐ Ⓑ Ⓒ Ⓓ ●
34. Ⓐ Ⓑ Ⓒ Ⓓ Ⓔ
35. Ⓐ Ⓑ Ⓒ Ⓓ Ⓔ
36. Ⓐ Ⓑ Ⓒ Ⓓ ●
37. Ⓐ Ⓑ Ⓒ Ⓓ Ⓔ
38. Ⓐ Ⓑ Ⓒ Ⓓ Ⓔ
39. Ⓐ Ⓑ Ⓒ Ⓓ ●
40. Ⓐ Ⓑ Ⓒ Ⓓ Ⓔ
41. Ⓐ Ⓑ Ⓒ Ⓓ Ⓔ
42. Ⓐ Ⓑ Ⓒ Ⓓ Ⓔ
43. Ⓐ Ⓑ Ⓒ Ⓓ Ⓔ
44. Ⓐ Ⓑ ● Ⓓ Ⓔ
45. Ⓐ Ⓑ Ⓒ Ⓓ Ⓔ
46. Ⓐ Ⓑ Ⓒ Ⓓ Ⓔ
47. Ⓐ Ⓑ Ⓒ Ⓓ Ⓔ
48. Ⓐ Ⓑ Ⓒ Ⓓ Ⓔ
49. Ⓐ Ⓑ ● Ⓓ Ⓔ
50. Ⓐ Ⓑ Ⓒ Ⓓ Ⓔ
51. Ⓐ Ⓑ Ⓒ Ⓓ ●
52. Ⓐ Ⓑ Ⓒ Ⓓ Ⓔ
53. Ⓐ Ⓑ Ⓒ Ⓓ Ⓔ
54. ● Ⓑ Ⓒ Ⓓ Ⓔ
55. Ⓐ Ⓑ Ⓒ Ⓓ Ⓔ
56. Ⓐ Ⓑ Ⓒ Ⓓ Ⓔ
57. Ⓐ Ⓑ Ⓒ Ⓓ Ⓔ
58. Ⓐ Ⓑ Ⓒ Ⓓ Ⓔ
59. Ⓐ Ⓑ Ⓒ Ⓓ Ⓔ
60. Ⓐ Ⓑ Ⓒ Ⓓ Ⓔ
61. Ⓐ Ⓑ Ⓒ Ⓓ Ⓔ
62. Ⓐ Ⓑ Ⓒ ● Ⓔ
63. Ⓐ Ⓑ Ⓒ Ⓓ Ⓔ
64. Ⓐ ● Ⓒ Ⓓ Ⓔ

65. Ⓐ Ⓑ Ⓒ Ⓓ Ⓔ
66. Ⓐ Ⓑ Ⓒ Ⓓ Ⓔ
67. Ⓐ Ⓑ Ⓒ Ⓓ Ⓔ
68. Ⓐ Ⓑ Ⓒ Ⓓ Ⓔ
69. Ⓐ Ⓑ Ⓒ Ⓓ Ⓔ
70. Ⓐ Ⓑ Ⓒ Ⓓ Ⓔ
71. Ⓐ Ⓑ Ⓒ Ⓓ ●
72. Ⓐ Ⓑ Ⓒ Ⓓ Ⓔ
73. Ⓐ Ⓑ Ⓒ Ⓓ Ⓔ
74. Ⓐ Ⓑ Ⓒ Ⓓ Ⓔ
75. ● Ⓑ Ⓒ Ⓓ Ⓔ
76. Ⓐ Ⓑ Ⓒ Ⓓ Ⓔ
77. Ⓐ Ⓑ Ⓒ Ⓓ Ⓔ
78. Ⓐ ● Ⓒ Ⓓ Ⓔ
79. ● Ⓑ Ⓒ Ⓓ Ⓔ
80. Ⓐ Ⓑ Ⓒ Ⓓ Ⓔ
81. Ⓐ Ⓑ Ⓒ Ⓓ Ⓔ
82. Ⓐ ● Ⓒ Ⓓ Ⓔ
83. Ⓐ Ⓑ Ⓒ Ⓓ Ⓔ
84. Ⓐ Ⓑ Ⓒ Ⓓ Ⓔ
85. Ⓐ Ⓑ Ⓒ Ⓓ Ⓔ
86. Ⓐ Ⓑ Ⓒ Ⓓ Ⓔ
87. Ⓐ Ⓑ Ⓒ Ⓓ Ⓔ
88. Ⓐ ● Ⓒ Ⓓ Ⓔ
89. Ⓐ Ⓑ Ⓒ Ⓓ Ⓔ
90. Ⓐ Ⓑ Ⓒ Ⓓ Ⓔ
91. Ⓐ Ⓑ Ⓒ Ⓓ Ⓔ
92. Ⓐ Ⓑ Ⓒ Ⓓ Ⓔ
93. Ⓐ Ⓑ Ⓒ Ⓓ Ⓔ
94. Ⓐ Ⓑ Ⓒ Ⓓ Ⓔ
95. Ⓐ Ⓑ Ⓒ Ⓓ Ⓔ

1. 11A
2. 78B
3. 3A
4. 82B
5. 8A
6. 5B
7. 27A
8. 4C
9. 9D
10. 36E
11. 2B, 33E
12. 62D
13. 54A
14. 10E
15. 44C
16. 64B
17. 17D, 39E
18. 6B
19. 75A
20. 79A, 51E
21. 49C, 1D
22. 22C
23. 12B
24. 71E
25. 88B
26. 7C

End of Practice Exam 460 #3

Notes:

Practice Exam 460 #4

Before beginning, tear out or photocopy the answer grid for each section of the exam.

Address Checking – Practice Exam 460 #4

(You have 6 minutes to complete this section.)

1.	3539 North Causeway	3593 North Causeway
2.	Plainsville, IL 36962	Plainvile, IL 36929
3.	352 N. 5th Ave.	352 N. 5th Ave.
4.	Saunemin, MD 20584	Saumenin, MD 20584
5.	#255 Apt. D-45	#255 Apt. D-45
6.	Zalma, MO	Zalma, MO
7.	1558 Cuevas Estates	1558 Cuevas Estates
8.	312 Jackson Square Notting	313 Jackson Square Notting
9.	Morris Landing, WY 80399	Morris Landing, WY 80399
10.	82499 West Plum Rd.	82499 East Plum Rd.
11.	104 Runnels Ave. South	114 Runnels Ave. North
12.	Collinsville, ND 34569	Collinsville, NH 93658
13.	#790 Royal Oak Roadway	#790 Royal Oak Roadway
14.	137 Beach Park Place	138 Beach Park Place
15.	130 Richards Ave.	130 Richard Ave.
16.	503 Cypress Cove	530 Cypress Cove
17.	#56 Alexander Rd.	#56 Alexander Rd.
18.	14334 Jo Ellen End	1434 Jo Ellen End
19.	Opal, OH 55334	Opal, OH 55335
20.	1011-B Ladd Cir.	1101-B Ladd Cir.
21.	2423 Middlecoffe Dr.	2423 Middlecoffee Dr.
22.	Bullis, LA 22856	Bullis, LA 22856
23.	97 West 58th Ave. NW	97 West 59th Ave NW
24.	Billings, MT	Billings, MT
25.	7345 East Overhead Dr.	7354 East Overhead Dr.
26.	46-D Bridgeport St.	46-D Bridgeport Cir
27.	369 New Haven Ave. E	396 New Haven Ave. W
28.	Staten Island, NY 95874	Staten Island, NY 95784
29.	303 Marice Drive NW	303 Marice Drive NW
30.	3906 Castille Dr.	3906 Castille Dr.
31.	Parkwood, DE 20648	Parkwood, DE 20649
32.	#44 Racquet Club	#44 Racquet Club
33.	1700 John Quincy Adams W	1700 John Quincy Adams E
34.	Bel-Aire Mobile Home Pk.	Bel-Aire Mobil Home Pk.
35.	3712 Reynosa Road	3712 Reynosa Pk
36.	Crest View, WA	Crest View, VA
37.	1415 Avolone-Topango Rd	1415 Avolone-Topango Rd
38.	1800 E. Beach Blvd.	1800 E. Beach Blvd.
39.	Daemions, NC 75498	Daemions, NC 57498
40.	813 Allendale St.	813 Allendale St.
41.	1412 Genevieve Race	1412 Genevieve Race
42.	#4 Carondelet Apt	#3 Carondlet Apt
43.	1910 Switzer Dr.	1910 Switzer Dr.
44.	3432 Washington Sq	3432 Washington Sq
45.	602 West Pass	602 West Pass
46.	4686 Virginia Blvd NE	4686 Virginia Blvd NW
47.	517 Jefferson Davis Ave.	715 Jefferson Davis Blvd.
48.	Howard, FL 74469	Howard, FL 47469

49. 101 Beauvoir Manor Apts	101 Beauvoir Manor Apts
50. 16485 Lorraine Cir	16485 Lorraine Cir
51. 8714-B 29th St. S.	8714-B 29th St. W.
52. Redding, WV 73996	Reeding, WV 73996
53. 14220 Lemoyne Blvd.	14220 Lemoyne Blvd.
54. 7778 Tower Hill	7778 Tower Hill
55. Tiffany Gardens Apt #101	Tiffany Gardens Apt #110
56. Metamorassa, FL 78232	Metamorassa, FL 78232
57. 975 Mission South NW	976 Mission South NW
58. del Amos Hwy. 57 S	del Amos Hwy. 57 S
59. 5275 West Water Way	5725 West Water Way
60. North Ridge, GA 43189	North Ridge, GA 43189
61. 545 Hews Ave. SW	545 Hewes Ave. SW
62. 14 Fair Lawn & Paramus N.	14 Fair Lawn & Paramus N.
63. Alden Manor, West Virginia	Alden Manor, West Virginia
64. 1976 Colonial Rd.	1796 Colonial Rd.
65. 1475 North Shore Parkway	1475 North Shore Parkway
66. 1786 Empire St. NE	1786 Empire St. NE
67. Rockchester, NY 73593	Rockchester, NJ 73593
68. Congress, Washington, DC	Congress, Washington, DC
69. 10004 St. Charles	1004 St. Charles
70. 678500 Independence Blvd.	678500 Independence Blvd.
71. Reno, NV 70900	Reno, NV 70900
72. 1212 Rual del Haban	1221 Rual del Haban
73. 1106 East Old Pass Rd.	1106 West Old Pass Rd.
74. 3992 Leigh High Blvd.	3992 Lehigh Blvd.
75. 45 Townhall Express Way	45 Townhall Express Way
76. Lake Byron, MN 40025	Lake Pyron, MA 00425
77. 67439 Ethel Ave.	67439 Ethel Ave.
78. St. John, ME 67985	St. John, ME 67891
79. 2745 Cookie Ct.	2745 Cookie Ct.
80. Juneville, NC 57684	Juneville, NC 57684
81. Rustway Blvd. 69 NE	Rustway Blvd. 69 NE
82. Flagg, MN 74925	Flagg, MN 74925
83. 88B Cinnamon Circle	88 Cinnamon Circle
84. 1684 Mushroom Blvd. NW	1684 Mushroom Blvd. NW
85. Wheatsdale, OH 45264	Wheatsdale, OH 45264
86. Coronet, NY 95847	Coronet, NY 95847
87. 147 Flower St.	147 Flower St.
88. 1647 Clearview St. Apt 6	1647 Clearview St. Apt 6
89. Sherwood Village, ID 69008	Sherwood Village, IA 69008
90. Maison D'Orleans Apt 72	Maison D'Orleans Apt 75
91. 537 Delauney Cir North	537 Delauney Cir North
92. 6809 Mescalero	6809 Mescalero
93. Santa Maria Del Mar SW	Santa Maria Del Mar SW
94. 875 Gorenflo Ave.	875 Gorenflo Ave.
95. 1234 Pineview Dr.	1234 Pineview Dr.

Address Checking – Practice Exam 460 #4

1. Ⓐ Ⓓ	33. Ⓐ Ⓓ	65. Ⓐ Ⓓ
2. Ⓐ Ⓓ	34. Ⓐ Ⓓ	66. Ⓐ Ⓓ
3. Ⓐ Ⓓ	35. Ⓐ Ⓓ	67. Ⓐ Ⓓ
4. Ⓐ Ⓓ	36. Ⓐ Ⓓ	68. Ⓐ Ⓓ
5. Ⓐ Ⓓ	37. Ⓐ Ⓓ	69. Ⓐ Ⓓ
6. Ⓐ Ⓓ	38. Ⓐ Ⓓ	70. Ⓐ Ⓓ
7. Ⓐ Ⓓ	39. Ⓐ Ⓓ	71. Ⓐ Ⓓ
8. Ⓐ Ⓓ	40. Ⓐ Ⓓ	72. Ⓐ Ⓓ
9. Ⓐ Ⓓ	41. Ⓐ Ⓓ	73. Ⓐ Ⓓ
10. Ⓐ Ⓓ	42. Ⓐ Ⓓ	74. Ⓐ Ⓓ
11. Ⓐ Ⓓ	43. Ⓐ Ⓓ	75. Ⓐ Ⓓ
12. Ⓐ Ⓓ	44. Ⓐ Ⓓ	76. Ⓐ Ⓓ
13. Ⓐ Ⓓ	45. Ⓐ Ⓓ	77. Ⓐ Ⓓ
14. Ⓐ Ⓓ	46. Ⓐ Ⓓ	78. Ⓐ Ⓓ
15. Ⓐ Ⓓ	47. Ⓐ Ⓓ	79. Ⓐ Ⓓ
16. Ⓐ Ⓓ	48. Ⓐ Ⓓ	80. Ⓐ Ⓓ
17. Ⓐ Ⓓ	49. Ⓐ Ⓓ	81. Ⓐ Ⓓ
18. Ⓐ Ⓓ	50. Ⓐ Ⓓ	82. Ⓐ Ⓓ
19. Ⓐ Ⓓ	51. Ⓐ Ⓓ	83. Ⓐ Ⓓ
20. Ⓐ Ⓓ	52. Ⓐ Ⓓ	84. Ⓐ Ⓓ
21. Ⓐ Ⓓ	53. Ⓐ Ⓓ	85. Ⓐ Ⓓ
22. Ⓐ Ⓓ	54. Ⓐ Ⓓ	86. Ⓐ Ⓓ
23. Ⓐ Ⓓ	55. Ⓐ Ⓓ	87. Ⓐ Ⓓ
24. Ⓐ Ⓓ	56. Ⓐ Ⓓ	88. Ⓐ Ⓓ
25. Ⓐ Ⓓ	57. Ⓐ Ⓓ	89. Ⓐ Ⓓ
26. Ⓐ Ⓓ	58. Ⓐ Ⓓ	90. Ⓐ Ⓓ
27. Ⓐ Ⓓ	59. Ⓐ Ⓓ	91. Ⓐ Ⓓ
28. Ⓐ Ⓓ	60. Ⓐ Ⓓ	92. Ⓐ Ⓓ
29. Ⓐ Ⓓ	61. Ⓐ Ⓓ	93. Ⓐ Ⓓ
30. Ⓐ Ⓓ	62. Ⓐ Ⓓ	94. Ⓐ Ⓓ
31. Ⓐ Ⓓ	63. Ⓐ Ⓓ	95. Ⓐ Ⓓ
32. Ⓐ Ⓓ	64. Ⓐ Ⓓ	

Notes:

Directions: Study the addresses below for 11 minutes, then turn the page and *from memory* match each address to the correct box.

A	B	C	D	E
1500-2399 Savannah	3600-3999 Savannah	2400-3299 Savannah	3300-3599 Savannah	1200-1499 Savannah
Grafton	Dambrino	Casper	Richardson	Maxey
2400-3299 Candy	3300-3599 Candy	3600-3999 Candy	1200-1499 Candy	1500-2399 Candy
Cleveland	Ridge	Mills	Lewis	Boggs
1200-1499 Latil	2400-3299 Latil	3300-3599 Latil	1500-2399 Latil	3600-3999 Latil

Memory for Addresses – Practice Exam 460 #4

(You will have 5 minutes to complete this section.)

1. Ridge
2. 3600 – 3999 Savannah
3. 1200 – 1499 Latil
4. Lewis
5. 2400 – 3299 Latil
6. 1200 – 1499 Savannah
7. Dambrino
8. 3600 – 3999 Latil
9. 2400 – 3299 Candy
10. 1500 – 2399 Candy
11. 3300 – 3599 Savannah
12. 2400 – 3299 Latil
13. Boggs
14. Mills
15. 1500 – 2399 Savannah
16. 1200 – 1499 Latil
17. 1200 – 1499 Savannah
18. 1200 – 1499 Latil
19. Mills
20. 3300 – 3599 Latil
21. 2400 –3299 Savannah
22. 1200 – 1499 Candy
23. 3600 – 3999 Latil
24. 2400 – 3299 Latil
25. 3300 – 3599 Candy
26. 2400 – 3299 Savannah
27. 1200 – 1499 Candy
28. Maxey
29. Grafton
30. Casper
31. 1500 – 2399 Latil
32. Cleveland
33. 3300 – 3599 Latil
34. Maxey
35. Dambrino
36. 1500 – 2399 Latil
37. 3600 – 3999 Savannah
38. Grafton
39. Lewis
40. 2400 – 3299 Candy
41. 3300 – 3599 Savannah
42. Dambrino
43. 3300 – 3599 Candy
44. Cleveland
45. Ridge
46. Richardson
47. 1500 – 2399 Savannah
48. Casper
49. 3600 – 3999 Candy
50. Boggs
51. 1200 – 1499 Candy
52. 1200 – 1499 Savannah
53. 2400 – 3299 Latil
54. Grafton
55. 2400 – 3299 Candy
56. 3600 – 3999 Latil
57. 1200 – 1499 Latil
58. 1500 – 3299 Savannah
59. 3300 – 3599 Savannah
60. 1200 – 1499 Savannah
61. Mills
62. Richardson
63. 3300 – 3599 Candy
64. Dambrino
65. 3300 – 3599 Latil
66. 2400 – 3299 Candy
67. 2400 – 3299 Savannah
68. Lewis
69. 1500 – 2399 Candy
70. Ridge
71. Mills
72. Maxey
73. Ridge
74. 2400 – 3299 Savannah
75. Lewis
76. 3300 – 3599 Latil
77. 1500 – 2399 Latil
78. 1500 – 2399 Candy
79. Maxey
80. 3600 – 3999 Savannah
81. 2400 – 3299 Candy
82. 1500 – 2399 Latil
83. 1200 – 1499 Candy
84. Grafton
85. Cleveland
86. Casper
87. 3600 – 3999 Latil
88. 2400 – 3299 Latil

1. Ⓐ Ⓑ Ⓒ Ⓓ Ⓔ	31. Ⓐ Ⓑ Ⓒ Ⓓ Ⓔ	61. Ⓐ Ⓑ Ⓒ Ⓓ Ⓔ	
2. Ⓐ Ⓑ Ⓒ Ⓓ Ⓔ	32. Ⓐ Ⓑ Ⓒ Ⓓ Ⓔ	62. Ⓐ Ⓑ Ⓒ Ⓓ Ⓔ	
3. Ⓐ Ⓑ Ⓒ Ⓓ Ⓔ	33. Ⓐ Ⓑ Ⓒ Ⓓ Ⓔ	63. Ⓐ Ⓑ Ⓒ Ⓓ Ⓔ	
4. Ⓐ Ⓑ Ⓒ Ⓓ Ⓔ	34. Ⓐ Ⓑ Ⓒ Ⓓ Ⓔ	64. Ⓐ Ⓑ Ⓒ Ⓓ Ⓔ	
5. Ⓐ Ⓑ Ⓒ Ⓓ Ⓔ	35. Ⓐ Ⓑ Ⓒ Ⓓ Ⓔ	65. Ⓐ Ⓑ Ⓒ Ⓓ Ⓔ	
6. Ⓐ Ⓑ Ⓒ Ⓓ Ⓔ	36. Ⓐ Ⓑ Ⓒ Ⓓ Ⓔ	66. Ⓐ Ⓑ Ⓒ Ⓓ Ⓔ	
7. Ⓐ Ⓑ Ⓒ Ⓓ Ⓔ	37. Ⓐ Ⓑ Ⓒ Ⓓ Ⓔ	67. Ⓐ Ⓑ Ⓒ Ⓓ Ⓔ	
8. Ⓐ Ⓑ Ⓒ Ⓓ Ⓔ	38. Ⓐ Ⓑ Ⓒ Ⓓ Ⓔ	68. Ⓐ Ⓑ Ⓒ Ⓓ Ⓔ	
9. Ⓐ Ⓑ Ⓒ Ⓓ Ⓔ	39. Ⓐ Ⓑ Ⓒ Ⓓ Ⓔ	69. Ⓐ Ⓑ Ⓒ Ⓓ Ⓔ	
10. Ⓐ Ⓑ Ⓒ Ⓓ Ⓔ	40. Ⓐ Ⓑ Ⓒ Ⓓ Ⓔ	70. Ⓐ Ⓑ Ⓒ Ⓓ Ⓔ	
11. Ⓐ Ⓑ Ⓒ Ⓓ Ⓔ	41. Ⓐ Ⓑ Ⓒ Ⓓ Ⓔ	71. Ⓐ Ⓑ Ⓒ Ⓓ Ⓔ	
12. Ⓐ Ⓑ Ⓒ Ⓓ Ⓔ	42. Ⓐ Ⓑ Ⓒ Ⓓ Ⓔ	72. Ⓐ Ⓑ Ⓒ Ⓓ Ⓔ	
13. Ⓐ Ⓑ Ⓒ Ⓓ Ⓔ	43. Ⓐ Ⓑ Ⓒ Ⓓ Ⓔ	73. Ⓐ Ⓑ Ⓒ Ⓓ Ⓔ	
14. Ⓐ Ⓑ Ⓒ Ⓓ Ⓔ	44. Ⓐ Ⓑ Ⓒ Ⓓ Ⓔ	74. Ⓐ Ⓑ Ⓒ Ⓓ Ⓔ	
15. Ⓐ Ⓑ Ⓒ Ⓓ Ⓔ	45. Ⓐ Ⓑ Ⓒ Ⓓ Ⓔ	75. Ⓐ Ⓑ Ⓒ Ⓓ Ⓔ	
16. Ⓐ Ⓑ Ⓒ Ⓓ Ⓔ	46. Ⓐ Ⓑ Ⓒ Ⓓ Ⓔ	76. Ⓐ Ⓑ Ⓒ Ⓓ Ⓔ	
17. Ⓐ Ⓑ Ⓒ Ⓓ Ⓔ	47. Ⓐ Ⓑ Ⓒ Ⓓ Ⓔ	77. Ⓐ Ⓑ Ⓒ Ⓓ Ⓔ	
18. Ⓐ Ⓑ Ⓒ Ⓓ Ⓔ	48. Ⓐ Ⓑ Ⓒ Ⓓ Ⓔ	78. Ⓐ Ⓑ Ⓒ Ⓓ Ⓔ	
19. Ⓐ Ⓑ Ⓒ Ⓓ Ⓔ	49. Ⓐ Ⓑ Ⓒ Ⓓ Ⓔ	79. Ⓐ Ⓑ Ⓒ Ⓓ Ⓔ	
20. Ⓐ Ⓑ Ⓒ Ⓓ Ⓔ	50. Ⓐ Ⓑ Ⓒ Ⓓ Ⓔ	80. Ⓐ Ⓑ Ⓒ Ⓓ Ⓔ	
21. Ⓐ Ⓑ Ⓒ Ⓓ Ⓔ	51. Ⓐ Ⓑ Ⓒ Ⓓ Ⓔ	81. Ⓐ Ⓑ Ⓒ Ⓓ Ⓔ	
22. Ⓐ Ⓑ Ⓒ Ⓓ Ⓔ	52. Ⓐ Ⓑ Ⓒ Ⓓ Ⓔ	82. Ⓐ Ⓑ Ⓒ Ⓓ Ⓔ	
23. Ⓐ Ⓑ Ⓒ Ⓓ Ⓔ	53. Ⓐ Ⓑ Ⓒ Ⓓ Ⓔ	83. Ⓐ Ⓑ Ⓒ Ⓓ Ⓔ	
24. Ⓐ Ⓑ Ⓒ Ⓓ Ⓔ	54. Ⓐ Ⓑ Ⓒ Ⓓ Ⓔ	84. Ⓐ Ⓑ Ⓒ Ⓓ Ⓔ	
25. Ⓐ Ⓑ Ⓒ Ⓓ Ⓔ	55. Ⓐ Ⓑ Ⓒ Ⓓ Ⓔ	85. Ⓐ Ⓑ Ⓒ Ⓓ Ⓔ	
26. Ⓐ Ⓑ Ⓒ Ⓓ Ⓔ	56. Ⓐ Ⓑ Ⓒ Ⓓ Ⓔ	86. Ⓐ Ⓑ Ⓒ Ⓓ Ⓔ	
27. Ⓐ Ⓑ Ⓒ Ⓓ Ⓔ	57. Ⓐ Ⓑ Ⓒ Ⓓ Ⓔ	87. Ⓐ Ⓑ Ⓒ Ⓓ Ⓔ	
28. Ⓐ Ⓑ Ⓒ Ⓓ Ⓔ	58. Ⓐ Ⓑ Ⓒ Ⓓ Ⓔ	88. Ⓐ Ⓑ Ⓒ Ⓓ Ⓔ	
29. Ⓐ Ⓑ Ⓒ Ⓓ Ⓔ	59. Ⓐ Ⓑ Ⓒ Ⓓ Ⓔ		
30. Ⓐ Ⓑ Ⓒ Ⓓ Ⓔ	60. Ⓐ Ⓑ Ⓒ Ⓓ Ⓔ		

(You will have 20 minutes to complete this section.)

1.   **3**   **5**   **7**   **9**   **11**   **13**   **15**   ___   ___

    A) 18   21   B) 19   23   C) 17   19   D) 16   17   E) 39   41

2.   **1**   **7**   **13**   **19**   **25**   **31**   **37**   ___   ___

    A) 38   45   B) 43   50   C) 38   46   D) 47   57   E) 43   49

3.   **12**   **15**   **18**   **21**   **24**   **27**   **30**   ___   ___

    A) 33   36   B) 34   37   C) 33   38   D) 40   50   E) 30   36

4.   **21**   **28**   **35**   **42**   **49**   **56**   **63**   ___   ___

    A) 72   79   B) 70   77   C) 70   80   D) 70   78   E) 73   83

5.   **62**   **60**   **58**   **56**   **54**   **52**   **50**   ___   ___

    A) 48   44   B) 52   54   C) 46   44   D) 48   46   E) 42   40

6.   **82**   **71**   **60**   **49**   **38**   **27**   ___   ___

    A) 16   5   B) 15   4   C) 17   6   D) 18   8   E) 19   9

7.   **16**   **20**   **24**   **28**   **32**   **36**   **40**   ___   ___

    A) 42   44   B) 43   47   C) 45   49   D) 50   54   E) 44   48

8.   **58**   **55**   **52**   **49**   **46**   **43**   **40**   ___   ___

    A) 36   33   B) 38   35   C) 37   34   D) 40   37   E) 42   39

9.   **4**   **5**   **8**   **6**   **7**   **11**   **8**   ___   ___

    A) 8   13   B) 9   14   C) 10   15   D) 16   18   E) 12   17

10.   **19**   **21**   **50**   **23**   **25**   **47**   **27**   ___   ___

    A) 30   45   B) 28   43   C) 27   42   D) 29   44   E) 25   45

11.   **3**   **9**   **15**   **21**   **27**   **33**   **39**   ___   ___

    A) 45   51   B) 35   41   C) 55   61   D) 56   66   E) 56   63

12.   **12**   **11**   **10**   **37**   **9**   **8**   **7**   **36**   ___   ___

    A) 9   2   B) 9   3   C) 8   4   D) 7   5   E) 6   5

13.   **42**   **37**   **64**   **69**   **32**   **27**   **74**   ___   ___

    A) 79   20   B) 80   21   C) 82   17   D) 76   20   E) 79   22

14. **71**   **76**   **31**   **29**   **81**   **86**   **27**   __   __

A) 24 90   B) 26 92   C) 25 91   D) 26 91   E) 26 93

15. **1**   **13**   **7**   **19**   **13**   **25**   **19**   __   __

A) 30 24   B) 31 25   C) 32 26   D) 34 28   E) 30 20

16. **21**   **21**   **14**   **18**   **18**   **52**   **15**   __   __

A) 15 92   B) 16 40   C) 14 52   D) 15 90   E) 45 90

17. **36**   **7**   **5**   **39**   **39**   **3**   **1**   __   __

A) 47 47   B) 42 42   C) 42 1   D) 3 42   E) 0 48

18. **27**   **37**   **61**   **21**   **85**   **109**   **15**   __   __

A) 133 157   B) 133 1589   C) 132 159   D) 159 165   E) 131 150

19. **11**   **17**   **7**   **7**   **7**   **23**   **3**   **3**   __   __

A) 3 28   B) 3 3   C) 27 3   D) 29 28   E) 3 29

20. **80**   **14**   **32**   **69**   **65**   **17**   **35**   **54**   **50**   **20**   __   __

A) 37 38   B) 18 39   C) 38 39   D) 36 38   E) 32 40

21. **15**   **22**   **25**   **32**   **35**   **42**   **45**   __   __

A) 52 55   B) 53 54   C) 54 60   D) 52 59   E) 55 60

22. **96**   **96**   **11**   **75**   **75**   **14**   **54**   __   __

A) 17 54   B) 54 54   C) 14 54   D) 54 17   E) 75 17

23. **27**   **42**   **57**   **72**   **87**   __   __

A) 92 107   B) 103 116   C) 102 117   D) 103 118   E) 101 126

24. **6**   **7**   **21**   **10**   **11**   **26**   **15** __ __

A) 16 30   B) 17 25   C) 18 33   D) 31 17   E) 16 31

Notes:

186

1. Ⓐ Ⓑ Ⓒ Ⓓ Ⓔ
2. Ⓐ Ⓑ Ⓒ Ⓓ Ⓔ
3. Ⓐ Ⓑ Ⓒ Ⓓ Ⓔ
4. Ⓐ Ⓑ Ⓒ Ⓓ Ⓔ
5. Ⓐ Ⓑ Ⓒ Ⓓ Ⓔ
6. Ⓐ Ⓑ Ⓒ Ⓓ Ⓔ
7. Ⓐ Ⓑ Ⓒ Ⓓ Ⓔ
8. Ⓐ Ⓑ Ⓒ Ⓓ Ⓔ
9. Ⓐ Ⓑ Ⓒ Ⓓ Ⓔ
10. Ⓐ Ⓑ Ⓒ Ⓓ Ⓔ
11. Ⓐ Ⓑ Ⓒ Ⓓ Ⓔ
12. Ⓐ Ⓑ Ⓒ Ⓓ Ⓔ
13. Ⓐ Ⓑ Ⓒ Ⓓ Ⓔ
14. Ⓐ Ⓑ Ⓒ Ⓓ Ⓔ
15. Ⓐ Ⓑ Ⓒ Ⓓ Ⓔ
16. Ⓐ Ⓑ Ⓒ Ⓓ Ⓔ
17. Ⓐ Ⓑ Ⓒ Ⓓ Ⓔ
18. Ⓐ Ⓑ Ⓒ Ⓓ Ⓔ
19. Ⓐ Ⓑ Ⓒ Ⓓ Ⓔ
20. Ⓐ Ⓑ Ⓒ Ⓓ Ⓔ
21. Ⓐ Ⓑ Ⓒ Ⓓ Ⓔ
22. Ⓐ Ⓑ Ⓒ Ⓓ Ⓔ
23. Ⓐ Ⓑ Ⓒ Ⓓ Ⓔ
24. Ⓐ Ⓑ Ⓒ Ⓓ Ⓔ

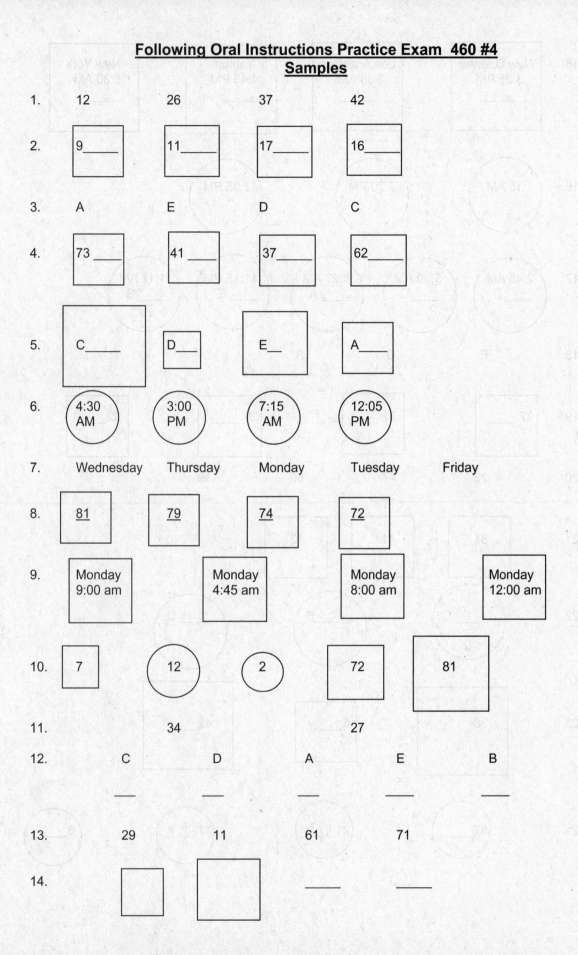

1.   12   26   37   42

2.   9____   11____   17____   16____

3.   A   E   D   C

4.   73____   41____   37____   62____

5.   C____   D___   E__   A____

6.   4:30 AM   3:00 PM   7:15 AM   12:05 PM

7.   Wednesday   Thursday   Monday   Tuesday   Friday

8.   81   79   74   72

9.   Monday   Monday   Monday   Monday
     9:00 am   4:45 am   8:00 am   12:00 am

10. 7   12   2   72   81

11.   34   27

12.   C   D   A   E   B
          __   __   __   __   __

13.   29   11   61   71

14.

15.

| New Orleans 3:25 PM ___ | Los Angeles 7:35 AM ___ | Tampa 4:45 PM ___ | New York 5:30 AM ___ |

16.

1:15 AM   3:20 PM   12:05 PM

17.

2:45 AM ___ D   5:00 AM ___ C   4:27 AM ___ A   11:15 PM ___ E   1:17 AM ___ B

18.   E   C   R   S   T

19.

27 ___   32 ___   20 ___   82 ___

20.   28   47   56   19
         __   __   __   __

21.

81   41   12

22.

___ C   ___ B   ___ D

23.

38 ___   5 ___   42 ___

24.

67 ___   81 ___   17 ___   6 ___

190

Answer Grid – Following Oral Instructions – Practice Exam 460 #4

1. Ⓐ Ⓑ Ⓒ Ⓓ Ⓔ
2. Ⓐ Ⓑ Ⓒ Ⓓ Ⓔ
3. Ⓐ Ⓑ Ⓒ Ⓓ Ⓔ
4. Ⓐ Ⓑ Ⓒ Ⓓ Ⓔ
5. Ⓐ Ⓑ Ⓒ Ⓓ Ⓔ
6. Ⓐ Ⓑ Ⓒ Ⓓ Ⓔ
7. Ⓐ Ⓑ Ⓒ Ⓓ Ⓔ
8. Ⓐ Ⓑ Ⓒ Ⓓ Ⓔ
9. Ⓐ Ⓑ Ⓒ Ⓓ Ⓔ
10. Ⓐ Ⓑ Ⓒ Ⓓ Ⓔ
11. Ⓐ Ⓑ Ⓒ Ⓓ Ⓔ
12. Ⓐ Ⓑ Ⓒ Ⓓ Ⓔ
13. Ⓐ Ⓑ Ⓒ Ⓓ Ⓔ
14. Ⓐ Ⓑ Ⓒ Ⓓ Ⓔ
15. Ⓐ Ⓑ Ⓒ Ⓓ Ⓔ
16. Ⓐ Ⓑ Ⓒ Ⓓ Ⓔ
17. Ⓐ Ⓑ Ⓒ Ⓓ Ⓔ
18. Ⓐ Ⓑ Ⓒ Ⓓ Ⓔ
19. Ⓐ Ⓑ Ⓒ Ⓓ Ⓔ
20. Ⓐ Ⓑ Ⓒ Ⓓ Ⓔ
21. Ⓐ Ⓑ Ⓒ Ⓓ Ⓔ
22. Ⓐ Ⓑ Ⓒ Ⓓ Ⓔ
23. Ⓐ Ⓑ Ⓒ Ⓓ Ⓔ
24. Ⓐ Ⓑ Ⓒ Ⓓ Ⓔ
25. Ⓐ Ⓑ Ⓒ Ⓓ Ⓔ
26. Ⓐ Ⓑ Ⓒ Ⓓ Ⓔ
27. Ⓐ Ⓑ Ⓒ Ⓓ Ⓔ
28. Ⓐ Ⓑ Ⓒ Ⓓ Ⓔ
29. Ⓐ Ⓑ Ⓒ Ⓓ Ⓔ
30. Ⓐ Ⓑ Ⓒ Ⓓ Ⓔ
31. Ⓐ Ⓑ Ⓒ Ⓓ Ⓔ
32. Ⓐ Ⓑ Ⓒ Ⓓ Ⓔ
33. Ⓐ Ⓑ Ⓒ Ⓓ Ⓔ
34. Ⓐ Ⓑ Ⓒ Ⓓ Ⓔ
35. Ⓐ Ⓑ Ⓒ Ⓓ Ⓔ
36. Ⓐ Ⓑ Ⓒ Ⓓ Ⓔ
37. Ⓐ Ⓑ Ⓒ Ⓓ Ⓔ
38. Ⓐ Ⓑ Ⓒ Ⓓ Ⓔ
39. Ⓐ Ⓑ Ⓒ Ⓓ Ⓔ
40. Ⓐ Ⓑ Ⓒ Ⓓ Ⓔ
41. Ⓐ Ⓑ Ⓒ Ⓓ Ⓔ
42. Ⓐ Ⓑ Ⓒ Ⓓ Ⓔ
43. Ⓐ Ⓑ Ⓒ Ⓓ Ⓔ
44. Ⓐ Ⓑ Ⓒ Ⓓ Ⓔ
45. Ⓐ Ⓑ Ⓒ Ⓓ Ⓔ
46. Ⓐ Ⓑ Ⓒ Ⓓ Ⓔ
47. Ⓐ Ⓑ Ⓒ Ⓓ Ⓔ
48. Ⓐ Ⓑ Ⓒ Ⓓ Ⓔ
49. Ⓐ Ⓑ Ⓒ Ⓓ Ⓔ
50. Ⓐ Ⓑ Ⓒ Ⓓ Ⓔ
51. Ⓐ Ⓑ Ⓒ Ⓓ Ⓔ
52. Ⓐ Ⓑ Ⓒ Ⓓ Ⓔ
53. Ⓐ Ⓑ Ⓒ Ⓓ Ⓔ
54. Ⓐ Ⓑ Ⓒ Ⓓ Ⓔ
55. Ⓐ Ⓑ Ⓒ Ⓓ Ⓔ
56. Ⓐ Ⓑ Ⓒ Ⓓ Ⓔ
57. Ⓐ Ⓑ Ⓒ Ⓓ Ⓔ
58. Ⓐ Ⓑ Ⓒ Ⓓ Ⓔ
59. Ⓐ Ⓑ Ⓒ Ⓓ Ⓔ
60. Ⓐ Ⓑ Ⓒ Ⓓ Ⓔ
61. Ⓐ Ⓑ Ⓒ Ⓓ Ⓔ
62. Ⓐ Ⓑ Ⓒ Ⓓ Ⓔ
63. Ⓐ Ⓑ Ⓒ Ⓓ Ⓔ
64. Ⓐ Ⓑ Ⓒ Ⓓ Ⓔ
65. Ⓐ Ⓑ Ⓒ Ⓓ Ⓔ
66. Ⓐ Ⓑ Ⓒ Ⓓ Ⓔ
67. Ⓐ Ⓑ Ⓒ Ⓓ Ⓔ
68. Ⓐ Ⓑ Ⓒ Ⓓ Ⓔ
69. Ⓐ Ⓑ Ⓒ Ⓓ Ⓔ
70. Ⓐ Ⓑ Ⓒ Ⓓ Ⓔ
71. Ⓐ Ⓑ Ⓒ Ⓓ Ⓔ
72. Ⓐ Ⓑ Ⓒ Ⓓ Ⓔ
73. Ⓐ Ⓑ Ⓒ Ⓓ Ⓔ
74. Ⓐ Ⓑ Ⓒ Ⓓ Ⓔ
75. Ⓐ Ⓑ Ⓒ Ⓓ Ⓔ
76. Ⓐ Ⓑ Ⓒ Ⓓ Ⓔ
77. Ⓐ Ⓑ Ⓒ Ⓓ Ⓔ
78. Ⓐ Ⓑ Ⓒ Ⓓ Ⓔ
79. Ⓐ Ⓑ Ⓒ Ⓓ Ⓔ
80. Ⓐ Ⓑ Ⓒ Ⓓ Ⓔ
81. Ⓐ Ⓑ Ⓒ Ⓓ Ⓔ
82. Ⓐ Ⓑ Ⓒ Ⓓ Ⓔ
83. Ⓐ Ⓑ Ⓒ Ⓓ Ⓔ
84. Ⓐ Ⓑ Ⓒ Ⓓ Ⓔ
85. Ⓐ Ⓑ Ⓒ Ⓓ Ⓔ
86. Ⓐ Ⓑ Ⓒ Ⓓ Ⓔ
87. Ⓐ Ⓑ Ⓒ Ⓓ Ⓔ
88. Ⓐ Ⓑ Ⓒ Ⓓ Ⓔ

Notes:

Following Oral Instructions – Practice Exam 460 #4

(Directions to be Read Aloud)

1. **Look at Sample 1.** (Pause slightly.) Draw a line under the fourth number. (Pause 2 seconds.) On the Answer Grid, darken the letter C as in Cat for the number you underlined. (Pause 5 seconds.)

2. **Look at Sample 2.** (Pause slightly.) Write the letter D as in Dog in the second box. (Pause 3 seconds.) On the Answer Grid, darken the number-letter combination you have made. (Pause 5 seconds.)

3. **Look at Sample 3.** (Pause slightly.) You should see four letters. (Pause slightly.) Draw a circle around the second letter. (Pause 2 seconds.) Find the number 35 on the Answer Grid and darken the letter you circled. (Pause 5 seconds.)

4. **Look at Sample 4.** (Pause slightly.) There are four boxes. (Pause slightly.) In each box there is a number of parcels to be delivered. (Pause slightly.) In the box with the most parcels, write the letter E as in Egg. (Pause 3 seconds.) On the Answer Grid, darken the number-letter combination you have made. (Pause 5 seconds.)

5. **Look at Sample 4 again.** (Pause slightly.) If the number 44 is greater than 48, write the letter A as in Apple in the box with the lowest number. (Pause 3 seconds.) Otherwise, write the letter D as in Dog in that box. (Pause 3 seconds.) On the Answer Grid, darken the number-letter combination you have made. (Pause 5 seconds.)

6. **Look at Sample 5.** (Pause slightly.) There are four boxes of different sizes with a letter in each. (Pause slightly.) Write the number 68 in the smallest box. (Pause 3 seconds.) On the Answer Grid, darken the number-letter combination you have just made. (Pause 5 seconds.)

7. **Look at Sample 5 again.** (Pause slightly.) Find the next-to-smallest box. If 22 is less than 67, write the number 8 in that box.(Pause 4 seconds.) Otherwise, write the number 8 in the last box. (Pause 3 seconds.) On the Answer Grid, find the number 85 and darken the letter A as in Apple. (Pause 5 seconds.)

8. **Look at Sample 6.** (Pause slightly.) In Sample 6, there are four circles with the time of day in each. (Pause slightly.) In the circle with the earliest time, write the letter D as in Dog. (Pause 3 seconds.) On the Answer Grid, find the number that would be created by using the last two digits of the earliest time and darken the letter D as in Dog. (Pause 5 seconds.)

9. **Look at Sample 7.** (Pause slightly.) In Sample 7, five days of the week are listed. (Pause slightly.) If 44 is greater than 39, underline the second letter of the first day listed. (Pause 3 seconds.) If not, underline the seventh letter of the second day listed. (Pause 3 seconds.) On the Answer Grid, find the number 36 and darken the letter you underlined. (Pause 5 seconds.)

10. **Look at Sample 7 again.** (Pause slightly.) If the name of the last day listed begins with R as in rat, draw a line under the last letter of the first day listed. (Pause 5 seconds.) Otherwise, darken A as in Apple at number 83 on the Answer Grid. (Pause 5 seconds.)

11. **Look at Sample 8.** (Pause slightly.) There are four boxes with a number in each. (Pause slightly.) Write the letter C as in Cat in the box with the number closest to 77. (Pause 4 seconds.) On the Answer Grid, darken the number-letter combination you have made. (Pause 5 seconds.)

12. **Look at Sample 9.** (Pause slightly.) Each box contains a mail delivery time. (Pause slightly.) If any of the mail delivery times is after 5:55 pm, darken the letter E as in Egg at number 38 on the Answer Grid. (Pause 4 seconds.) Otherwise, darken the letter B as in Boy at that number. (Pause 5 seconds.)

13. **Look at Sample 10.** (Pause slightly.) There are three boxes and two circles of different sizes. (Pause slightly.) If B as in Boy comes before D as in Dog in the alphabet, and if 23 is less than 34, darken the letter as in Apple on the Answer Grid at the number found in the smallest box. (Pause 4 seconds.) Otherwise, darken the letter E as in Egg at the number found in the smaller circle. (Pause 5 seconds.)

14. **Look at Sample 10 again.** (Pause slightly.) If the number in the largest box is smaller than the numbe in the largest circle, darken the letter B as in Boy on the Answer Grid at the number found in the largest circl (Pause 5 seconds.) Otherwise, darken the letter A as in Apple at the number found in the smaller circle. (Pause 5 seconds.)

15. **Look at Sample 11.** (Pause slightly.) If the second number is an odd number and the first number is a even number, underline the first number. (Pause 4 seconds.) On the Answer Grid, find the number you underlined and darken the letter A as in Apple. (Pause 4 seconds.) Otherwise, find the second number on t Answer Grid and darken the letter B as in Boy. (Pause 5 seconds.)

16. **Look at Sample 12.** (Pause slightly.) Look at the letters. (Pause slightly.) There are 5 lines, one for each letter. Circle the letter E as in Egg and write the number 58 under the fourth letter. (Pause 3 seconds. If the number you just wrote on the underline is under the number you just circled, darken that number-letter combination on the Answer Grid. (Pause 5 seconds.) Otherwise, at number 58 on the Answer Grid darken th letter above the number 58. (Pause 5 seconds.)

17. **Look at Sample 13.** (Pause slightly.) Draw a circle around the second number. (Pause 2 seconds.) Draw a circle around the last number. (Pause 2 seconds.) Draw a circle around the first number. (Pause 2 seconds.) On the Answer Grid, find the second number you circled and darken the letter D as in Dog. (Pau 5 seconds.)

18. **Look at Sample 13 again.** (Pause slightly.) If the number you did not circle is larger than the number 7 darken the letter A as in Apple on the Answer Grid at the number you did not circle. (Pause 3 seconds.) Otherwise, darken the letter E as in Egg on the Answer Grid at the number you did not circle. (Pause 5 seconds.)

19. **Look at Sample 14.** (Pause slightly.) There are two squares and two lines. (Pause slightly.) Write the letter E as in Egg in the smaller square. (Pause 3 seconds.) Write the number 72 on the first line. (Pause 2 seconds.) Darken this number-letter combination on the Answer Grid. (Pause 5 seconds.)

20. **Look at Sample 14 again.** (Pause slightly.) If 12 is more than 15, write the letter D as in Dog in the largest square and the number 42 on the last line. (Pause 3 seconds.) On the Answer Grid, darken this number-letter combination. (Pause 3 seconds.) Otherwise, darken 64C. (Pause 5 seconds.)

21. **Look at Sample 15.** (Pause slightly.) There are four boxes, each containing the name of a city, and a mail collection time. (Pause slightly.) Write the letter B as in Boy in the box that contains the city with the latest collection time. (Pause 3 seconds.) On the Answer Grid, find the number that would be created by using the last two digits of the time in that box, and darken the letter you have written in that box. (Pause 5 seconds.)

22. **Look at Sample 16.** (Pause slightly.) Each circle contains a mail delivery time. (Pause slightly.) Find th circle with the earliest time; in that circle write the first digit of that time. (Pause 3 seconds.) On the Answer Grid darken the letter D as in Dog for the number you just wrote. (Pause 5 seconds.)

23. **Look at Sample 17.** (Pause slightly.) Each of the five circles has a time and a letter in it. (Pause slightly.) On the line in the last circle write the last two digits of the time in that circle. (Pause 3 seconds.) O the Answer Grid, darken the number-letter combination you have made. (Pause 5 seconds.)

24. **Look at Sample 18.** (Pause slightly.) Draw a line under the second letter. (Pause 3 seconds.) Find th number 4 on the Answer Grid and darken the letter under which you drew a line. (Pause 5 seconds.)

25. **Look at Sample 19**. (Pause slightly.) Each box contains a number representing sacks of mail. (Pause slightly.) Find the box with the smallest number of sacks. (Pause 3 seconds.) On the line in that box, write the letter B as in Boy. (Pause 3 seconds.) On the Answer Grid, darken the number-letter combination in that box. (Pause 5 seconds.)

26. **Look at Sample 20**. Each number has a line under it. (Pause slightly.) If the first number is the largest, write the letter A as in Apple under the second number. (Pause 3 seconds.) Otherwise, write the letter C as in Cat under the third number. (Pause 3 seconds.) On the Answer Grid, darken the number-letter combination you have just made. (Pause 5 seconds.)

27. **Look at Sample 21**. Each box contains a number. (Pause slightly.) Write the letter D as in Dog next to the middle number. (Pause 3 seconds.) On the Answer Grid, darken the number-letter combination you just made. (Pause 5 seconds.)

28. **Look at Sample 22**. (Pause slightly.) If P as in Puddle comes before R as in Rain in the alphabet, write the number 14 in the first circle. (Pause 3 seconds.) If not, write the number 27 in the last circle. (Pause 3 seconds.) On the Answer Grid, darken the number-letter combination you have made. (Pause 5 seconds.)

29. **Look at Sample 23**. (Pause slightly.) Write the letter B as in Boy in the smallest box. (Pause 3 seconds.) On the Answer Grid, darken the number-letter combination you have made. (Pause 5 seconds.)

30. **Look at Sample 24**. (Pause slightly.) If 15 is less than 12, write the letter D as in Dog in the first circle. (Pause 3 seconds.) If not, write the letter E as in Egg in the last circle. (Pause 3 seconds.) On the Answer Grid, darken the number-letter combination you have just made. (Pause 5 seconds.)

End of Following Oral Instructions Practice Exam 460 #4

End of Practice Exam 460 #4. Use the answer keys on the next five pages to score your work.

1. D	33. D	65. A
2. D	34. D	66. A
3. D	35. D	67. D
4. D	36. D	68. A
5. A	37. A	69. D
6. A	38. A	70. A
7. A	39. D	71. A
8. D	40. A	72. D
9. A	41. A	73. D
10. D	42. D	74. D
11. D	43. A	75. A
12. D	44. A	76. D
13. A	45. A	77. A
14. D	46. A	78. D
15. D	47. D	79. A
16. D	48. D	80. A
17. A	49. A	81. A
18. D	50. A	82. A
19. D	51. D	83. D
20. D	52. D	84. A
21. D	53. A	85. A
22. A	54. A	86. A
23. D	55. D	87. A
24. A	56. A	88. A
25. D	57. D	89. D
26. D	58. A	90. D
27. D	59. D	91. A
28. D	60. A	92. A
29. A	61. D	93. A
30. A	62. A	94. A
31. D	63. A	95. A
32. A	64. D	

Correct Answers – Memory for Addresses – Practice Exam 460 #4

1. B	31. D	61. C
2. B	32. A	62. D
3. A	33. C	63. B
4. D	34. E	64. B
5. B	35. B	65. C
6. E	36. D	66. A
7. B	37. B	67. C
8. E	38. A	68. D
9. A	39. D	69. E
10. E	40. A	70. B
11. D	41. D	71. C
12. B	42. B	72. E
13. E	43. B	73. B
14. C	44. A	74. C
15. A	45. B	75. D
16. A	46. D	76. C
17. E	47. A	77. D
18. A	48. C	78. E
19. C	49. C	79. E
20. C	50. E	80. B
21. C	51. D	81. A
22. D	52. E	82. D
23. E	53. B	83. D
24. B	54. A	84. A
25. B	55. A	85. A
26. C	56. E	86. C
27. D	57. A	87. E
28. E	58. A	88. B
29. A	59. D	
30. C	60. E	

1. C   (3 5 7 9 11 13 15 **17 19**)
2. E   (1 7 13 19 25 31 37 **43 49**)
3. A   (12 15 18 21 24 27 30 **33 36**)
4. B   (21 28 35 42 49 56 63 **70 77**)
5. D   (62 60 58 56 54 52 50 **48 46**)
6. A   (82 71 60 49 38 27 **16 5**)
7. E   (16 20 24 28 32 36 40 **44 48**)
8. C   (58 55 52 49 46 43 40 **37 34**)
9. B   (4 5 8 6 7 11 8 **9 14**)
10. D   (19 21 50 23 25 47 27 **29 44**)
11. A   (3 9 15 21 27 33 39 **45 51**)
12. E   (12 11 10 37 9 8 7 36 **6 5**)
13. E   (42 37 64 69 32 27 74 **79 22**)
14. C   (71 76 31 29 81 86 27 **25 91**)
15. B   (1 13 7 19 13 25 19 **31 25**)
16. D   (21 21 14 18 18 52 15 **15 90**)
17. B   (36 7 5 39 39 3 1 **42 42**)
18. A   (27 37 61 21 85 109 15 **133 157**)
19. E   (11 17 7 7 7 23 3 3 **3 29**)
20. C   (80 14 32 69 65 17 35 54 50 20 **38 39**)
21. A   (15 22 25 32 35 42 45 **52 55**)
22. D   (96 96 11 75 75 14 54 **54 17**)
23. C   (27 42 57 72 87 **102 117**)
24. E   (6 7 21 10 11 26 15 16 31)

#	A	B	C	D	E
1.	A	B	C	●	E
2.	●	B	C	D	E
3.	A	B	C	D	E
4.	A	B	●	D	E
5.	A	●	C	D	E
6.	A	B	C	D	●
7.	●	B	C	D	E
8.	A	B	C	D	E
9.	A	B	C	D	E
10.	A	B	C	D	E
11.	A	B	C	●	E
12.	A	B	C	D	E
13.	A	B	C	D	E
14.	A	B	●	D	E
15.	A	B	C	D	E
16.	A	B	C	D	E
17.	A	●	C	D	E
18.	A	B	C	D	E
19.	A	B	C	D	E
20.	A	●	C	D	E
21.	A	B	C	D	E
22.	A	B	C	D	E
23.	A	B	C	D	E
24.	A	B	C	D	E
25.	A	B	C	D	E
26.	A	B	C	D	E
27.	A	B	C	D	E
28.	A	B	C	D	E
29.	A	B	C	D	E
30.	A	B	C	●	E
31.	A	B	C	D	E
32.	A	B	C	D	E
33.	A	B	C	D	E
34.	●	B	C	D	E
35.	A	B	C	D	●
36.	A	B	C	D	●
37.	A	B	C	●	E
38.	A	●	C	D	E
39.	A	B	C	D	E
40.	A	B	C	D	E
41.	A	B	C	●	E
42.	A	B	●	D	E
43.	A	B	C	D	E
44.	A	B	C	D	E
45.	A	●	C	D	E
46.	A	B	C	D	E
47.	A	B	C	D	E
48.	A	B	C	D	E
49.	A	B	C	D	E
50.	A	B	C	D	E
51.	A	B	C	D	E
52.	A	B	C	D	E
53.	A	B	C	D	E
54.	A	B	C	D	E
55.	A	B	C	D	E
56.	A	B	●	D	E
57.	A	B	C	D	E
58.	A	B	C	D	●
59.	A	B	C	D	E
60.	A	B	C	D	E
61.	A	B	C	D	●
62.	A	B	C	D	E
63.	A	B	C	D	E
64.	A	B	●	D	E
65.	A	B	C	D	E
66.	A	B	C	D	E
67.	A	B	C	D	E
68.	A	B	C	●	E
69.	A	B	C	D	E
70.	A	B	C	D	E
71.	A	B	C	●	E
72.	A	B	C	D	●
73.	A	B	C	D	●
74.	A	B	C	D	E
75.	A	B	C	D	E
76.	A	B	C	D	E
77.	A	B	C	D	E
78.	A	B	C	D	E
79.	A	B	●	D	E
80.	A	B	C	D	E
81.	A	B	C	D	E
82.	A	B	C	D	E
83.	●	B	C	D	E
84.	A	B	C	D	E
85.	●	B	C	D	E
86.	A	B	C	D	E
87.	A	B	C	D	E
88.	A	B	C	D	E

1. 42C
2. 11D
3. 35E
4. 73E, 37D
5. 68D, 85A
6. 30D
7. 36E, 83A
8. 79C
9. 38B
10. 7A, 2A
11. 34A
12. 58E
13. 71D, 61E
14. 72E, 64C
15. 45B
16. 1D
17. 17B
18. 4C
19. 20B
20. 56C
21. 41D
22. 14C
23. 5B
24. 6E

Chapter 7: Exam 473 Basics

The following section will help you prepare for Battery Exam 473 (If there is a high need for City carriers, this exam is called the 473-C exam). This is the test required for most entry level positions, including city carrier, distribution and processing positions.   Like Exam 460, Exam 473 consists of several different sections. These sections are Address Comparison, Forms Completion, Coding, Memory and a Personal Characteristics and Experience Inventory.   As in chapter 4, we will discuss each of the individual sections, provide sample questions and then, in chapter 8, we will provide full-length practice exams. We will not be cover the Personal Characteristics and Experience Inventory in the full-length exams, our reasons for not covering it multiple times will become clear as you go through these study materials.

Address Comparison

The Address Comparison section of Exam 473 will seem familiar to those of you who have already gone through the previous chapters of this book. However, for this exam you are not asked to simply determine if the addresses are different, but also to identify in what way the addresses differ. In this section of the exam, you are asked to compare 60 sets of addresses. You will be given 11 minutes to answer as many questions as possible. This is a test of your ability to compare two lists quickly and accurately. You will be shown a correct list that consists of addresses and ZIP codes. A list to be checked will appear next to the correct list. The list to be checked also contains addresses and ZIP codes. The list to be checked should be identical to the correct List. Your task is to compare the information in each row of the list to be checked with the correct list. Decide if there are no errors, an error in the address only, and error in the ZIP code only or an error in both the address and the ZIP code.

This section is scored based on the number of items that you answer correctly minus one-third of the number of items that you answer incorrectly. Your score depends on how many items you can accurately compare in the time allowed. You may not be able to finish all of the items before time runs out, but you should do your best to finish as many as you can as accurately as possible. There is a penalty for guessing on this part of the test. It will NOT be to your advantage to guess randomly.

Here are some tips on how to reduce errors:

- **Work as quickly and accurately as possible.** Although you are not expected to answer all items in the time allowed, do your best and answer as many as you can.
- **Identify the correct and incorrect information** in the address and/or ZIP code quickly (as expected on the job.). The speed comes from lots of practice!
- **Do not lose your place.** As you quickly answer items, it can be easy to lose your place. Consider holding your pencil on the Answer Grid directly on the item number being answered. After answering an item, move your pencil to the next number. Use your other index finger to keep track of items as they are answered.
- **Concentrate on the item you are working on.** Do not allow your eyes to wander around the page. Remain focused on one item at a time. Periodically, check to see that you are working on the same item that you are marking on your Answer Grid.

Directions:

If the combination of street address and ZIP codes are identical, select A for NO ERRORS. If the street addresses for both choices differ, but the ZIP codes are identical, mark B for STREET ADDRESS ONLY on your Answer Grid. If the street addresses are identical, but there is a difference in the ZIP code, mark C for ZIP CODE ONLY on your Answer Grid. And finally, if there are differences in both the street address and the ZIP code, you should mark D for BOTH.

Below is an abbreviated sample exercise so that you can practice before you begin timing yourself.

Sample Exercise - Address Comparison

Answer Key:
A) No Errors
B) Street Address Only
C) ZIP Code Only
D) Both

	Correct Addresses		Addresses to be Corrected	
	Address	**ZIP Code**	**Address**	**ZIP Code**
1.	154 E. 9th St. Seattle, WA	98755	154 E. 9th St. Seattle, WA	98755
2.	2061 S. Hwy 178 Cedar Falls, IA	50067	2061 S. Hwy 178 Cedar Falls, IA	50076
3.	16-A Sunset Blvd Phoenix, AZ	85037-4111	16-A Sunset Blvd Phoenix, AR	85037-4111
4.	20531 E. Cascade Trail Bend, OR	95112-3112	20531 E. Cascade Trail Bend, OR	95113-2112
5.	PO Box 9556 Rutland, VA	08563	PO Box 9556 Routland, VA	08563
6.	9716 West End Terrace Knoxville, TN	36152	9716 West End Terrace Knoxville, TN	36152
7.	7109 Deed St. Reno, NE	87412	7109 Deed St. Reno, NV	87422
8.	2525 Riverdale Rd. Nashua, NH	03060	2225 Riverdale Rd. Nashua, NH	03060
9.	1 Ocean Way Philadelphia, PA	19019	1 Ocean Way Philadelphia, PA	19019
10.	4 Vane Hwy Hollywood, CA	90068	4 Vein Hwy Hollywood, CA	90868
11.	4836 Capital St. Montpelier, VT	05603	4836 Capitol St. Montpelier, VT	05608
12.	6464 Springdale Dr. Veto, CA	99652	6464 Springdale Dr. Vito, CA	99652
13.	1717 W. 1st St. Little Bend, CO	54216	1717 W. 1st St. Little Bend, CO	54216
14.	PO Box 554782 Detroit, MI	48206	PO Box 554782 Detroit, MI	48206
15.	6 Gillman St. Rapid City, SD	57703	6 Giulman St. Rapid City, SD	57703
16.	258 Smith St. Boxborough, MA	01719	268 Smith St. Boxborough, MA	81719
17.	9001 Gliding Rd Bronx, NY	10452	9011 Gilding Rd Bronx, NY	10452
18.	555 Sweet Lane Clearwater, FL	33762	555 Sweet Lane Clearwater, FL	33762
19.	700 Oakhurst Street Little Rock, AR	72207	706 Oakhurst Street Little Rock, AR	72287
20.	1234 Spalding Dr. Norcross, GA	30095	1325 Spalding Dr. Norcross, GA	30095

Answer Grid – Sample Exercise – Address Comparison

1. Ⓐ Ⓑ Ⓒ Ⓓ
2. Ⓐ Ⓑ Ⓒ Ⓓ
3. Ⓐ Ⓑ Ⓒ Ⓓ
4. Ⓐ Ⓑ Ⓒ Ⓓ
5. Ⓐ Ⓑ Ⓒ Ⓓ
6. Ⓐ Ⓑ Ⓒ Ⓓ
7. Ⓐ Ⓑ Ⓒ Ⓓ
8. Ⓐ Ⓑ Ⓒ Ⓓ
9. Ⓐ Ⓑ Ⓒ Ⓓ
10. Ⓐ Ⓑ Ⓒ Ⓓ
11. Ⓐ Ⓑ Ⓒ Ⓓ
12. Ⓐ Ⓑ Ⓒ Ⓓ
13. Ⓐ Ⓑ Ⓒ Ⓓ
14. Ⓐ Ⓑ Ⓒ Ⓓ
15. Ⓐ Ⓑ Ⓒ Ⓓ
16. Ⓐ Ⓑ Ⓒ Ⓓ
17. Ⓐ Ⓑ Ⓒ Ⓓ
18. Ⓐ Ⓑ Ⓒ Ⓓ
19. Ⓐ Ⓑ Ⓒ Ⓓ
20. Ⓐ Ⓑ Ⓒ Ⓓ

Correct Answers – Sample Exercise

1. A
2. C
3. B
4. C
5. B
6. A
7. D
8. B
9. A
10. D
11. D
12. B
13. A
14. A
15. B
16. D
17. B
18. A
19. D
20. B

How many did you get right?

10 or more?	Awesome
5-10?	Still Good
1-5?	You should practice a bit more

As you can see, subtle differences in either the numbers or the spelling can be hard to catch at first glance. Most people, for one reason or another, can spot transposed numbers in either the ZIP code or the street address. However, applicants frequently overlook differences in addresses that sound the same. Be sure to pay close attention to addresses of this nature before marking your Answer Grid. Exercising caution here will pay off in terms of a higher test score.

You may have noticed, too, that while working on the sample exercises a straightedge or ruler could have helped reduce confusion. Unfortunately, such aids are not allowed in the examination. However, you are allowed two pencils, one of which can serve as a crude straightedge, if necessary.
One other helpful trick to reduce confusion while comparing a set of addresses is to place your index finger on one column of addresses and your little finger on the other column. As you proceed with each pair, move your fingers in unison down the page. This does essentially the same thing as a straightedge. Using this method makes it substantially easier to focus your attention on just the addresses you are comparing.

More practice exercises are provided on the following pages. Photocopy or tear the Answer Grid out of the book for your convenience in marking answers. To help you get a better idea of how the actual exam is conducted, you could use a kitchen timer or have someone time you for the allotted eleven minutes as you do this exercise. If you continue after the time has expired, you'll lose a true sense of what will be required of you on the actual exam, and you will only be cheating yourself.

On the following pages you will find two full-length address comparison exercises. These exercises are timed. You need either to have someone time you or to set your own timer to eleven minutes. Do not begin the exercise until your timer has begun. If the pair of addresses is alike, darken the circle A. If just the address is different, darken the circle B. If just the ZIP code is different, darken the circle C. If both the address and ZIP code are different, darken the circle D. Be sure to erase all your mistakes completely. If you are unsure, but can narrow your choices, you may take a guess to help increase your score. Keep in mind that wrong answers could count against right answers. As this section is timed, you should make the accurate decision quickly and mark the correct bubble neatly. Be sure to have some No. 2 pencils on hand. Once you've started your timer, you cannot stop it.

As with the Exam 460 Answer Grids, the Answer Grid immediately follows the questions and is blank on the back. This is done so that you may remove the Answer Grid and make copies so you can practice this exam over and over if needed. All of the practice exam Answer Grids will be done this way so that the book will still be complete with no pages of information missing.

The first of two full-length practice exercises is found on the next page. When you have finished taking the first practice exam, score yourself carefully and honestly. Once you have obtained your score, go back over your incorrect answers to better understand the subtleties of their differences.

Address Comparison – Full-length Practice #1

A) No Errors
B) Street Address Only

C) ZIP Code Only
D) Both

	Correct Addresses		Addresses to be Corrected	
	Address	**ZIP Code**	**Address**	**ZIP Code**
1.	12 Thomas Jefferson Pl. Worchester, MA	01499	12 Thomas Jefferson Pl. Worchester, MA	01489
2.	69665 Atlantic Ocean Dr. Boca Raton, FL	33428	69665 Atlantic Ocean Dr. Boca Raton, FL	33428
3.	1014 Herbert Pl. Ludlow, CA	98721	1014 Herbert Pl. Ludlow, CA	98721
4.	PO Box 10101 Glenview Station, NY	87246	PO Box 10111 Glenview Station, NY	87446
5.	1216 West End St. Finally, MI	56489	1216 West End St. Fenlly, MI	56489
6.	1 Johns Financial Blvd. Pittsburgh, PA	45621	1 Johns Financial Blvd. Pittsburgh, PA	45621
7.	8965 Ridge Rd Brentwood, TN	37219	8965 Ridge Rd Brentwood, TN	37219
8.	7293 Brittany Lane Charlotte, NC	28202	7298 Brittany Lane Charlotte, NC	26202
9.	576 Oak Hill Rd Indianapolis, IN	46108	576 Oak Hill Rd Indianapolis, IN	46188
10.	9000 Jiffy Lane Gardner, ME	04345	9000 Jiffy Lane Gardner, ME	04345
11.	187 Parker Hill Rd. Harvard, MA	01495	187 Parker Hill Rd. Harvard, MA	01495
12.	3001 Carver Way Fairland, OK	46456	3001 Carver Way Fairland, OK	45465
13.	20304 Government Pl. Braxton, IA	50042	20304 Government Pl. Broxton, IA	50642
14.	PO Box 457489 Myrtle Beach, SC	29587	PO Box 457499 Myrtle Beach, SC	29587
15.	558 Gilligan Lane Portland, OR	97217	558 Gilligan Lane Portland, OR	97217
16.	101 Park Place Lexington, KY	40512	11 Park Place Lexington, KY	40612
17.	PO Box 5147 Tempe, AZ	85285	PO Box 5147 Tampa, AZ	85285
18.	756 John Wayne Lane San Francisco, CA	94107	756 John Wayne Lane San Francisco, CA	94107
19.	999 Quincy St Owensville, AL	35427	888 Quincy St Owensville, AL	35427
20.	918 Truvoy Lane Campbell, CA	95008	918 Truvay Lane Campbell, CA	95018

21.	200 Central Ave. Diamond Rock Park, MS	39533		200 Central Ave. Diamond Rock Park, MA	39533
22.	42 Wilkinson Way Beach, VA	23832		42 Wilkinson Way Beach, VA	23832
23.	77 Lincoln Park Blvd. Little Rock, AR	72222		77 Lincoln Park Blvd. Little Rock, AR	76222
24.	2929 Hammer Rd. Omaha, NE	68154		2828 Hammer Rd. Omaha, NE	66154
25.	14 Brockton St. Zephyrhills, FL	33539		14 Brockton St. Zephyrhills, FL	33539
26.	123 1st Street Minneapolis, MN	55401		123 1st Street Minneapolis, MN	55411
27.	800 King Street Macon, GA	31201-1267		800 Kong Street Macon, GA	31201-1267
28.	1919 Jackson Ave. Sun Park, CA	93966		1919 Jackson Ave. Sun Park, CA	93966
29.	214 Macy Ave. Brighton, TX	79411		214 Macy Ave. New Brighton, TX	79911
30.	4259 Mahoney Ct. Charlottesville, VA	22902-2299		4259 Mahoney Ln. Charlottesville, VA	22902-0299
31.	7328 Woodruff Cir. Seattle, WA	98104		7823 Woodruff Cir Seattle, WA	98104
32.	1425 Rainbow Rd. Wichita, KS	67271-4257		1425 Rainbow Curve Wichita, KS	67271-4257
33.	3125 Ebel Terrace Barrow, AK	72999-3794		3125 Ebel Terrace Barrow, AK	72999-3749
34.	14 Heather Cir. #315 Portland, OR	97204-3195		14 Heather Cir. #315 Portland, OR	97204-3195
35.	27145 49th Ave. S. Springfield, IL	62797		27145 49th Ave. S. Springfield, IL	62797
36.	10 Wentworth Way Little Rock, AR	72259		10 Wentworth Way Little Rock, AR	72259
37.	5549 E. Riverwalk Ln. Meridian, MS	39302-9942		5549 E. Riverwalk Ln. Meridian, MS	39320-9942
38.	65 Stilfield Pkwy. Portland, ME	04102		65 Silfield Pkwy. Parker, ME	04101
39.	155 42nd St. New York, NY	10005-1267		155 52nd St. New York, NY	10005-1267
40.	12000 Myers Road Fort Myers, FL	33906-0001		12000 Myers Rd Fort Myers, FL	33906-0001
41.	PO Box 41 Cooperstown, MA	01911		PO Box 14 Cooperstown, MA	01911
42.	888 79th Street Detroit, MI	48203-5341		666 79th Street Detroit, MI	48203-5341
43.	9972 Harris Dr. Lakeland, FL	33879-1199		9972 Harris Dr. Lakeland, FL	33879-0099
44.	1000 Woodley Place Newcastle, PA	15504		1000 Woodland Place Newcastle, PA	15504
45.	1425 Chain Bridge Rd. Eustis, KS	67248-0001		1425 Chain Bridge Dr. Eustis, KS	67248-0001
46.	9679 Angoff Terrace Centerdale, RI	02908-3494		9679 Angoff Terrace Centerdale, RI	02909-3794
47.	14 Fraternity Cir. Kingston, ME	05145-1222		14 Fraternity Cir. Kingston, ME	05145-1223
48.	55541 First Ave. S. Springfield, MO	65863		55541 Front Ave. S. Springfield, MO	65863

49.	54 Wellesley Ave. Middleton, CA	95436	54 Wellesley Ave. Middletown, CA	95436
50.	1095 Ave. of the Americas New York, NY	10004-4872	1095 Ave. of the Americas New York, NY	10004-4872
51.	PO Box 9811 New Brunswick, ME	04873	PO Box 91811 New Brunswick, ME	04783
52.	22 Liberty St. Meriden, CT	06450	22 Liberty St. Meriden, CT	06450
53.	266 Main St. Cumberland, ME	04021-9754	267 Main St. Cumberland, ME	04021-9754
54.	1530 Harden St. Anderson, SC	29201	1530 Harden St. Anderson, SC	29201
55.	1400 Kettering Tower Dayton, OH	45423	1400 Ketering Tower Dayton, OH	45423
56.	340 Ocean Dr. Juno Beach, FL	33408	340 Ocean Dr. Juno Beach, FL	33408
57.	263 Tompkins Ave. Brooklyn, NY	11221	263 Tompkins Ave. Brookline, NY	11121
58.	282 Avenue A Warren, MI	48092	1282 Avenue A Warren, MI	48092
59.	9240 West Ironwood Dr. Lisle, IL	60532	9240 West Ironwood Dr. Lisle, IL	60532
60.	675 Heritage Drive Durant, MS	39063	675 Heritage Drive Durant, MS	39063

Answer Grid – Address Comparison – Full-length Practice #1

(You will have 11 minutes to complete this section.)

1. Ⓐ Ⓑ Ⓒ Ⓓ
2. Ⓐ Ⓑ Ⓒ Ⓓ
3. Ⓐ Ⓑ Ⓒ Ⓓ
4. Ⓐ Ⓑ Ⓒ Ⓓ
5. Ⓐ Ⓑ Ⓒ Ⓓ
6. Ⓐ Ⓑ Ⓒ Ⓓ
7. Ⓐ Ⓑ Ⓒ Ⓓ
8. Ⓐ Ⓑ Ⓒ Ⓓ
9. Ⓐ Ⓑ Ⓒ Ⓓ
10. Ⓐ Ⓑ Ⓒ Ⓓ
11. Ⓐ Ⓑ Ⓒ Ⓓ
12. Ⓐ Ⓑ Ⓒ Ⓓ
13. Ⓐ Ⓑ Ⓒ Ⓓ
14. Ⓐ Ⓑ Ⓒ Ⓓ
15. Ⓐ Ⓑ Ⓒ Ⓓ
16. Ⓐ Ⓑ Ⓒ Ⓓ
17. Ⓐ Ⓑ Ⓒ Ⓓ
18. Ⓐ Ⓑ Ⓒ Ⓓ
19. Ⓐ Ⓑ Ⓒ Ⓓ
20. Ⓐ Ⓑ Ⓒ Ⓓ
21. Ⓐ Ⓑ Ⓒ Ⓓ
22. Ⓐ Ⓑ Ⓒ Ⓓ
23. Ⓐ Ⓑ Ⓒ Ⓓ
24. Ⓐ Ⓑ Ⓒ Ⓓ
25. Ⓐ Ⓑ Ⓒ Ⓓ
26. Ⓐ Ⓑ Ⓒ Ⓓ
27. Ⓐ Ⓑ Ⓒ Ⓓ
28. Ⓐ Ⓑ Ⓒ Ⓓ
29. Ⓐ Ⓑ Ⓒ Ⓓ
30. Ⓐ Ⓑ Ⓒ Ⓓ
31. Ⓐ Ⓑ Ⓒ Ⓓ
32. Ⓐ Ⓑ Ⓒ Ⓓ
33. Ⓐ Ⓑ Ⓒ Ⓓ

34. Ⓐ Ⓑ Ⓒ Ⓓ
35. Ⓐ Ⓑ Ⓒ Ⓓ
36. Ⓐ Ⓑ Ⓒ Ⓓ
37. Ⓐ Ⓑ Ⓒ Ⓓ
38. Ⓐ Ⓑ Ⓒ Ⓓ
39. Ⓐ Ⓑ Ⓒ Ⓓ
40. Ⓐ Ⓑ Ⓒ Ⓓ
41. Ⓐ Ⓑ Ⓒ Ⓓ
42. Ⓐ Ⓑ Ⓒ Ⓓ
43. Ⓐ Ⓑ Ⓒ Ⓓ
44. Ⓐ Ⓑ Ⓒ Ⓓ
45. Ⓐ Ⓑ Ⓒ Ⓓ
46. Ⓐ Ⓑ Ⓒ Ⓓ
47. Ⓐ Ⓑ Ⓒ Ⓓ
48. Ⓐ Ⓑ Ⓒ Ⓓ
49. Ⓐ Ⓑ Ⓒ Ⓓ
50. Ⓐ Ⓑ Ⓒ Ⓓ
51. Ⓐ Ⓑ Ⓒ Ⓓ
52. Ⓐ Ⓑ Ⓒ Ⓓ
53. Ⓐ Ⓑ Ⓒ Ⓓ
54. Ⓐ Ⓑ Ⓒ Ⓓ
55. Ⓐ Ⓑ Ⓒ Ⓓ
56. Ⓐ Ⓑ Ⓒ Ⓓ
57. Ⓐ Ⓑ Ⓒ Ⓓ
58. Ⓐ Ⓑ Ⓒ Ⓓ
59. Ⓐ Ⓑ Ⓒ Ⓓ
60. Ⓐ Ⓑ Ⓒ Ⓓ

Notes:

210

Correct Answers – Address Comparison – Full-length Practice #1

1.	C	31.	B
2.	A	32.	B
3.	A	33.	C
4.	D	34.	A
5.	B	35.	A
6.	A	36.	A
7.	A	37.	C
8.	D	38.	D
9.	C	39.	B
10.	A	40.	B
11.	A	41.	B
12.	C	42.	B
13.	D	43.	C
14.	B	44.	B
15.	A	45.	B
16.	D	46.	C
17.	B	47.	C
18.	A	48.	B
19.	B	49.	B
20.	D	50.	A
21.	B	51.	D
22.	A	52.	A
23.	C	53.	B
24.	D	54.	A
25.	A	55.	B
26.	C	56.	A
27.	B	57.	D
28.	A	58.	B
29.	D	59.	A
30.	D	60.	A

How many did you get right?

10 or more?   **Awesome**
5-10?   **Still Good**
1-5?   **You should practice a bit more**

Address Comparison – Full-length Practice # 2

Answer Key:

A) No Errors   C) ZIP Code Only
B) Street Address Only   D) Both

	Correct Address		Address to be Corrected	
	Address	**ZIP Code**	**Address**	**ZIP Code**
1.	1989 Green Leaf Dr. Lynnwood, WA	98037	989 Green Leaf Dr. Lynnwood, WA	98037
2.	6101 N. Sheridan Road E. Chicago, IL	60660	6101 N. Sheridan Road E. Chicago, IL	60660
3.	1642 Days Run Rd. Apt A Moreno Valley, CA	92553	1642 Days Run Rd. Apt A1 Moreno Valley, CA	92553
4.	6016 Portico Dr. Silver Springs, FL	10904	6016 Portico Dr. Silver Springs, FL	10904
5.	16 Wolcott Ave Old Bridge, NJ	08857	16 Wolcott Ave Old Bridge, NJ	08857
6.	282 Avenue A Warren, MI	48092	1282 Avenue A Warren, MI	48092
7.	8104 Bangor Dr. Owenton, KY	40359	8104 Bangor Dr. Owenston, KY	40359
8.	4374 Winters Chapel Road Sandy, UT	84090	4374 Winters Chapel Road Sandy, UT	84090
9.	1035 Gaslight Ct. Woonsocket, RI	02895	1035 Gaslight Ct. Woonsocket, RI	02895
10.	975 Heritage Drive Durant, MS	39063	675 Heritage Drive Durant, MS	39063
11.	1411 Old Cottondale Road Broomfield, CO	80020	1411 Old Cottondale Road Broomfield, CO	80028
12.	PO Box 121 Wailuku, HI	96793	PO Box 1212 Wailuku, HI	96793
13.	806 French Street Burden, WA	98146	806 French Street Darien, WA	98146
14.	56 Kenway Dr. Hamilton, OH	45015	156 Kenway Dr. Hamilton, OH	25015
15.	2721 W. 12th St. Rigby, ID	83442	2721 W. 12th St. Rigby, ID	83442
16.	PO Box 5350 Newton Grove, NC	28366	PO Box 5350 Newton Grove, NC	28366
17.	2475 Walker Road Galveston, TX	77550	2457 Walken Rd Galveston, TX	77550
18.	5262 Horizon Drive Mount Juliet, TN	37122	5262 Horizon Drive Mount Juliet, TN	37122
19.	1265 Yates St. Mankato, MN	56001	1265 Yates St. Mankato, MN	56881
20.	1414 White Plains Rd. Columbus, OH	43185	1441 White Plains Rd. Columbus, OH	43185

21.	18-C Black Hawk Ct. Statesville, NC	28561		18-C Black Hawk Ct. Statesville, NH	28561
22.	8087 Lynwood Dr. Henderson, NV	89701-1611		8087 Lynwood Dr. Henderson, NV	89701-1611
23.	378 Abbeyville Blvd Buffalo, NY	14152-1378		378 Abbotsville Blvd Buffalo, NY	14152-1373
24.	A-149 Birch Pkwy Nashville, TN	38714		A-149 Birch Pkwy Nashville, KY	38741
25.	10371 Bramblebrook Way Fort Worth, TX	71625-4038		10371 Bramblebrook Place Fort Worth, TX	71625-4038
26.	5751 Green Willow Trail Leesburg, VA	20079		5751 Green Willow Trail Leesburg, VA	20709
27.	Box 162, State Hwy 17 Plano, TX	71649		Box 162, State Rt. 17 Plano, TX	71694
28.	1313 Blacksmith Ln Florence, SC	29057-3500		1313 Blacksmith Ln Florence, SC	29056-3500
29.	12 Deerfield Ave Woodstock, OH	44497		12 Deerfield Ave Woodstock, OH	44497
30.	9307 Montrose Dr. Newark, NJ	09712-0571		9307 Montrose Dr. Newark, NE	09217-0571
31.	902 Eaglemont Place Rochester, NY	16497-5608		902 Eaglemont Place Rothchester, NY	16497-5608
32.	D-705 Ferguson Cr Farmington, NM	84071		D-705 Ferguson Cr Farmington, NM	80471
33.	1616 Havencrest Rd. Beaverton, OR	90717		1616 Havencrest Rd Beaverton, OR	91707
34.	50 Eldridge Ln Abingdon, VA	24412		50 Eldridge Ln Abington, VA	24412
35.	30117 Grandview Pl. Greenwich, CT	08157-7997		30117 Grandview Pl Greenwich, Ct	08157-7997
36.	4072 Colony St. Apt 101 San Mateo, CA	95407-0302		4027 Colony St. Apt 101 San Mateo, CA	95407-0302
37.	91 Ericson Way Bella Vista, AR	77214		91 Erikson Way Bella Vista, AR	77214
38.	2000 London Circle Tuscaloosa, AL	34571		2000 London Circle Tuscaloosa, AL	34571-7110
39.	4949 S. Fairmont Dr. Wichita, KS	67018-1300		4949 S. Fairmont Ave. Wichita, KS	67018-3100
40.	700-L Clare St. Indianapolis, IN	42671-1584		700-L S. Cleer St. Indianapolis, IN	42671-1584
41.	14 Cedar Park Dr. Valdosta, GA	37159		14 Cedar Park Dr. Valdosta, GA	37158
42.	13599 Burton Ln Chicago, IL	60069-1409		13995 Burton Ln Chicago, IL	60097-1409
43.	3060 Stanly Ct. Idaho Falls, ID	38715		3060 Stanley Ct. Idaho Falls, ID	38715
44.	12792 Central Ave. Baltimore, MD	22257-6789		12792 Central Ave. Baltimore, MD	20257-6789
45.	7-B Sanctuary Ln Atlanta, GA	30511-7102		708 Sanctuary Ln Atlanta, GA	30511-7102
46.	18300 NW 8th Ave Apt C. Longmont, CO	81023-3001		381800 NW 8th Ave Apt C Longmont, CO	81023-3001
47.	4710 W. Osego Rd Commerce, GA	39157		4710 W Oswego Rd Commerce, GA	39157
48.	10520 Chrysopolis Ln Walnut Creek, CA	90571		10250 Crysopolis Ln Walnut Creek, CA	90571

49.	D-4091 Valencia Pkwy Delray Beach FL	37215	D-4091 Valencia Pkwy Delray Beach FL	37125
50.	697 Gardenia Lane Oak Park, IL	60952-4017	697 Gardenia Lane Oak Park, IL	60952-4017
51.	168-R Rivermist Dr. Palm Desert, CA	91215	168-R Rivermist Dr. Palm Desert, CA	91215
52.	911 Rio Grand Ave Hendersonville, NC	25910	911 Rio Grande Ave Hendersonville, NC	29510
53.	189-D NE Industrial Rd Atlantic City, NJ	04801	198-D SE Industrial Rd Atlantic City, NJ	04801
54.	1219 SW Manchester Ave Staten Island, NY	13051-5211	1219 SW Manchester Ave Staten Island, NY	13051-5211
55.	14701 S. Cypress Dr Plainfield, NY	10001-1472	14701 S. Cypress Dr Plainfield, NY	10001-1472
56.	1850 Princeton Blvd. Laramie, WY	87511	1850 Princeton Blvd. Laramie, WY	87511
57.	13 S. Madison Ave. La Crosse, WI	55641	13 S. Madison Ave. La Crosse, WI	55641
58.	A-417 Millbrook Rd Richmond, VA	22398	A-417 Millbrook Rd Richmond, VA	22398
59.	170 Panterra Way San Marcos, CA	94015-6711	170 Panterra Way San Marcos, CA	94015-6711
60.	100 Raceway Blvd. Talledega, AL	34475	101 Racepark Dr. Talledega, AL	34475

Answer Grid – Address Comparison – Full-length Practice #2

(You will have 11 minutes to complete this section.)

1. Ⓐ Ⓑ Ⓒ Ⓓ
2. Ⓐ Ⓑ Ⓒ Ⓓ
3. Ⓐ Ⓑ Ⓒ Ⓓ
4. Ⓐ Ⓑ Ⓒ Ⓓ
5. Ⓐ Ⓑ Ⓒ Ⓓ
6. Ⓐ Ⓑ Ⓒ Ⓓ
7. Ⓐ Ⓑ Ⓒ Ⓓ
8. Ⓐ Ⓑ Ⓒ Ⓓ
9. Ⓐ Ⓑ Ⓒ Ⓓ
10. Ⓐ Ⓑ Ⓒ Ⓓ
11. Ⓐ Ⓑ Ⓒ Ⓓ
12. Ⓐ Ⓑ Ⓒ Ⓓ
13. Ⓐ Ⓑ Ⓒ Ⓓ
14. Ⓐ Ⓑ Ⓒ Ⓓ
15. Ⓐ Ⓑ Ⓒ Ⓓ
16. Ⓐ Ⓑ Ⓒ Ⓓ
17. Ⓐ Ⓑ Ⓒ Ⓓ
18. Ⓐ Ⓑ Ⓒ Ⓓ
19. Ⓐ Ⓑ Ⓒ Ⓓ
20. Ⓐ Ⓑ Ⓒ Ⓓ
21. Ⓐ Ⓑ Ⓒ Ⓓ
22. Ⓐ Ⓑ Ⓒ Ⓓ
23. Ⓐ Ⓑ Ⓒ Ⓓ
24. Ⓐ Ⓑ Ⓒ Ⓓ
25. Ⓐ Ⓑ Ⓒ Ⓓ
26. Ⓐ Ⓑ Ⓒ Ⓓ
27. Ⓐ Ⓑ Ⓒ Ⓓ
28. Ⓐ Ⓑ Ⓒ Ⓓ
29. Ⓐ Ⓑ Ⓒ Ⓓ
30. Ⓐ Ⓑ Ⓒ Ⓓ
31. Ⓐ Ⓑ Ⓒ Ⓓ
32. Ⓐ Ⓑ Ⓒ Ⓓ
33. Ⓐ Ⓑ Ⓒ Ⓓ

34. Ⓐ Ⓑ Ⓒ Ⓓ
35. Ⓐ Ⓑ Ⓒ Ⓓ
36. Ⓐ Ⓑ Ⓒ Ⓓ
37. Ⓐ Ⓑ Ⓒ Ⓓ
38. Ⓐ Ⓑ Ⓒ Ⓓ
39. Ⓐ Ⓑ Ⓒ Ⓓ
40. Ⓐ Ⓑ Ⓒ Ⓓ
41. Ⓐ Ⓑ Ⓒ Ⓓ
42. Ⓐ Ⓑ Ⓒ Ⓓ
43. Ⓐ Ⓑ Ⓒ Ⓓ
44. Ⓐ Ⓑ Ⓒ Ⓓ
45. Ⓐ Ⓑ Ⓒ Ⓓ
46. Ⓐ Ⓑ Ⓒ Ⓓ
47. Ⓐ Ⓑ Ⓒ Ⓓ
48. Ⓐ Ⓑ Ⓒ Ⓓ
49. Ⓐ Ⓑ Ⓒ Ⓓ
50. Ⓐ Ⓑ Ⓒ Ⓓ
51. Ⓐ Ⓑ Ⓒ Ⓓ
52. Ⓐ Ⓑ Ⓒ Ⓓ
53. Ⓐ Ⓑ Ⓒ Ⓓ
54. Ⓐ Ⓑ Ⓒ Ⓓ
55. Ⓐ Ⓑ Ⓒ Ⓓ
56. Ⓐ Ⓑ Ⓒ Ⓓ
57. Ⓐ Ⓑ Ⓒ Ⓓ
58. Ⓐ Ⓑ Ⓒ Ⓓ
59. Ⓐ Ⓑ Ⓒ Ⓓ
60. Ⓐ Ⓑ Ⓒ Ⓓ

Notes:

Correct Answers – Address Comparison – Full-length Practice #2

1. B		31. B	
2. A		32. C	
3. B		33. C	
4. A		34. B	
5. A		35. B	
6. B		36. B	
7. B		37. B	
8. A		38. C	
9. A		39. D	
10. B		40. B	
11. C		41. C	
12. B		42. D	
13. B		43. B	
14. D		44. C	
15. A		45. B	
16. A		46. B	
17. B		47. B	
18. A		48. B	
19. C		49. C	
20. B		50. A	
21. B		51. A	
22. A		52. D	
23. D		53. B	
24. D		54. A	
25. B		55. A	
26. C		56. A	
27. D		57. A	
28. C		58. A	
29. A		59. B	
30. D		60. B	

How many did you get right?

10 or more?   **Awesome**
5-10?   **Still Good**
1-5?   **You should practice a bit more**

Forms Completion

This is a test of your ability to identify information needed to complete forms similar to those used by the Postal Service. Most positions with the Postal Service require applicants to fill out forms and accuracy is extremely important. You will be given 15 minutes to answer 30 questions. This section of the exam is scored based on the number of items that you answer correctly. It is generally to your advantage to respond to each item, even if you have to guess.

This part of the exam is really about common sense. You are asked what information should be entered on a form and/or where it should be entered. You look at the form and find the answer. You do not have to memorize or remember anything.

As with any multiple choice exam, the questions can be tricky. Be sure to read over all the answer possibilities before answering the question. That being said, don't let the format of the answers confuse you. For example, you are answering question 4 and you look at the form and find that the correct answer for this question is Box 5a, which is choice C for question 4. At this point you are working with several numbers and letters…5, A, 4 and C…as in Box 5a, question 4, and answer C. If you rush to the answer sheet you may become confused. Are you supposed to be marking 5A, 4C, 5C, or 4A, or what? You are working at maximum speed dealing with what may seem to be eighty million different numbers, letters, boxes, answer choices, dates, ZIP codes, addresses, etc., etc., etc. It's a wonder that you can get your name straight, much less the answer to question 4. The bottom line is that you must mark your answers carefully, making sure that you are marking the proper question number and answer choice (4C), not a box number (5a) that was involved in the question or answer.

Hopefully, as you practice, these hints will help to give you an advantage in answering as many questions as possible in the 15 minutes allowed.

Before you begin answering questions, take a few seconds to glance over the form in question. Although you don't want to memorize the form, being familiar with it will make answering the questions easier.

Sample questions that you can use to practice before you take a timed test follow the form.

Authorization to Hold Mail

NOTE: *Complete and give to your letter carrier or mail to the post office that delivers your mail.*

We can hold your mail for a minimum of **3**, but not for more than **30 days**.

Postmaster: Please hold mail for:

Name(s)

1.

☐ **A.** Please deliver all accumulated mail and resume normal delivery on the ending date shown below.

Address *(Number, street, apt./suite no., city, state, ZIP + 4)*

2.

☐ **B.** I will pick up all accumulated mail when I return and understand that mail delivery will not resume until I do.

Beginning Date	Ending Date *(May only be changed by the customer in writing)*	Customer Signature
3a.	**3b.**	**3c.**

For Post Office Use Only

Date Received	**4a.**		
Clerk	**4b.**	Bin Number	
Carrier	**4c.**	Route Number	

(Complete this section only if customer selected option B)

☐ Accumulated mail has been picked up.	Resume Delivery of Mail *(Date)* **5.**	By

PS Form **8076**, April 2001

1. Where is the address entered on the form on the previous page?

     A. Box 4a
     B. Box 2
     C. Box 4c
     D. Box 1

2. Which of these is a correct entry for Box 3?

     A. Date received
     B. Customer Address
     C. Customer Signature
     D. Carrier's name

3. In which box would 6/7/96 be an appropriate entry?

     A. 3a
     B. 3b and 5
     C. 4a
     D. 3a, 3b, 4a, and 5

Here are the correct answers:

    1.   B, Box 2
    2.   C, Customer Signature
    3.   D, 3a, 3b, 4a, and 5

This section is scored on the number of questions you get correct. There is no penalty, however, for answering incorrectly. The best technique is to answer all the easier questions and then return to the more difficult ones. If you are not sure of a particular answer, work through all the questions and then go back to make an educated guess for the ones you're not sure about. Try to eliminate the answers that are obviously incorrect. Even though incorrect answers do not count against you, it is important to answer all questions in this section.

Forms Completion – Full-length Practice #1

				Note Mail Arrival Date & Time
				4.

Use this form for either First-Class Mail or Priority Mail.

Mailer	Permit Holder's Name and Address and Email Address If Any 1a.	Telephone 1b.	Name and Address of Mailing Agent (If other than permit holder) 2a.	Telephone 2b.	Name and Address of Individual or Organization for Which Mailing Is Prepared (If other than permit holder) 3.

1. Where would the mail arrival date and time go?

        A. Box 1b
        B. Box 2a
        C. Box 2a
        D. Box 4

2. What is a correct entry for Box 1b?

        A. 1716 South Street
        B. 207-555-1212
        C. $3.50
        D. 8:30 pm

3. Where would the telephone number of the mailing agent go?

        A. Box 4
        B. Box 2b
        C. Box 3a
        D. Box 3b

1. Customer Information

Customer Name
1.

Company Name

Address 1
2a.

Address 2

City

State
2b.

ZIP + 4
2c.

2. Product Information

Quantity

Express Mail _____

4.

Global Express Guaranteed _____

Priority Mail _____

Parcel Post _____
(Domestic or International)

Estimated total weight
of all packages _____
(In pounds)

3.

4. What would an appropriate entry in Box 4 be?

    A. 4
    B. Jeff Spencer
    C. 7:00 pm
    D. Green

5. In what box would the estimated total weight of all packages go?

    A. Box 1
    B. Box 2b
    C. Box 3
    D. Box 4

6. Trevor Washington is the customer. Where does his name go?

    A. Box 1
    B. Box 2c
    C. Box 3
    D. Box 4

7. What would an appropriate entry in Box 2c be?

    A. 738-555-1212
    B. Sarah Connor
    C. 145 South Bend Street
    D. 10285-3437

Customer		Postal Service Representative	
Name 1.		Accepted by 9.	
Title 2.		Title	
Company Name 3.		Date 10.	
Address (No., street, apt./ste. no.) 4.			
City, state, ZIP + 4® 5.			
Email Address 6a.			
Telephone (include area code) 6b.			
Signature 7.			
Date 8.			

8. What is an appropriate entry for Box 8?

    A. 6/11/05
    B. Gordon Shumway
    C. 678-555-1212
    D. 344 Main Street

9. Where does the customer's name go?

    A. Box 6a
    B. Box 4
    C. Box 7
    D. Box 1

10. Where does the accepting Postal Service Representative's name go?

    A. Box 1
    B. Box 5
    C. Box 9
    D. Box 10

11. You could put a name in any of the following boxes EXCEPT:

    A. Box 1
    B. Box 3
    C. Box 5
    D. Box 9

12. How would a Postal Service Representative acknowledge receipt of this form?

    A. Sign in Box 9
    B. Drawing a big X on the form
    C. Calling a Postal Service supervisor
    D. There is no way to acknowledge receipt

Publication Title		Publication Number
1.						–				

Issue Frequency	Issue Verified
2.	

Authorization Section	Type of Advertising Authorized	Contact Name and Telephone Number	Date
	☐ General ☐ Pub Only ☐ None	3.	4.

Print Order or Press Run *(Total copies printed)*	
5.	1. Total Copies Mailed 6. _____
	2. Other Distribution _____
	3. Remaining Copies _____
	Total *(1 + 2 + 3)* _____

13. In what box does the Issue Frequency number go?

    A. Box 1
    B. Box 2
    C. Box 5
    D. Box 6

14. "First Class Mail Procedures" would be an appropriate entry in which box?

    A. Box 6
    B. Box 3
    C. Box 1
    D. Box 5

15. Where would you indicate that Philip Marlowe is the contact person?

    A. Box 3
    B. Box 4
    C. Box 5
    D. Box 6

16. The total number of copies mailed was 7,000. Where does this number go?

    A. Box 3
    B. Box 4
    C. Box 5
    D. Box 6

17. What would be an appropriate entry in Box 4?

    A. November 26, 2005
    B. Julio Velasquez
    C. 93849-0394
    D. Bi-monthly

Address		Adhesive Stamp ☐	Postage Meter Stamp ☐	Other ☐

☐ Handwritten

☐ Typewritten   1.

or

☐ Other (Describe)

(Return Address)

Name _____ 2a.

Street and Number _____ 2b.

Post Office _____ 2c.

State and ZIP Code _____ 2d.

I deposit herewith $ ___ 3. ___ to pay for expenses incurred for necessary telegrams, postage, etc.

Signature of Applicant	Applicant's Address	Telephone No.
4.	5.	6.

Application Received By (Name of employee)	Hour Received		Date Received
7.	8.	A.M. P.M.	9.

Telephoned To	Copies To	Returned By (Name of employee)
10.	11.	12.

18. Where does the applicant's address go?

A. Box 3
B. Box 4
C. Box 5
D. Box 6

19. Numbers would be part of a correct response in the following boxes EXCEPT:

A. Box 6
B. Box 8
C. Box 9
D. Box 12

20. The application was received by Declan MacManus. Where would this name go?

A. Box 2a
B. Box 7
C. Box 11
D. Box 12

21. Choose an appropriate entry for Box 3:

A. Daniel Stephen
B. $42.40
C. 432-555-1212
D. 8:00 am

22. Where would you indicate that the address was hand-written?

A. Box 1
B. Box 5
C. Box 9
D. Box 11

23. Where would the signature of the applicant go?

    A. Box 4
    B. Box 5
    C. Box 7
    D. Box 12

24. This application was received at 9:43 am. Where should this be noted?

    A. Box 3
    B. Box 5
    C. Box 8
    D. Box 9

25. Copies of this application need to go to John Winston. Where would this be noted?

    A. Box 2a
    B. Box 8
    C. Box 11
    D. Box 12

Complainant Information		
Your Name **1.**	SSN* **2.**	Year of Birth* **3.**
Address **4.**		
City **5.**	State **6.** ZIP Code **7.**	Country **8.**
Home Phone No. *(Include Area Code)* **9.**	Work Phone No. *(Include Area Code)* **10.**	E-Mail **11.**

26. Where would the Social Security Number go?

    A. Box 1
    B. Box 2
    C. Box 3
    D. Box 4

27. Misty Sullivan is filling out this form. Where does her name go?

    A. Box 1
    B. Box 6
    C. Box 8
    D. Box 11

28. What must you include in Box 9 and Box 10?

    A. First name
    B. Contact time
    C. ZIP code
    D. Area code

29. Numbers would be part of a correct response in the following boxes EXCEPT

    A. Box 2
    B. Box 3
    C. Box 6
    D. Box 7

30. The email address is xyz@email.com. Where is this noted?

        A. Box 2
        B. Box 3
        C. Box 10
        D. Box 11

Answer Grid – Forms Completion – Full-length Practice #1

(You have 15 minutes to complete this section.)

1. Ⓐ Ⓑ Ⓒ Ⓓ
2. Ⓐ Ⓑ Ⓒ Ⓓ
3. Ⓐ Ⓑ Ⓒ Ⓓ
4. Ⓐ Ⓑ Ⓒ Ⓓ
5. Ⓐ Ⓑ Ⓒ Ⓓ
6. Ⓐ Ⓑ Ⓒ Ⓓ
7. Ⓐ Ⓑ Ⓒ Ⓓ
8. Ⓐ Ⓑ Ⓒ Ⓓ
9. Ⓐ Ⓑ Ⓒ Ⓓ
10. Ⓐ Ⓑ Ⓒ Ⓓ
11. Ⓐ Ⓑ Ⓒ Ⓓ
12. Ⓐ Ⓑ Ⓒ Ⓓ
13. Ⓐ Ⓑ Ⓒ Ⓓ
14. Ⓐ Ⓑ Ⓒ Ⓓ
15. Ⓐ Ⓑ Ⓒ Ⓓ
16. Ⓐ Ⓑ Ⓒ Ⓓ
17. Ⓐ Ⓑ Ⓒ Ⓓ
18. Ⓐ Ⓑ Ⓒ Ⓓ
19. Ⓐ Ⓑ Ⓒ Ⓓ
20. Ⓐ Ⓑ Ⓒ Ⓓ
21. Ⓐ Ⓑ Ⓒ Ⓓ
22. Ⓐ Ⓑ Ⓒ Ⓓ
23. Ⓐ Ⓑ Ⓒ Ⓓ
24. Ⓐ Ⓑ Ⓒ Ⓓ
25. Ⓐ Ⓑ Ⓒ Ⓓ
26. Ⓐ Ⓑ Ⓒ Ⓓ
27. Ⓐ Ⓑ Ⓒ Ⓓ
28. Ⓐ Ⓑ Ⓒ Ⓓ
29. Ⓐ Ⓑ Ⓒ Ⓓ
30. Ⓐ Ⓑ Ⓒ Ⓓ

Notes:

228

1. D
2. B
3. B
4. A
5. C
6. A
7. D
8. A
9. D
10. C
11. C
12. A
13. B
14. C
15. A
16. D
17. A
18. C
19. D
20. B
21. B
22. A
23. A
24. C
25. C
26. B
27. A
28. D
29. C
30. D

Forms Completion – Full-length Practice #2

Authorization to Hold Mail

➤ We can hold your mail for a minimum of **3**, but not for more than **30 days.**

NOTE: *Complete and give to your letter carrier or mail to the post office that delivers your mail.*

Postmaster: Please hold mail for:

Name(s) 1.	
	☐ A. Please deliver all accumulated mail and resume normal delivery on the ending date shown below. 2.
Address (Number, street, apt./suite no., city, state, ZIP + 4) 3.	☐ B. I will pick up all accumulated mail when I return and understand that mail delivery will not resume until I do.

Beginning Date 4.	Ending Date *(May only be changed by the customer in writing)* 5.	Customer Signature 6.

For Post Office Use Only

Date Received 7.	
Clerk 8.	Bin Number 9.
Carrier 10.	Route Number 11.

(Complete this section only if customer selected option B)

12. ☐ Accumulated mail has been picked up.	Resume Delivery of Mail *(Date)* 13.	By 14.

1. What is the maximum time that mail will be held?

   A. 3 days
   B. 15 days
   C. 20 days
   D. 30 days

2. What would be an appropriate entry for box 12?

   A. John Smith
   B. June 5, 2007
   C. A Check mark
   D. 1257 S. North Street

3. The customer would like 2 or 3 days after their return to "decompress. " Which box should the check mark go in?

   A. 2A
   B. 6
   C. 9
   D. 2B

4. In which box does the carrier designate the date they began re-delivering the mail?

   A. 4
   B. 13
   C. 7
   D. 5

230

5. In which box does the mail recipient sign to give permission for mail to be held?

    A. 6
    B. 14
    C. 8
    D. 10

United States Postal Service

Postage Statement - Extra Services

Not all extra services are available with all classes of mail.

MAILER: This postage statement must be used with a separate postage statement for the class of mail indicated. After computing the fees below, enter the total onto the appropriate postage statement and attach this form. For all extra services, PS Form 3877, *Firm Mailing Book for Accountable Mail*, also must be completed. Domestic mail and International mail must be reported on separate copies of this form.

Mailer	Permit Holder's Name, Address, and Email Address, If Any 1.	Telephone 2.	Post Office of Mailing 3a.	Form Number of Attached Postage Statement 4.	
			Mailing Date 3b.	**For Domestic** ☐ First-Class Mail	**For International** ☐ Letter Post (LP)
			Permit Number 3c.	☐ Priority Mail ☐ Standard Mail	☐ Parcel Post (PP) 5. ☐ Express Mail (EMS)
			Statement Sequence No. 3d.	☐ Package Services	

6. What would be an appropriate response for box 2?

    A. 678-555-1247
    B. 3/27/06
    C. Check mark
    D. Gil Grissom

7. The Statement Sequence Number is entered into which box?

    A. 1
    B. 3b
    C. 3d
    D. 4

8. The mailer's e-mail address is 123xyz@examservices.us. In which box should this be entered?

    A. 3b
    B. 5
    C. 4
    D. 1

13a. Describe Support Required

X Logon ID (Circle one): (New) Change Delete
□ DDE/DR: Access Code: _____ User Type: _____

X Facility Where Access Is Required: **Eagan Data Center**
San Mateo Data Center
□ List Existing Logon IDs & Facilities: _____

Access for Delivery Confirmation System	Access for Confirm System
□ PPP Dial-up Account Access to: PTSMFTP.USPS.GOV □ Internet Access **1a.**	□ Web Site Access □ File Transmission Account **1b.**
Access for Entry Information System	**Access for Performance Reporting System**
□ Web Site Access □ File Transmission Account **1c.**	□ Web Site Access **1d.**

13b. Resource Name (Additional room is available on the reverse side)	13c. Sensitive or Proprietary	13d. Access Level Required (See instructions)
2a.	**2b.**	**2c.**

9. Viola White wants to request computer access to proprietary or sensitive items. Which box should be marked?

    A. 1a
    B. 1c
    C. 2b
    D. 1b

10. Where can you put additional information if needed?

    A. On a separate sheet of paper.
    B. Box 2c
    C. Box 2a
    D. On the reverse side of the form.

Certification Program (Check the applicable certification program)

1.
□ Delivery Confirmation™   □ Parcel Barcodes   □ Signature Confirmation™
□ Express Mail®   □ Parcel Return Services (PRS)   □ Special Services
□ Flat Container Label   □ Sack Container Label   □ Tray Container Label
□ International Customs

Customer Information (Please print)

Company Name
2.

Customer Identification Number (e.g., DUNS® number, Mailer ID, etc.)
3.

Contact Name
4.

Street Address (P.O. Box, Rural/Hwy Contract, or Route Number) **5a.**		Apt/Suite **5b.**
City **6a.**	State **6b.**	ZIP + 4® **6c.**

Telephone Number (Include area code) **7a.**	Fax Number (Include area code) **7b.**	Email Address **7c.**	
Signature of Contact Person **8a.**			Date **8b.**

NOTE: To obtain a unique 9-digit DUNS number, contact Dun & Bradstreet at 1-800-333-0505 or at www.dnb.com.

11. The company requesting certification is located in Nebraska. Where should this be noted?

    A. Box 8a
    B. Box 4
    C. Box 6a
    D. Box 6b

12. In which box should the customer's DUNS number be noted?

    A. 5a
    B. 3
    C. 4
    D. 2

13. What would be an appropriate entry in box 1?

    A. Check mark
    B. Quickie Mart
    C. 803-555-1212
    D. John Smith

1a. Name of Addressee 1.			2a. Name of Mailer 2.		
1b. Street Address (No., street, apt./ste./PO box no.) 3.			2b. Street Address (No., street, apt./ste./PO box no.) 4.		
1c. City 5.	1d. State 6.	1e. ZIP +4® 7.	2c. City 8.	2d. State 9.	2e. ZIP + 4 10.
1f. Telephone Number (Include area code) 11.			2f. Telephone Number (Include area code) 12.		
3. Date Mailed 13.			4. Mailed at (Location, city, state, ZIP + 4) 14.		

14. The package was mailed to Jane Doe. In which box should this information be entered?

    A. 6
    B. 14
    C. 5
    D. 1

15. The package was mailed to San Francisco. In which box should this information be entered?

    A. 12
    B. 14
    C. 10
    D. 5

16. The addressee lives at ZIP code 29223-4815. Where is this information entered on this form?

    A. Box 10
    B. Box 7
    C. Box 13
    D. Box 12

B. Casual (Non-Career) Job Information

8. Casual Position Applied For:

☐ Clerk **1.**   ☐ Mail Handler   ☐ Carrier   ☐ Other *(Position Title)*: _____

9. Postal Facility Name and Location *(City/State)* **2.**	10. Earliest Date You Are Available **3.**

C. Prior Casual Work History

11. Dates of Last Casual Employment **4** From _____ To _____	12. Salary **5.** $ _____ per hour	13. Title of Former Casual Position ☐ Clerk ☐ Mail Handler ☐ Carrier ☐	Other *(Position Title)*: **6.**

14. Postal Facility Name and Location *(City/State)* **7.**	15. Name of Supervisor **8.**	16. Telephone No. *(If known)* **9.**

17. Reason Assignment Ended:

☐ Expiration of Appointment ☐ Resignation *(Give Reason)*: _____ ☐ Termination *(Give Reason)*: _____

17. The applicant's last casual employment ended on May 7, 2007. In which box should this be entered?

    A. Box 1
    B. Box 7
    C. Box 4
    D. Box 8

18. What would be a proper response to box 6?

    A. Check mark
    B. James Jones
    C. 800-555-1212
    D. $5.25

19. The applicant is applying for a carrier position. In which box should this be entered?

    A. 6
    B. 7
    C. 1
    D. 2

20. In which box would the name of the applicant's previous supervisor entered?

    A. 1
    B. 4
    C. 8
    D. 7

1. Mailer's Name **1.**	2. Mailer's Address *(No., street., ste. no., city, state, ZIP + 4)* **2.**	
3. Contact Person **3.**		
4a. Telephone No. *(Include area code)* **4a.**		
4b. Fax No. *(Include area code)* **4b.**		
5. Destination Country **5.**	6. Date Notified **6.**	7. Global Direct Customer ID No. **7.**

21. The package was mailed to France. In which box should this be entered?

    A. 5
    B. 7
    C. 4a
    D. 2

22. Which of the following is an appropriate entry for box 6?

    A. June 7, 1996
    B. 678-542-3912
    C. Charles Horn
    D. 123 S. North St, Seneca, SC 30024

23. The parcel was mailed by C & C Technologies. In which box should this be noted?

    A. 1
    B. 3
    C. 4a
    D. 2

No application fee is required. *(All information must be complete and typewritten or printed legibly.)*   **1.**

1. Complete Name of Organization *(If voting registration official, include title)*   **2.**

2. Street Address of Organization *(Include apartment or suite number)*   **3.**

3. City, State, ZIP+4® Code   **4.**

4. Telephone *(Include area code)* **5.**	5. Name of Applicant *(Must represent applying organization)* **6.**

6. Type of Organization *(Check only one)*

7.

☐ (01) Religious	☐ (03) Scientific	☐ (05) Agricultural	☐ (07) Veterans	☐ (09) Qualified political committee *(Go to item 9)*
☐ (02) Educational	☐ (04) Philanthropic	☐ (06) Labor	☐ (08) Fraternal	☐ (10) Voting registration official *(Go to item 9)*

Not all nonprofit organizations are eligible for the Nonprofit Standard Mail rates. Domestic Mail Manual® 703.1 lists certain organizations (such as busines‹ leagues, chambers of commerce, civic improvement associations, social and hobby clubs, governmental bodies, and others) that, although nonprofit, do n‹ qualify for the Nonprofit Standard Mail rates.

---

24. The organization requesting this service is a church. In which box would this be marked?

    A. 4
    B. 1
    C. 7
    D. 3

25. The organization's representative's name is Jane White. Where should this be noted?

    A. Box 1
    B. Box 6
    C. Box 4
    D. Box 7

26. In which box does it state whether or not there is an application fee?

    A. Box 5
    B. Box 1
    C. Box 6
    D. Box 4

27. This particular organization is located in Anderson, SC. Where should this be filled in on the form?

    A. Box 4
    B. Box 2
    C. Box 5
    D. Box 3

	Permit Holder's Name and Address and Email Address, If Any	Telephone 1b.	Name and Address of Mailing Agent *(If other than permit holder)*	Telephone 2b.	Name and Address of Individual or Organization for Which Mailing Is Prepared *(If other than permit holder)*
Mailer	1a. CAPS Cust. Ref. No. _____ Dun & Bradstreet No.		2a. Dun & Bradstreet No.		3. Dun & Bradstreet No.

Mailing	Post Office of Mailing 4a.	Processing Category 4b. ☐ Letters ☐ CMM ☐ Flats ☐ Automation Flats (DMM 301.3) ☐ Parcels	Mailing Date 4d.	Federal Agency Cost Code 4f.	Statement Seq. No. 5a.	No. and type of Containers 6.
	Type of Postage ☐ Permit Imprint ☐ Precanceled Stamps ☐ Metered		Weight of a Single Piece 0._____ 4e. pounds		Total Pieces 5b	
	Permit # 4c.	For Mail Enclosed within Another Class ☐ Bound Printed Matter ☐ Library Mail ☐ Media Mail ☐ Parcel Post ☐ Periodicals		If Sacked, Based on ☐ 125 pcs ☐ 15 lbs. ☐ both	Total Weight 5c.	Detached Address Lables? *(DMM 602.4)* ☐ Yes ☐ No 7.

28. Each piece to be mailed weighs 3 ounces. In which box should this be written?

    A. Box 5c
    B. Box 4e
    C. Box 6
    D. Box 2a

29. The permit holder's e-mail address is 123@yourisp.com. Where should this be entered?

    A. Box 2a
    B. Box 1a
    C. Box 3
    D. Box 6

30. What is the best entry for box 4b?

    A. Check mark
    B. James Fenimore Cooper
    C. 321-555-7982
    D. 52

Answer Grid – Forms Completion – Full-length Practice #2

(You will have 15 minutes to complete this section.)

1. Ⓐ Ⓑ Ⓒ Ⓓ
2. Ⓐ Ⓑ Ⓒ Ⓓ
3. Ⓐ Ⓑ Ⓒ Ⓓ
4. Ⓐ Ⓑ Ⓒ Ⓓ
5. Ⓐ Ⓑ Ⓒ Ⓓ
6. Ⓐ Ⓑ Ⓒ Ⓓ
7. Ⓐ Ⓑ Ⓒ Ⓓ
8. Ⓐ Ⓑ Ⓒ Ⓓ
9. Ⓐ Ⓑ Ⓒ Ⓓ
10. Ⓐ Ⓑ Ⓒ Ⓓ
11. Ⓐ Ⓑ Ⓒ Ⓓ
12. Ⓐ Ⓑ Ⓒ Ⓓ
13. Ⓐ Ⓑ Ⓒ Ⓓ
14. Ⓐ Ⓑ Ⓒ Ⓓ
15. Ⓐ Ⓑ Ⓒ Ⓓ
16. Ⓐ Ⓑ Ⓒ Ⓓ
17. Ⓐ Ⓑ Ⓒ Ⓓ
18. Ⓐ Ⓑ Ⓒ Ⓓ
19. Ⓐ Ⓑ Ⓒ Ⓓ
20. Ⓐ Ⓑ Ⓒ Ⓓ
21. Ⓐ Ⓑ Ⓒ Ⓓ
22. Ⓐ Ⓑ Ⓒ Ⓓ
23. Ⓐ Ⓑ Ⓒ Ⓓ
24. Ⓐ Ⓑ Ⓒ Ⓓ
25. Ⓐ Ⓑ Ⓒ Ⓓ
26. Ⓐ Ⓑ Ⓒ Ⓓ
27. Ⓐ Ⓑ Ⓒ Ⓓ
28. Ⓐ Ⓑ Ⓒ Ⓓ
29. Ⓐ Ⓑ Ⓒ Ⓓ
30. Ⓐ Ⓑ Ⓒ Ⓓ

Correct Answers – Forms Completion – Full-length Practice #2

1. D
2. C
3. D
4. B
5. A
6. A
7. C
8. D
9. C
10. D
11. D
12. B
13. A
14. D
15. D
16. B
17. C
18. A
19. C
20. C
21. A
22. A
23. A
24. C
25. B
26. B
27. A
28. B
29. B
30. A

Coding & Memory

This is a test of your ability to use codes quickly and accurately, both with a coding guide visible and from memory without using a guide. You will be shown a coding guide, along with several items that must be assigned a code. To the best of your ability, you must look up the correct code for each item and record your response on the Answer Grid accurately and quickly. During the first section of the test, you will be allowed to look at the coding guide while you assign codes. During the second section of the test, you must assign codes based on your memory of the same coding guide. While the coding guide is visible, try to memorize as many of the codes as you can. These are the same codes that will be used in the memory section.

During the actual test you are not permitted to look at the codes when answering the items in the memory section, nor are you permitted to write down any addresses during the memory period.

This section of the exam is scored based on the number of items that you answer correctly minus one-third of the number of items that you answer incorrectly. In both sections of this test, your score depends on how many items you can accurately assign a code in the time allowed. You may not be able to assign a code to all of the items before time runs out, but you should do your best to assign codes to as many items as you can as accurately as possible. There is a penalty for guessing on this test. It will NOT be to your advantage to guess randomly.

For convenience in practice, in this chapter ONLY, the coding and memory sections are separated and do not use the same coding guides. When you practice with the full-length exams and when you take the actual exam, these two sections are given as one part of the exam and will use the same coding guides.

Coding

In the coding section of Exam 473 you are asked to identify the correct code to assign for an address. You will be asked to answer 36 questions in 6 minutes.

Following is a sample coding guide and some tips on how to use it.

Coding Guide	
Address Range	**Delivery Route**
1 - 99 Anywhere Lane 10 – 200 Calico Avenue 5 – 15 N 42nd Street	A
100 – 200 Anywhere Lane 16 – 30 N 42nd Street	B
10000 – 12000 Graham Avenue 1 – 10 Rural Route 1 200 – 1500 Calico Ave.	C
All mail that doesn't fall in one of the address ranges listed above	D

The same coding guide will be used throughout the test. The guide presented here, although similar to that used on the actual test, contains different information.

The first column of the coding guide shows each address range. The second column shows the one-letter code for the delivery route that serves those addresses. Some of the street names appear twice, each time with a different range of address numbers associated with a different delivery route. For example, Anywhere Lane is served by delivery route A for address numbers ranging from 1 – 99 and by route B for address numbers from 100 – 200. Also notice that delivery route D serves all addresses that do not fall in one of the address ranges listed for Delivery Routes A, B, or C.

Following are some sample questions you can practice on before you take a timed exam.

Coding Sample Exercise

Coding Guide	
Address Range	**Delivery Route**
1 - 99 Anywhere Lane 10 – 200 Calico Avenue 5 – 15 N 42nd Street	A
100 – 200 Anywhere Lane 16 – 30 N 42nd Street	B
10000 – 12000 Graham Avenue 1 – 10 Rural Route 1 200 – 1500 Calico Ave.	C
All mail that doesn't fall in one of the address ranges listed above.	D

	Address		Delivery Route			
1.	82 Calico Ave.		A	B	C	D
2.	20 N 42nd Street		A	B	C	D
3.	29 Rural Route 1		A	B	C	D
4.	11000 Graves Ave.		A	B	C	D
5.	5 Anywhere Lane		A	B	C	D
6.	102 Amity lane		A	B	C	D
7.	1250 Calico Ave.		A	B	C	D
8.	23 N 42nd Street		A	B	C	D
9.	14 N 42nd Street		A	B	C	D
10.	119 Anywhere Lane		A	B	C	D
11.	9 Rural Route 1		A	B	C	D
12.	15 Rural Route 1		A	B	C	D
13.	10191 Rural Route 1		A	B	C	D
14.	5 N 42nd Street		A	B	C	D
15.	195 Anyplace Lane		A	B	C	D
16.	12500 Graham Lane		A	B	C	D
17.	10 N 42nd Street		A	B	C	D
18.	135 Anywhere Lane		A	B	C	D
19.	1061 Calico Ave.		A	B	C	D
20.	72 Rural Route 1		A	B	C	D

1. (A) (B) (C) (D)
2. (A) (B) (C) (D)
3. (A) (B) (C) (D)
4. (A) (B) (C) (D)
5. (A) (B) (C) (D)
6. (A) (B) (C) (D)
7. (A) (B) (C) (D)
8. (A) (B) (C) (D)
9. (A) (B) (C) (D)
10. (A) (B) (C) (D)
11. (A) (B) (C) (D)
12. (A) (B) (C) (D)
13. (A) (B) (C) (D)
14. (A) (B) (C) (D)
15. (A) (B) (C) (D)
16. (A) (B) (C) (D)
17. (A) (B) (C) (D)
18. (A) (B) (C) (D)
19. (A) (B) (C) (D)
20. (A) (B) (C) (D)

Correct Answers – Coding – Sample Exercise

1. A
2. B
3. D
4. D
5. A
6. D
7. C
8. B
9. A
10. B
11. C
12. D
13. D
14. A
15. D
16. D
17. A
18. B
19. C
20. D

Coding – Full-length Practice #1

(You will have 6 minutes to complete this section.)

Coding Guide	
Address Range	**Delivery Route**
1500 – 7999 Bloomdale Ave 455-1699 S.W. 12th St. 199 – 500 Herstad Ave	A
899 – 1499 Bloomdale Ave 21099-34099 Hwy 105 501-1375 Herstad Ave	B
34100 – 38999 Hwy 105 290-898 Bloomdale Ave	C
All mail that doesn't fall in one of the address ranges listed above.	D

	Address	Delivery Route			
1.	492 Herstad Ave.	A	B	C	D
2.	399 Bloomdale Ave.	A	B	C	D
3.	1301 Bloomdale Ave.	A	B	C	D
4.	131 Crystal Lake Rd.	A	B	C	D
5.	37523 Hwy 105	A	B	C	D
6.	900 S.W. 12th St.	A	B	C	D
7.	2750 Bloomdale Ave.	A	B	C	D
8.	305 Bloomdale Ave.	A	B	C	D
9.	677 Herstad Ave.	A	B	C	D
10.	890 Bloomdale Ave	A	B	C	D
11.	14-C Holiday Ln.	A	B	C	D
12.	1232 Bloomdale Ave.	A	B	C	D
13.	471 Herstad Ave.	A	B	C	D
14.	1649 S.W 14th St.	A	B	C	D
15.	1542 SW 12th St.	A	B	C	D
16.	32015 Hwy 105	A	B	C	D
17.	37999 Hwy 105	A	B	C	D
18.	1572 Bloomdale Ave.	A	B	C	D
19.	500 Herstad St.	A	B	C	D
20.	1403 Bloomdale Ave.	A	B	C	D
21.	36051 Hwy 105	A	B	C	D
22.	1106 SW 12th St	A	B	C	D
23.	809 Herstad Ave.	A	B	C	D
24.	2200 Hwy 105	A	B	C	D
25.	293 Bloomdale Ave.	A	B	C	D
26.	6092 Heston Ln.	A	B	C	D
27.	1905 S.W. 12th St.	A	B	C	D
28.	318 Herstad Ave.	A	B	C	D
29.	29072 Hwy 101	A	B	C	D
30.	1350 Bloomdale Ave.	A	B	C	D

31. 600 Herstad Ave.   A   B   C   D
32. 335 Bloomdale Ave.   A   B   C   D
33. 531 S.W. 12th St.   A   B   C   D
34. 6715 Tricia Pl   A   B   C   D
35. 1212 Herstad Ave.   A   B   C   D
36. 34200 Hwy 109   A   B   C   D

Notes:

246

Answer Grid – Coding – Full-length Practice #1

(You have 6 minutes to complete this section.)

1. Ⓐ Ⓑ Ⓒ Ⓓ
2. Ⓐ Ⓑ Ⓒ Ⓓ
3. Ⓐ Ⓑ Ⓒ Ⓓ
4. Ⓐ Ⓑ Ⓒ Ⓓ
5. Ⓐ Ⓑ Ⓒ Ⓓ
6. Ⓐ Ⓑ Ⓒ Ⓓ
7. Ⓐ Ⓑ Ⓒ Ⓓ
8. Ⓐ Ⓑ Ⓒ Ⓓ
9. Ⓐ Ⓑ Ⓒ Ⓓ
10. Ⓐ Ⓑ Ⓒ Ⓓ
11. Ⓐ Ⓑ Ⓒ Ⓓ
12. Ⓐ Ⓑ Ⓒ Ⓓ
13. Ⓐ Ⓑ Ⓒ Ⓓ
14. Ⓐ Ⓑ Ⓒ Ⓓ
15. Ⓐ Ⓑ Ⓒ Ⓓ
16. Ⓐ Ⓑ Ⓒ Ⓓ
17. Ⓐ Ⓑ Ⓒ Ⓓ
18. Ⓐ Ⓑ Ⓒ Ⓓ

19. Ⓐ Ⓑ Ⓒ Ⓓ
20. Ⓐ Ⓑ Ⓒ Ⓓ
21. Ⓐ Ⓑ Ⓒ Ⓓ
22. Ⓐ Ⓑ Ⓒ Ⓓ
23. Ⓐ Ⓑ Ⓒ Ⓓ
24. Ⓐ Ⓑ Ⓒ Ⓓ
25. Ⓐ Ⓑ Ⓒ Ⓓ
26. Ⓐ Ⓑ Ⓒ Ⓓ
27. Ⓐ Ⓑ Ⓒ Ⓓ
28. Ⓐ Ⓑ Ⓒ Ⓓ
29. Ⓐ Ⓑ Ⓒ Ⓓ
30. Ⓐ Ⓑ Ⓒ Ⓓ
31. Ⓐ Ⓑ Ⓒ Ⓓ
32. Ⓐ Ⓑ Ⓒ Ⓓ
33. Ⓐ Ⓑ Ⓒ Ⓓ
34. Ⓐ Ⓑ Ⓒ Ⓓ
35. Ⓐ Ⓑ Ⓒ Ⓓ
36. Ⓐ Ⓑ Ⓒ Ⓓ

Notes:

1. A
2. C
3. B
4. D
5. C
6. A
7. A
8. C
9. B
10. C
11. D
12. B
13. A
14. D
15. A
16. B
17. C
18. A
19. D
20. B
21. C
22. A
23. B
24. D
25. C
26. D
27. D
28. A
29. D
30. B
31. B
32. C
33. A
34. D
35. B
36. D

Coding – Full-length Practice #2

Coding Guide	
Address Range	**Delivery Route**
590 - 680 Turner Dr 4100 – 8760 N 63rd St. 5299 – 6399 Hampshire Ct	A
8761 – 9599 N. 63rd St 215 – 589 Turner Drive 2000 – 4590 Gardner Blvd	B
3000 – 4099 N. 63rd St. 5491-7050 Gardner Blvd.	C
All mail that doesn't fall in one of the address ranges listed above	D

Address   **Delivery Route**

#	Address				
1.	670 Turner Dr.	A	B	C	D
2.	2001 Gardner Blvd.	A	B	C	D
3.	7060 Gardner Blvd	A	B	C	D
4.	3500 N. 63rd St.	A	B	C	D
5.	275 Turner Dr.	A	B	C	D
6.	9502 N. 63rd Ave.	A	B	C	D
7.	6000 Hampshire Ct.	A	B	C	D
8.	3007 N. 63rd St.	A	B	C	D
9.	3999 Gardner Blvd.	A	B	C	D
10.	5789 Hampshire Ct.	A	B	C	D
11.	4205 N. 63rd St.	A	B	C	D
12.	6203 Gardner Blvd.	A	B	C	D
13.	8777 N. 63rd St.	A	B	C	D
14.	315 Turner Dr.	A	B	C	D
15.	1812 Lakemont Ave	A	B	C	D
16.	103 James River Blvd	A	B	C	D
17.	5000 Gardner Blvd	A	B	C	D
18.	3025 Gardner Blvd	A	B	C	D
19.	681 Turner Dr.	A	B	C	D
20.	4091 N. 63rd St	A	B	C	D
21.	5300 Hampshire Ct	A	B	C	D
22.	707 Turner Dr.	A	B	C	D
23.	4309 N. 63rd St.	A	B	C	D
24.	4219 Gardner Blvd.	A	B	C	D
25.	4875 Gardner Blvd.	A	B	C	D
26.	175 Woodland St.	A	B	C	D
27.	5407 Hampshire Ct.	A	B	C	D
28.	382 Turner Dr.	A	B	C	D
29.	9400 N. 63rd St.	A	B	C	D
30.	619 Turner Dr.	A	B	C	D
31.	4806 Gardner Blvd.	A	B	C	D

32. 3010 N. 63rd St.   A   B   C   D

33. 5444 Hampshire Ct.   A   B   C   D

34. 20500 Gardner Blvd   A   B   C   D

35. 8889 N. 63rd St.   A   B   C   D

36. 621 Turner Ave.   A   B   C   D

Notes:

Answer Grid – Coding – Full-length Practice #2

(You have 6 minutes to complete this section.)

1. Ⓐ Ⓑ Ⓒ Ⓓ
2. Ⓐ Ⓑ Ⓒ Ⓓ
3. Ⓐ Ⓑ Ⓒ Ⓓ
4. Ⓐ Ⓑ Ⓒ Ⓓ
5. Ⓐ Ⓑ Ⓒ Ⓓ
6. Ⓐ Ⓑ Ⓒ Ⓓ
7. Ⓐ Ⓑ Ⓒ Ⓓ
8. Ⓐ Ⓑ Ⓒ Ⓓ
9. Ⓐ Ⓑ Ⓒ Ⓓ
10. Ⓐ Ⓑ Ⓒ Ⓓ
11. Ⓐ Ⓑ Ⓒ Ⓓ
12. Ⓐ Ⓑ Ⓒ Ⓓ
13. Ⓐ Ⓑ Ⓒ Ⓓ
14. Ⓐ Ⓑ Ⓒ Ⓓ
15. Ⓐ Ⓑ Ⓒ Ⓓ
16. Ⓐ Ⓑ Ⓒ Ⓓ
17. Ⓐ Ⓑ Ⓒ Ⓓ
18. Ⓐ Ⓑ Ⓒ Ⓓ

19. Ⓐ Ⓑ Ⓒ Ⓓ
20. Ⓐ Ⓑ Ⓒ Ⓓ
21. Ⓐ Ⓑ Ⓒ Ⓓ
22. Ⓐ Ⓑ Ⓒ Ⓓ
23. Ⓐ Ⓑ Ⓒ Ⓓ
24. Ⓐ Ⓑ Ⓒ Ⓓ
25. Ⓐ Ⓑ Ⓒ Ⓓ
26. Ⓐ Ⓑ Ⓒ Ⓓ
27. Ⓐ Ⓑ Ⓒ Ⓓ
28. Ⓐ Ⓑ Ⓒ Ⓓ
29. Ⓐ Ⓑ Ⓒ Ⓓ
30. Ⓐ Ⓑ Ⓒ Ⓓ
31. Ⓐ Ⓑ Ⓒ Ⓓ
32. Ⓐ Ⓑ Ⓒ Ⓓ
33. Ⓐ Ⓑ Ⓒ Ⓓ
34. Ⓐ Ⓑ Ⓒ Ⓓ
35. Ⓐ Ⓑ Ⓒ Ⓓ
36. Ⓐ Ⓑ Ⓒ Ⓓ

Notes:

254

1. A
2. B
3. D
4. C
5. B
6. B
7. A
8. C
9. B
10. A
11. A
12. C
13. B
14. B
15. D
16. D
17. D
18. B
19. D
20. C
21. A
22. D
23. A
24. B
25. D
26. D
27. A
28. B
29. B
30. A
31. D
32. C
33. A
34. D
35. B
36. A

Memory

In the memory section of Exam 473 you are asked to memorize a series of codes that are then assigned to range of addresses. You will be asked to answer 36 questions in 7 minutes. If you thoroughly studied the section on Memory for Exam 460 you already have some memorization strategies under your belt. Before we present any new strategies, here are a few things you should notice about the coding guides:

1. Some of the street names repeat. For instance, in the coding guide below, La Place Hwy. appears in both routes A and B, and Farmerville Lane appears in both Routes A and C. So, you must plan on memorizing two different address ranges for each of these streets. Notice that when a street name repeats, the addresses increase. The numbers in the second range for a particular street are larger than the numbers in the first range. Notice also that when a street name repeats, the second range for that street usually to picks up exactly where the first range stopped.

2. The ranges can fit different descriptions. Some end in a zero like 800-900. But when the first range for a particular street ends with a zero, then the next range for the same street must end with "1" like 901-1200. Other ranges for a particular street end with a "9" like 1200-1579. When the first range ends with a "9", then the first number in the next range for the same street will end with a zero number like 1580-1800. Some ranges are smaller like 1-10 or 61-99; other ranges are large address numbers like 10000-15000; and yet other ranges fit somewhere in the middle.

Now that you have seen how the ranges are formatted, let's look at how to memorize the first street, La Place Hwy., along with its two address ranges.

- The address range for La Place Hwy in Route A is 1991–3200, you want to memorize this range as is.
- The address range for La Place Hwy in Route B is 3201– 900, you want to memorize this as 3200–3900. The reason for remembering this particular route this way is simply to reduce the amount of "stuff" you need to memorize. Instead of having to memorize 1991, 3200, 3201, and 3900, you only need to memorize 1991, 3200 and 3900.
- Now, let's put this all together. Memorize the line below by silently repeating it over and over…

La Place Hwy.   1991-3200-A   3200-3900-B

- Now that you have memorized this sequence, how do you use it? Simply, repeat the sequence to yourself every time you see a La Place Hwy address given as a question.

Use the same strategy when memorizing the Farmerville Lane and Chattanooga Drive addresses. The remaining addresses do not repeat and should be memorized as written. We have now reduced the amount of material to be recalled from eight pieces of information to five.

La Place Hwy   1991-3200 A   3200-3900 B
Farmerville Ln   15-30 A   30-60 C
Chattanooga Dr   100-400 A   400-699 B
830-900 CR 228
9000–15000 Alta Vista Ave

Remember that the memory section will use the same coding guide as the coding section of the exam so you will get some familiarity with the coding guide as you take the coding section of the exam as well. Also, as with the memory section of Exam 460, you are given a few chances to practice before you take the actual memory exam. On the following pages are two practice memory sections; apply these strategies and see how you do. Good luck!

Memory – Full-length Practice #1

Coding Guide

Address Range	Delivery Route
1991–3200 La Place Hwy 15–30 Farmerville Ln 100–399 Chattanooga Dr.	A
3201–3900 La Place Hwy 400–699 Chattanooga Dr.	B
830-900 CR 228 9000–15000 Alta Vista Ave. 31–60 Farmerville Ln	C
All mail that doesn't fall in one of the address ranges listed above	D

Take 5 minutes to study this coding guide. Use this guide to answer the questions on the next page FROM MEMORY.

Memory – Full-length Practice #1

(You have 7 minutes to complete this section.)

	Address	Delivery Route			
1.	15 Farmerville Ln	A	B	C	D
2.	660 Chattanooga Dr.	A	B	C	D
3.	831 CR 228	A	B	C	D
4.	2000 La Place Hwy	A	B	C	D
5.	13840 Alta Vista Ave.	A	B	C	D
6.	270 Chattanooga Dr.	A	B	C	D
7.	55 Farmerville Ln	A	B	C	D
8.	624 Chattanooga Dr	A	B	C	D
9.	8000 Alta Vista Ave.	A	B	C	D
10.	42 Farmerville Ln	A	B	C	D
11.	3790 La Place Hwy	A	B	C	D
12.	872 CR 228	A	B	C	D
13.	120 Chattanooga Dr.	A	B	C	D
14.	3642 La Place Hwy	A	B	C	D
15.	14100 Alta Vista Ave	A	B	C	D
16.	3000 La Place Hwy	A	B	C	D
17.	29 Farmerville Ln	A	B	C	D
18.	720 Chattanooga Dr.	A	B	C	D
19.	1400 Alta Vista Ave.	A	B	C	D
20.	380 Chattanooga Dr.	A	B	C	D
21.	14000 Alta Vista Ave.	A	B	C	D
22.	46 Farmerville Ln	A	B	C	D
23.	3150 La Place Hwy	A	B	C	D
24.	600 Chattanooga Dr	A	B	C	D
25.	890 CR 228	A	B	C	D
26.	16 Farmerville Ln	A	B	C	D
27.	500 Chattanooga Dr	A	B	C	D
28.	3800 La Place Parkway	A	B	C	D
29.	28 Farmerville Ln	A	B	C	D
30.	3600 La Place Hwy	A	B	C	D
31.	388 Chattanooga Dr.	A	B	C	D
32.	25 Farmerdale Ln	A	B	C	D
33.	2890 La Place Hwy	A	B	C	D
34.	8794 Alta Vista Dr.	A	B	C	D
35.	1000 Farmerville Ln	A	B	C	D
36.	828 CR 228	A	B	C	D

(You will have 5 minutes to complete this section.)

1. Ⓐ Ⓑ Ⓒ Ⓓ
2. Ⓐ Ⓑ Ⓒ Ⓓ
3. Ⓐ Ⓑ Ⓒ Ⓓ
4. Ⓐ Ⓑ Ⓒ Ⓓ
5. Ⓐ Ⓑ Ⓒ Ⓓ
6. Ⓐ Ⓑ Ⓒ Ⓓ
7. Ⓐ Ⓑ Ⓒ Ⓓ
8. Ⓐ Ⓑ Ⓒ Ⓓ
9. Ⓐ Ⓑ Ⓒ Ⓓ
10. Ⓐ Ⓑ Ⓒ Ⓓ
11. Ⓐ Ⓑ Ⓒ Ⓓ
12. Ⓐ Ⓑ Ⓒ Ⓓ
13. Ⓐ Ⓑ Ⓒ Ⓓ
14. Ⓐ Ⓑ Ⓒ Ⓓ
15. Ⓐ Ⓑ Ⓒ Ⓓ
16. Ⓐ Ⓑ Ⓒ Ⓓ
17. Ⓐ Ⓑ Ⓒ Ⓓ
18. Ⓐ Ⓑ Ⓒ Ⓓ

19. Ⓐ Ⓑ Ⓒ Ⓓ
20. Ⓐ Ⓑ Ⓒ Ⓓ
21. Ⓐ Ⓑ Ⓒ Ⓓ
22. Ⓐ Ⓑ Ⓒ Ⓓ
23. Ⓐ Ⓑ Ⓒ Ⓓ
24. Ⓐ Ⓑ Ⓒ Ⓓ
25. Ⓐ Ⓑ Ⓒ Ⓓ
26. Ⓐ Ⓑ Ⓒ Ⓓ
27. Ⓐ Ⓑ Ⓒ Ⓓ
28. Ⓐ Ⓑ Ⓒ Ⓓ
29. Ⓐ Ⓑ Ⓒ Ⓓ
30. Ⓐ Ⓑ Ⓒ Ⓓ
31. Ⓐ Ⓑ Ⓒ Ⓓ
32. Ⓐ Ⓑ Ⓒ Ⓓ
33. Ⓐ Ⓑ Ⓒ Ⓓ
34. Ⓐ Ⓑ Ⓒ Ⓓ
35. Ⓐ Ⓑ Ⓒ Ⓓ
36. Ⓐ Ⓑ Ⓒ Ⓓ

Notes:

Correct Answers – Memory – Full-length Practice #1

1. A
2. B
3. C
4. A
5. C
6. A
7. C
8. B
9. D
10. C
11. B
12. C
13. A
14. B
15. C
16. A
17. A
18. D
19. D
20. A
21. C
22. C
23. A
24. B
25. C
26. A
27. B
28. D
29. A
30. B
31. A
32. D
33. A
34. D
35. D
36. D

Memory – Full-length Practice #2

Coding Guide	
Address Range	**Delivery Route**
1701–2700 Lapalco Blvd. 950–1349 Beach Blvd. 8600–9399 Elkhorn Dr.	A
2701–3700 Lapalco Blvd. 9400–9899 Elkhorn Dr.	B
11000–17000 RR 148 19–60 Raceway Blvd 1350–1949 Beach Blvd	C
All mail that doesn't fall in one of the address ranges listed above	D

Take 5 minutes to study this coding guide. Use this guide to answer the questions on the next page FROM MEMORY.

<u>Memory – Full-length Practice #2</u>

(You will have 5 minutes to complete this section.)

Address   **Delivery Route**

1. 8794 Elkhorn Dr.   A   B   C   D
2. 1500 Beach Blvd.   A   B   C   D
3. 9443 Elkhorn Dr.   A   B   C   D
4. 975 Beach Blvd.   A   B   C   D
5. 14982 RR 148   A   B   C   D
6. 65 Raceway Rd.   A   B   C   D
7. 930 Beach Blvd.   A   B   C   D
8. 2900 Lapalco Blvd.   A   B   C   D
9. 9792 Elkhorn Dr.   A   B   C   D
10. 16500 RR 148   A   B   C   D
11. 3100 Lapalco Blvd   A   B   C   D
12. 50 Raceway Blvd.   A   B   C   D
13. 1300 Beach Blvd.   A   B   C   D
14. 9782 Elkhorn Dr.   A   B   C   D
15. 13940 RR 148   A   B   C   D
16. 21 Raceway Blvd.   A   B   C   D
17. 2461 Lapalco Blvd.   A   B   C   D
18. 1000 RR 148   A   B   C   D
19. 2596 Lapalco Blvd.   A   B   C   D
20. 1659 Lapalco Blvd   A   B   C   D
21. 1268 Beach Blvd.   A   B   C   D
22. 13940 RR 148   A   B   C   D
23. 8499 Elkhorn Dr.   A   B   C   D
24. 8711 Elkhorn Dr.   A   B   C   D
25. 46 Raceway Blvd.   A   B   C   D
26. 9598 Lapalco Blvd.   A   B   C   D
27. 949 Beach Blvd.   A   B   C   D
28. 2300 Lapalco Blvd.   A   B   C   D
29. 2856 Lapalco Blvd.   A   B   C   D
30. 14000 RR 148   A   B   C   D
31. 1741 Beach Blvd.   A   B   C   D
32. 48 Rice Cay Rd.   A   B   C   D
33. 9800 Elkhorn Dr.   A   B   C   D
34. 20 Raceway Blvd.   A   B   C   D
35. 175 Beach Blvd.   A   B   C   D
36. 2955 Lapalco Blvd.   A   B   C   D

1. Ⓐ Ⓑ Ⓒ Ⓓ
2. Ⓐ Ⓑ Ⓒ Ⓓ
3. Ⓐ Ⓑ Ⓒ Ⓓ
4. Ⓐ Ⓑ Ⓒ Ⓓ
5. Ⓐ Ⓑ Ⓒ Ⓓ
6. Ⓐ Ⓑ Ⓒ Ⓓ
7. Ⓐ Ⓑ Ⓒ Ⓓ
8. Ⓐ Ⓑ Ⓒ Ⓓ
9. Ⓐ Ⓑ Ⓒ Ⓓ
10. Ⓐ Ⓑ Ⓒ Ⓓ
11. Ⓐ Ⓑ Ⓒ Ⓓ
12. Ⓐ Ⓑ Ⓒ Ⓓ
13. Ⓐ Ⓑ Ⓒ Ⓓ
14. Ⓐ Ⓑ Ⓒ Ⓓ
15. Ⓐ Ⓑ Ⓒ Ⓓ
16. Ⓐ Ⓑ Ⓒ Ⓓ
17. Ⓐ Ⓑ Ⓒ Ⓓ
18. Ⓐ Ⓑ Ⓒ Ⓓ

19. Ⓐ Ⓑ Ⓒ Ⓓ
20. Ⓐ Ⓑ Ⓒ Ⓓ
21. Ⓐ Ⓑ Ⓒ Ⓓ
22. Ⓐ Ⓑ Ⓒ Ⓓ
23. Ⓐ Ⓑ Ⓒ Ⓓ
24. Ⓐ Ⓑ Ⓒ Ⓓ
25. Ⓐ Ⓑ Ⓒ Ⓓ
26. Ⓐ Ⓑ Ⓒ Ⓓ
27. Ⓐ Ⓑ Ⓒ Ⓓ
28. Ⓐ Ⓑ Ⓒ Ⓓ
29. Ⓐ Ⓑ Ⓒ Ⓓ
30. Ⓐ Ⓑ Ⓒ Ⓓ
31. Ⓐ Ⓑ Ⓒ Ⓓ
32. Ⓐ Ⓑ Ⓒ Ⓓ
33. Ⓐ Ⓑ Ⓒ Ⓓ
34. Ⓐ Ⓑ Ⓒ Ⓓ
35. Ⓐ Ⓑ Ⓒ Ⓓ
36. Ⓐ Ⓑ Ⓒ Ⓓ

Notes:

1. A
2. C
3. B
4. A
5. C
6. D
7. D
8. B
9. B
10. C
11. B
12. C
13. A
14. B
15. C
16. C
17. A
18. D
19. A
20. D
21. A
22. C
23. D
24. A
25. C
26. D
27. D
28. A
29. B
30. C
31. C
32. D
33. B
34. C
35. D
36. B

Personal Characteristics and Experience Inventory

This is the final part of the exam. This inventory is used to determine if you will be a good fit for the Postal Service. You apply for a position because you see yourself as perfect for the job, but the employer is looking for the applicant whose personality and character best fit the company's business model.

This particular section of the book by no means represents the exact questions you will be asked; it is intended to give you an idea of the types of questions to expect when you reach this part of the exam. By that time, you will be tired, perhaps a bit frustrated, and ready to go home. However, we believe that this is the most important part of the exam, so answer the questions as truthfully as possible. There are no right or wrong answers to these questions; they are used to measure your ability to work with others and your strengths and weaknesses in the workplace.

The next questions are offered only to give you an idea of the types of questions that will be asked so that you will not be caught off guard. When you take the actual exam you will be given 90 minutes to answer 236 questions; you must answer them honestly and sincerely. Remember, there are no right or wrong answers, and the following questions are only presented to give you an idea of the TYPES of questions you may be asked on this section of the exam.

1. Even under a great deal of stress, I am still able to perform efficiently on the job.

    A. Strongly agree
    B. Agree
    C. Disagree
    D. Strongly disagree

2. On-the-job safety is very important to the success of any operation.

    A. Strongly agree
    B. Agree
    C. Disagree
    D. Strongly disagree

3. Theft of any kind should immediately be reported to a supervisor.

    A. Strongly agree
    B. Agree
    C. Disagree
    D. Strongly disagree

4. Even when I know I am right, I will always listen to other people's opinions.

    A. Strongly agree
    B. Agree
    C. Disagree
    D. Strongly disagree

5. Speaking to a large group of people is very uncomfortable for me.

    A. Strongly agree
    B. Agree
    C. Disagree
    D. Strongly disagree

6. I work well with established deadlines.

    A. Strongly agree
    B. Agree
    C. Disagree
    D. Strongly disagree

7. I enjoy working at a faster pace than others do.

    A. Strongly agree
    B. Agree
    C. Disagree
    D. Strongly disagree

8. Boring or monotonous jobs can have a detrimental effect on my morale.

    A. Strongly agree
    B. Agree
    C. Disagree
    D. Strongly disagree

9. While trying to focus on a particular task, I prefer not to have constant interruptions.

    A. Strongly agree
    B. Agree
    C. Disagree
    D. Strongly disagree

10. If a co-worker suggests a better way to do something, it is very easy for me to change an established work habit.

    A. Strongly agree
    B. Agree
    C. Disagree
    D. Strongly disagree

11. People who are close to me would say I am an optimist

    A. Strongly agree
    B. Agree
    C. Disagree
    D. Strongly disagree

12. If I do not agree with the handling of a work issue, I allow my frustrations to affect my attitude at work.

    A. Strongly agree
    B. Agree
    C. Disagree
    D. Strongly disagree

13. I am not beyond taking a calculated risk to accomplish a given task.

    A. Strongly agree
    B. Agree
    C. Disagree
    D. Strongly disagree

14. It is extremely irritating to hear criticism from a co-worker.

   A. Strongly agree
   B. Agree
   C. Disagree
   D. Strongly disagree

15. I prefer not to wear seatbelts because they are too constrictive and uncomfortable.

   A. Strongly agree
   B. Agree
   C. Disagree
   D. Strongly disagree

16. People who have worked with me would testify that I have a superior work ethic.

   A. Strongly agree
   B. Agree
   C. Disagree
   D. Strongly disagree

17. I get along with almost everybody.

   A. Strongly agree
   B. Agree
   C. Disagree
   D. Strongly disagree

18. Standing or walking for a long period of time would not be a problem for me.

   A. Strongly agree
   B. Agree
   C. Disagree
   D. Strongly disagree

19. I never have to be reminded to attend meetings.

   A. Strongly agree
   B. Agree
   C. Disagree
   D. Strongly disagree

20. It is important to me that my work performance is recognized.

   A. Strongly agree
   B. Agree
   C. Disagree
   D. Strongly disagree

21. The quality of my work actually improves under tight deadlines

   A. Strongly agree
   B. Agree
   C. Disagree
   D. Strongly disagree

22. Once I begin a project, it is important to me to see it through to its end.

    A. Strongly agree
    B. Agree
    C. Disagree
    D. Strongly disagree

23. If I had a choice, I would prefer not to travel long distances for on-the-job training.

    A. Strongly agree
    B. Agree
    C. Disagree
    D. Strongly disagree

24. I prefer to work nights and weekends.

    A. Strongly agree
    B. Agree
    C. Disagree
    D. Strongly disagree

25. I consistently outperformed my classmates in school.

    A. Strongly agree
    B. Agree
    C. Disagree
    D. Strongly disagree

26. I do better when I work on one project at a time than when I multitask.

    A. Strongly agree
    B. Agree
    C. Disagree
    D. Strongly disagree

27. It is easy to be courteous when dealing with an angry customer.

    A. Strongly agree
    B. Agree
    C. Disagree
    D. Strongly disagree

28. I am always willing to go the extra distance to get the job completed.

    A. Strongly agree
    B. Agree
    C. Disagree
    D. Strongly disagree

29. I consider myself to be detail oriented.

    A. Strongly agree
    B. Agree
    C. Disagree
    D. Strongly disagree

30. If I witnessed a safety violation, I would bring it to my supervisor's attention immediately, regardless of how busy we might be.

    A. Strongly agree
    B. Agree
    C. Disagree
    D. Strongly disagree

31. It is very easy for me to deal with an unpleasant co-worker.

    A. Strongly agree
    B. Agree
    C. Disagree
    D. Strongly disagree

32. Co-workers would agree that I work well under pressure.

    A. Strongly agree
    B. Agree
    C. Disagree
    D. Strongly disagree

33. While I was in school, I regularly dressed better than my classmates did.

    A. Strongly agree
    B. Agree
    C. Disagree
    D. Strongly disagree

34. I look forward to working with people who have a common goal.

    A. Strongly agree
    B. Agree
    C. Disagree
    D. Strongly disagree

35. I struggle to remain courteous toward co-workers who tend to interrupt my conversations with others.

    A. Strongly agree
    B. Agree
    C. Disagree
    D. Strongly disagree

36. I find it very aggravating when others do not respect my opinion.

    A. Strongly agree
    B. Agree
    C. Disagree
    D. Strongly disagree

37. I have a genuine respect for authority.

    A. Strongly agree
    B. Agree
    C. Disagree
    D. Strongly disagree

38. I find it very discouraging when something does not go my way.

   A. Strongly agree
   B. Agree
   C. Disagree
   D. Strongly disagree

39. I enjoy change when it enhances my work performance.

   A. Strongly agree
   B. Agree
   C. Disagree
   D. Strongly disagree

40. I carefully weigh all the risks before making a decision that affects others.

   A. Strongly agree
   B. Agree
   C. Disagree
   D. Strongly disagree

41. I do not allow the poor attitude of a co-worker to affect my performance.

   A. Strongly agree
   B. Agree
   C. Disagree
   D. Strongly disagree

42. If a co-worker were struggling with a personal problem, I would offer encouragement and support.

   A. Strongly agree
   B. Agree
   C. Disagree
   D. Strongly disagree

43. I don't hesitate to make my co-workers aware of their mistakes.

   A. Strongly agree
   B. Agree
   C. Disagree
   D. Strongly disagree

44. When necessary, I always wear hearing protection and safety goggles.

   A. Strongly agree
   B. Agree
   C. Disagree
   D. Strongly disagree

45. I am more interested in doing my job the way that works best for me than in following supervisory directives.

   A. Strongly agree
   B. Agree
   C. Disagree
   D. Strongly disagree

273

46. I prefer work that involves direct contact with customers.

    A. Strongly agree
    B. Agree
    C. Disagree
    D. Strongly disagree

47. I would not let a stressful week affect the quality of my work performance.

    A. Strongly agree
    B. Agree
    C. Disagree
    D. Strongly disagree

48. When a supervisor does not listen to the others' opinions, I become frustrated.

    A. Strongly agree
    B. Agree
    C. Disagree
    D. Strongly disagree

49. I would not hesitate to purchase an item that was priced lower than it should have been. After all, setting prices is the store's responsibility, not mine.

    A. Strongly agree
    B. Agree
    C. Disagree
    D. Strongly disagree

50. I consistently strive to improve my job performance.

    A. Strongly agree
    B. Agree
    C. Disagree
    D. Strongly disagree

51. If I did not like the personal habits of a co-worker, I would let it be known to both the co-worker and my supervisor.

    A. Strongly agree
    B. Agree
    C. Disagree
    D. Strongly disagree

52. I am open to suggestions from co-workers.

    A. Strongly agree
    B. Agree
    C. Disagree
    D. Strongly disagree

53. I always wear my seatbelt when I ride in a motor vehicle.

    A. Strongly agree
    B. Agree
    C. Disagree
    D. Strongly disagree

54. I enjoy working on projects that take a lot of my time and effort.

    A. Strongly agree
    B. Agree
    C. Disagree
    D. Strongly disagree

55. I would not enjoy completing a job that someone else had left unfinished.

    A. Strongly agree
    B. Agree
    C. Disagree
    D. Strongly disagree

56. I need to be told to do a specific task only once.

    A. Strongly agree
    B. Agree
    C. Disagree
    D. Strongly disagree

57. I am not bothered by doing the same kind of task every day.

    A. Strongly agree
    B. Agree
    C. Disagree
    D. Strongly disagree

58. It is important to me to have some say about office policy.

    A. Strongly agree
    B. Agree
    C. Disagree
    D. Strongly disagree

59. It is okay to keep the collection of government pens that I have inadvertently brought home.

    A. Strongly agree
    B. Agree
    C. Disagree
    D. Strongly disagree

60. I do not like it when someone misconstrues something I have said.

    A. Strongly agree
    B. Agree
    C. Disagree
    D. Strongly disagree

61. If I finish a particular job ahead of schedule, I will look for something else to do without being asked.

    A. Strongly agree
    B. Agree
    C. Disagree
    D. Strongly disagree

62. A supervisor should be kept well informed of mistakes made by fellow workers.

   A. Strongly agree
   B. Agree
   C. Disagree
   D. Strongly disagree

63. Supervisory directions should be followed without exception.

   A. Strongly agree
   B. Agree
   C. Disagree
   D. Strongly disagree

64. I rarely have disagreements with other people.

   A. Strongly agree
   B. Agree
   C. Disagree
   D. Strongly disagree

65. No matter how busy I may be, I will take the time needed to report a safety violation to an immediate supervisor.

   A. Strongly agree
   B. Agree
   C. Disagree
   D. Strongly disagree

66. I treat co-workers and customers the way they treat me.

   A. Strongly agree
   B. Agree
   C. Disagree
   D. Strongly disagree

67. I work better alone than I do in a group.

   A. Strongly agree
   B. Agree
   C. Disagree
   D. Strongly disagree

68. If management grants a special favor to one person, then everyone else should get the same benefit.

   A. Strongly agree
   B. Agree
   C. Disagree
   D. Strongly disagree

69. No matter how tired I might be, I make customer service a priority.

   A. Strongly agree
   B. Agree
   C. Disagree
   D. Strongly disagree

70. If a co-worker received undeserved praise, it would be important to me to set the record straight.

    A. Strongly agree
    B. Agree
    C. Disagree
    D. Strongly disagree

71. I look for new and better ways to enhance my job performance.

    A. Very Often
    B. Often
    C. Sometimes
    D. Never

72. I assist co-workers in need, even if they do not ask for help.

    A. Very often
    B. Often
    C. Sometimes
    D. Never

73. I have used sick time for personal time off.

    A. Very often
    B. Often
    C. Sometimes
    D. Never

74. I am quick to respond in kind to co-workers' criticisms.

    A. Very often
    B. Often
    C. Sometimes
    D. Never

75. I have received citations for speeding.

    A. Very often
    B. Often
    C. Sometimes
    D. Never

76. I was involved in fights with classmates when in school.

    A. Very often
    B. Often
    C. Sometimes
    D. Never

77. I take issue with co-workers who do not show up for work on time.

    A. Very often
    B. Often
    C. Sometimes
    D. Never

78. I get discouraged when a job has to be finished within an unrealistic time frame.

    A. Very often
    B. Often
    C. Sometimes
    D. Never

79. I like to plan things in advance and have contingencies in place, just in case.

    A. Very often
    B. Often
    C. Sometimes
    D. Never

80. I apologize for other people's mistakes.

    A. Very often
    B. Often
    C. Sometimes
    D. Never

81. Co-workers look to me for leadership.

    A. Very often
    B. Often
    C. Sometimes
    D. Never

82. I will do tedious work that others neglect.

    A. Very often
    B. Often
    C. Sometimes
    D. Never

83. I get irritated when I do not receive credit for my production- or cost-saving ideas.

    A. Very often
    B. Often
    C. Sometimes
    D. Never

84. I use abusive language when I am frustrated.

    A. Very often
    B. Often
    C. Sometimes
    D. Never

85. I regularly maintain my personal vehicle with the intention of avoiding both safety hazards and costly repairs.

    A. Very often
    B. Often
    C. Sometimes
    D. Never

86. I willfully avoid conversations that can be construed as gossip.

    A. Very often
    B. Often
    C. Sometimes
    D. Never

87. I express concerns or problems as well as share successes with co-workers.

    A. Very often
    B. Often
    C. Sometimes
    D. Never

88. I would resent not being personally informed of managerial decisions that directly affect the workplace.

    A. Very often
    B. Often
    C. Sometimes
    D. Never

89. Regardless of what I am in the middle of, I am inclined to take a lunch break at a specific time.

    A. Very often
    B. Often
    C. Sometimes
    D. Never

90. I will challenge managerial policies that do not seem to make sense.

    A. Very often
    B. Often
    C. Sometimes
    D. Never

91. I make compromises in order to get projects completed.

    A. Very often
    B. Often
    C. Sometimes
    D. Never

92. I invite constructive feedback from others when work-related issues are discussed.

    A. Very often
    B. Often
    C. Sometimes
    D. Never

93. I use sarcasm to deflect other people's criticisms.

    A. Very often
    B. Often
    C. Sometimes
    D. Never

94. Without reservation, I will perform duties outside my job description.

    A. Very often
    B. Often
    C. Sometimes
    D. Never

95. I am flexible and accepting of frequent changes at work.

    A. Very often
    B. Often
    C. Sometimes
    D. Never

96. I work long hours without complaint.

    A. Very often
    B. Often
    C. Sometimes
    D. Never

These questions are very useful in telling a prospective employer about an applicant's personality and learning style. Personality profile and learning style assessment resources are available online as provided by your reseller or for a small fee from the publisher at www.endeavormediallc.com. The personality profile uses new, sophisticated technology to match you with your career choice. This assessment is completed in the privacy and comfort of your own home. You will receive a report which will indicate the areas where you will excel as well as areas where you may need to overcome obstacles. The Learning Styles assessment was developed by faculty at North Carolina State University and will help you to understand the way you can best learn new information, at the very least it will help you to understand why you learn the way you do. As with the personality assessment, this survey is conducted in the privacy and comfort of your own home and you receive a report which discusses the results. We here at Endeavor Media hope that you find both of these assessments of great value in your job search, no matter what your eventual career.

Chapter 8: Practice Exam 473

On the following pages you will find two full-length practice exams to help you prepare for Exam 473. The Sections of these practice exams are set up in the order they were introduced in the manual and may not reflect the order of the actual exam given.

There are no hints or formulas to use in this section. You will have to rely on what you have learned in Chapter 7 of this manual.

The answers for all sections of each practice exam are located at the end of that exam.

Good Luck!!!!

Practice Exam 473 #1

Before beginning, tear out or photocopy the answer grid for each section of the exam.

Address Comparison – Practice Exam 473 #1

Answer Key:
A) No Errors
B) Street Address Only
C) ZIP Code Only
D) Both

	Correct Addresses			Addresses to be Corrected	
	Address	**ZIP Code**		**Address**	**ZIP code**
1.	613 Key Street Espanola, NM	87532		613 Key Street Espanola, NM	87532
2.	7205 Tacoma Avenue South Bladensburg, MD	20710		7205 Tacoma Avenue South Bladensburg, MD	20718
3.	2833 Grapefruit Dr. McAllen, TX	78503		2833 Grapefruit Dr. McAllen, TX	78503
4.	250 Mountain Ct. Apt 7B Hendersonville, TN	37075		250 Mountain Ct. Apt. 6C Hendersonville, TN	37875
5.	6155 Glenmore Ave Baden, PA	15005		6155 Glenmore Ave Baden, PA	15605
6.	157-12 45th Avenue South St. Paul, MN	55075		157-12 45th Avenue South St. Paul, MN	65075
7.	11 Carnen St. Greenville, SC	29615		11 Carnen St. Greenville, SC	29615
8.	215 Delight Road Winnedago, IL	61088		215 Delite Road Winnebago, IL	61088
9.	862 Six Avenue North Racine, WI	53402		362 Six Avenue North Racine, WI	53402
10.	60 Kingdom Hall Lane Woodburn, NY	12788		60 Kingdom Hall Lane Woodburn, NY	12788
11.	5323 Effex Court Auburn, NE	68305		5323 Effects Court Auburn, NE	68305
12.	8585 John McKeever Ave. Baton Rough, LA	70814		8686 John McKeever Ave. Baton Rouge, LA	70814
13.	5319 West 119th Terrace Rossville, GA	30741		5319 West 119th Terrace Rossville, GA	30741
14.	PO Box 3222 Sun Prairie, WI	53590		PO Box 3322 Sun Prairie, WI	53590
15.	Rt. 3 Box 363 A Hayward, CA	94544		Rt. 3 Box 363 Hayward, CA	94547
16.	50 Austin Ave. Ogden, UT	84401		60 Austin Ave. Ogden, UT	84402
17.	43 Buttermilk Dr. Camp Hill, PA	17011		43 Buttermilk Drive Camp Hill, PA	17011
18.	310 Lopax Rd. Mullica Hill, NJ	08062		310 Lopax Rd. Mullica Hill, NJ	08062
19.	19852 Wheelwright Dr. Shelbyville, KY	40065		19852 Wheelwright Dr. Shelbyville, KY	40065
20.	1107 State Route 209 Albuquerque, NM	87102		1107 State Route 209 Albuquerque, NM	87103

#	Address (Left)	ZIP	Address (Right)	ZIP
21.	1102 Green Tree Ct Gilbert AZ	85234	1102 Green Tree Ct Gilvert AZ	85234
22.	301 N. Progress Ave. Newton, IA	50208	301 N. Progress Ave. Newton, IA	50208
23.	4516 Nalley View Ave Aurora, IL	60504	4516 Nalley Ave Aurora, IL	60504
24.	6039 Crafton Dr. Marlboro, MA	01752	6039 Crofton Dr Marlboro, MA	01752
25.	PO Box 76A St. James, MO	65559	PO Box 76A St. James, MO	65559
26.	3285 Coco Plum Circle Enfield, CT	06082	3285 Coco Plum Circle Enfield, CT	06083
27.	100 Clarksville St Fort Worth, TX	76135	1000 Clarksville St. Fort Worth, TX	76135
28.	18 Ferry Rd. Cheyenne, WY	82001	18 Ferry Rd. Cheyenne, WY	82002
29.	1245 Woodcrest Lane Warrenville, SC	29857	1245 Woodcrest Lane Warrenville, SC	29857
30.	119 Cooley Road Detroit, MI	48239	119 Cooley Road Detroit, MI	48237
31.	RR1 Box 230 Willingboro, NJ	08046	RR1 Box 238 Willingboro, NJ	08046
32.	Number 5 Country Hill Court Temecula, CA	92592	Number 5 Country Court Temecula, CA	92593
33.	997 Heather Lane Harrisburg, OR	97446	1997 Heather Lane Harrisburg, OR	97446
34.	231 Hedrick Dr. Johnson City, TX	78636	231 Hendrick Dr. Johnson City, TX	78636
35.	610 W 24th St. Apt F Birmingham, AL	85214	610 W 24th St. Apt F Birmingham, AL	85214
36.	1408 Locust St Taiser, MO	65047	1408 Locust St Taiser, MO	65047
37.	131 Otis Ave. Rockford, IL	61109	131 Otis Ave. Rockford, IL	61109
38.	30012 Quail Run Drive Lincoln, NE	68503	30012 Quail Run Drive Lincoln, NE	66503
39.	92 Painters Drive Logansport, IN	46947	92 Painters Drive Logansport, IN	46944
40.	2211 Lost Oak Trail Thornton, CO	80241	2211 Lost Oak Trail Thornton, CO	80241
41.	15 Ashmont St. 1st Floor Lake Forest Park, WA	98155	15 Ashmont St. 1st Floor Lake Forest Park, WA	98155
42.	2208 Brighton Place Florence, MS	39073	2028 Brighton Place Florence, MS	39073
43.	PO Box 1776 Wantage, NJ	07461	PO Box 1776 Wantage, NJ	07461
44.	2321 Idle Hour Rd. Tunnel Hill, GA	30755	2321 Idle Hour Rd. Tunnel Hill, GA	03557
45.	4 Hodges Street Charlotte, NC	28208	4 Hodges Street Charlotte, NC	28203
46.	90 East 19th Street Edmond, OK	73003	93 19th Street Edmond, OK	73003
47.	2200 Mary St. Augusta, ME	04330	2200 Merry St Augusta, GA	04330
48.	44 Truelight Rd. Chantilly, VA	20151	44 Truelight Rd. Chantilly, VA	20151

49.	5111 Alameda Ave. Chino Hills, CA	91709		5113 Alameda Ave. China Halls, CA	92709
50.	1 Miramar Ave. Denver, CO	80219		1 Miramar Ave. Denver, CO	80219
51.	503 Wildwind Rd Belleview, WA	98006		503 Wildwind Rd Belleview, WA	98006
52.	8915 Laisy Ave. Cettering, OH	45420		8915 Daisy Ave. Cettering, OH	45420
53.	2617 Levic St. Lake Worth, FL	33460		2617 Levick St. Lake Worth, FL	33460
54.	433 Beaver Dam Road Hattiesburg, MS	39402		433 Beaver's Dam Rd. Hattiesburg, MS	39402
55.	1419 Sophie Blvd Avon, NY	14414		1419 Sophie Blvd Avon, NY	14414
56.	PO Box 1784 Gastonia, NC	28045		PO Box 1784 Gastonia, NC	28045
57.	245 E High St Springfield, MA	01105		245 E High St Springfield, MA	01105
58.	927 Richard St. Clearfield, UT	84015		927 Richard St. Clearfield, UT	84015
59.	786 Dell Ave. Nashville, TN	37221		786 Dell Ave. Nashville, TN	37221
60.	RR 4 Box 421 Bangor, PA	18013		RR 4 Box 1421 Bangor, PA	18013

Notes:

286

Answer Grid – Address Comparison – Practice Exam 473 #1

1. Ⓐ Ⓑ Ⓒ Ⓓ
2. Ⓐ Ⓑ Ⓒ Ⓓ
3. Ⓐ Ⓑ Ⓒ Ⓓ
4. Ⓐ Ⓑ Ⓒ Ⓓ
5. Ⓐ Ⓑ Ⓒ Ⓓ
6. Ⓐ Ⓑ Ⓒ Ⓓ
7. Ⓐ Ⓑ Ⓒ Ⓓ
8. Ⓐ Ⓑ Ⓒ Ⓓ
9. Ⓐ Ⓑ Ⓒ Ⓓ
10. Ⓐ Ⓑ Ⓒ Ⓓ
11. Ⓐ Ⓑ Ⓒ Ⓓ
12. Ⓐ Ⓑ Ⓒ Ⓓ
13. Ⓐ Ⓑ Ⓒ Ⓓ
14. Ⓐ Ⓑ Ⓒ Ⓓ
15. Ⓐ Ⓑ Ⓒ Ⓓ
16. Ⓐ Ⓑ Ⓒ Ⓓ
17. Ⓐ Ⓑ Ⓒ Ⓓ
18. Ⓐ Ⓑ Ⓒ Ⓓ
19. Ⓐ Ⓑ Ⓒ Ⓓ
20. Ⓐ Ⓑ Ⓒ Ⓓ
21. Ⓐ Ⓑ Ⓒ Ⓓ
22. Ⓐ Ⓑ Ⓒ Ⓓ
23. Ⓐ Ⓑ Ⓒ Ⓓ
24. Ⓐ Ⓑ Ⓒ Ⓓ
25. Ⓐ Ⓑ Ⓒ Ⓓ
26. Ⓐ Ⓑ Ⓒ Ⓓ
27. Ⓐ Ⓑ Ⓒ Ⓓ
28. Ⓐ Ⓑ Ⓒ Ⓓ
29. Ⓐ Ⓑ Ⓒ Ⓓ
30. Ⓐ Ⓑ Ⓒ Ⓓ

31. Ⓐ Ⓑ Ⓒ Ⓓ
32. Ⓐ Ⓑ Ⓒ Ⓓ
33. Ⓐ Ⓑ Ⓒ Ⓓ
34. Ⓐ Ⓑ Ⓒ Ⓓ
35. Ⓐ Ⓑ Ⓒ Ⓓ
36. Ⓐ Ⓑ Ⓒ Ⓓ
37. Ⓐ Ⓑ Ⓒ Ⓓ
38. Ⓐ Ⓑ Ⓒ Ⓓ
39. Ⓐ Ⓑ Ⓒ Ⓓ
40. Ⓐ Ⓑ Ⓒ Ⓓ
41. Ⓐ Ⓑ Ⓒ Ⓓ
42. Ⓐ Ⓑ Ⓒ Ⓓ
43. Ⓐ Ⓑ Ⓒ Ⓓ
44. Ⓐ Ⓑ Ⓒ Ⓓ
45. Ⓐ Ⓑ Ⓒ Ⓓ
46. Ⓐ Ⓑ Ⓒ Ⓓ
47. Ⓐ Ⓑ Ⓒ Ⓓ
48. Ⓐ Ⓑ Ⓒ Ⓓ
49. Ⓐ Ⓑ Ⓒ Ⓓ
50. Ⓐ Ⓑ Ⓒ Ⓓ
51. Ⓐ Ⓑ Ⓒ Ⓓ
52. Ⓐ Ⓑ Ⓒ Ⓓ
53. Ⓐ Ⓑ Ⓒ Ⓓ
54. Ⓐ Ⓑ Ⓒ Ⓓ
55. Ⓐ Ⓑ Ⓒ Ⓓ
56. Ⓐ Ⓑ Ⓒ Ⓓ
57. Ⓐ Ⓑ Ⓒ Ⓓ
58. Ⓐ Ⓑ Ⓒ Ⓓ
59. Ⓐ Ⓑ Ⓒ Ⓓ
60. Ⓐ Ⓑ Ⓒ Ⓓ

Notes:

Forms Completion – Practice Exam 473 #1

(You will have 15 minutes to complete this section.)

Attention: 1.			
Company: 2.			
Complete Street Address, PO Box, or Rural Hwy Contract Route and Box #: 3.			Apt/Suite #: 4.
City: 5.		State: 6.	ZIP+4® Code: 7.
Foreign Country (*If applicable*): 8.		Foreign Postal Code (*If applicable*): 9.	
Phone Number: 10.	Fax Number: 11.	Email Address (*Required for Web download*): 12.	

1. Numbers would NOT be part of an appropriate entry for which box?

    A. Box 11
    B. Box 6
    C. Box3
    D. Box 10

2. What is required for Web download?

    A. Phone number
    B. Name
    C. Email address
    D. City

3. An apartment or suite number would go in which box?

    A. Box 4
    B. Box 11
    C. Box 5
    D. Box 8

4. This form is to the attention of Tori Malmstrom. Where does her name go?

    A. Box1
    B. Box 7
    C. Box 3
    D. Box 10

5. What would an appropriate entry be for Box 6?

    A. 775-240-1798
    B. Jill Holloway
    C. 30096
    D. WA

Contact (If known) 1.					Phone Number 2. ( )

Type of Mail 3.	☐ Letter ☐ Postcard	☐ Folded Self-mailer	☐ Window Envelope	☐ Other *(Specify)*:

Paper Color 4.	☐ White	☐ Other *(Describe)*:

Barcode Ink Color 5.	☐ Black	☐ Other *(Describe)*:

Destination Ink Color 6.	☐ Black	☐ Other *(Describe)*:

Return Address Ink Color 7.	☐ Black	☐ Other *(Describe)*:

Estimated Volume 8.	☐ < 50	☐ 50-100	☐ 100-200	☐ 201-300	☐ Other *(Specify)*:

Frequency of Problem 9.	☐ Daily	☐ Twice Weekly	☐ Weekly	☐ Monthly	☐ Other *(Specify)*:

6. In what box would the Estimated Volume be indicated?

    A. Box 2
    B. Box 8
    C. Box 7
    D. Box 9

7. What would be an appropriate entry for Box 2?

    A. Check mark
    B. Name
    C. Phone number
    D. Date

8. The option "Weekly" can be found in which box?

    A. Box 4
    B. Box 2
    C. Box 9
    D. Box 7

9. Tyrone Fisher is the contact. Where would you enter his name?

    A. Box 8
    B. Box 1
    C. Box 3
    D. Box 6

10. "Black" is NOT a selection for which box?

    A. Box 4
    B. Box 5
    C. Box 6
    D. Box 7

Origin ZIP Code	Day of Delivery	Flat Rate
1.	2. ☐ Next ☐ Second	3.
Date In Mo. 4. Day Yr.	5. ☐ 12 Noon ☐ 3 PM	Postage $ 6.
Time In 7. ☐ AM ☐ PM	Addressed to PO Box 8.	Return Receipt Fee 9.
Weight 10. Lbs. Oz.	International Code 11.	COD Fee 12.
No Delivery Requested 13. ☐ Weekend ☐ Holiday	Acceptance Clerk 14.	Total Postage $ 15.
Tracking Number 16.		Destination ZIP 17.

11. Numbers would NOT be an appropriate entry for which box?

    A. Box 16
    B. Box 17
    C. Box 4
    D. Box 14

12. Where would the total postage due be noted?

    A. Box 14
    B. Box 6
    C. Box 15
    D. Box 16

13. The destination ZIP code is 33790. Where would this be noted?

    A. Box 9
    B. Box 1
    C. Box 17
    D. Box 13

14. Which box requires an answer other than a check mark?
    A. Box 2
    B. Box 4
    C. Box 7
    D. Box 13

15. What would be an appropriate entry for Box 8?

    A. PO Box 9659
    B. Drew Curtis
    C. 8:14 am
    D. 17

Post Office		Mailing Date		Statement Sequence No.		Receipt Number	
1.		2.		3.		4.	
Permit Number		Customer Agreement No.		Reference No.		Container Quantity	
5.		6.		7.		8a. ___ Sacks	8b. ___ Pallets
Address Accuracy Rate		Delivery Mode	Single-Piece Weight	Total Pieces	Total Weight (lbs.) (Less Tare)		Total Tare Weight (lbs.)
9. ___ %		10.	11.	12.	13.		14.
Mailer's Name and Address (Include ZIP Code)				Mailing Agent's Name and Address (Include ZIP Code)			
15.				16.			
☐ Check if Permit Holder				☐ Check if Permit Holder			

16. The address accuracy rate is 14%. Where would this be entered?

        A. Box 7
        B. Box 11
        C. Box 16
        D. Box 9

17. The mailing agent's name is Susie Sintillo. Where would this be entered?

        A. Box 5
        B. Box 6
        C. Box 15
        D. Box 16

18. Where would you enter the Total Tare Weight?

        A. Box 14
        B. Box 13
        C. Box 12
        D. Box 11

19. Which response would be appropriate for Box 12?

        A. Tracy Elliot
        B. Reference number 679B458
        C. 7
        D. A check mark

20. Where would you note that the container quantity was four sacks?

        A. Box 5
        B. Box 8a
        C. Box 12
        D. Box 14

Post Office of Mailing 1.	Processing Category 4. ☐ Flats ☐ Irregular Parcels ☐ Machinable Parcels	Mailing Date 5.	Cost Code 6.	Seq. No. 9.	Number of Containers 12.
Permit No. 2.		Weight of a Single Piece 7. _____ pounds		Total Pieces 10.	
Packaging Based on ☐ Piece Count ☐ Weight 3.	☐ Nonmachinable Parcels	If Sacked, Based on ☐ Piece Count ☐ 20 lbs. 8.		Total Weight 11.	

21. A check mark would be used in the following boxes EXCEPT:

    A. Box 3
    B. Box 4
    C. Box 8
    D. Box 9

22. The sequence number is 9384852. Where would this be entered?

    A. Box 8
    B. Box 10
    C. Box 9
    D. Box 4

23. Where would you note that the items were irregular parcels?

    A. Box 4
    B. Box 7
    C. Box 2
    D. Box 10

24. Numbers would NOT be an appropriate entry in which box?

    A. Box 2
    B. Box 4
    C. Box 10
    D. Box 12

25. A check would be an appropriate response in which box?

    A. Box 1
    B. Box 2
    C. Box 4
    D. Box 5

Weight of a Single Piece 1. 0 _____ pound		Are figures at left adjusted? ☐ Yes ☐ No If "Yes," Reason 6.			Stamp (Required) 14.
Total Pieces 2.	Total Weight 3.				
Total Postage 4.					
Check One ☐ Presort Verification Not Scheduled 5. ☐ Presort Verification Performed as Scheduled		Date Mailer Notified 7.	Contact 8.	By (Initials) 9.	
I CERTIFY that this mailing has been inspected 10.					
Verifying Employee's Signature 11.		Verifying Employee's Name 12.		Time 13. AM PM	

26. Where is the Presort Verification noted?

        A. Box 5
        B. Box 3
        C. Box 11
        D. Box 9

27. Where would the stamp be placed?

        A. Box 6
        B. Box 9
        C. Box 14
        D. Box 4

28. The mailer was notified on 6/11/05. Where would this be noted?

        A. Box 12
        B. Box 2
        C. Box 13
        D. Box 7

29. What would be a correct entry in Box 9?

        A. Full name
        B. Initials
        C. Date
        D. Time

30. Where would the verifying employee's signature be entered?

        A. Box 11
        B. Box 1
        C. Box 12
        D. Box 4

Answer Grid – Forms Completion – Practice Exam 473 #1

1. Ⓐ Ⓑ Ⓒ Ⓓ
2. Ⓐ Ⓑ Ⓒ Ⓓ
3. Ⓐ Ⓑ Ⓒ Ⓓ
4. Ⓐ Ⓑ Ⓒ Ⓓ
5. Ⓐ Ⓑ Ⓒ Ⓓ
6. Ⓐ Ⓑ Ⓒ Ⓓ
7. Ⓐ Ⓑ Ⓒ Ⓓ
8. Ⓐ Ⓑ Ⓒ Ⓓ
9. Ⓐ Ⓑ Ⓒ Ⓓ
10. Ⓐ Ⓑ Ⓒ Ⓓ
11. Ⓐ Ⓑ Ⓒ Ⓓ
12. Ⓐ Ⓑ Ⓒ Ⓓ
13. Ⓐ Ⓑ Ⓒ Ⓓ
14. Ⓐ Ⓑ Ⓒ Ⓓ
15. Ⓐ Ⓑ Ⓒ Ⓓ

16. Ⓐ Ⓑ Ⓒ Ⓓ
17. Ⓐ Ⓑ Ⓒ Ⓓ
18. Ⓐ Ⓑ Ⓒ Ⓓ
19. Ⓐ Ⓑ Ⓒ Ⓓ
20. Ⓐ Ⓑ Ⓒ Ⓓ
21. Ⓐ Ⓑ Ⓒ Ⓓ
22. Ⓐ Ⓑ Ⓒ Ⓓ
23. Ⓐ Ⓑ Ⓒ Ⓓ
24. Ⓐ Ⓑ Ⓒ Ⓓ
25. Ⓐ Ⓑ Ⓒ Ⓓ
26. Ⓐ Ⓑ Ⓒ Ⓓ
27. Ⓐ Ⓑ Ⓒ Ⓓ
28. Ⓐ Ⓑ Ⓒ Ⓓ
29. Ⓐ Ⓑ Ⓒ Ⓓ
30. Ⓐ Ⓑ Ⓒ Ⓓ

Notes:

Coding – Practice Exam 473 #1

(You will have 6 minutes to complete this section.)

Coding Guide	
Address Range	**Delivery Route**
1101–1400 Louetta Cir. 770–929 Ella Rd. 8300–8399 State Rt 16	A
1401–1900 Louetta Cir 8400–8499 State Rt 16	B
20–50 ALT 90 W 19000–22000 Dogwood Trace 930–1420 Ella Rd.	C
All mail that doesn't fall in one of the address ranges listed above	D

	Address	Delivery Route			
1.	30 ALT 90 W	A	B	C	D
2.	760 Ella Rd	A	B	C	D
3.	1107 Louetta Cir.	A	B	C	D
4.	8432 State Rt 16	A	B	C	D
5.	1492 Louetta Cir	A	B	C	D
6.	785 Ella Rd.	A	B	C	D
7.	8368 State Rt. 16	A	B	C	D
8.	19562 Dogwood Trace	A	B	C	D
9.	1000 Louetta Cir	A	B	C	D
10.	941 Ella Rd.	A	B	C	D
11.	8466 State Rt. 16	A	B	C	D
12.	23000 Dogwood Trace	A	B	C	D
13.	42 ALT 90 W	A	B	C	D
14.	1842 Louetta Cir	A	B	C	D
15.	1367 Ella Rd	A	B	C	D
16.	1188 Louetta Cir	A	B	C	D
17.	919 Ella Rd.	A	B	C	D
18.	19681 Dagwood Race	A	B	C	D
19.	1690 Louetta Cir	A	B	C	D
20.	8345 State Rt 16	A	B	C	D
21.	21541 Dogwood Trace	A	B	C	D
22.	1296 Louetta Cir.	A	B	C	D
23.	39 ALT 90 W	A	B	C	D
24.	864 Ella Rd.	A	B	C	D
25.	8413 State Rt 16	A	B	C	D
26.	8370 State Rt 16	A	B	C	D
27.	1800 Louetta Cir	A	B	C	D
28.	20500 Dogwood Trace	A	B	C	D

29. 8472 Louetta Cir   A   B   C   D
30. 1300 Louetta Cir   A   B   C   D
31. 8488 State Rt 16   A   B   C   D
32. 40 ALT 90 W   A   B   C   D
33. 1803 Louetta Cir   A   B   C   D
34. 7300 State Rt 16   A   B   C   D
35. 1568 Louetta Cir   A   B   C   D
36. 21000 Dogwood Trace   A   B   C   D

Answer Grid – Coding – Practice Exam 473 #1

1. Ⓐ Ⓑ Ⓒ Ⓓ
2. Ⓐ Ⓑ Ⓒ Ⓓ
3. Ⓐ Ⓑ Ⓒ Ⓓ
4. Ⓐ Ⓑ Ⓒ Ⓓ
5. Ⓐ Ⓑ Ⓒ Ⓓ
6. Ⓐ Ⓑ Ⓒ Ⓓ
7. Ⓐ Ⓑ Ⓒ Ⓓ
8. Ⓐ Ⓑ Ⓒ Ⓓ
9. Ⓐ Ⓑ Ⓒ Ⓓ
10. Ⓐ Ⓑ Ⓒ Ⓓ
11. Ⓐ Ⓑ Ⓒ Ⓓ
12. Ⓐ Ⓑ Ⓒ Ⓓ
13. Ⓐ Ⓑ Ⓒ Ⓓ
14. Ⓐ Ⓑ Ⓒ Ⓓ
15. Ⓐ Ⓑ Ⓒ Ⓓ
16. Ⓐ Ⓑ Ⓒ Ⓓ
17. Ⓐ Ⓑ Ⓒ Ⓓ
18. Ⓐ Ⓑ Ⓒ Ⓓ

19. Ⓐ Ⓑ Ⓒ Ⓓ
20. Ⓐ Ⓑ Ⓒ Ⓓ
21. Ⓐ Ⓑ Ⓒ Ⓓ
22. Ⓐ Ⓑ Ⓒ Ⓓ
23. Ⓐ Ⓑ Ⓒ Ⓓ
24. Ⓐ Ⓑ Ⓒ Ⓓ
25. Ⓐ Ⓑ Ⓒ Ⓓ
26. Ⓐ Ⓑ Ⓒ Ⓓ
27. Ⓐ Ⓑ Ⓒ Ⓓ
28. Ⓐ Ⓑ Ⓒ Ⓓ
29. Ⓐ Ⓑ Ⓒ Ⓓ
30. Ⓐ Ⓑ Ⓒ Ⓓ
31. Ⓐ Ⓑ Ⓒ Ⓓ
32. Ⓐ Ⓑ Ⓒ Ⓓ
33. Ⓐ Ⓑ Ⓒ Ⓓ
34. Ⓐ Ⓑ Ⓒ Ⓓ
35. Ⓐ Ⓑ Ⓒ Ⓓ
36. Ⓐ Ⓑ Ⓒ Ⓓ

Notes:

Memory – Practice Exam 473 #1

(You have 5 minutes to complete this section.)

Coding Guide	
Address Range	**Delivery Route**
1101–1400 Louetta Cir. 770–929 Ella Rd. 8300–8399 State Rt 16	A
1401–1900 Louetta Cir 8400–8499 State Rt 16	B
20–50 ALT 90 W 19000–22000 Dogwood Trace 930–1420 Ella Rd.	C
All mail that doesn't fall in one of the address ranges listed above	D

Take 5 minutes to study from this coding guide. Use this guide to answer the questions on the next page FROM MEMORY.

Address	Delivery Route
37. 670 Ella Rd	A B C D
38. 1741 Louetta Cir	A B C D
39. 46 ALT 90 W	A B C D
40. 8462 State Rd. 16	A B C D
41. 1346 Louetta Cir.	A B C D
42. 790 Ella Rd.	A B C D
43. 20999 Dogwood Trace	A B C D
44. 15 ALT 90 W	A B C D
45. 8420 State Rt 16	A B C D
46. 35 ALT 90 W	A B C D
47. 120 Louetta Cir	A B C D
48. 1220 Ellen Rd.	A B C D
49. 8331 State Rt. 16	A B C D
50. 37 ALT 90 W	A B C D
51. 1100 Ella Rd.	A B C D
52. 8370 State Rt 16	A B C D
53. 20641 Dogwood Trace	A B C D
54. 1894 Louetta Cir	A B C D
55. 920 Ella Rd	A B C D
56. 8404 State Rt 16	A B C D
57. 1367 Louetta Cir	A B C D
58. 29 ALT 90 W	A B C D
59. 915 Ella Rd.	A B C D
60. 1522 Louetta Cir	A B C D
61. 21682 Dogwood Trace	A B C D
62. 1320 Ella Rd.	A B C D
63. 8302 State Rt 16	A B C D
64. 39 ALT 90 W	A B C D
65. 21222 Dogwood Trace	A B C D
66. 1121 Ella Rd	A B C D
67. 1210 Louetta Cir	A B C D
68. 8490 State Rt 16	A B C D
69. 1010 Louetta Ct	A B C D
70. 8391 State Rt 16	A B C D
71. 19644 Dogwood Raceway	A B C D
72. 859 Baker Rd.	A B C D

Answer Grid – Memory – Practice Exam #1

1. Ⓐ Ⓑ Ⓒ Ⓓ
2. Ⓐ Ⓑ Ⓒ Ⓓ
3. Ⓐ Ⓑ Ⓒ Ⓓ
4. Ⓐ Ⓑ Ⓒ Ⓓ
5. Ⓐ Ⓑ Ⓒ Ⓓ
6. Ⓐ Ⓑ Ⓒ Ⓓ
7. Ⓐ Ⓑ Ⓒ Ⓓ
8. Ⓐ Ⓑ Ⓒ Ⓓ
9. Ⓐ Ⓑ Ⓒ Ⓓ
10. Ⓐ Ⓑ Ⓒ Ⓓ
11. Ⓐ Ⓑ Ⓒ Ⓓ
12. Ⓐ Ⓑ Ⓒ Ⓓ
13. Ⓐ Ⓑ Ⓒ Ⓓ
14. Ⓐ Ⓑ Ⓒ Ⓓ
15. Ⓐ Ⓑ Ⓒ Ⓓ
16. Ⓐ Ⓑ Ⓒ Ⓓ
17. Ⓐ Ⓑ Ⓒ Ⓓ

18. Ⓐ Ⓑ Ⓒ Ⓓ
19. Ⓐ Ⓑ Ⓒ Ⓓ
20. Ⓐ Ⓑ Ⓒ Ⓓ
21. Ⓐ Ⓑ Ⓒ Ⓓ
22. Ⓐ Ⓑ Ⓒ Ⓓ
23. Ⓐ Ⓑ Ⓒ Ⓓ
24. Ⓐ Ⓑ Ⓒ Ⓓ
25. Ⓐ Ⓑ Ⓒ Ⓓ
26. Ⓐ Ⓑ Ⓒ Ⓓ
27. Ⓐ Ⓑ Ⓒ Ⓓ
28. Ⓐ Ⓑ Ⓒ Ⓓ
29. Ⓐ Ⓑ Ⓒ Ⓓ
30. Ⓐ Ⓑ Ⓒ Ⓓ
31. Ⓐ Ⓑ Ⓒ Ⓓ
32. Ⓐ Ⓑ Ⓒ Ⓓ
33. Ⓐ Ⓑ Ⓒ Ⓓ
34. Ⓐ Ⓑ Ⓒ Ⓓ
35. Ⓐ Ⓑ Ⓒ Ⓓ

This concludes Practice Exam 473 #1.

Please move onto the answer keys on the next few pages to see how well you have done.

1.	A	31.	B
2.	C	32.	D
3.	A	33.	B
4.	D	34.	B
5.	C	35.	A
6.	C	36.	A
7.	A	37.	A
8.	B	38.	C
9.	B	39.	C
10.	A	40.	A
11.	B	41.	A
12.	B	42.	B
13.	A	43.	A
14.	B	44.	C
15.	D	45.	C
16.	D	46.	B
17.	B	47.	B
18.	A	48.	A
19.	A	49.	D
20.	C	50.	A
21.	B	51.	A
22.	A	52.	B
23.	B	53.	B
24.	B	54.	B
25.	A	55.	A
26.	C	56.	A
27.	B	57.	A
28.	C	58.	A
29.	A	59.	A
30.	C	60.	B

1. B
2. C
3. A
4. A
5. D
6. B
7. C
8. C
9. B
10. A
11. D
12. C
13. C
14. B
15. A
16. D
17. D
18. A
19. C
20. B
21. D
22. C
23. A
24. B
25. C
26. A
27. C
28. D
29. B
30. A

Correct Answers – Coding – Practice Exam 473 #1

1. C
2. D
3. A
4. B
5. B
6. A
7. A
8. C
9. D
10. C
11. B
12. D
13. C
14. B
15. C
16. A
17. A
18. D
19. B
20. A
21. C
22. A
23. C
24. A
25. B
26. A
27. B
28. C
29. D
30. A
31. B
32. C
33. B
34. D
35. B
36. C

End of Practice Exam 473 #1

You should be able to see your strengths and weaknesses after scoring this Practice Exam. You may want to review areas that you are weak in, to improve your score on the next Practice Exam.

Before proceeding to the next Practice Exam, you should go back and study the point, which will help you to answer correctly. Remember, you are not expected to answer all of the questions, but every correct answer will increase your score.

307

37. D
38. B
39. C
40. B
41. A
42. A
43. C
44. D
45. B
46. C
47. D
48. D
49. A
50. C
51. C
52. A
53. C
54. B
55. A
56. B
57. A
58. C
59. A
60. B
61. C
62. C
63. A
64. C
65. C
66. C
67. A
68. B
69. D
70. A
71. D
72. D

End of Practice Exam 473 #1

You should be able to see your strengths and weaknesses after scoring this Practice Exam. You may want to review areas that you are weak in, to improve your score on the next Practice Exam.

Before proceeding to the next Practice Exam, you should go back and study the points which will help you to answer correctly. Remember, you are not expected to answer all of the questions, but every correct answer will increase your score

Practice Exam 473 #2

Before beginning, tear out or photocopy the answer grid for each section of the exam.

Address Comparison – Practice Exam 473 #2

Answer Key:

A) No Errors
B) Street Address Only

C) ZIP Code Only
D) Both

	Correct Addresses		Addresses to be Corrected	
	Address	**ZIP Code**	**Address**	**ZIP Code**
1.	4300 Vista Rd. Princeton, NJ	84457-3214	4300 Vista Rd. Princeton, NY	84457-3214
2.	5390 S Gessner St. Grand Rapids, MI	38310-8496	5390 S Gessner St Grand Rapids, MI	3931-9406
3.	3115 W Loop South Lexington, KY	54006	3115 W Loop South Lexington, KY	54086
4.	7079 Allison Dr Shreveport, LA	67938-3541	7070 Allison Dr Shreveport, LA	67938-3541
5.	1987 Jenson Ave. Biloxi, MS	39440-4812	19871 Jensen Ave. Biloxi, MS	39440-4812
6.	9418 Tally Ho St Queens, NY	48621-0489	9418 Tally Ho St Queens, NY	46621-0489
7.	133120 Misty Oak Nashville, TN	74509	131120 Misty Oak Nashville, TN	74509
8.	PO Box 126581 York, SC	28903-6581	PO Box 162581 York, SC	28903-6581
9.	4300 Vista Rd Kimball, TN	60458-2973	43000 Vista Rd Kimball, TN	69458-2973
10.	106211 Crystal Dr. Ennis Tx	60084-1056	106211 Krystal Dr Ennis, TX	70088-1065
11.	2631 Fountain Blue Grafton, WV	59067-8221	2631 Fountain Blue Grafton, WV	59067-8221
12.	92 Beachnut Ct. Rock Springs, WY	81006-7312	92 Beechnut Ct. Rock Springs, WY	81006-7312
13.	124 W 17th Street Fond du Lac, WI	20913-5542	124 W 17th Street Fond du Lac, WI	20913-5542
14.	4825 Fry Rd. Apt 39 Santa Ana, CA	30995	4825 Fry Rd. Apt 30 Santa Ana, CA	30995
15.	7250 Harwin Aberdeen, SD	94183-5349	5250 Harwin Aberdeen, SC	94183-5349
16.	601 N. Lincoln Waterbury, CT	03012-9120	601-S. Lincoln Waterbury, CT	03012-9120
17.	4740 Mail Dr Owatonna, MN	28945-1003	4470 Mail Dr Owatonna, MN	28945-1004
18.	3301 Pontiac Trail Rd Howell, MI	61039-2163	3301 Pontiac Trail Rd Howell, MI	61039-2163
19.	9750 Gaylord Ave Anchorage, AK	90975-8826	9750 Gaylord Ave Anchorage, AL	90975-8266

20.	2518 Tangley St. Fresno, CA	95469-3578		2518 Dangy St Fresno, CA	95469-3578
21.	6156 S Loop East Silverton, CO	80469-4002		6156 S Loop East Silver City, CO	80469-4002
22.	167 Northshore Blvd White Marsh, MD	49760		167 Northshore Blvd White Marsh, MD	49160-49160
23.	218 Cumberline Skowhegan, ME	02498-6543		218 Cumberland Snowhaven, ME	02498-6543
24.	210 E Tower Park Bastrop, LA	38369-1975		210 E Tower Park Bastrop, LA	38369-1975
25.	PO Box 23513 Pratt, KS	51349-3513		PO Box 25313 Pratt, KS	51349-5313
26.	5401 Beacon Rd Florence, KY	70694-3729		5401 Beacon Rd. Florence, KY	70694-3729
27.	1095 Industrial Pky Eagle River, AK	30158-7649		1095 Industrial Pky Eagle River, AK	30158-7649
28.	4701 N Stone Ave Mesa, AZ	59127		4701 N Stone Ave Mesa, AK	59127-8437
29.	801 Hover Apt 24B Hattiesburg, MS	32719-1002		801 Hover Apt 24B Hattiesburg, MS	32179-1002
30.	9499 Sheridan Ct. Bartow, FL	43005-7512		9499 Sheridan Ct. Bartow, FL	43005-7512
31.	3855 S. Hwy 59 Waterford, CT	00154-3719		3855 S. Hwy 59 Waterford, CT	00159-3719
32.	1340 Randall Rd New Castle, DE	26792-7631		1340 Randall Rd New Castle, Delaware	26792-7631
33.	1201 S Division St Joliet, IL	77463-1026		1201 S Division St Joliet, IL	77463-1026
34.	4501 Quail Hollow Dr. Christiansburg, VA	49485		4501 Quail Hollow Dr. Christiansburg, VA	49485
35.	60 Short Rd. Mt. Pleasant Mills, PA	17853		60 Short Rd. Mt. Pleasant, PA	17853
36.	330 Red Cedar Bremerton, WA	73021-7625		300 Red Cedar Bremerton, WA	73021-7625
37.	PO Box 3287 American Fork, UT	60085-3287		PO Drawer 3287 American Fork, UT	60085-3287
38.	4419 Ironwood Ave Auburn, GA	43012		4419 Ironwood Ave Auburn, GA	43012
39.	2402 Camillia Apt. B McCalla, AL	32156-4378		2402 Camilla Apt. B McCalla, AL	32156-4378
40.	800 Birdsong St. Morro Bay, CA	96521-4457		800 Birdsong St. Morro Bay, CA	96521-4457
41.	1828 125th Ave Hammond, IN	52136		1828 125th Ave Hammond, IN	52136
42.	3701 Portage Dr Bogalusa, LA	79612-8431		3701 Portage Dr Bogalusa, LA	79612-8431
43.	403 E. Oskaloosa Festus, MO	56321		403 E. Oskaloosa Festus, MO	56231
44.	1436 Dogwood Apt B Hartford, CT	99452		1432 Dogwood Apt B Hartford, CT	99452-1006
45.	PO Box 2674 Muskogee, OK	70345-2674		PO Box 2674 Muskogee, OK	70345-2674
46.	18 Moore Street Shenandoah, IA	59134-8453		18 Moore Street Shenandoah, IA	59134-8453
47.	2005 Long Beach Blvd. Oceanside, CA	42913-8825		2005 Long Beach Blvd. Oceanside, CA	42913-8825

48.	#19 Bakersfield, Apt 29 Fargo, ND	37619	#19 Bakersfield, Apt 29 Fargo, ND	37619
49.	9045 Glen Court Salt Lake City, UT	83194-9712	9045 Glen Court Salt Lake City, UT	83194-9812
50.	110 Village Place St. Springfield, VT	62210-5491	110 Village Place St. Springfield, VT	62210-5491
51.	89 Coe Rd. Apt 9 Pleasantville, TX	78210-6513	89 Coe Rd. Apt 9 Pleasantville, TX	79210-6513
52.	5403 Kirby Ln Gallatin, TN	23984-9546	5403 Kirby Ln Gallatin, TX	23984-9546
53.	1225 Campbell Ave. York, SC	49907-3819	1225 Campbell Ave. York, SC	49907-3819
54.	6043 Selinsky Eugene, OR	99378	6043 Selinsky Eugene, OR	99378
55.	10056 Sheldon Dr. Dime Box, AL	65792-5917	10056 Sheldon Dr. Dime Box, AL	65792-5917
56.	550 Sherwood Forest Tampa, FL	33094-7391	550 Sherwood Forest Tampa, FL	33094-7391
57.	15600 John F. Kennedy San Bernardino, CA	90137-4672	15600 John F. Kennedy San Bernardino, CA	90137-4672
58.	4511 Cherry St Hartford, CT	20065-2613	4511 Cherry St Hartford, CT	20056-2613
59.	3703 Irvington Pl Providence, RI	11079-3917	3703 Irvington Pl Providence, RI	11079-3919
60.	24 Lake June Rd. Lake Placid, FL	33853	29 Lake June Rd. Lake Placid, FL	33853

Notes:

Answer Grid – Address Comparison – Practice Exam 473 #2

(You will have 11 minutes to complete this section.)

1. Ⓐ Ⓑ Ⓒ Ⓓ
2. Ⓐ Ⓑ Ⓒ Ⓓ
3. Ⓐ Ⓑ Ⓒ Ⓓ
4. Ⓐ Ⓑ Ⓒ Ⓓ
5. Ⓐ Ⓑ Ⓒ Ⓓ
6. Ⓐ Ⓑ Ⓒ Ⓓ
7. Ⓐ Ⓑ Ⓒ Ⓓ
8. Ⓐ Ⓑ Ⓒ Ⓓ
9. Ⓐ Ⓑ Ⓒ Ⓓ
10. Ⓐ Ⓑ Ⓒ Ⓓ
11. Ⓐ Ⓑ Ⓒ Ⓓ
12. Ⓐ Ⓑ Ⓒ Ⓓ
13. Ⓐ Ⓑ Ⓒ Ⓓ
14. Ⓐ Ⓑ Ⓒ Ⓓ
15. Ⓐ Ⓑ Ⓒ Ⓓ
16. Ⓐ Ⓑ Ⓒ Ⓓ
17. Ⓐ Ⓑ Ⓒ Ⓓ
18. Ⓐ Ⓑ Ⓒ Ⓓ
19. Ⓐ Ⓑ Ⓒ Ⓓ
20. Ⓐ Ⓑ Ⓒ Ⓓ
21. Ⓐ Ⓑ Ⓒ Ⓓ
22. Ⓐ Ⓑ Ⓒ Ⓓ
23. Ⓐ Ⓑ Ⓒ Ⓓ
24. Ⓐ Ⓑ Ⓒ Ⓓ
25. Ⓐ Ⓑ Ⓒ Ⓓ
26. Ⓐ Ⓑ Ⓒ Ⓓ
27. Ⓐ Ⓑ Ⓒ Ⓓ
28. Ⓐ Ⓑ Ⓒ Ⓓ
29. Ⓐ Ⓑ Ⓒ Ⓓ
30. Ⓐ Ⓑ Ⓒ Ⓓ
31. Ⓐ Ⓑ Ⓒ Ⓓ
32. Ⓐ Ⓑ Ⓒ Ⓓ
33. Ⓐ Ⓑ Ⓒ Ⓓ
34. Ⓐ Ⓑ Ⓒ Ⓓ

35. Ⓐ Ⓑ Ⓒ Ⓓ
36. Ⓐ Ⓑ Ⓒ Ⓓ
37. Ⓐ Ⓑ Ⓒ Ⓓ
38. Ⓐ Ⓑ Ⓒ Ⓓ
39. Ⓐ Ⓑ Ⓒ Ⓓ
40. Ⓐ Ⓑ Ⓒ Ⓓ
41. Ⓐ Ⓑ Ⓒ Ⓓ
42. Ⓐ Ⓑ Ⓒ Ⓓ
43. Ⓐ Ⓑ Ⓒ Ⓓ
44. Ⓐ Ⓑ Ⓒ Ⓓ
45. Ⓐ Ⓑ Ⓒ Ⓓ
46. Ⓐ Ⓑ Ⓒ Ⓓ
47. Ⓐ Ⓑ Ⓒ Ⓓ
48. Ⓐ Ⓑ Ⓒ Ⓓ
49. Ⓐ Ⓑ Ⓒ Ⓓ
50. Ⓐ Ⓑ Ⓒ Ⓓ
51. Ⓐ Ⓑ Ⓒ Ⓓ
52. Ⓐ Ⓑ Ⓒ Ⓓ
53. Ⓐ Ⓑ Ⓒ Ⓓ
54. Ⓐ Ⓑ Ⓒ Ⓓ
55. Ⓐ Ⓑ Ⓒ Ⓓ
56. Ⓐ Ⓑ Ⓒ Ⓓ
57. Ⓐ Ⓑ Ⓒ Ⓓ
58. Ⓐ Ⓑ Ⓒ Ⓓ
59. Ⓐ Ⓑ Ⓒ Ⓓ
60. Ⓐ Ⓑ Ⓒ Ⓓ

Notes:

Forms Completion – Practice Exam 473 #2

Applicant Information

Name (Last, First, MI) 1.	Title of Present Position 2.			
Mailing Address 3.	Name and Location of Employing Office 4.			
Home Phone (Area Code) 5.	Work Phone 6.	Social Security Number 7.	Grade 8.	Years of Service 9.

Information About Vacant Position

Vacancy Announcement Number 10.	Closing Date 11.	Position Applied For 12.	Grade
Name of Vacancy Office 13.		Location of Vacancy Office 14.	

1. 416384 is the Vacancy Announcement Number. Where would you enter this?

    A. Box 9
    B. Box 8
    C. Box 3
    D. Box 10

2. Where would you enter the Years of Service?

    A. Box 9
    B. Box 3
    C. Box 14
    D. Box 5

3. Marcy Darden is the applicant. Where does her name go?

    A. Box 7
    B. Box 14
    C. Box 1
    D. Box 13

4. Marcy is applying for a Clerk/Carrier position. Where would she enter this?

    A. Box 12
    B. Box 5
    C. Box 8
    D. Box 9

5. Marcy is currently a Rural Carrier. Where would this be entered?

    A. Box 11
    B. Box 2
    C. Box 12
    D. Box 3

Address			Adhesive Stamp □	Postage Meter Stamp □	Other □

Address

☐ Handwritten

☐ Typewritten

1.

or

☐ Other *(Describe)*

_____

_____
_____
(Return Address)

Name   2a. _____

Street and Number 2b. _____

Post Office 2c. _____

State and ZIP Code 2d. _____

I deposit herewith $ 3. _____ to pay for expenses incurred for necessary telegrams, postage, etc.

Signature of Applicant	Applicant's Address	Telephone No.
4.	5.	6.

►

Application Received By *(Name of employee)*		Hour Received		Date Received
7.		8.	A.M. P.M.	9.
Telephoned To	Copies To		Returned By *(Name of employee)*	
10.	11.		12.	

6. Dean Guild received this form. Where would his name go?

     A. Box 2a
     B. Box 5
     C. Box 7
     D. Box 3

7. What would be an appropriate entry for Box 1?

     A. Julie Johnson
     B. 584-555-1212
     C. Check mark
     D. 10:11 am

8. A payment of $20.00 was deposited to cover expenses. Where would this be noted?

     A. Box 3
     B. Box 5
     C. Box 2d
     D. Box 1

9. Where does the applicant's signature go?

     A. Box 2c
     B. Box 2a
     C. Box 7
     D. Box 4

10. A number is NOT an appropriate entry for which box?

    A. Box 6
    B. Box 12
    C. Box 9
    D. Box 3

Weight of a Single Piece 0 . 1. _____ pound	Are figures at left adjusted? ☐ Yes ☐ No If "Yes," Reason 6.		Stamp (Required) 14.
Total Pieces 2.	Total Weight 3.		
Total Postage 4.			
Check One ☐ Presort Verification Not Scheduled 5 ☐ Presort Verification Performed as Scheduled	Date Mailer Notified 7.	Contact 8. By (Initials) 9.	
I CERTIFY that this mailing has been inspected 10.			
Verifying Employee's Signature 11.	Verifying Employee's Name 12.	Time 13. AM PM	

11. Where would the stamp be placed?

    A. Box 3
    B. Box 7
    C. Box 10
    D. Box 14

12. A person's initials would be the correct response in which box?

    A. Box 11
    B. Box 4
    C. Box 9
    D. Box 12

13. What would be an appropriate entry for Box 2?

    A. 7:14 am
    B. 50 pieces
    C. Salena Gutierrez
    D. Blue

14. The mailer was notified on 8/17/05. Where would this be entered?

    A. Box 7
    B. Box 3
    C. Box 5
    D. Box 12

15. Where would the total weight of the inspected shipment be entered?

    A. Box 3
    B. Box 1
    C. Box 7
    D. Box 2

Post Office of Mailing 1.	Processing Category 4.	Mailing Date 5.	Cost Code 6.	Seq. No. 9.	Number of Containers
	☐ Flats				12.
Permit No. 2.	☐ Irregular Parcels	Weight of a Single Piece 7.		Total Pieces 10.	
	☐ Machinable Parcels	_____ pounds			
Packaging Based on ☐ Piece Count ☐ Weight 3.	☐ Nonmachinable Parcels	If Sacked, Based on ☐ Piece Count ☐ 20 lbs. 8.		Total Weight 11.	

16. The cost code is 579c3. Where would this be entered?

       A. Box 2
       B. Box 11
       C. Box 6
       D. Box 10

17. A check mark would NOT be an appropriate entry for which box?

       A. Box 3
       B. Box 7
       C. Box 4
       D. Box 8

18. Where would you note that the packaging is based on piece count?

       A. Box 3
       B. Box 7
       C. Box 6
       D. Box 2

19. Which would be an appropriate response for Box 8?

       A. 613-555-1212
       B. Permit number 7B
       C. 40 lbs.
       D. A check mark

20. Where would you note that the sacked weight is based on piece count?

       A. Box 8
       B. Box 4
       C. Box 9
       D. Box 2

Post Office 1.	Mailing Date 2.	Statement Sequence No. 3.	Receipt Number 4.		
Permit Number 5.	Customer Agreement No. 6.	Reference No. 7.	Container Quantity 8a. Sacks	8b. Pallets	
Address Accuracy Rate 9. %	Delivery Mode 10.	Single-Piece Weight 11.	Total Pieces 12.	Total Weight (lbs.) (Less Tare) 13.	Total Tare Weight (lbs.) 14.
Mailer's Name and Address (Include ZIP Code) 15. ☐ Check if Permit Holder			Mailing Agent's Name and Address (Include ZIP Code) 16. ☐ Check if Permit Holder		

21. Where would you note that the Mailer is the permit holder?

   A. Box 16
   B. Box 13
   C. Box 15
   D. Box 6

22. The Customer Agreement Number is 14-652. Where would this be entered?

   A. Box 6
   B. Box 2
   C. Box 7
   D. Box 10

23. Where would you note the number of sacks?

   A. Box 9
   B. Box 8a
   C. Box 16
   D. Box 5

24. The shipment was mailed on 6/17/05. Where is this noted?

   A. Box 14
   B. Box 7
   C. Box 2
   D. Box 8b

25. Where would the total weight (less tare) be noted?

   A. Box 9
   B. Box 13
   C. Box 10
   D. Box 14

Origin ZIP Code	Day of Delivery	Flat Rate
1.	2. ☐ Next ☐ Second	3.

Date In				Postage
Mo. 4. Day Yr.	5. ☐ 12 Noon ☐ 3 PM			$ 6.

Time In	Addressed to PO Box	Return Receipt Fee
7. ☐ AM ☐ PM	8.	9.

Weight	International Code	COD Fee
10. Lbs. Oz.	11.	12.

No Delivery Requested	Acceptance Clerk	Total Postage
13. ☐ Weekend ☐ Holiday	14.	$ 15.

Tracking Number	Destination ZIP
16.	17.

26. The COD fee is $10.00. Where is this noted?

        A. Box 15
        B. Box 4
        C. Box 12
        D. Box 10

27. The Day of Delivery time is 3 pm. Where is this noted?

        A. Box 5
        B. Box 14
        C. Box 4
        D. Box 10

28. What would be a correct entry for Box 17?

        A. $6.50
        B. J. Peterson
        C. 2/15/05
        D. 49495

29. Where would the total postage of $1.50 be entered?

        A. Box 7
        B. Box 15
        C. Box 10
        D. Box 3

30. This is addressed to PO Box 4004. Where would this be noted?

        A. Box 5
        B. Box 8
        C. Box 1
        D. Box 12

(You will have 15 minutes to complete this section.)

1. Ⓐ Ⓑ Ⓒ Ⓓ
2. Ⓐ Ⓑ Ⓒ Ⓓ
3. Ⓐ Ⓑ Ⓒ Ⓓ
4. Ⓐ Ⓑ Ⓒ Ⓓ
5. Ⓐ Ⓑ Ⓒ Ⓓ
6. Ⓐ Ⓑ Ⓒ Ⓓ
7. Ⓐ Ⓑ Ⓒ Ⓓ
8. Ⓐ Ⓑ Ⓒ Ⓓ
9. Ⓐ Ⓑ Ⓒ Ⓓ
10. Ⓐ Ⓑ Ⓒ Ⓓ
11. Ⓐ Ⓑ Ⓒ Ⓓ
12. Ⓐ Ⓑ Ⓒ Ⓓ
13. Ⓐ Ⓑ Ⓒ Ⓓ
14. Ⓐ Ⓑ Ⓒ Ⓓ
15. Ⓐ Ⓑ Ⓒ Ⓓ
16. Ⓐ Ⓑ Ⓒ Ⓓ
17. Ⓐ Ⓑ Ⓒ Ⓓ
18. Ⓐ Ⓑ Ⓒ Ⓓ
19. Ⓐ Ⓑ Ⓒ Ⓓ
20. Ⓐ Ⓑ Ⓒ Ⓓ
21. Ⓐ Ⓑ Ⓒ Ⓓ
22. Ⓐ Ⓑ Ⓒ Ⓓ
23. Ⓐ Ⓑ Ⓒ Ⓓ
24. Ⓐ Ⓑ Ⓒ Ⓓ
25. Ⓐ Ⓑ Ⓒ Ⓓ
26. Ⓐ Ⓑ Ⓒ Ⓓ
27. Ⓐ Ⓑ Ⓒ Ⓓ
28. Ⓐ Ⓑ Ⓒ Ⓓ
29. Ⓐ Ⓑ Ⓒ Ⓓ
30. Ⓐ Ⓑ Ⓒ Ⓓ

Notes:

Coding – Practice Exam 473 #2

(You will have 6 minutes to complete this section.)

Coding Guide	
Address Range	**Delivery Route**
801-1240 Monmouth Dr. 3300-3699 Ince Blvd. 1-149 Ellington Ln	A
1241-1300 Monmouth Dr. 150-299 Ellington Ln	B
22-82 Tolling Wood Terrace 14500-16500 Sam Houston Toll Rd 3700-3999 Ince Blvd.	C
All mail that doesn't fall in one of the address ranges listed above	D

Address Range **Delivery Route**

1. 670 Ella Rd	A B C D
2. 3607 Ince Blvd	A B C D
3. 199 Ellington Ln	A B C D
4. 80 Tolling Wood Terrace	A B C D
5. 822 Monmouth Dr.	A B C D
6. 17500 Sam Houston Toll Rd	A B C D
7. 3906 Ince Blvd	A B C D
8. 92 Ellington Ln	A B C D
9. 1262 Monmouth Dr.	A B C D
10. 25 Tolling Wild Dr	A B C D
11. 111 Ellington Ln	A B C D
12. 3489 Ince Blvd	A B C D
13. 1294 Monmouth Dr.	A B C D
14. 3820 Ince Blvd	A B C D
15. 1100 Monmouth Dr	A B C D
16. 253 Ellington Ln	A B C D
17. 16218 Sam Houston Toll Rd	A B C D
18. 3762 Ince Blvd	A B C D
19. 1258 Monmouth Dr.	A B C D
20. 29 Tolling Wood Terrace	A B C D
21. 967 Monmouth Dr.	A B C D
22. 153 Wellington Ln	A B C D
23. 3456 Ince Blvd.	A B C D
24. 20 Tolling Wood Terrace	A B C D
25. 178 Ellington Ln	A B C D
26. 934 Monmouth Dr.	A B C D
27. 41 Tolling Wood Terrace	A B C D
28. 290 Ellington Ln	A B C D

29. 1650 Sam Houston Toll Rd   A   B   C   D
30. 3890 Ince. Blvd   A   B   C   D
31. 1225 Monmouth Dr.   A   B   C   D
32. 227 Ellington Ln   A   B   C   D
33. 3584 Ince Blvd   A   B   C   D
34. 16400 Sam Houston Toll Rd   A   B   C   D
35. 27 Ellington Ln   A   B   C   D
36. 54 Tolling Wood Terrace   A   B   C   D

Answer Grid – Coding – Practice Exam 473 #2

1. Ⓐ Ⓑ Ⓒ Ⓓ
2. Ⓐ Ⓑ Ⓒ Ⓓ
3. Ⓐ Ⓑ Ⓒ Ⓓ
4. Ⓐ Ⓑ Ⓒ Ⓓ
5. Ⓐ Ⓑ Ⓒ Ⓓ
6. Ⓐ Ⓑ Ⓒ Ⓓ
7. Ⓐ Ⓑ Ⓒ Ⓓ
8. Ⓐ Ⓑ Ⓒ Ⓓ
9. Ⓐ Ⓑ Ⓒ Ⓓ
10. Ⓐ Ⓑ Ⓒ Ⓓ
11. Ⓐ Ⓑ Ⓒ Ⓓ
12. Ⓐ Ⓑ Ⓒ Ⓓ
13. Ⓐ Ⓑ Ⓒ Ⓓ
14. Ⓐ Ⓑ Ⓒ Ⓓ
15. Ⓐ Ⓑ Ⓒ Ⓓ
16. Ⓐ Ⓑ Ⓒ Ⓓ
17. Ⓐ Ⓑ Ⓒ Ⓓ
18. Ⓐ Ⓑ Ⓒ Ⓓ
19. Ⓐ Ⓑ Ⓒ Ⓓ
20. Ⓐ Ⓑ Ⓒ Ⓓ
21. Ⓐ Ⓑ Ⓒ Ⓓ
22. Ⓐ Ⓑ Ⓒ Ⓓ
23. Ⓐ Ⓑ Ⓒ Ⓓ
24. Ⓐ Ⓑ Ⓒ Ⓓ
25. Ⓐ Ⓑ Ⓒ Ⓓ
26. Ⓐ Ⓑ Ⓒ Ⓓ
27. Ⓐ Ⓑ Ⓒ Ⓓ
28. Ⓐ Ⓑ Ⓒ Ⓓ
29. Ⓐ Ⓑ Ⓒ Ⓓ
30. Ⓐ Ⓑ Ⓒ Ⓓ
31. Ⓐ Ⓑ Ⓒ Ⓓ
32. Ⓐ Ⓑ Ⓒ Ⓓ

33. Ⓐ Ⓑ Ⓒ Ⓓ
34. Ⓐ Ⓑ Ⓒ Ⓓ
35. Ⓐ Ⓑ Ⓒ Ⓓ
36. Ⓐ Ⓑ Ⓒ Ⓓ

326

Coding Guide

Address Range	Delivery Route
801-1240 Monmouth Dr. 3300-3699 Ince Blvd. 1-149 Ellington Ln	A
1241-1300 Monmouth Dr. 150-299 Ellington Ln	B
22-82 Tolling Wood Terrace 14500-16500 Sam Houston Toll Rd 3700-3999 Ince Blvd.	C
All mail that doesn't fall in one of the address ranges listed above	D

Take 5 minutes to study from this coding guide. Use this guide to answer the questions on the next page FROM MEMORY.

Memory – Practice Exam 473 #2

(You will have 5 minutes to complete this section.)

Address Range   **Delivery Route**

#	Address				
37.	3940 Ince Blvd	A	B	C	D
38.	136 Ellington Ln	A	B	C	D
39.	31 Tolling Wood Terrace	A	B	C	D
40.	122 Mammoth Dr.	A	B	C	D
41.	184 Ellington Ln	A	B	C	D
42.	3352 Ince Blvd.	A	B	C	D
43.	1350 Sam Houston Toll Rd	A	B	C	D
44.	1266 Monmouth Dr.	A	B	C	D
45.	52 Tolling Wood Terrace	A	B	C	D
46.	129 Ellington Ln	A	B	C	D
47.	16234 Sam Houston Toll Rd	A	B	C	D
48.	196 Ellington Ln	A	B	C	D
49.	3367 Inch St.	A	B	C	D
50.	812 Monmouth Dr.	A	B	C	D
51.	16550 Sam Houston Toll Rd.	A	B	C	D
52.	51 Ellington Ln	A	B	C	D
53.	1271 Monmouth Dr.	A	B	C	D
54.	3390 Ince Blvd	A	B	C	D
55.	72 Tolling Wood Terrace	A	B	C	D
56.	1204 Monmouth Dr.	A	B	C	D
57.	279 Ellington Ln	A	B	C	D
58.	16000 Sam Houston Toll Rd	A	B	C	D
59.	3480 Ince Blvd.	A	B	C	D
60.	35 Tolling Wood Place	A	B	C	D
61.	1290 Monmouth Dr.	A	B	C	D
62.	3900 Ince Blvd.	A	B	C	D
63.	282 Ellington Ln	A	B	C	D
64.	987 Monmouth Dr.	A	B	C	D
65.	15500 Sam Houston Toll Rd.	A	B	C	D
66.	81 Rolling Wood Terrace	A	B	C	D
67.	1140 Monmouth Dr.	A	B	C	D
68.	3730 Ince Blvd.	A	B	C	D
69.	2849 Main St.	A	B	C	D
70.	1280 Monmouth Dr.	A	B	C	D
71.	3841 Inch Blvd.	A	B	C	D
72.	1670 Ellington Ln	A	B	C	D

37. Ⓐ Ⓑ Ⓒ Ⓓ
38. Ⓐ Ⓑ Ⓒ Ⓓ
39. Ⓐ Ⓑ Ⓒ Ⓓ
40. Ⓐ Ⓑ Ⓒ Ⓓ
41. Ⓐ Ⓑ Ⓒ Ⓓ
42. Ⓐ Ⓑ Ⓒ Ⓓ
43. Ⓐ Ⓑ Ⓒ Ⓓ
44. Ⓐ Ⓑ Ⓒ Ⓓ
45. Ⓐ Ⓑ Ⓒ Ⓓ
46. Ⓐ Ⓑ Ⓒ Ⓓ
47. Ⓐ Ⓑ Ⓒ Ⓓ
48. Ⓐ Ⓑ Ⓒ Ⓓ
49. Ⓐ Ⓑ Ⓒ Ⓓ
50. Ⓐ Ⓑ Ⓒ Ⓓ
51. Ⓐ Ⓑ Ⓒ Ⓓ
52. Ⓐ Ⓑ Ⓒ Ⓓ
53. Ⓐ Ⓑ Ⓒ Ⓓ
54. Ⓐ Ⓑ Ⓒ Ⓓ
55. Ⓐ Ⓑ Ⓒ Ⓓ

56. Ⓐ Ⓑ Ⓒ Ⓓ
57. Ⓐ Ⓑ Ⓒ Ⓓ
58. Ⓐ Ⓑ Ⓒ Ⓓ
59. Ⓐ Ⓑ Ⓒ Ⓓ
60. Ⓐ Ⓑ Ⓒ Ⓓ
61. Ⓐ Ⓑ Ⓒ Ⓓ
62. Ⓐ Ⓑ Ⓒ Ⓓ
63. Ⓐ Ⓑ Ⓒ Ⓓ
64. Ⓐ Ⓑ Ⓒ Ⓓ
65. Ⓐ Ⓑ Ⓒ Ⓓ
66. Ⓐ Ⓑ Ⓒ Ⓓ
67. Ⓐ Ⓑ Ⓒ Ⓓ
68. Ⓐ Ⓑ Ⓒ Ⓓ
69. Ⓐ Ⓑ Ⓒ Ⓓ
70. Ⓐ Ⓑ Ⓒ Ⓓ
71. Ⓐ Ⓑ Ⓒ Ⓓ
72. Ⓐ Ⓑ Ⓒ Ⓓ

End of Practice Exam 473 #2

The correct answers for Practice Exam 473 #2 are found on the next four pages.

330

<u>Correct Answers – Address Correction – Practice Exam 473 #2</u>

1.	B	31.	C
2.	D	32.	B
3.	C	33.	A
4.	B	34.	A
5.	B	35.	B
6.	C	36.	B
7.	B	37.	B
8.	B	38.	A
9.	D	39.	B
10.	D	40.	A
11.	A	41.	A
12.	B	42.	A
13.	A	43.	C
14.	B	44.	D
15.	B	45.	A
16.	B	46.	A
17.	D	47.	A
18.	A	48.	A
19.	D	49.	C
20.	B	50.	A
21.	B	51.	C
22.	C	52.	B
23.	B	53.	A
24.	A	54.	A
25.	D	55.	A
26.	A	56.	A
27.	A	57.	A
28.	D	58.	C
29.	C	59.	C
30.	A	60.	B

<u>Correct Answers – Forms Completion – Practice Exam 473 #2</u>

1. D
2. A
3. C
4. A
5. B
6. C
7. C
8. A
9. D
10. B
11. D
12. C
13. B
14. A
15. A
16. C
17. B
18. A
19. D
20. A
21. C
22. A
23. B
24. C
25. B
26. C
27. A
28. D
29. B
30. B

Correct Answers – Coding – Practice Exam 473 #2

1. D
2. A
3. B
4. C
5. A
6. D
7. C
8. A
9. B
10. D
11. A
12. A
13. B
14. C
15. A
16. B
17. C
18. C
19. B
20. C
21. A
22. D
23. A
24. D
25. B
26. A
27. C
28. B
29. D
30. C
31. A
32. B
33. A
34. C
35. A
36. C

37. C
38. A
39. C
40. D
41. B
42. A
43. D
44. B
45. C
46. A
47. C
48. B
49. D
50. A
51. D
52. A
53. B
54. A
55. C
56. A
57. B
58. C
59. A
60. D
61. B
62. C
63. B
64. A
65. C
66. D
67. A
68. C
69. D
70. B
71. D
72. D

By now, you should be able to pass the actual exam with a higher score. If you feel you need more preparation, you may take these exams again with the copies you made of each Answer Grid. If you feel you need new material to work with, you can ask a friend or relative to assist you in compiling additional practice tests.

Chapter 9: The Final Step

If you read the earlier sections of this book carefully, what we are about to discuss was your first task. But, just in case, we will now cover the process of applying to take either Exam 460 or Exam 473.

The easiest way to apply for the exam is by using the Internet. Our website, www.endeavormediallc.com, has a link to the USPS site so that you can apply for the exam of your choice, in the location of your choice. It takes about 2 minutes to register for an exam using this system. You do not need an announcement number to apply using this method. Simply follow the instructions on our site and in the instructions included in your packet. If you need help setting up your login, please contact the Customer Care Department for the company you ordered the book from. This information should have been part of your original packet.

The next easiest way to apply is the USPS Job line. The number for this service is 1-478-757-3199, this is not a toll free number and long distance charges may apply. It takes approximately 8-15 minutes to register for an exam using this number. You will need an announcement number to apply using this method.

Regardless of the method, once you have applied, you will receive a confirmation packet. (Remember, this could take up to six months from the date of your application.) The packet will include some more information on the contents of the exam, the date, time, and place of the exam. Pay close attention to the date, time, and place; you don't want to be late.

Remember, these scores are kept on record for two years, good or bad. You want to make the first time the best time.

Soon, you may be employed by one of the largest employers in the United States. Study hard and good luck! You should have the edge needed to excel beyond other applicants if you use all the information within this book.